Architectural Involutions

Rethinking the Early Modern

Series Editors

Architectural Involutions

Writing, Staging, and Building Space, c. 1435–1650

Mimi Yiu

Northwestern University Press
Evanston, Illinois

Northwestern University Press
www.nupress.northwestern.edu

Printed in the United States of America

10 9 8 7 6 5 4 3 2 1

ISBN 978-0-8101-3659-5

The Library of Congress has cataloged the original, hardcover edition as follows:

Yiu, Mimi, author.
Architectural involutions : writing, staging, and building space, c. 1435–1650 / Mimi Yiu.
pages cm. — (Rethinking the Early Modern)
ISBN 978-0-8101-2986-3 (cloth : alk. paper)
1. English drama—Early modern and Elizabethan, 1500–1600—History and criticism. 2. Architecture, Domestic, in literature. 3. Dwellings—Social aspects—England—History—16th century. 4. Architecture, Domestic—Social aspects—England—History—16th century. 5. Theaters—Stage-setting and scenery—England—History—16th century. I. Title. II. Series: Rethinking the Early Modern.
PR658.D65Y58 2014
822.309357—dc23

2014012467

CONTENTS

FIGURES

Architectural Involutions

INTRODUCTION

Building Platforms

> To continue and finish, is not so great a matter in building, as to attempt and laie the foundation or platforme.
>
> —Raphael Holinshed, *Chronicles*

To "laie the foundation or platforme" for a book requires clearing a space for writing, marking the outlines of a design that will slowly be realized, performed, inscribed materially. On a much grander scale, early modern England strove to "laie the foundation or platforme" for a novel field: architecture. This foreign term, derived from the Greek αρχι (head) and τέκτων (maker), entered the English lexicon with the advent of treatises such as John Shute's *The First and Chief Grounds of Architecture* (1563).[1] Staking out new "grounds" to build a discourse on space, these sixteenth- and seventeenth-century treatises promoted architecture as a discipline based on intellect rather than manual labor. The architect who serves as "head maker" (αρχιτέκτων) thus directs the efforts of others who construct while devoting himself to reading and inscribing in multiple forms—sketches, maps, notes, letters, even treatises.

By defining the architect as a proto-Cartesian subject who builds inside his head, who edifies his mind, England joined a critical dialogue that flowered after a complete manuscript of Vitruvius's *De architectura* surfaced in the early fifteenth century. As the only treatise on architecture extant from classical antiquity, *De architectura* (first century B.C.E.) inspired humanist scholars across Europe to ponder how spatial design affects the relation between a subject and the external world. Given fresh purpose as an early modern genre, the architectural treatise offered a platform that could address not only the physical need for shelter, but also the social and psychic impact of building. Such attention to the intangible properties of architecture extended into a parallel arena of plotting in England: the playhouse. Blending textual and actual building, theater provided an alternative platform for working through competing paradigms of space, continuing the discourse of architectural treatises in dramatic fashion.

The term *platform* already suggests a conceptual slippage between architecture and theater in this period: as a flat (plat) structure, a *platform* in early modern usage indicates a stage, scaffold, or draftsman's sketch. A *platform* thus switches—with the blink of a mind's eye—from a static drawing into a vibrant piece of theater, subsuming the bones of architecture into something rich and strange. Indeed, these valences of *platform* evoke Michel de Certeau's opposition between a proper, univocal place (*lieu*) and an improper, volatile space (*espace*). While a named place (*lieu*) conforms to its prescribed shape and function, a more undefined space (*espace*) opens itself to chance and change as different social vectors collide: "space is a practised place."[2] Always in the process of becoming, de Certeau's *espace* provides a theater for the unscripted events that comprise everyday life.

Such a dynamic platform may be linked to Robert Weimann's concept of the *platea,* a liminal ground between actors and audience in medieval theater. Working in tandem with the *locus,* a purpose-built structure dedicated to performance, the *platea* extends the playing space into "a street, a village green, or a marketplace surrounded by spectators."[3] While the *locus* remains distant from the common viewer, the *platea* supplies a contact zone where actors and nonactors come into proximity, if not actually mingle. In the *platea*'s socially charged space, "the play world continues to be frankly treated as a theatrical dimension of the real world."[4] Weimann's *locus,* in contrast, adheres more closely to our modern notion of a stage by indexing a "fixed, symbolic" locale, such as a palace, throne, or other place of authority.[5] That is, while the *locus* draws upon mimetic techniques to construct a fictive setting, the *platea* converts readymade architectural sites into ad hoc platforms for theater, infusing legibly familiar spaces with layers of fantasy. Quite literally, the *platea* levels the playing field between actors and nonactors, troubling the distinction between theater and reality. *Architectural Involutions* delves into similar encounters between formal and informal spaces of performance (Weimann's "localized" and "unlocalized" sites), exploring the hinge between theater meant to signify as architecture and architecture meant to signify as theater.

To clarify the nuances of *platform* that concern this book, we might begin with the curious example of Antonello da Messina's *St. Jerome in his Study* (c. 1475), a painting that transforms private architecture into public theater (figure I.1). Antonello envisions Jerome in a cathedral-like

Figure I.1. Antonello da Messina, *St. Jerome in His Study* (c. 1475). National Gallery (London)/Bridgeman Art Library.

setting with vaulted ceilings, rendering this interior space with a delicate and detailed touch that recalls Jan van Eyck. Yet Antonello grounds his ethereal space in the geometry of linear perspective, a technique that creates the illusion of three-dimensional space using a two-dimensional surface (a *plat* form). Following a paradigm that emerged only decades earlier in the fifteenth century, Antonello divides the floor into square tiles that recede toward an unseen point on the horizon; everything placed on this coordinate plane, including an arcade to the right, converges toward the same point at infinity. Yet in his desire to play architect, to depict a realistic space in depth, Antonello leaves Jerome adrift upon an ocean of tiles, a scholar lost in his raft of books like Prospero. Not only a mortal dwarfed by his divine milieu, Jerome also finds himself scaled down by the dictates of perspective, distanced from viewers by a stone portal and expanse of floor. Indeed, Antonello reduces Jerome to a rather small figure in a rather small painting (45.7 × 36.2 cm); seen in profile, the cleric stands out mainly due to the cascade of his scarlet robes. While such a posture denies viewers the usual vehicle of interior expression—the face—Antonello offers an alternative route to the psyche: he situates

Jerome within a series of nested spaces that register as ever more private. As our gaze passes through the portal, skims along the lines of tiles, then finally penetrates the sanctum of Jerome's study, our inward journey aspires to reach straight into his soul.

Despite revealing Jerome's interior state through the external correlative of architecture, Antonello does not place his subject at the center of his own portrait. Diagonal lines drawn from the portal's four corners intersect at the *book* in Jerome's hands—perhaps the Vulgate, his seminal effort to translate the Bible into Latin. To sanctify the drama of reading that occupies the painting's heart, to build the ultimate bookcase for the ultimate book, Antonello devises a cubicle enclosed by shelves along the back and left sides only. Not based on any known model, this peeled-open study within a church resembles a chapel dedicated to Jerome, a shrine for a saint already turned statue by his formal pose; after all, Jerome had become less a man than a monument by the fifteenth century, more than a millennium after his death. Building upon a wooden platform whose contours govern the closet's shape, Antonello creates a vitrine for the sacred relic of a bookish saint: to borrow a phrase from Jerome's Vulgate, *ecce homo,* behold the man. Tucked inside the larger stage of a church, Jerome's study functions as a discovery space where spectators can bear witness as he performs a ritual of solitude. To achieve this quasi-religious privacy, Jerome has removed his shoes before mounting the short flight of stairs to his study, arriving like an actor upon a platform, ready to inhabit an open book of a room. Jerome's removal to a privileged space, a raised scaffold, resembles a journey from *platea* to *locus*. Antonello breaks down any such binary, however, since the painting allows visual access to an ostensibly private study, thereby enlisting a public gaze to produce a subject defined by performance. Only by setting foot on this inner stage can Jerome assume his proper identity as scholar, unlocking the secret of his portrait by sitting down and plugging a book—his key attribute—into the center of this cosmos.

The platform closet thus renders Jerome's being legible by telling the story of his becoming, by staging the book of himself as a book of open secrets. Yet just as Antonello displaces the saint's body to feature an event of reading, viewers must also negate their bodies in the search for visual meaning. Since linear perspective demands that viewers occupy a precise location to satisfy its optical geometry, only a perfectly stilled body can access and chart the illusory world. In return, the painting unfolds its secrets to the gaze like a book of architecture, inviting viewers to peruse its well-wrought lines, turning its spatial poetics into a visual performance. At first glance, Antonello seems to exploit the logic of coordinate space by stuffing the closet with Euclidean shapes: the curved lectern, the cutout shapes beneath the raised floor, the semicircular chair with its rectangular voids, the boxy cabinets and bench, even the arched doorway that promises to extend this figural dance beyond the frame. While showing off the structure of single-point perspective, these ideal forms also promote a nonlinear interplay among motifs that repeat with a mysterious rhythm, urging viewers to trace desultory paths across a mystical landscape. Like a Ptolemaic universe, Antonello's fanciful world thrums with the harmony of a higher order, its intervals of space coded with meanings that should transfix the viewer. In this painterly equivalent of magical realism, the platform supports both the objective, transparent space of perspective and the opaque, private space of a subject. Just as the portrait features a textual artifact both central and inscrutable, a material book that may contain the ineffable words of God, the platform inscribes a subject whose psychic space resonates against a physical interior.

In a similar vein, *Architectural Involutions* examines a series of early modern platforms where visual, textual, and spatial elements collide to create an architecture of the self. Like Jerome's book, spaces form a complex semiotic system whose meanings derive, in part, from their cultural and historical context; like Jerome, the subject assumes a social position determined by a performance of reading—a performance that always situates and is read by another. As a species of conscious design that literally builds communities, materially reshaping human relationships, architecture provides a signifying space par excellence, as Vitruvius realized:

> Both in general and especially in architecture are these two things found; that which signifies and that which is signified. (Cum in omnibus enim rebus, tum maxime etiam in architectura haec duo insunt, quod significatur et quod significat.)[6]

This definition near the beginning of Vitruvius's treatise establishes a foundation that allows early modern thinkers to conceive architecture as a social discourse, as a blend of *techne* and text. Such a recourse to language would appeal to a writer who urges architects to pursue a broad array of liberal arts, a writer who includes both Plato and plaster in his purview. By claiming a semiotic basis for space from the outset, Vitruvius notifies readers that what follows should not be regarded simply as a technical manual, but rather a far-reaching exploration of architecture's role in a culture entirely constituted by signs (*in omnibus enim rebus*).

Some interpreters parallel Vitrivius's signifier and signified with *ratiocinatio* (theory) and *fabrica* (practice), thus linking an architect's intellectual activity to the physical construction that follows.[7] Although *ratiocinatio* and *fabrica* appear only several lines above "quod significatur et quod significat," recent scholarship has forged a more obvious linkage with the signifier and signified found in Greek linguistics.[8] However, Vitruvius avoids the Stoics' tripartite system of signifier, signified, and referent to adopt the dualism of Epicurean thought, dropping the term usually perceived as most architectural—the referent, the material structure.[9] Rather than conflate the referent and signified, confusing the building in the world with the building in the mind, Vitruvius plunges architecture headlong into language:

> That which is signified is the thing proposed about which we speak; that which signifies is the demonstration unfolded in systems of precepts. (Significatur proposita res, de qua dicitur; hanc autem significat demonstratio rationibus doctrinarum explicata.)[10]

Vitruvius carefully defines the signified not as some actual building, but as a matter proposed and spoken of using words (*proposita res, de qua dicitur*).[11] In contrast to *fabrica,* which is "carried out by the hands" (*quae manibus perficitur*), Vitruvius posits an architectural signified that develops as the subject of discourse, not least his own.[12] Indeed, by clearing a space for this field and *topos* called architecture, the author cannily ensures that his words signify.

Architectural Involutions examines the outcome of this moment as Vitruvius and his early modern interlocutors unfold systems of precepts that define the intangible matter of architecture. Though such treatises attempt to secure a linguistic foundation for architecture, Henri Lefebvre cautions that space resists being merely a passive tablet for writing.[13] Just as every piece of writing must grapple with context to achieve meaning, edifices can never stand on a neutral tabula rasa no matter how neatly plotted their design. The best-laid plans of writers and draftsmen must contend with a ground that resists yielding a clean inscription, a ground whose constant movement prevents any imprint from settling into absolute clarity. Thus when Vitruvian treatises came into vogue in early modern England, conflicts arose between a *space* defined by social practice and a *place* regulated by imported tenets. While spatiality always involves a struggle among competing interests, the growth of an English print culture enabled a Vitruvian discourse to engage more people in debate than ever before. Such interest in the semiotics of architecture informed not only the theater of everyday life, but also the dramas mounted on London stages.

Lefebvre argues that "representations of space have a practical impact, that they intervene in and modify spatial *textures* which are informed by effective knowledge and ideology."[14] Beyond altering how a culture perceives the abstract texture of space, however, aspects of theater crucially structured the early modern home in England. Tracing an inward journey from facades to closets, from physical to psychic space, *Architectural Involutions* reveals how the meeting of theater and architecture helped to construct an early modern sense of interiority. For starters, as Geoffrey Broadbent notes, "walls, enclosures, and façades serve to define both a *scene* (where something takes place) and an *obscene* area to which everything that cannot or may not happen on the scene is relegated: whatever is inadmissible, be it malefic or forbidden, thus has its own hidden space on the near or the far side of a frontier."[15] In Leon Battista Alberti's *De re aedificatoria* (1485), the first treatise-length response to Vitruvius since antiquity, the creation of this frontier between scene and obscene defines architecture itself. Chapter 1 explores how Alberti redirects the Vitruvian dialogue with his concept of a facade (*facies*), an aesthetic "face" that makes the building cohere and thus signify on the public stage.

Does Alberti's facade, hailing the viewer with a quasi-human face, provide an alternative model of early modern subjectivity? At first glance, the facade's upright surface evokes a picture plane, the focus of Alberti's treatise on painting, *De pictura* (1435). In this earlier text, Alberti codifies the method of single-point or linear perspective, which yokes vision to space through optical geometry. By locking viewers opposite the vanishing point, single-point perspective creates a "stereometric 'cage'" that enables the most realistic illusion of spatial depth; Alberti thus seems to envision a subject who attains a rightful sense of place in the world by sacrificing mobility and freedom.[16] Yet when Alberti the armchair theorist became an architect in the latter portion of his career, this paradigm needed to evolve since neither buildings nor viewers can negate their bodies for visual pleasure. In designs for the Tempio Malatestiano, Santa Maria Novella, and Palazzo Rucellai, Alberti gradually abandoned the notion of a facade that produces an ideal but static picture. Instead, adapting to the fluid urban context, Alberti began to fracture the building's face to achieve a social interface. By attending to other platforms that embrace the public, including facade benches that function as impromptu stages, Alberti finally turned perspective into theater.

Chapter 2 examines how Alberti's facade translates into England after the Reformation, whose ravages inspired a period of intense construction known as the Great Rebuilding. Yet English builders often suffer a reputation as provincial bumblers who enter belatedly into the *Bildungsroman* of Western architecture. Despite the absence of a major conceptual framework like Alberti's, a neglected textual corpus from this period disproves the notion that English builders were "rude mechanicals" unable to articulate their own thoughts, unaware of the latest advances on the Continent. On the contrary, English writers feared that adopting a facade in the Albertian mode would imperil a native solidity, turning their buildings into pictures, their homes into theaters. With an iconoclastic zeal befitting their newly converted nation, these writers castigate an "Italianate" falsity that weakens English masculinity with cosmetic flourishes. As a matter of fact, architecture did perform a dramatic change in early modern England, but not only from the outside: in a process of architectural involution, an inward-looking courtyard module refolded, like origami, into an outward-looking compact design finished with a public facade.

Turning itself inside out, the traditional English pile underwent a structural inversion that paralleled a social rebuilding throughout the sixteenth and seventeenth centuries. While the great hall once anchored a feudal household, this large central space now dissolves into a network of hallways that values circulation over assembly. These "public" corridors through the house prevent sudden incursions upon the monadic subject, tucked into newly "private" rooms. By driving a wedge between proper spaces, the hallway inserts a pause that turns entrances and exits into theatrical rituals, redefining the scene (and seen) from the obscene. In short, unlike medieval buildings that fortified their exteriors, the early modern home defends against internal threats by placing facades along every hallway. Such a tactic reaches its logical end with the double-pile layout, which features two layers of rooms divided by hallways that cross at the house's center. Ironically, the emerging nuclear family inhabits a home without a nucleus, a home alienated from itself internally.

With a circuit of transitional spaces that radiates from an empty heart, the early modern home assumes a structure based on principles of absence and dissemination—qualities that Jacques Derrida identifies as intrinsic to writing. Before an epistemic shift toward hallways begins in the latter decades of the sixteenth century, most buildings ordered rooms in a chain from public to private, rendering an exit from one room an entrance into the next. Such a paradigm, like speech, requires a presence at every point along a single axis, offering a linear path forward like an expelled breath. Yet if writing derives meaning from the differential *spacing* between words, then the English home that inserts a skeletal frame of hallways begins to articulate itself in written form. The density of a double-pile house, for instance, embraces *différance* with hallways that distinguish between rooms, defer to monadic privacy, and delay arrival at the proper destination. Architecture's profound relation to writing reaches thus beyond the textual sources that inspire design (the books that Vaughan Hart calls "paper palaces"), or even the built-in emblems and mottoes that, in Mark Girouard's terms, make a building speak.[17] Instead, English architecture seizes upon a syntax and semiotics that uncannily mirror those of writing, thus realizing in material form the metaphor of an inscriptional ground. Standing upon the English landscape as a textual icon, the early modern house not only performs a spatial writing, but also renders every footstep inside its frame a species of inscription.

As the word transforms into spatial flesh, how does this affect the subject who moves through a congeries of liminal spaces described repeatedly by critics as a "no man's land"? While treatises often figure architecture as a book of secrets, conjuring a magus-like architect who unveils some interior mystery in print and practice, what the English home reveals most plangently is a subject's interior in the process of becoming. If the structure of our homes opens a window onto how we conceive and perform our selves daily, our *habitus,* then the architectural involution that rearranges a domestic interior also rearranges a psychic interior. As the home orients itself around a central void that disperses, the subject must negotiate a growing array of spaces abjected as "no man's land" before stepping across the threshold to social legibility, to the scene/seen. Indeed, while houses always behave as heterotopias with multiple functions,[18] the early modern architect must ensure a certain *spacing* among various subjects as they perform their everyday routines, balancing the cohesion of a household against the staging of interiority.

The inevitable fears and frictions arising from these changes in sociality found the perfect outlet in drama. As Henry Turner argues, "the English drama of the late sixteenth and early seventeenth centuries must be considered above all as a highly spatialized mode of representation."[19] While Turner's excellent study on "poetics and geometry" explores the technologies of spatial plotting,[20] especially the impact of proto-scientific discourse and methods on staging, *Architectural Involutions* queries how a desire to examine interior spaces, both physical and psychic, drove the rapid ascent of drama in early modern England. After all, theater supplied the perfect, self-reflexive crucible for making sense of a home that seemed no different from a playhouse, and thus a person who seemed no different from a player. Given a four-fold increase in London's population between 1500 and 1700, the plotting of domestic space was perhaps an obvious point of concern for new plays staged in the capital. At the same time, rejecting the archetypes found in medieval drama, playwrights began looking inward to chart the human psyche, investing brave new worlds inside their characters. *Architectural Involutions* selects for analysis a key tragedy and comedy—Shakespeare's *Hamlet* and Jonson's *Epicoene*—that ponder the outcome of subjects whose interiority, what Hamlet calls his "heart of heart," seem as hollow as the center of their homes. Moreover, by framing these plays within a matrix of related platforms, *Architectural Involutions* suggests a method for spatial mapping that crosses academic fields to produce a broader cultural history.

Chapter 3 examines the most famous portrait of subjective crisis in early modern drama: *Hamlet* (1600). Agonizing over the demise of an authentic self, mourning the passing of "that within that passes show," Hamlet searches for an interior space of inscription that remains true. Shakespeare locates this "heart of heart" in Gertrude's closet, where Hamlet forces his mother to confront her spotted soul by turning her eyes inward; spatial interiority thus becomes complicit in staging the human psyche. But how did personal closets become the ultimate signifier of interiority? Most scholars regard Gertrude's closet as some erotic retreat, or perhaps the final sanctum of an enfilade that ranges from public to private. Yet royal closets, derived from chapels, anchor a spatial complex that renders privacy a staged domestic ritual. From the religious *secretarium* to the humanist study, from the practical cabinet for storage to the rhetorical "closet of the heart," the early modern closet defines an interiority based on shared practices that include reading and writing. By collapsing gender binaries that conceive women's spaces only as lockable, chaste enclosures, Gertrude's closet reveals itself as a place of sovereign power, not least the power of theater.

Not simply an "unweeded garden" that nurtures female desire, Gertrude's closet evokes a deeply rooted tradition of conceiving space itself as a maternal ground of inscription. In the *Timaeus,* Plato describes space as a womb-like receptacle called *chora,* a third type (*genos*) that enables ideals to assume material bodies. Like a soft piece of wax, the feminine chora passively accepts a paternal imprint from the ideal, providing a mere vessel that holds in place a concept, a script, a body, a subject. As theorists such as Jacques Derrida, Luce Irigaray, and Judith Butler observe, this unthinking, unknowing chora provides a blank ground upon which Plato inscribes his own ideas, plotting his own *topoi.* Though the philosopher hopes to build his logical edifice on a stable but silent platform, we should recall that space, even distilled into the most abstract state, resists providing a neutral medium for a single form of writing. As a result, modern cartography became a contested ground when a more scientific model of space began to emerge, one that espoused an impersonal, coordinate universe. In response, Plato's chora was assigned to the mapping of intimate places with names, meanings, histories, and dreams. Taking a similarly non-empirical approach, Alison Findlay reclaims a feminist chora for the domestic spaces that functioned as both theatrical venues and fictional settings in this period: "Drama is, like the *chora,* an incubator in which new worldly forms, new places and identities for women can be engendered."[21]

Chapter 4 widens the scope of this domestic, dramatic chora to examine the theater of Great Britain, the center of an aspiring empire. Unlike travelers to exotic outposts who returned with stories of alterity, chorographers such as William Camden and William Lambarde sought to define "home" for their fellow Britons, to make coherent a nation of disparate regions, cultures, languages, and politics. The discipline of chorography—literally, the inscribing or graphing of chora—flourished in early modern Europe precisely as a means to represent a locality with nuanced depth, to stage a place often close to the heart. Blending history, anecdotes, folklore, maps, tables, and assorted images, chorographers attempted to endow a feminized "Britannia" with a unified identity as their motherland. In this figural birth of a nation, Queen Elizabeth's virginal womb served as the chora that produced British subjects, her chaste yet fecund body pressed into sanctioning an ideology of empire. Ultimately, though Findlay confers upon the chora a "fuller maternal, corporeal presence,"[22] Plato's legacy ensnared the female subject in a nonplace of impossible maternity, caught between having and being interior space.

Opening the door from a mother's closet to a father's, from Elizabethan to Jacobean space, chapter 5 revisits the theater to consider how a city comedy can function as a mode of chorography. First staged at the Whitefriars theater, Ben Jonson's *Epicoene* (1609) features a misanthropic "bad architect" named Morose who seals his London townhouse against common noise, turning Turk against his neighbors as he orients himself inward. Yet since the play's action occurs almost entirely inside characters' homes, Jonson builds an imagined architecture that mirrors the intimate Whitefriars theater, a new type of indoor venue known as a "private house." Moreover, the theater's location, in a pocket "liberty" just outside city walls, invites viewers to enter the very region of London depicted in *Epicoene*. Jonson thus conceives a site-specific performance that resonates with local audiences, devising a comedy whose bitter laughter depends upon an awareness of theatrical space. *Epicoene* deepens these parallels between the actual and staged worlds when Morose foolishly marries an ideal silent woman—whose facade soon crumbles to reveal a boy, an actor trained to perform femininity. As this marital travesty queers his closeted house, calling into question the most interior of spaces, an invading mob forces Morose to declare himself an impotent "no man." Despite turning Morose's home into a literal "no man's land," Jonson's comedy suggests a resolution that would allow this patriarchal subject, no longer accepted in Jacobean culture, to rebuild his interiority. To achieve a proper social place, however, Morose must renounce the fantasy of inscribing on a silent womb and master instead the *epicoene* techniques of theater.

After the turmoil of an architectural involution, what future awaits the subject? Chapter 6 glimpses a possible outcome inside the perspective box of Samuel van Hoogstraten, a Dutch artist who worked in 1650s London. Testing the limits of optical geometry, Hoogstraten has painted the inner surfaces of this trunk-like box to resemble the inside of an ordinary house: a bedroom where a woman sleeps, a front room where another woman reads quietly, a salon that contains a letter addressed to himself. Two peepholes drilled into opposite panels ensure that visitors access this domestic interior from the optimal vantage points, one eye at a time; when viewers stand rooted at their allotted subject positions, the anamorphoses within resolve into larger-than-life focus, creating the illusion of a coherent home. While Alberti endows architecture with an external face, Hoogstraten inscribes a facade that extends, unbroken, across the box's *internal* surfaces. Ironically, Hoogstraten flattens the interior into a picture to satisfy the desire for a wondrous secret depth, an ever-deeper heart of heart.

Yet such an illusion cannot be sustained without the complicity of viewers who circulate from one peephole to another, seeking fruitlessly to complete their sense of a holistic space. Barred from the center, from coming home, the subject must suture together two opposed views while tracing a circuit of endless transition. Pushing Alberti's philosophy to its logical extreme, Hoogstraten's indoor theater makes subjects perform their already riven status, showing how interiors have already become facades. Locked outside any position of control in this reverse camera obscura, the subject can never go home again; on the contrary, stuck in a "no man's land" that requires constant motion, the subject must keep writing home in every sense. Ultimately, by launching off a series of related platforms, *Architectural Involutions* suggests possible avenues for conceiving not only the writing *of* space—that is, by realizing a graphic design or executing a textual philosophy—but also writing *as* space.

Chapter One

Refacing Alberti

The Arrest of the Facade

Architecture may be dead as a doornail, but the dead still open doors. Since design always molds itself around a society's desires and anxieties, we can study the contours of buildings to recover some fragment, some *figure* of an evanescent human condition. We can stroll through cast-off skins of brick and stone, walking alongside specters from bygone days. We can listen to walls that reveal how they connect and divide, what they contain and deny. Passed from failing hands, these storied places of the dead possess a certain spatial memory of everyday practice, as though retaining the impress of bodies on every surface. Yet architecture does not only serve as a backdrop for social drama, offering an artificial dermis that wraps around the social corpus. Instead, architecture itself takes on a material and textual body to perform as a quasi-subject, following Bruno Latour's definition of an entity that behaves like an agent within a network.[1] More specifically, Michel Serres argues that a quasi-subject "marks or designates a subject who, without it, would not be a subject."[2]

In fifteenth-century Europe, architecture began to make visible this agential function by adopting a facade, a constructed face that allows the building to project a coherent, legible identity. First theorized by Leon Battista Alberti in his treatise *De re aedificatoria* (1485), the facade turns architectural space into an aesthetic body that invites the human gaze—but also looks back. Alberti's notion of the facade inspired scholars and builders alike to restage the interface between human and building, to rethink space as drama. Even as architecture became the subject of discourse in treatises, reviving a genre of writing fallen into obscurity since Vitruvius, architecture became visible as a quasi-subject upon the social landscape, a monad whose windows look upon the world. Bodied forth in books that create faces and faces that read like books, early modern buildings engage viewers in an endless series of tête-à-têtes, remapping the contact zones between public and private, interior and exterior. In this awakening to consciousness, so to speak, architecture moves beyond a material presence to become a signifier invested with the power to solicit into being a person who might be called an architectural subject. While buildings have always furnished a place for the subject, a physical address, the facade that now envelops the bones of architecture begins to address this subject on social terms. In the network of relations that arise between human and humanlike faces, in the mirroring of physical and psychic spaces, early modern culture questions the sanctity of human interiority itself. Can we regard the human body and mind as anything more than another built space, a plotted interior finished off with a public face? Can we read ourselves as architecture, and vice versa?

Alberti's legacy comes across forcibly in a seventeenth-century etching by the French artist and theorist Abraham Bosse, which attempts to illustrate the scene of architectural representation. Bosse depicts a solitary draftsman seated at a worktable, compass in hand, who seems absorbed in drawing an arcade that stands across from him (figure 1.1). His shoulders hunched over his work, his arms folded around a world of inner space, this draftsman forms the epitome of inward focus, a microcosm so intensely self-oriented that his upper body almost describes an enclosed sphere. Below the waist, however, the draftsman's figure dissolves murkily into ruffles that register almost as an extension of the fringed tablecloth—a nice finishing touch, but hardly vital to the task at hand. Despite this schism between his shadowy bottom half and his spotlighted head, his negated mobility and his prized intellect, the draftsman achieves bodily coherence by resonating with an *architectural* figure. Even as he traces the contours of an arch onto paper, he himself traces those same contours onto the paper that he inhabits. The draftsman's head and arms sketch out a curve that his own compass might have issued, thus capping an upright trunk with a vault; even the four bands of ribbon loops across his breeches evoke the four broad steps that lead into the arcade. While Friedrich Nietzsche warns that "if you gaze for long into an abyss, the abyss gazes back into you,"[3] architecture seems to produce the same mirroring effect between the viewing subject and object. Indeed, Bosse's etching reveals a subconscious fear and fantasy that architecture could reshape the viewer, rather than vice versa, hinting that the vaunted interiority of humanism may comprise only an abyssal ground.

Bosse's draftsman comes from a 1664 treatise that urges readers to construct space through vision, thus seeing rather than setting foot in

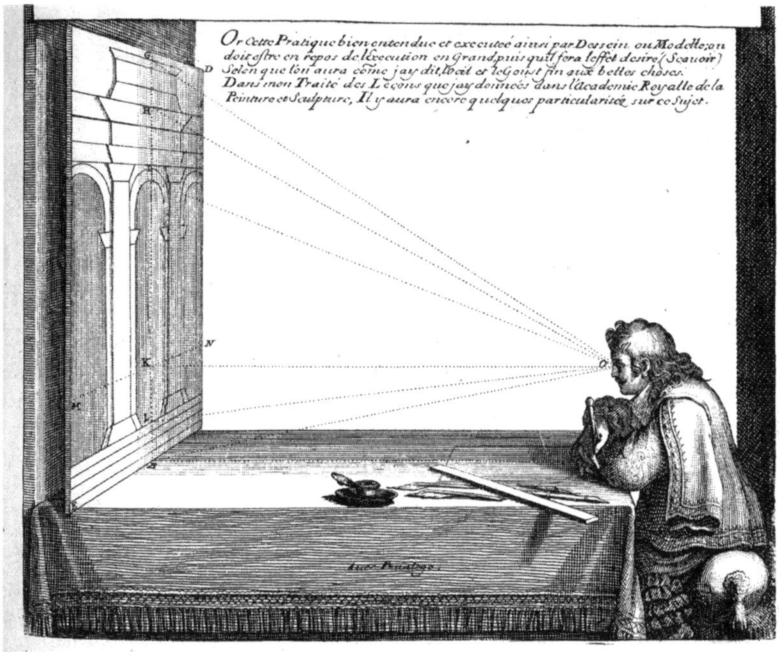

Figure 1.1. Draftsman with perspectival drawing, from Abraham Bosse's *Traité des manières de dessiner les ordres de l'architecture antique* (Paris, 1664), xliii. Rosenwald Collection, Library of Congress.

buildings. Such a claim would seem absurd unless we appreciate the profound impact of Alberti's single-point perspective, a technique initially devised for painters, which joins actual and imagined space to create a seamless visual world.[4] As codified in Alberti's treatise *De pictura* (1435), single-point perspective treats the viewer as a disembodied eye that remains fixed in place, reducing the subject to a precise locus from which sightlines radiate. To capture the event of seeing in Albertian terms, Bosse diagrams the draftsman's gaze with dotted lines that emanate from a point marked O for *oeil* (eye); in contrast to the immobile, inward-turned O of his posture, this ocular O marks an outward expansion across space that brings the subject into contact with objects in the world. Vision occupies such a central position in this paradigm that both the subject and object of architecture must be pushed to the margins, all the better to transform the process of seeing into a spatialized field. Indeed, the drama of seeing defines the role of a draftsman whose gaze has been so neatly drafted by an unseen hand—and whose main activity seems not to involve drafting at all. While his folded arms suggest an attempt to obscure the paper before him, a greater sleight of hand soon emerges as an open secret: the facade being sketched is already a sketch.

Thanks to the diffusion of Alberti's single-point perspective across disciplines, architecture became easily conflated with a picture of architecture by the seventeenth century. Bosse's treatise thus counsels builders to construct on paper before incurring the expense of breaking ground, offering readers a perspectival method that accurately renders architecture in miniature (*une pratique d'arrester en petit*).[5] Since visuality governs spatial relations, a scale drawing adequately substitutes for a physical edifice by showing architects the ocular impact of their designs: "Il fasse à l'Oeil l'effet que l'on s'est proposé par l'arresté de ce petit" (This small drawing would effect upon the eye what has been proposed).[6] Indeed, what Bosse terms "l'arresté de ce petit" may indicate not only a certain spatial essence that the image captures (*l'arresté:* what has been arrested, stopped), but also the perspectival code that enables such visual realism (*l'arresté:* a decree, law, accord).[7] If Bosse's etching depicts this practice of testing designs in advance, then the draftsman may be projecting a future building onto the screen before him, propelling onto a blank surface—an architectural ground for inscription—some inchoate structure glimpsed in his mind's eye. Copying an image without a discernible original, the draftsman engages in a recursive creation of sketches that may never produce tangible architecture. As buildings arise on cardboard and canvas to satisfy the ocular sense, architects become artists who strive to house the restless gaze.

By enabling the proliferation of images disconnected from bricks-and-mortar reality, the regime of single-point perspective renders architecture the deferred copy of a visual template, enacting what Jean Baudrillard calls the precession of simulacra.[8] Like the portrait of a person as yet unborn, or the map of a region as yet unknown, the perspectival drawing precedes and subsumes the architecture that should ostensibly be primary. The very success of single-point perspective in spatial deception thus requires new modes of policing. To avoid confusion between actual and imagined architecture, between present and future construction, Bosse inserts a lacuna that distances the backing wall from the "building" now identified as a maquette, a shallow mock-up that forms the ultimate facade. Foreseeing the viewer's difficulty in separating the image of a building from the image of an image of one, Bosse avoids a frontal view that suppresses the maquette's difference from material architecture, not least from the wall behind. Like the viewing subject and object, the architectural signifier and signified must be prized apart to clarify their essential contrast, thus staving off a semiotic collapse.

Bosse's anxious tactics reveal how single-point perspective radically undercuts a belief in depth, tainting architecture with the artifice of scenography, debunking faces as empty masks. Even the supporting wall—a nondescript backdrop that shows the aesthetic facade to advantage—cannot pass muster as solidly upstanding. Despite providing a substratum marked as reality, this shadowy wall closely resembles the maquette as a surface truncated on three sides by the etching's borders. Given the chance to peek beyond the print's left edge, might we discover that even this piece of built space, this wall that anchors our sense of reality, proves to be nothing more than trompe l'oeil? Such a question remains moot, of course, for the cut that unmoors Bosse's wall is the cut of representation: indeed, the first cut that transforms a building into a flattened maquette echoes the second cut of the etching's frame. As though to emphasize how absolutely an image should break from reality, Bosse detaches his maquette from the wall to produce a floating signifier, a simulacrum that disdains even the slightest contact with actual building. Harnessed only in the dotted lines of an ethereal optical matrix, Bosse's facade stands through the sheer force of visual attention, drawn upright by the draftsman's magnetic gaze.

Yet even as single-point perspective releases architecture from physical constraints, the eye remains arrested by the *arresté* of a facade that demands a constant, unwavering gaze. Evoking Louis Althusser's famous example of interpellation in which a policeman hails a subject into being,[9] this arrest of the facade snaps into place an architectural subject defined by visuality, a subject who enters an illusory world of spatial plenitude to revel in the most intense ocular pleasure: "la capitale satisfaction a l'Oeil, est de voir d'abord son Object d'une seule Oeillade, et en suite tout son detail" (the main satisfaction of the Eye is to view first of all its Object in a single glance, and then in all its detail).[10] To make the architectural image stand up for itself, to come fully into being, Bosse demands complete allegiance to a visual ideology that immobilizes and interpellates. By locking both viewer and viewed into what Martin Kemp calls the "stereometric 'cage'" of single-point perspective,[11] Bosse proposes a "draftsman's contract"—to riff on the title of Peter Greenaway's film—in which the body sold belongs to the draftsman himself.

Such an enraptured gaze helps to plaster over the cracks when single-point perspective fails to cohere, when competing desires propel the artificer's hand in multiple directions. If we imagine a vertical line that bisects the scene through the inkwell, structural asymmetries emerge when we cover the two sections in alternation. For instance, Bosse's draftsman works on a surface that seems to form a trapezoid rather than a rectangle.

Despite seating the draftsman at right angles to the viewer, a stance that simplifies the plotting of sightlines, Bosse gently rotates the etching's left side to reveal more of the maquette's front. This maneuver destroys the rigorous geometry of perspective, but permits viewers to share the draftsman's "capital satisfaction" in beholding a classical facade. Yet the subtlety of Bosse's skewed geometry suggests a desire to maintain the veneer of spatial coherence while reveling in the sheer pleasure of seeing, uninhibited by the dictates of rulers and compasses. As though building a partly raked stage that looks perfectly level to the audience, Bosse queers a coordinate plane to suture together a makeshift spatial integrity: the deceptive facade, we discover to our discomfort, merely distracts from this more insidious tampering with the etching's spatial paradigm.

Such pervasive duplicity subverts the diagram's intention to show perspective not merely as an artistic technique, but as a science that reproduces how the eye actually perceives the world. Rather than study a model draftsman who performs the correct way to visualize space, we become slowly aware that Bosse's etching offers just another illusory surface, twisted to serve the artist's purposes—mocking the process of making a maquette as shown by the draftsman. In this sense, Bosse's inkwell splashes onto the picture what Slavoj Žižek calls a visual blot, "a point from which the image itself looks at the spectator, the point of the 'gaze of the Other,'" a point that "throws the harmony of my vision off-balance."[12] Both marking and suturing over a symbolic crevice, the blot of Bosse's inkwell jostles us into realizing our complicity in forging a sense of spatial rightness. Our gaze thus redounds upon ourselves as we examine our cognitive faculties alongside the external world. If an unseen hand has already drawn lines that extend outward from the draftsman's eye, then Bosse's inkwell reverses this function by inscribing lines that radiate backward from the viewer's eye into the mind.

To reinforce this concept of a reflective interiority, of a mind arrested within its own gaze, Bosse inserts a facade where artists traditionally place a window upon the world. Hieronymus Rodler's 1531 treatise exemplifies how single-point perspective usually positions the artist in relation to the object. Rodler's woodcut shows an artist, seated at a worktable indoors, who sketches while looking outward through a gridded window (figure 1.2). By copying the visible landscape onto a drawing surface, gridded similarly, the artist produces an image that can be hung on another wall as a false window. Single-point perspective, as we shall see, develops from this basic notion of the two-dimensional artwork as a window that breaks through an enclosed interiority, freeing the gaze from material barriers to explore an illusory space. Despite

Figure 1.2. Perspectival artist, from Hieronymus Rodler's *Eyn schön nützlich büchlin und underweisung der kunst des Messens, mit dem Zirkel, Richtscheidt oder Lineal* (Simmern, 1531), H2v. Woodcut variously attributed to Master H. H. and Johann von Pfalz-Simmern. Spencer Collection, the New York Public Library, Astor, Lenox and Tilden Foundations.

obvious similarities between Rodler's artist and Bosse's draftsman, the latter figure does not gaze through a window to find a suitable object to sketch; on the contrary, Bosse replaces this aperture with a maquette that has already brought architecture indoors as a drawing. Why should the draftsman need to *transform* architecture into a picture, since Bosse readily conflates the two? Bosse not only removes that initial stage of reading the outside world, but also positions architecture as a deeply interiorizing mechanism. By inserting a maquette that serves as a false window, but stands as a real second wall, Bosse provides the illusion of external access while doubling the number of barriers that limit the draftsman's gaze. More importantly, the maquette traps viewers in a visual semiotics that permits no outside, a circuit that loops seamlessly between actual and imagined spaces.

How did architecture become so deeply engaged with this aesthetic system? Vitruvius, writing in the first century B.C.E., exhorts potential architects to heed what Greek philosophers termed the *logos opticos* (optical discourse).[13] In the heady crucible of Renaissance humanism, the *logos* of space and vision grew even closer together with the science of optics. As the spatial theorist Henri Lefebvre notes, fifteenth-century Tuscany nurtured a cluster of artists and thinkers who advanced a radically effective technique to represent spatial depth, a technique that "became enshrined in architectural and urbanistic practice as the *code* of linear perspective."[14] This early modern building code established a consistent, calibrated method for creating the illusion of three-dimensional space, usually on two-dimensional surfaces. Based on a principle of recession in which parallel orthogonal lines converge toward a vanishing point, single-point (or linear) perspective situates the viewer and viewed in a shared geometric space that seems to extend unto infinity. While critics like Martin Jay caution against treating single-point perspective as a monolithic force in the "scopic regime of modernity,"[15] the advent of this artistic technique impacts a broader cultural history by raising questions about the nature of interior space, both physical and psychic. But does single-point perspective literally pave the way—as we shall see, by inscribing a *pavimentum*—for a Cartesian subject situated in coordinate space?

According to Erwin Panofsky's seminal essay on symbolic form, visual paradigms reveal how a given culture perceives and represents the world.[16] Despite a tendency to naturalize single-point perspective as replicating the eye's own process of seeing, Panofsky's mandate to historicize and localize every construct makes evident the social dimension of this "scientific" visuality, and hence of the viewing subject. In mapping the cultural milieu of perspective, we must somehow account for the central figure of Leon Battista Alberti (1404–72), a Florentine humanist who moved among the intellectual circles mentioned by Lefebvre. Alberti's treatise *De pictura* initiated readers into the workings of linear perspective, while *De re aedificatoria* sparked the renewal of a Vitruvian discourse on the semiotics of architecture.[17] Despite breaking ground in distinct realms of knowledge, both treatises relate vision to a theory of the surface: how the eye looks upon a picture plane, how the eye sees a facade. Yet with the exception of Anne Friedberg's careful explication of Alberti's window trope,[18] few art or architectural historians have studied the treatises side-by-side to question whether the visual paradigm in *De pictura* applies to built spaces as well.

Critics often assume that Alberti's painterly teachings color his later architectural works, as though the same brushstroke of thought extended linearly across his canon, as though an afterimage of *De pictura* still hovered in the mind's eye. Yet Alberti does not use the term *perspectiva* or *prospettiva* anywhere in *De re aedificatoria;*[19] this omission arises not because Alberti discounts the visuality of architecture, but because he realizes that built spaces require thinking outside the perspectival box. Especially when Alberti moves from theory to actual building in the latter part of his career, the conflation of facade and picture plane becomes untenable in the theater of urban streets. As the viewing experience itself escapes from a static interior, the mobile subject confronts a facade that masks a spatial body, a signifying face that provokes a crisis of recognition. By examining Alberti's built works against his two surface-oriented texts—sometimes reading against the grain by teasing out the architectural in *De pictura* and the visual in *De re aedificatoria*—we emerge from the critical tunnel vision that locks Alberti's *logos opticos* into a single totalizing stance. By freeing the subject from a single viewing position, a more nuanced theory of Alberti's facialized surface comes into focus.

Through a Veil

For Alberti, the construction of single-point perspective begins with an act of inscription:

> First of all, on the surface on which I am going to paint, I draw [*inscribo*] a rectangle of whatever size I want, which I regard as an open window [*aperta finestra*] through which the subject to be painted [*historia*] is seen.[20]

As Joseph Masheck reminds us, Alberti's default painting surface (*superficies pingendi*) would have been a wooden panel rather than the stretched canvas popular with later Renaissance artists.[21] On the inscriptional ground of single-point perspective, then, Alberti responds to the materiality of his wooden panel by performing an architectural gesture; plotting a delimited space that the mind must bore through, Alberti punches a metaphorical aperture through a miniature wall. Yet the picture plane also stands as an optical intersection (*intercisio*),[22] a vertical plane that slices through the imagined pyramid radiating from a viewer's eye to a distant object. Alberti thus encloses the gaze with a *double* cut: while the incised rectangle marks the edges of a visual field, the panel itself arrests the gaze from probing in depth. Only with this foundational inscription (*inscribo*) and in(ter)cision (*intercisio*) can the artist transform an opaque panel into a machine for generating views, an optical prosthesis that enables the gaze to penetrate into a substitute, transcendent world.

Alberti's act of inscription thus operates on three levels: by writing on the pages of *De pictura,* by drawing or scoring lines on a picture plane, and by breaking conceptual ground to install a perspectival *logos opticos.* To impress on these multiple surfaces the tenets of an emerging visual ideology, Alberti appropriates scientific discoveries about *prospettiva naturalis,* the optics governing how an eye actually sees, to create an artistic *perspectiva artificialis,* a mimetic representation of that ocular process.[23] Anchored upon a "centric point" that the painter arbitrarily selects and marks within the pictorial window, this perspectival regime strives to produce the *effect* of spatial depth even as physical depth remains effaced. To achieve this illusion, *De pictura* nominates the surface as the ultimate carrier of meaning: "I call a sign [*signum*] anything which exists on a surface so that it is visible to the eye."[24] Alberti thus regards single-point perspective not merely as a workshop technique, but as a species of visual semiotics.

To create a surface that signifies in single-point perspective, artists inscribe both an external frame and an internal framework ordered around the centric point ("unicum punctum . . . constituo"),[25] a *punctum* that Roland Barthes might have recognized as piercing the viewer.[26] The centric point, Alberti explains, can be found where the viewer's "centric ray" (*centricus radius*) meets the pictorial surface "in such a way that it makes equal angles on all sides."[27] Like the medieval *axis visualis,* Alberti's centric ray was believed to transmit the most direct sensory data to the brain. Yet while the *axis visualis* traces a linear route from the optic nerve through the center of a viewer's pupil to reach an object's surface, Alberti defines his centric ray as forming right angles to the *picture* rather than to the cornea.[28] To locate this centric ray, Alberti's viewer must search for a position exactly opposite the centric point, moving through physical space to identify that sweet spot from which an illusory world coheres. Ironically, even as the pictorial surface became more disengaged from the built environment during the Renaissance—devolving from walls, panels, and furniture to a malleable, movable canvas—linear perspective imposed a new internal architectonic that fixed the viewer in place.

Once riveted into the correct position, viewers unlock the Albertian window to discover a uniform spatial matrix established a priori, a Cartesian universe that seems to radiate from a single point. Choosing to build this world from the bottom up, Albert details a novel method that begins filling the window frame with a gridded "floor," a literal ground for artistic inscription. *De pictura* instructs painters to notch regular units along the window's bottom axis, then draw orthogonal lines that connect each notch to the centric point. These orthogonals represent parallel lines that seem to converge at some infinitely distant location, now termed the vanishing point. Although the treatise lapses into unclear diction at this juncture, Alberti seems to enjoin the addition of diagonals from these baseline notches to a "distance point," situated on the pictorial frame along the same horizon as the centric point. Where these diagonals and orthogonals intersect, the artist draws a series of transversal lines, parallel to the window's base, which appear to recede into the distance (figure 1.3).[29] Since the resultant pattern of orthogonal and transversal lines resembles a floor of square tiles, Alberti refers to this spatial foundation as a *pavimentum* (pavement), a platform on which artists can more precisely situate objects to mimic a three-dimensional environment.

While Jacques Lacan dismisses single-point perspective as "simply the mapping of space, not sight,"[30] Alberti's keenest insight derives precisely from his marriage of space and vision, his single-minded siting of sight (a quality that also undergirds Lacan's own work, ironically). Rather than follow natural philosophers who dissect the process of seeing, probing into anatomy and physics, Alberti constructs an optical scaffolding that yokes the viewer and object into the same coordinate space.[31] Ignoring the question of whether the eye transmits or receives optical rays, Alberti balances actual and illusory space across the threshold of a picture's surface, an interface that looks both ways. This symmetry allows the subject and object to dance a visual pas de deux across a checked floor, with neither partner given primacy. Indeed, even while *De pictura* asserts that first and foremost "when we look at a thing, we see it as an object which occupies a space," further that "no objects in a painting can appear like real objects, unless they stand to each other in a determined relationship,"[32] these criteria defining an object apply equally to the subject. After all, *De pictura* treats the viewer as a situated eye that comes into being when arrested in space, caught within a *pavimentum* that sweeps across the picture plane and secures a network of calibrated relations. At heart, Alberti's open window renders the viewer deeply vulnerable not only to the gaze of another, but also to the space of another. Ensnared in a universe whose center remains beyond mastery, located at some imagined and unattainable infinity beyond the picture plane, the viewer must concede a kind of subjective arrest.

By making the eye's *axis visualis* align with a centric ray defined in relation to the picture, Alberti sutures a viewer's ocular rays onto the

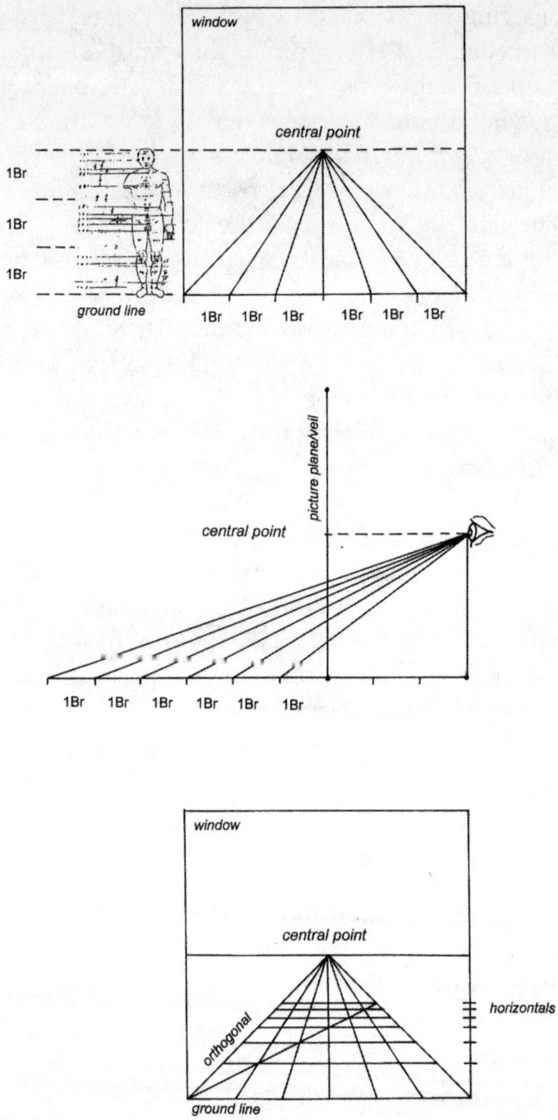

Figure 1.3. Alberti's perspectival construction. *Top:* frontal view scaled to a human figure; *middle:* side view; *bottom:* frontal view. Reprinted from Robert Tavernor, *On Alberti and the Art of Building* (1998), 8, with permission of Yale University Press and Robert Tavernor.

orthogonal lines of a *pavimentum,* blazing an unbroken track for the gaze across the picture plane. After an optical cut that encloses the subject comes the healing suture of perspective; after a negation of depth comes the promise of infinite extension, the wonder of an opaque panel made "transparent and like glass."[33] However, finding this escape route through a window entails accepting the centric point as a geometric double for the viewer's eye,[34] a specular other calling the subject to a preordained location. David Summers argues that *De pictura* turns away from a model of the eye as a living mirror (*speculum animatum*), espoused by Brunelleschi among others, to embrace a metaphor of the eye as a window through which the soul, the *virtù visiva,* contemplates the world.[35] Yet since the pictorial surface, like a wooden shutter, blocks the viewer's eye physically, the subject gazing out through an ocular window finds only the centric point gazing back through a virtual window. This doubled gaze recalls John Donne's account of looking into his lover's eyes: "Our eye-beams twisted, and did thread/Our eyes upon one double string."[36] Likewise, twisting eye-beams with the centric point along a doubled ray, Alberti's viewer stands transfixed by strings of perspective that stretch tautly in either direction.

Despite an interpretive tradition that frames Alberti's window as looking outward, *De pictura* eschews such a binary orientation. Instead, the treatise promotes a regular, reversible geometry that almost negates the division between interior and exterior, subject and object. Beyond honoring a Euclidean principle, however, Alberti builds his pictorial space upon the measure of human bodies, making his illusory landscape a mirror of the viewer's own proportions. For example, *De pictura* specifies that units marked on the window's bottom axis should be gauged against the *braccio,* defined as one-third of an average man's height; moreover, the centric point must be "no higher from the base line than the height of the man to be represented in the painting, for in this way both the viewers and the objects in the painting will seem to be on the same plane."[37] Intended to produce greater empathy, this spatial resonance between the viewer and viewed underscores how the Albertian window functions as a metaphor (Greek for "to carry across, through"), transporting the viewer into a similar but simulated world. In this sense, Alberti's cut of inscription also defines the borders of a stage, a wooden platform that deploys perspective to reveal a drama in progress.[38]

Indeed, to furnish this scenographic frame, Alberti rejects a tableau of abstract shapes to embrace a genre called *historia.* As the "great work of a painter," the "most important part of the painter's work," the very "subject to be painted," a *historia* should present a narrative that includes the broadest variety of human figures, showing "every abundance and beauty."[39] Urging painters to choose a ground "as near as possible in size to the actual object,"[40] Alberti envisions his window as a hinge between the viewer's space and a life-size stage filled with actors. Such continuity allows the painted figures to reach into a viewer's affective space, thus inducing catharsis; for Alberti, a *historia* should aspire to "move spectators when the men painted in the picture outwardly demonstrate their own feelings as clearly as possible."[41] The painted figures thus perform their interior state to arouse the viewer's own interiority, miming "their own feelings" to provoke a similarly humane response. Since these daubs of pigment exhibit a psychic depth that echoes the subject's own, Alberti suggests that both external and internal space extend across the picture plane: "Everything the people in the painting do among themselves, or *perform in relation to the spectators,* must fit together to represent and explain the 'historia'" (emphasis mine).[42] Allowed to perform "among themselves" without any relation to viewers, the painted figures assume a sociality of their own. At the same time, Alberti parallels the viewer to the painted figures in space and syntax, as though every figure could interact with the viewer or another painted figure.[43] Breaking the fourth wall of theater, Alberti's figures solicit the viewer's support to fulfill the project of *historia,* folding the viewer into a diverse community that "must fit together" to serve a greater narrative. In short, the spectator must also perform in relation to the painted figures.

Indeed, to further place the viewer and painted figures on an equal footing, in every sense, Alberti counsels artists to include "someone in the 'historia' who tells the spectators what is going on" through hand gestures, facial expressions, or even a "forbidding glance [*torvis oculis*]" (83). Like a Greek chorus who mediates between stage and audience by framing the performed actions, by stringing discrete events into a coherent narrative, this Albertian guide occupies a third space that disrupts the linear relation between a centric point and viewer. As a semantic anchor usually located to one side of the main action—not unlike the distance point, which also serves to verify the perspectival scene—the Albertian chorus provides a humane contrast to the centric point, warping the geometric stasis of perspective. Drawn away from the centric point, the viewer fulfills the guide's silent request to sustain an ocular journey around the picture, to analyze the *historia*'s narrative ("what is going on") rather than enjoy a purely spatial rapture.[44] Alberti's painted chorus, an alter ego for the artist, thus implicates viewers in a *historia* that refuses to stay arrested for the gaze, but rather demands to come alive through performance.

As the viewer supplies a crucial piece of the *historia*'s semiotic puzzle, the process of building a meaningful world activates the viewer as a subject with agency and affect. Though a mobile, embodied gaze thus throws off-kilter the spatial mastery offered by the centric point, Alberti builds into *De pictura* just such a counter to the regime of perspective. Following Alhazen's influential theory of optics in *De aspectibus*,[45] and as Bosse would reiterate in his own treatise, *De pictura* divides the visual experience into spatial and narrative segments: an overall gaze that provides a sense of holistic depth, then an itinerant glance that explores how disparate elements create meaning together. To borrow Roman Jakobson's semiotic terms, the viewer initially enters a simulacral world founded upon a metaphoric relation of likeness, then embarks on a more desultory journey over the pictorial surface that endorses a metonymic relation of displacement and difference. While Norman Bryson contrasts the fixed, ahistorical gaze of perspective with the "irregular, unpredictable, and intermittent" glance,[46] *De pictura* always hinges these visual modes together, not least because Alberti values *historia* rather than landscape. From his earliest writings on vision, Alberti situates the viewer not only in space but also within a staged narrative.

Indeed, even when opening a portal into another world, single-point perspective regards space as an open textile to be read. To visualize how objects can be plotted on a vertical intersection, Alberti insists that painters use a "veil [*velum*] loosely woven of fine thread, dyed whatever color you please, divided up by thicker threads into as many parallel square sections as you like, and stretched on a frame."[47] By placing this device before an object, the artist easily perceives how even difficult shapes such as those "round and in relief [are] represented on the flat surface of the veil."[48] In Albrecht Dürer's treatise on artistic measurement, a woodcut depicts how a male artist tames an unruly curved object—a woman—using an Albertian *velum* divided into squares (figure 1.4). As a prosthetic that filters the painter's fallible sight, this open veil converts the visible world into packets of data that can be framed, mapped, and transferred to a pictorial surface.[49] Alberti thus interrupts a direct pathway between what the painter's eye perceives and what the painter's hand produces, inserting a coordinate plane between the material object and its artistic signifier. By adding a self-conscious pause where an object enters the semiotic realm, Alberti's veil makes visible the liminal position of an artistic signified: partly enmeshed with the object, partly inscribed in the artist's mind. In other words, this double-faced screen reveals the contours of a seductive world beyond, but also distances and flattens that world for entrance into a symbolic economy. If the *pavimentum* supplies

Figure 1.4. Woman mapped through a screen; woodcut from Albrecht Dürer's *Underweysung der Messung mit dem Zirckel und Richtscheyt* (Nuremberg, 1525). Bridgeman Art Library.

a foundational platform that enables the staging of a perspectival scene, then the *velum* constructs an architectural elevation that transforms the world into a depthless facade. By translating organic landscapes into the graphic language of perspective, Alberti veils not just the naked object but also the body of space.

Although *De pictura* strongly asserts the veil's centrality to every painter—"I do not understand how anyone could even moderately achieve this [perspectival effect] without the help of the veil"[50]—the treatise withholds any proofs or diagrams that explain the precepts behind this practical tool. *De pictura* thus inserts a rhetorical veil that dissuades readers from querying a method stated "briefly and . . . in a not altogether obscure fashion."[51] Assuming a feigned bonhomie as "a painter speaking to painters," Alberti implores that *De pictura* "be accepted not as the product of a pure mathematician but only of a painter."[52] Readers who desire clarity should await other treatises, Alberti explains: "We will explain the theory behind this if ever we write about the demonstrations of painting" (Cuius rei rationem explicabimus, siquando de his demonstrationibus picturae conscribemus).[53] Using terms that evoke Vitruvius, who defines the architectural signifier as "the demonstration unfolded in systems of precepts" (demonstratio rationibus doctrinarum explicata),[54] Alberti disavows the process of rational unfolding to present an already constructed signified. Despite revealing that he "used to demonstrate these things at greater length to my friends with some geometrical explanation,"[55] Alberti occludes the logical structure that underlies perspective, and indeed the whole edifice of *De pictura.* Alberti thus dresses his treatise in a facade whose meaning has already been worked out by the master theorist offstage, off-site, outside the frame.

Making Faces in Architecture

Unveiling, then veiling, the process of representation, *De pictura* brushes aside the need for logical demonstration by offering a heuristic technique whose results, the text implies, prove their own validity to the untrained eye. As this "self-evident" paradigm achieved a dominant status across early modern Europe, Piero della Francesca, the fifteenth-century painter, naturalized single-point perspective as the *costruzione legittima,* the "legitimate" method of constructing space.[56] Given the enduring success of this *costruzione legittima,* we might expect Alberti's architectural theory to simply translate the pictorial surface into a facade, shifting from one grid system to another. Undoubtedly, *De pictura*'s emphasis on a coherent, illusionistic surface provides a necessary stepping-stone to a modern architectural discourse that dwells on the facade. Could there indeed be an architectural equivalent of the *velum*?

One major clue emerges in the contrast between *De pictura*'s usage of *superficies* to describe the painted surface and the *facies* that appears at the start of *De re aedificatoria:*

> Let us therefore begin thus: the whole matter of building is composed of lineaments and structure. All the intent and purpose of lineaments lies in finding the correct, infallible way of joining and fitting together those lines and angles which define and enclose the surfaces of the building [*quibus aedificii facies comprehendatur atque concludatur*].[57]

A hierarchy instantly arises on the inscriptional ground of *De re aedificatoria:* Alberti subordinates internal structure to a singular element called the building's "face" (*aedificii facies*), a novel concept better known today as the facade.[58] Making his primal cut between interior and exterior rather than front and back, Alberti construes this facade as an outward-facing surface that stretches over the structural bones, thus giving material definition to the "lineaments" of design.[59] Just as *De pictura* valorizes the pictorial surface for its ability to carry meaning—"I call a sign [*signum*] anything which exists on a surface so that it is visible to the eye"[60]—*De re aedificatoria* creates a facade that permits architecture to signify. Perhaps this function explains why "all the intent and purpose of lineaments" should drive toward an architectural version of *costruzione legittima,* "the correct, infallible way of joining and fitting together those lines and angles." As Alberti develops a semiotics based on this syntax of lines and angles, a certain surface tension becomes evident:

while a centripetal force pushes the facade outward, a reciprocal force braces this architectural face in position as the most fetishized part of any building.

In the transition between two-dimensional grids and three-dimensional lineaments, Alberti's treatise must negotiate between the visual system in *De pictura* and the spatial philosophy of Vitruvius's *De architectura.* Alberti likely composed *De re aedificatoria* in the 1440s and early 1450s, the decades following his work on *De pictura,* possibly to fulfill a commission from Leonello d'Este to provide a commentary on Vitruvius. Although portions of *De architectura* had circulated throughout the medieval period,[61] the discovery of a complete manuscript around 1415 spurred humanists to reclaim Vitruvius as their intellectual forefather. As the first sustained response to classical architectural theory in the Renaissance, Alberti's treatise closely parallels Vitruvius's in theme and adopts the same ten-book structure.[62] Yet as Françoise Choay observes, Alberti's sudden first-person *I* in the ninth line of the Prologue establishes a strong authorial voice that diverges from his precursor's; in contrast, *De pictura* often resorts to the plural *we* to soften its didactic agenda.[63] Despite projecting this more forceful persona from the outset, Alberti does not condescend to readers by holding back abstract concepts, nor does he claim insider status as a practitioner. On the contrary, Alberti confesses his own insecurities about rescuing the principles of building from the "vast shipwreck" of time,[64] indeed from *De architectura*'s corrupt language. Noting Vitruvius's "pidgin" lexicon—"his speech such that the Latins might think that he wanted to appear Greek, while the Greeks would think that he babbled Latin"[65]—Alberti struggles to achieve the "correct, infallible way" to build upon classical ruins, starting with finding the right words ("frequentes difficultates . . . nominum inveniendorum").[66]

While early readers often lamented *De architectura*'s obscure terminology and absence of images, Alberti wishes not simply to repair these faults, to restore Vitruvius to health, but rather to construct a discourse that resonates with his own historical context. Given such a Janus-faced undertaking, *De re aedificatoria* fittingly promotes a facade that reflects upon its internal framework of geometric lineaments while looking outward to the viewer. On the one hand, to propel architecture toward a visually based exterior, a surface more than purely structural, Alberti devotes four books in *De re aedificatoria* to issues of ornament. However, with the debut of an architectural *facies* in Book I, Alberti decisively breaks from *De architectura* and dispels his anxiety of influence, turning his face away from Vitruvius's.[67] While *facies* appears only four times in

De architectura, three times to describe people and once to describe the facing of stone,[68] Alberti scatters thirty allusions to *facies* through his treatise, mostly in relation to a building's appearance, surface elements, or setting.[69] Alberti thus orients the building toward the outside by crafting a face that echoes the viewer's (and writer's) own. For example, Book IX suggests that a building "will be most attractive, if it presents a cheerful appearance [*facies*] . . . as if to attract and expect visitors"; further in the passage, Alberti promotes a "whole outer face and address of a building of whatever kind, bright and conspicuous on every side, since that increases its grace. . . . Let everything smile at the visitor and greet him as he arrives."[70] While Vitruvius bemoans his own elderly face (*facies*),[71] Alberti graces the building with a "bright and conspicuous" face that welcomes visitors like a host's embrace. In this face-lift from architect to architecture, early modern builders project a civic persona onto their brick-and-mortar surrogates, effacing their own bodies and labor behind a smiling facade.

Just as *De pictura* troubles the contrast between inner and outer, subject and object, *De re aedificatoria* posits a building that returns the viewer's gaze with a face shining and bright—not unlike the sardine can that seems to watch Lacan from the sea. To explain how the subject can be arrested by the gaze of another, even if that other radically lacks the faculty of sight, Lacan recounts a fishing excursion during which a floating sardine can, glinting with sunlight, catches his eye. As Lacan realizes from this incident, he is "not simply that punctiform being located at the geometral point from which the perspective is grasped. . . . That which is light looks at me, and by means of that light in the depths of my eye, something is painted . . . an impression, the shimmering of a surface."[72] The facade similarly captures viewers with a surface whose brightness, literal and figural, creates an impression outside the realm of geometric perspective, forging an affective bond between a quasi-subject and subject. Designed to address the viewer, the facade positions itself halfway between a passive materiality and an artificial vitality that appears sentient, always looking. If Alberti the supporter of *historia* wishes that "men painted in the picture outwardly demonstrate their own feelings as clearly as possible," then Alberti the architectural theorist displaces that emotive and theatrical function onto a building.

Indeed, while *De pictura* calibrates space using somatic units, *De re aedificatoria* extends the age-old logic that buildings should mirror human bodies to house an interior selfhood as well. For Vitruvius, the perfect body—male by default—subtends both a circle and a square; from head to foot, every component must exhibit the correct

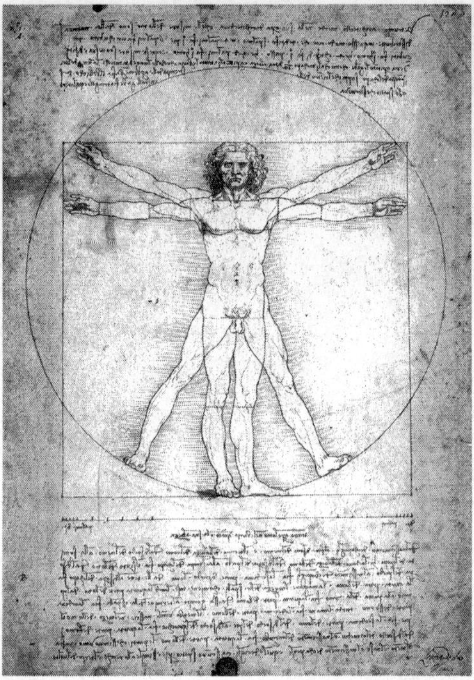

Figure 1.5. Leonardo da Vinci, "Vitruvian Man" (c. 1492). Galleria dell'Accademia (Venice)/Bridgeman Art Library.

proportions to achieve an organic, even cosmic harmony when joined together.[73] Renaissance artists, newly invested in anatomy, revived this model of a centered, measured, but notably flattened body, resulting most famously in Leonardo da Vinci's sketch of the "Vitruvian Man" (figure 1.5).[74] Applying this concept of bodily consonance to architecture, Vitruvius asserts that *decor* or *decorum* should constitute one of the six major criteria of building. Defined as the "faultless ensemble of a work,"[75] *decorum* affirms the principle that a well-composed building should form a cohesive whole rather than a collection of assorted parts. Translated into Alberti's treatise, however, this philosophy of balance and integrity becomes an aesthetics "in which beauty shines full face [*quo tota pulchritudinis facies mirifice collucescat*]: our term for this is *concinnitas.*"[76] While the lineaments provide a geometric skeleton for the built structure, Alberti locates *concinnitas* in a beautiful face that inspires visual wonder (*mirifice*), evoking a lantern-like facade that radiates light and ensnares the gaze. Although *concinnitas* should express a "critical sympathy of the parts" where nothing can be added, subtracted, or shifted without deleterious effects,[77] this perfect harmony evidently regards some bodily parts as more equal than others.

By promoting a facade that supplements the building, by wrapping a signifying ribbon around a radically blank interior, Alberti transforms architecture into what Gilles Deleuze and Félix Guattari term an "abstract machine of faciality,"[78] an impersonal device that produces faces. As Deleuze and Guattari contend, the face defines a plane of expressivity where the white wall of signification intersects the black hole of subjectivity; that is, the face serves as an inscriptional ground for the interplay of social meaning and subjective illegibility. For Deleuze and Guattari, a face "constructs the wall that the signifier needs in order to bounce off of; it constitutes the wall of the signifier, the frame or screen."[79] Architecture thus "positions its ensembles . . . to function like faces in the landscape they transform."[80] In this dynamic encounter, however, facades assume some of the nomadic, changing qualities of a landscape (*paysagéité*), while the landscape becomes more facial: recognizable, domesticated, mapped.

Single-point perspective creates a face precisely where the white wall of inscription (the panel or pictorial surface) meets the black hole of a centric point, a point that organizes the viewing subject. While Alberti's *velum* filters, converts, and frames the world into a tamed landscape, that landscape ultimately looks back across the picture plane with a face measured in human *braccia,* with a centric point that is both arbitrarily chosen and an uncanny lock for the viewer's eye. To prevent the viewer from slipping into this black hole of subjectivity, into a trance of self-fascination, Alberti supplies a choric double—by definition a redundant figure, at once inside and outside history—who seizes the gaze and impels a journey over a narrative topography. In so doing, Alberti invites the viewing subject to perform in a shared ritual that produces meaning, to exchange glances that bounce off and thus define a wall of social signification. Extending *De pictura*'s regime of spatial facialization, *De re aedificatoria* proposes a facade that can achieve universal *decorum* by knitting viewer and viewed ever closer on the same plane, by explicitly cutting both from the same organic fabric. Nevertheless, grafting this dazzling new skin onto architecture does not conclude and close off the building's play of meanings (*comprehendatur atque concludatur*) like a loving but sealed missive to the viewer. As Alberti discovers during his first major building project,[81] the irresolvable lines of tension emanating from a black hole/white wall dichotomy threaten to fatally undermine the cosmetically sutured face.

Architectural Facials: Massaging the Metaphor

The noble ideals of *concinnitas* may govern imagined cities built with philosophers' stones, but what happens to architecture in the mundane world? Since Alberti did not embark seriously on a building career until after 1452, when he presented a version of *De re aedificatoria* to Pope Nicholas V,[82] critics often maintain that Alberti places theoretical rigor ahead of practical execution.[83] Certainly, Alberti's credentials display the perfect *concinnitas* for a "counsellor-at-antiquity":[84] youthful education from a leading humanist in Padua, a degree in canon law from Bologna, various roles in the papal court, extensive knowledge of classical ruins, prolific writings on everything from family structure to satire to mathematics to statuary.[85] Yet this scholarly career takes a sharp detour into the material present when Alberti decides to construct actual buildings.[86] While Alberti's scant artistic output may reveal little to readers of *De pictura,* despite the author's choice to identify as *pictor,*[87] his three facade-only projects in Rimini and Florence illumine how the novel concepts in *De re aedificatoria* can be applied—and reassessed.

Alberti writes *De pictura* as a painter speaking to other painters, leaving aside scholarly proofs irrelevant to studio practice, but the budding architect who writes *De re aedificatoria* must demonstrate his ideas before the public eye. Yet the densely stratified cities of quattrocento Italy rarely afforded the luxury of building *ex novo,* of clearing ground to inscribe a wholly new design. Forced instead to repurpose and reconfigure existing structures, architects entered into an aesthetic dialogue with a richly polyvocal history, performing on the uneven platform of a spatial palimpsest. Such logistical exigencies may explain the popularity of a facade that smoothes over eclectic layers of construction to project a single legible *historia,* providing a synedochal marker of internal order that must be taken at face value. While *De re aedificatoria* espouses a *concinnitas* between interior and exterior, a transparent harmony, Alberti's first building project instantly challenged him to practice what he preaches. Working on the Tempio Malatestiano in the early 1450s, Alberti confronted the specter of a facade that refuses any organic relation to its internal structure, a facade that demands an absolute exteriority.

The Tempio Malatestiano in Rimini stands on the largely thirteenth- and fourteenth-century church of San Francesco, itself built upon the even older church of Santa Maria in Trivio. Starting in the 1440s, Sigismondo Malatesta, ruler of Rimini, embarked on a series of construction projects that eclipsed the original single-nave church. The bodies of various Malatesta relatives had already found resting places within the

Figure 1.6. Castel Sismondo, begun c. 1437. Photo: Mimi Yiu.

church when Sigismondo decided to transform the building into a family monument and mausoleum, turning a sacred locale into a largely secular homage to himself.[88] In the early phases of this building campaign, the artists Matteo de' Pasti and Agostino di Duccio carried out major changes to the interior scheme, including the addition of side funerary chapels for Sigismondo and his mistress, Isotta degli Atti.[89] Beyond this provision for a Malatesta bodily presence, Matteo and Agostino made the interior signify by weaving every variant of their patron's family emblem into the ornamental fabric; for instance, viewers could admire virtually everywhere an intertwined *S* and *I* that stood for Sigismondo and Isotta. However, when the building finally stood ready for the crowning touch of a facade, Sigismondo reached beyond his capable team in Rimini to request the services of Alberti, then a noted scholar but unproven architect in faraway Rome.

Alberti well understood his patron's desire for a bespoke face that boldly proclaims its identity, an outward statement that inverts the dark, inward orientation of medieval churches. The radical nature of Alberti's vision can be usefully contrasted with Sigismondo's nearby residence, the hulking Castel Sismondo, which models a species of anti-*concinnitas* with its sprawling mass of extra-thick walls, arrow slits, and scattered windows (figure 1.6). Begun only about fifteen years earlier, the moated

Figure 1.7. Arch of Augustus, at the entrance to Rimini's center. Photo: Mimi Yiu.

Castel Sismondo crouches in a classic medieval posture of defense, presenting an inscrutable nonface befitting the home of a notorious *condottiere*. After all, Sigismondo acquired more than a few enemies during his career of military conquest and political intrigue, not to mention his many romantic affairs. One powerful nemesis, Pope Pius II, branded him "the worst of all men who have lived or ever will live, the shame of Italy, the disgrace of our age"; in 1462, effigies of Sigismondo were burned in Rome to punish him for alleged crimes, while a bizarre papal edict consigned this sinner directly to hell.[90] The fortified Castel Sismondo thus reflects the everyday stress of a warlord's lifestyle, but for his final resting place, Sigismondo lowered his guard to stage a rebirth into light and grace—or at least, to depart the world in damned fine style. For someone who wished to restore his image, his body, his *historia* through a parallel renewal of architecture, could there be a more suitable choice of builder than Alberti?

Cannily linking his patron's lineage to the glories of imperial Rome, Alberti proposed a symmetrical exterior whose motifs evoke a nearby triumphal arch, the Vitruvian-era Arch of Augustus (figures 1.7 and 1.8).[91]

Figure 1.8. Tempio Malatestiano, front. A harsh cleaning in the Jubilee Year 2000 has whitewashed the medieval layer, which still registers as a yellowish stone around the door. Photo: Mimi Yiu.

With columns across the front, a grandly arched entrance, and an arcade running along one side, Alberti's classical vision sparked a trend for redressing Christian churches in the guise of antique temples. Such a radical mixture of past and present justifies the building's informal moniker, the Tempio Malatestiano (Malatesta Temple). Yet to realize what Vasari called one of the finest and most famous temples in Italy,[92] Alberti needed to literally surmount the irregular body produced by San Francesco's piecemeal growth during the Middle Ages, and even during earlier stages of Sigismondo's renovation.[93] The west-facing wall, for instance, features pointed Gothic windows that break the surface at uneven intervals; as the obverse of side chapels added by Matteo only several years ago, this stone exterior situates windows to serve the demands of internal lighting rather than the pleasure of external viewers. To preserve the ancient principles of Greeks and Romans, however, Alberti utterly rejects a building envelope from this more recent period in history, a surface that violates his standards of geometric harmony. Though dumbly useful in daily function, Matteo's surface forms a less-than-signifying face that Alberti exiles to architectural hell.

Alberti thus elevates his own marble facade above such a muddy ground, inserting a space between the two surfaces that reflects the aesthetic lacuna between Renaissance and Gothic.[94] Obeying a clear policy of segregation, what remains today of Alberti's unfinished facade gingerly encircles—but does not touch—the church beneath. For Alberti, mere resurfacing could never remedy a structure whose lineaments fail to achieve the "critical sympathy" demanded by *concinnitas*. Writing from Rome to Matteo, who continued to oversee building activity in Rimini, Alberti quashes any doubt about his divide-and-conquer strategy: "remember that I told you that this façade [*faccia*] must be entirely independent, because these widths and heights of the chapels cause me some concern."[95] Just as the Tempio's classical facade keeps a haughty distance from Matteo's walls, Alberti displays an alpha dominance by turning his face away from a colleague regarded as a lesser architect. Indeed, despite addressing the letter to "the eminent Matteo de' Pasti our very dear friend,"[96] Alberti's patient but inflexible manner implies that Matteo's limited, local *savoir* could not possibly match the penetrating gaze of a humanist looking all the way from Rome, both ancient and Renaissance.

Alberti's forceful will-to-power evinces his belief, noted in Book VI of *De re aedificatoria,* that builders must "adhere to a consistent theory; for to follow a consistent theory is the mark of true art."[97] Perhaps the most dramatic proof of Alberti's conceptual rigor emerges along the Tempio's west side, where the regular openings of an arcade recognize but refuse to align with the Gothic windows underneath (figure 1.9).[98] In these and other areas of opening where Alberti's facade does not totally mask the old church, unexpected vistas puncture the surface to reveal one building uneasily caged within another, as though a dark wolf lurked within a fine marble fleece. While Alberti's letter warns that inexact geometry would perturb the Tempio's architectural music ("ciò che tu muti, si discorda tutta quella musica"), a plangent discord strikes the viewer who observes two surfaces marching to their own drummers.[99] At the side arcade where even sunlight must stumble through mismatched apertures, our constantly stymied and rerouted gaze flounders between surfaces, finding one wall to be a bad echo of the other—but which is which?

In a series of poems known as the Malatesta Cantos, Ezra Pound astutely describes the Tempio's double-layering as "the filigree hiding the gothic,/with a touch of rhetoric in the whole."[100] For a purely superficial project that negates the possibility of organic growth, Alberti seems to define *concinnitas* not as the congruence of interior and exterior but rather as a desperate masking of masks, a muting of dissonant voices by

Figure 1.9. Tempio Malatestiano's side arcade with misaligned windows. Note the gap between Alberti's shell and the medieval layer underneath. Photo: Mimi Yiu.

an uppermost face that always speaks the final word. Yet by infusing his facade with a "touch of rhetoric," Alberti also positions exterior surfaces in conversation with each other and with the viewer, casting quasi-subjects and subjects as interlocutors to bring attention to the process of change. Alina Payne observes that Alberti's notion of the facade depends crucially on a relation to history, since he "declares the face of buildings to be the principal domain of appropriation and singles it out as the principal site of an eloquent dialogue with the past."[101] While Payne refers to Alberti's intertextual play with classical antiquity, a similar relationship obtains in his dialogue with a more abjected, recent history still marking the landscape. Although the Tempio's two exterior surfaces may not touch physically, a rhetorical touch develops as openings in Alberti's facade expose a *historia* of social and aesthetic change, showing viewers the density of meaning hidden within this architectural palimpsest. Because facades can never blanket a structure without leaving apertures for interaction with the outside, a dynamic rhythm emerges in those places of access where—regardless of the architect's intention—one layer plays against another, where overtones deepen the harmonic scheme.

Indeed, while Rudolf Wittkower describes Alberti as "screening the old walls with his Roman arches,"[102] this sieve-like screen so ineptly conceals what rests beneath that every arched opening actually frames the difference between the two strata: in this sense, the Tempio sounds not an overarching but an intra-arching harmony, with strategic pockets of silence where alternative voices break through. As Alberto Cassani argues, Alberti's *concinnitas* goes beyond "a completely banal harmony" to embrace "the difficult consonance" of naturally warring elements; Matteo's irregular elements, then, constitute "false notes left well in sight by Alberti, among the side arches, from *pietas* or from sadism."[103] By allowing conflicting melodies to resonate in tandem, by intertwining competing systems of signification, Alberti literally deconstructs the Tempio's facade to expose alternative methods of articulation. In linguistic terms, Alberti selects nodal points along the facade's own syntax to display paradigmatically—in depth—a range of architectural options. Instead of presenting the viewer with a compelling, coherent worldview like single-point perspective, the Tempio structures dialogic counterpoint into its semantic production. By undoing the logic of a unitary face, Alberti suggests that meaning arises from a process of deferral and difference, that architecture itself should be treated as a matter of *différance.* Aptly, then, Alberti's grandiose design remained incomplete when building ceased upon Sigismondo's death in 1468. As a half-built dream of enclosure that keeps failing to reach closure, Alberti's first attempt at creating a facade stands today in memory of productive difference.

Beyond the adverse conditions specific to San Francesco, however, Book VI of *De re aedificatoria* posits a general principle of superimposition that holds wherever:

> one wall is backed by another, like a pelt on top of clothing [*paries parieti quasi pellis vesti affulcitur*], and a kind of opening is formed that does not continue through but is blocked off by the intervening wall: it would therefore not be inappropriate to call this a "false opening."[104]

Curiously labeling this useless aperture as "a kind of ornament," Alberti clarifies his point by adducing that most well-known feature of classical architecture: columns arranged along a facade, either engaged or detached.[105] By regarding this line of columns as an extremely porous wall with large areas excised,[106] in effect creating a trans-parietal transparency, *De re aedificatoria* proposes a basic architectural unit composed of two superimposed planes, one reduced to skeletal vertical supports while the other provides a solid backing.

Abandoning a figure/ground, ornament/wall dichotomy, Alberti syncopates the rhythm of blockages and openings to construct a spatial depth of field purely for ocular pleasure. As a result, even the columns and blind niches across the Tempio's front should be regarded as following the same tactic of adding levels that governs the facade as a whole. By sculpting an architectural face more nuanced than a cellular layer of skin, Alberti seems to regard ornament as an intricate slicing away of strata, a teasing dance that unveils rather than a cosmetic plastering over. Yet with his analogy of the blocked opening to a pelt over clothing,[107] Alberti also suggests that this ensemble of ornamental clothing serves to conceal an elusive architectural body, perpetually hidden behind a false opening that thwarts the gaze. Evidently, in a postlapsarian world, even a church must sometimes dress—and redress—before addressing its public, pulling an extra pelt over a body now seen as shamefully deformed and inadequately clothed, a body no longer easily sighted or sited. As a second skin (*pellis*) that supplements the building's own, the pelt necessarily calls into question the idea of organic wholeness, indeed the function of enclosure itself as a determinant of identity.

In the nineteenth century, German architectural historian Gottfried Semper postulated that textiles rather than solid walls formed the first dividers of space, that hanging mats and carpets furnished a kind of primitive enclosure. Developed later only to supplement textiles, rather than vice versa, the much less supple walls of masonry and timber "were necessary for reasons that had nothing to do with the creation of space; they were needed for security, for supporting a load, for their permanence."[108] Noting that the German *Wand* (wall) and *Gewand* (dress) derive from a common root, Semper imagines architects as wall-fitters who dress space in textiles—"the true and legitimate representative of the wall"—to construct flexible, ornamented, nomadic dwellings.[109] Whether layering a pelt over clothing, or lace filigree over dark bones, the wall-fitter drapes textile partitions to define an always changing body of space, a body not fixed into the rictus of facialization.

Alberti's conception of the wall, particularly the facade, wavers between an awareness and erasure of textile construction. After defining ornament as a visual blockage, *De re aedificatoria* instantly attempts to reinstate a smoothly flowing surface:

> Any of these openings would be more beautiful for having its bones made entirely from one stone. Next best would be to compose all the parts so that there do not appear to be any joints.[110]

The paradoxical beauty of ornament thus hinges on a balance of visibility and invisibility, shifting between a seamlessly sutured sameness and an undulating topography of difference. In a further discussion of revetment, "the main ornament" of a wall with the exception of columns,[111] Alberti declares again that all surfaces should be covered with multiple coats (*tunicae*) of plaster to create a fine white skin (*cutis*).[112] As Mark Wigley notes, this white skin of plaster creates a mask that covers the imposition of masculine order on feminine materiality, while drawing a strict division between structure and ornament.[113] Yet this division becomes unstable even in Alberti's own lexicon, where a slippage emerges between the structural body and its external ornament: the *tunicae* (tunics) of plaster that beautify the wall should be finished off with a final *cutis* (skin) that gleams wonderfully like white marble ("splendentes marmorei candoris sintillulas mirifice referet").[114] Piling skin upon clothing like *pellis* over *vesti,* Alberti carelessly mixes organic and inorganic membranes to reinforce a bodily integrity, repeatedly whitewashing the building's structure to create a shining, hardened screen of signification (*mirifice referet*). Unlike the Vitruvian man, however, the feminine Albertian body cannot be chastely bound within a perfectly concordant geometry.

To expose this failure of corporeal limits, the Tempio Malatestiano removes patches of its cosmetic white dermis to reveal the disordered, "feminine" matter of its dark Gothic corpus, airing by design its own dirty secrets, its architectural underwear. Pulled apart by the desire for both an evenly polished surface and a finely contoured depth, the Tempio betrays its disjointed body at those shadowy, abjected orifices—the central portal, the side arches—where the building proves most difficult to enclose. Yet for viewers who choose not to plunge into the Tempio's seamy underbelly, Alberti provides discrete viewing positions that occlude these horrific apertures, using single-point perspective to engineer a sublime enjoyment of his classical mask. Standing directly across from the church's main entrance, for example, or looking obliquely at the west arcade from the piazza in front, viewers occupy those select locations that most successfully produce the illusion of a pristine, coherent temple (figures 1.8, 1.10).[115] Only with such a distanced, immobile viewer can the Tempio maintain this perfect image, however. When viewers draw near the front entrance, cross the threshold, or stroll along the side,[116] the Tempio's scarred inner surface inevitably appears in close-up like the ravaged face of Norma Desmond in *Sunset Boulevard*. At the same time, Matteo's older surface exudes its own grotesque allure for viewers who pursue glimpses of this body through the porous exterior,

Figure 1.10. Tempio Malatestiano's side arcade, viewed obliquely from the piazza in front. Photo: Mimi Yiu.

drawn to the darker side, to half-buried secrets. Driven by conflicting desires, viewers either occupy specific locations to enjoy the coherent upper facade or circle the building to explore its stratified history.

By propelling spectators around the perimeter, thus revealing a Gothic skeleton within an open marble closet, the Tempio allows its textile face to become frayed at the edges. That is, Alberti's facade solicits not only the static, metaphoric gaze of linear perspective but also a series of darting metonymic glances. Stitching together these quasi-cinematic sequences of metaphoric and metonymic images to construct a personal *historia,* the spectator negotiates between a marble screen of signification and the interstitial black holes into which an unwary gaze plummets. Caught off guard by the sight of windows not quite concealed behind an arcade, or by a darkened inner entrance not quite obscured behind the large Renaissance arch, viewers enter a psychic free fall that casts doubt upon their own faces, their own subjective coherence. Like the anamorphic skull that occupies the center of Hans Holbein's *The Ambassadors,* a vision of impending ruin confronts the viewer who looks even slightly awry at the Tempio's exterior; in this sense, the front entrance forms a kind of death's head that warns viewers of the building's decay from within, and of their own innate mortality. Indeed, the building almost demands that viewers employ an angled, anamorphic gaze to reflect upon the faciality of the facade, to recognize the beautiful artifice of Alberti's frame. Yet at these vulnerable places where the frame's limitations become all too apparent, where the architectural fabric comes too loosely undone, the facade loses its ability to signify as a coherent face.

The density of a facade's weave thus matters in keeping black holes from swallowing up the surface. After all, the facade behaves like a perspectival *velum* that dresses buildings to satisfy the dictates of architectural *decorum,* trying to domesticate resistant bodies into social readability.[117] Conversely, when a painter stretches a *velum* across a wooden frame, this pliable fabric transforms into a wall-like latticework with threads pressed against an object-made-image, not unlike columns strung across a facade. Indeed, single-point perspective constructs a false opening by separating the metaphoric window into two components: the loosely permeable *velum* that forms a textile screen and the solid (or more densely woven) pictorial surface that provides a supporting wall. Though sometimes pulled apart during the process of painting, as Dürer's grid implies, these two elements must ultimately be submerged under a glossy coat of paint, a shining face, an extra pelt that covers the unseemly, raw surface. To banish any notion of a black hole other than the centric point, the artistic facade that radiantly greets the viewer must efface its bodily depth to promote an illusory depth. Only when its layers remain tightly compressed can the false opening become facialized as an open window.

While Alberti construes both the architectural and artistic surfaces around a cluster of related concepts, the Tempio Malatestiano challenges the limits of translating from one discourse to another, the limits of metaphor in the literal sense of carrying across. Despite imposing a marble topcoat that mimics the screen of single-point perspective, the Tempio's unraveled facade cannot fully corset the abjected body within, the feminized matter that always occupies an interior and anterior position. As the irrational *mater* that gives birth to the masculine, Renaissance facade, this disavowed inner face nevertheless finds a measure of breathing room in the negative space between surfaces, a "no man's land" between aesthetic regimes. This architectural buffer thus creates an in-between space that affords a certain freedom, defining a third space between ideals and bodies that Plato termed *chora.*[118] Probing behind the sanctioned ideal of Alberti's facade, plunging toward the shameful body of Matteo's wall, the viewer's curious gaze enters this crevasse to blaze its own path, to assume the mantle of subjective agency. The viewer whose gaze switches from one surface to another necessarily constructs a dialogue between them, finding common ground in the interstices, in movement that

Figure 1.11. Matteo de' Pasti, medal of the Tempio Malatestiano (c. 1450). Münzkabinett, Staatliche Museen zu Berlin, #18217197. Photo: R. Saczewski.

follows impulse rather than mapped geometry. More than Alberti ever could, the viewing subject brings polar opposites into a common *historia,* eschewing dialectical synthesis for a rhetorical touching, a playful exploration of difference. In this sense, the Tempio recovers the ability of metaphor to signify.

The Face Gets New Lines

Ultimately, the seamless legibility that Alberti so desired in Rimini became possible only with a different kind of faciality: a medal struck by Matteo de' Pasti depicts a finished Tempio Malatestiano, an image likely based on a model that Alberti presented to his patron (figure 1.11). Isolated from history and locality to create an ideal Vitruvian body within a circle, the Tempio finally reaches its classical apotheosis in the currency of imagined architecture. Such a perfect union of vision and space eludes Alberti, however, despite his chosen emblem of a winged eye (figure 1.12). On the reverse of Alberti's portrait medal, also struck by Matteo de' Pasti, this winged eye appears beside the motto "Quid tum?" (What then?). After

Figure 1.12. Matteo de' Pasti, portrait medal of Alberti with a winged eye (c. 1450). © Trustees of the British Museum.

his frustrated efforts at Rimini,[119] a false opening of sorts in his budding career, Alberti might well ask: *Quid tum?* Turning away from the Tempio despite its fractured state, Alberti threw himself into two other facade-only projects in Florence under the patronage of Giovanni di Paolo Rucellai, a patriarch of the wealthy banking family. A brief analysis of these facades at Santa Maria Novella and the Palazzo Rucellai will help flesh out the contours of Alberti's evolving architectural face.

At the church of Santa Maria Novella, a religious center from the late thirteenth century onward, Rucellai charged Alberti with completing a medieval exterior whose cladding never advanced beyond the first cornice, leaving everything above blighted with unsightly bareness. Legally bound to retain the existing Gothic components,[120] including pointed arches that extend across the front and a large rose window in the upper story, Alberti designs a hybrid facade that derives *concinnitas* from the work of many hands and minds over the centuries. That is, Alberti forces disparate styles to merge on a slippery marble surface, discarding the Tempio's jangling layers for the harmony of a single integrated face (figure 1.13). While continuing a green-and-white pattern a touch more flamboyant than classically desirable, Alberti's facade imposes a spatial concord by using the module of a perfect square to unify conflicting aesthetic voices.[121] Alberti masks the architrave's faulty proportions by adding a high attic between the two levels, even though the rose window then rests upon the cornice itself. Pilasters and engaged columns are placed at musical intervals across the front, while scrolled volutes on either side connect the two stories and conceal the roofs over the

Figure 1.13. Santa Maria Novella, front. Photo: Mimi Yiu.

aisles. Likewise, Alberti inserts round arches in a Roman style above their pointed Gothic forebears, thus diffusing any medieval effect within a matrix of classical elements in the same color scheme. Most centrally, Alberti removes several blind arches to make room for a grand entrance that evokes the Pantheon, a much-admired exemplar of Roman architecture;[122] in so doing, he pulls back the building's skin to achieve a bright white smile. Indeed, Alberti's facade smoothes its medieval wrinkles by injecting *all'antica* fillers—old yet new—into available pockets of space. Realigning joints that no longer conform to prevailing standards of beauty, Alberti devises a solution that favors embedded simultaneity over layered temporal strata.

While Santa Maria Novella scatters the indecorous within the decorous to produce a glossy screen, a shining face that arrests viewers with wonder, this strategy of eliding difference could not succeed at the Palazzo Rucellai.[123] As the Rucellai family's housing compound, the palazzo was created from eight distinct buildings that clustered between the via della Vigna and via dei Palchetti (figure 1.14).[124] In his quest to rival the Medici, whose imposing palazzo was erected around 1444, Rucellai began crafting his architectural rejoinder from the heart: Bernardo Rossellino was hired to coalesce the eight buildings around an internal courtyard similar to the Palazzo Medici's. Yet perhaps because the

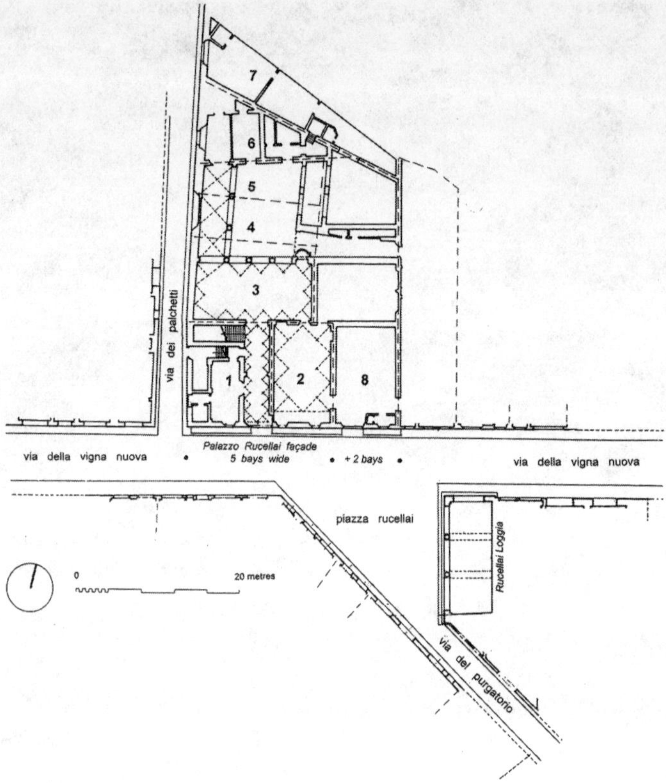

Figure 1.14. Palazzo Rucellai site map. Reprinted from Robert Tavernor, *On Alberti and the Art of Building* (1998), 82, with permission of Yale University Press and Robert Tavernor.

fledgling Rossellino lacked prestige among the Florentine upper classes,[125] Rucellai followed Sigismondo Malatesta's footsteps by entrusting the concluding architectural face to Alberti, who proposed a three-story, five-bay design.[126] Stretched across several buildings on the via della Vigna (figure 1.15), Alberti's facade again strongly echoes the Palazzo Medici with its rusticated sandstone, *bifore* windows, and classically inspired cornice.[127] However, Alberti softens the aesthetic by using pilasters to articulate the bays, adding panels of *opus reticulatum* (a diamond pattern) on the ground floor,[128] applying ornamented friezes between each story, and devising a humbler post-and-lintel entrance without arches. Yet the greatest contrast between the Rucellai and Medici homes arises from their differing inscriptional grounds, their respective locations that resulted in unequal viewing conditions. While the Palazzo Medici occupied a prime intersection along the spacious via Larga,

Figure 1.15. Palazzo Rucellai facade as seen from the piazza in front. Note the flattened pilasters to minimize depth and the jagged edge on the right for possible expansion. Photo: Mimi Yiu.

nestled into a scenic curve partly shaped by Medici power,[129] the Palazzo Rucellai squeezed into an awkward space that could not provide an expansive, dramatic vista. Unable to convey its intrinsic *concinnitas* to someone traveling along either the via della Vigna or the via del Purgatorio, a diagonal *allée* that stifled any frontal view (figure 1.16), this otherwise stately palazzo could offer only slivered, skewed glimpses to even the most determined admirer on the street.

Despite later attempts to rectify this situation by carving out a small triangular piazza and loggia across from the facade, the optimal angle of vision advocated by *De pictura* remained beyond reach in this densely serried locale. Robert Tavernor contends that, to mitigate the unflattering close-ups produced by urban constraints, Alberti "created the effect of a well-proportioned composition designed to be seen from key viewing positions."[130] On the one hand, Alberti presses the facade against

Figure 1.16. Palazzo Rucellai as seen from the tight confines of the via del Purgatorio. Photo: Mimi Yiu.

the street by flattening columns into pilasters, thus rendering the semblance of depth "fictive (as in a *trompe-l'oeil*)." More seriously, Alberti resorts to a panoply of visual tricks that make the building seem more balanced, especially when viewed from a sharp angle below: upper pilasters do not diminish in height and width as usual, for example, while window frames are adjusted to give more space above, between lintel and cornice.[131] These deceptions seem to violate the dictates of classical *decorum,* yet Vitruvius himself counsels architects to "produce a proper balance by adjustment, adding or subtracting from the symmetry of the design, so that it may *seem* to be rightly planned and the elevation may *lack* nothing" (emphasis added).[132] As the ideal viewer posited by single-point perspective vanishes in the wake of a typical passerby, glancing upward from time to time while hurrying elsewhere, the architect must dabble in optical illusion to assuage a sense of aesthetic lack, to conjure an effect of beauty in the urban congeries of blocked openings.

Leaving behind the concept of a winged eye that soars above mortal concerns, Alberti relocates ocular pleasure in what we might call a well-tempered perspective: a system that stitches together a series of mobile glances, preserving overall harmony by allowing individual elements to chime slightly out of tune. Thus, absent a piazza that affords a panorama of the facade, a staging area or *platea* that both the Tempio Malatestiano and Santa Maria Novella enjoy, the Palazzo Rucellai responds to an irregular urban pulse by marking its facade with a similar rhythm, shaping elements upon the exterior to interlock with the framing streetscape. While Santa Maria Novella carefully diffuses any discords so that, in a single coup d'oeil, the facade appears as a unified aesthetic entity, the Palazzo Rucellai repeats a perfectly regular module across five bays so that its surface can visually break up with minimal damage, parceled out to discrete viewers at a range of locations. To further offset a potentially off-kilter, partial glimpse, the palazzo's relatively uniform surface, only lightly rusticated for stylistic effect, promotes a fluent ocular itinerary that works in every direction. For viewers who approach from the west, Alberti wraps his facade around the corner to forestall a jarring peek behind the mask (figure 1.17). Such a maneuver also suggests a malleable facade that extends in multiple dimensions, a sentient face that pivots when hailed by its surroundings. Indeed, after Rucellai's purchase of adjacent properties, Alberti's graceful design proved flexible enough to build two more bays along what is now the via della Vigna Nuova. The jagged vertical edge that remains from this expansion, still visible today at the facade's right border, testifies to a mobile surface averse to neat enclosure.

A more potent unfinished edge pushes outward in the form of benches along the facade (figure 1.18), an addition that evokes the benches circling the Palazzo Medici's three street faces—a true benchmark in Florence. The facade bench occupies "a unique position in the nexus of interior and exterior space," Yvonne Elet argues, endowing Florentine palazzi with a palpable sense of civic authority, furnishing a semi-public arena where citizens gather to socialize or carry out business.[133] In this regard, the panels of *opus reticulatum* on the facade define the benches as places to build social networks, thus making the building's fabric into an open weave, the home into an open work.[134] Although these benches reduce pedestrian space, rendering viewing conditions even more restrictive, the Palazzo Rucellai physically reaches forward to embrace an anticipated public, claiming the street as an extension of domestic space. As the assembled visitors layer human faces upon their architectural counterpart, the palazzo's benches provide a social platform that

Figure 1.17. Palazzo Rucellai as seen from an acute angle on the via della Vigna Nuova. For a passerby, heightened spaces above the windows counter the effects of foreshortening, while a wraparound facade minimizes the sense of a shallow mask. Photo: Mimi Yiu.

Figure 1.18. Palazzo Rucellai benches in use today. Photo: Mimi Yiu.

relegates the facade to serving merely as a backrest and backdrop. By offering the public sphere an extendable horizon of benches that punctures the upright, uptight facade, the palazzo transforms a designed place (*lieu*) into a dynamic space (*espace*), reframing architecture as an event beyond the control of an architect, or even the powerful Rucellai.[135] Indeed, while the facade carefully regulates entrance into the palazzo's interior, the outward-facing benches invite a certain level of chaos by providing a stage open equally to friends and foes—perhaps even street performers like *cantimbanchi* (literally "bench singers").[136]

By attending to urban rhythms as well as the celestial harmony of proportions, by sustaining a dialogue with the present as well as the past, Alberti produces a double-faced *concinnitas* as sensitive to theoretical rigor within as environmental forces without. The early modern facade thus weaves itself into the open fabric of an emerging public sphere, blocked and unblocked by the pressures of a polis upon the private realm. After all, according to David Friedman, the first known usage of *facciata* in an architectural document pertains to a domestic building situated on an urban street: thus, the set phrase *facciata dinanzi a strada* (facade in front of the street) later simplifies to *facciata.*[137] While architecture often seems to represent the apotheosis of *costruzione legittima*—"faced with the geometry of the Ionian temple, the Glance finds in itself no counterpart to the enduring, motionless and august logic of architectural form"[138]—the reverently distanced facade in painting bears little relation to the architectural face that presses against a busy street rather than an empty *pavimentum.* Never simply a partner in the regime of perspective, Alberti's own facades undermine such a static purity with each successive project.

When released from serving as the paradigmatic form that comprehends and concludes the lineaments of *costruzione legittima,* architecture provides the space for a face-to-face encounter that exceeds an eye-to-eye geometry. In *De re aedificatoria,* Alberti imagines his ideal house in terms of just such a facial meeting. Forgoing his usual suave urbanity, Alberti dwells on the charm of a villa situated not far outside city limits, describing an idyllic locale marked by an unspoiled *hortus* (garden): "A building here will be most attractive, if it presents a cheerful overall appearance [*facies*] to anyone leaving the city, as if to attract and expect visitors."[139] As a traveler's gaze alights, perhaps through sheer luck, upon this beaming house along the way, Alberti envisions one face greeting another to establish a homely rapport, a bond of hospitality between a host and potential guest. In this implicitly gendered interaction that involves an ornamental house waiting for an anonymous spectator in motion, Alberti reveals his nostalgia for a facialized space governed not by geometry but interpellation, an architectural lure that readily turns public viewers into private visitors. In thus radiating invitations to move behind the veil, to cross the physical and social threshold, the signifying facade transcends its function as a boundary marker to domesticate the landscape in a network of affective relationships: "Let everything smile at the visitor and greet him as he arrives. And once he has entered, let him be unsure whether it would be more pleasurable to stay where he is or to venture further."[140]

While this utopian vignette draws upon three liminal elements—a cheerful facade, suburban locale, and roaming gaze—that each figure an outward motion from some type of body, Alberti's investment in a mobile, decentered visuality continues even when he enters the heart of a fortified community. While boulevards furnish a grand perspective through cities "renowned and powerful," *De re aedificatoria* praises an anti-geometric design that resists physical and visual invasion, urging towns to adopt a defensive plan where streets "meander gently like a river flowing now here, now there, from one bank to the other."[141] Since viewers borne by these organically curving streets must likewise career from here to there, Alberti makes clear the importance of building an unbroken line of facades along each route, thus preventing the trauma of stumbling upon a visual and spatial rupture: "it is no trifle that visitors at every step meet yet another façade [*facies*], or that the entrance to and view from every house should face directly onto the street."[142] On the one hand, this tactic ensures that no human or architectural face can turn away from the interface formed by the communal street, thus enfolding the external visitor within ribbons of facades interlocked in panoptical solidarity. Yet like a row of militiamen standing cheek by jowl, this phalanx of opaque screens also wards off the greater internal threat posed by subjective black holes that rend the social fabric, by spatial orifices that unexpectedly expose to citizens the abyss behind a public mask of order, cohesion, and security.

As the advent of facades transforms the world into a thicket of architectural screens, the subject internalizes a sense of being constantly looked at and positioned within a facialized space. Whether joyously beckoned or repelled with a forbidding glance, the viewer constructs a social face while moving through a landscape of quasi-faces. Alberti thus contends that every building should be designed

> so that one's gaze might flow freely and gently along the cornices, through the recessions, and over the entire interior and exterior face

> [*facies*] of the work, its every delight heightened by both similarity and contrast; and so that anyone who saw it would imagine that he could never be satiated by the view, but looking at it again and again in admiration, would glance back once more as he departed.[143]

Driven by an ocular desire that flows like a fluvial street, the viewer scans "the entire interior and exterior face [*facies*] of the work," charting a topography "heightened by both similarity and contrast." Despite the semiotic regime implied by this reading of space, Alberti stresses the viewer's sheer delight in gazing "freely and gently" without any sense of direction or closure. Indeed, consumed by the very process of consuming architecture, the viewer creates such an affective bond with the facade that even internal surfaces count as the "face of the work"; like a Möbius band, the facade keeps twisting upon itself, making the interior just as facialized a mask as the exterior, proving the building envelope to be self-addressed.

Strangely, this reversible facade effects a similar torsion in the viewer, who must always "glance back" over the shoulder when trying to leave. The building thus choreographs a dance—step, turn, glance—in which the facade's perceived gaze from behind prompts the viewer to recoil, to respond in similar fashion. However, rather than inscribe a geometric dance across the *pavimentum* of linear perspective, the viewer registers the facade as a series of discrete images gleaned from an ever-shifting location ("looking at it again and again . . . once more"), a series of glances that must be sutured together in the mind's eye like a reel of film. After all, Alberti's scenario implicitly describes a moving viewer who looks "over the entire interior and exterior face of the work," entering and exiting the building in the quest for ocular satisfaction. As the face that launched a thousand glances, Alberti's facade compels a masculine viewer to keep returning to the *mater* of visual pleasures, hailing a subject whose awakened desire will not be slaked. Unable to cease admiring his beloved's *facies,* to show his back to such a front, the viewer wants to mimic the facade in being all face, all the time, everywhere. His inability to become utterly facialized thus portends an enduring psychic lack ("imagine that he could never be satiated"), arresting his physical and affective progress. That is, as the masculine eye dresses the feminized architectural body in the fabric of his gaze, his signifying veil, the facade also undresses the viewer's unfulfilled desire for faciality—his own and others'. As chapter 2 will explore, this folding backward of the facade into the interior, even into the private spaces of the home, produces a subject acutely conscious of facing the world.

Chapter Two

How to Double Your Pile (in the Privacy of Your Own Home)

The English lexicon harbors a peculiar architectural label: the country pile. While the French have their *chateaux,* the Spanish their *casas,* the Italians their *villas,* the English have *piles.* Are these a spatial disease endemic to the British Isles? Did visitors once smile nervously upon hearing "my pile is your pile"? Though *pile* may bring to mind a spatial body that sprawls with wings akimbo, the term likely derives from the medieval *pele* (a fortified tower or castle keep), which in turn derives from the Latin *pila* (a stone wall or pillar). This etymology suggests a phallic verticality that epithets such as "this lofty pile" reinforce.[1] Yet the early modern pile also wrapped around the nucleus of a womb-like courtyard, embracing a negative space that oriented the building on a horizontal plane. Indeed, entering the sixteenth century, the most popular module in English architecture involved a courtyard framed by a single layer of rooms, a single chain where one room opened onto the next. This "single-pile" house, named in retrospect, activates a different network of concepts that associate *pile* with the French *pli* (fold, layer), a cognate to the modern English *ply.* A single-pile house thus comprises a single layer/fold of rooms, while the double-pile that arose later, as we shall see, remaps the interior by linking two layers of rooms.

As the dominant typology heading into the sixteenth century, the single-pile house inscribed a spatial and social code that forced traffic to proceed through every room in sequence, excepting strategic points of escape outdoors. Despite obviating a modern sense of privacy, larger houses often ranged from service areas at one end to sleeping quarters at the other (figure 2.1). While this orderly structure evokes an architectural chain of being, the domestic interior revolved around a central great hall whose hearth or fireplace provided the home's warm heart. As the anchor of every home, the great hall catered to diverse needs around the clock:

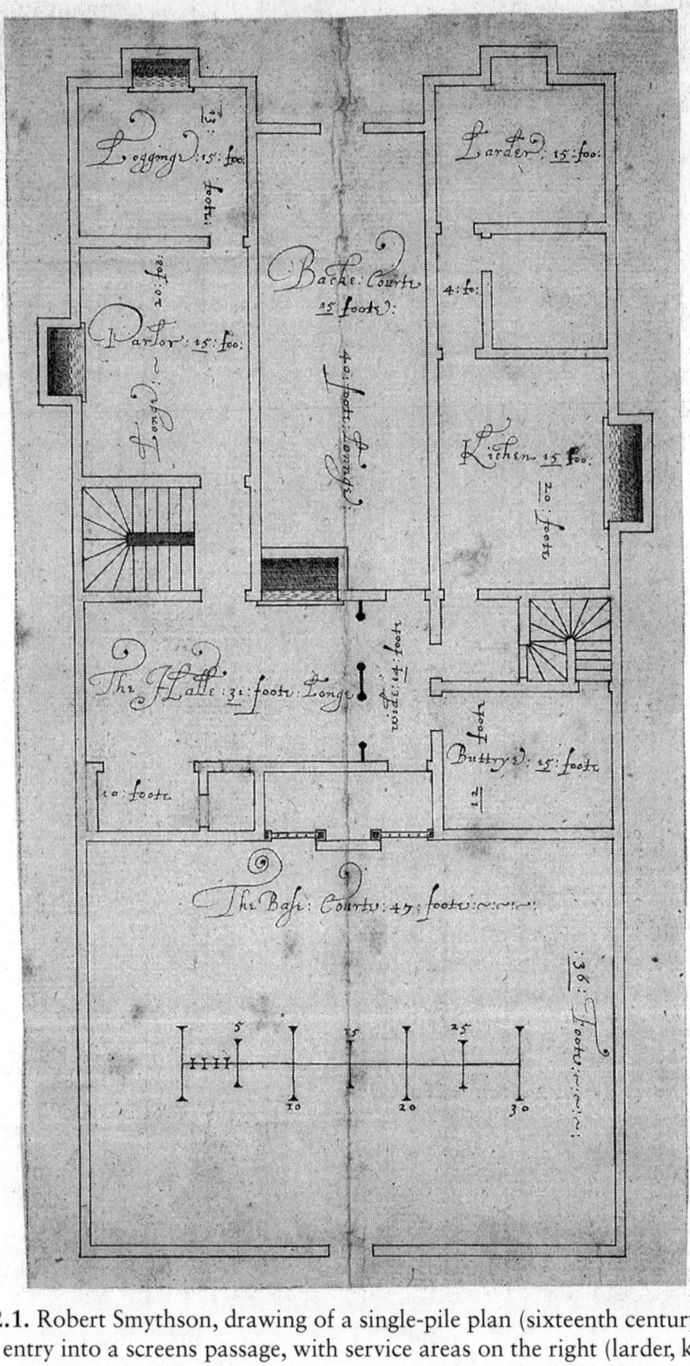

Figure 2.1. Robert Smythson, drawing of a single-pile plan (sixteenth century). Central entry into a screens passage, with service areas on the right (larder, kitchen, buttery) and family quarters to the left (lodging, parlor). RIBA Library Drawings and Archives Collection, #29155.

for example, receiving visitors, eating meals, staging entertainment, dealing with estate affairs, and sleeping.[2] Such radical openness maximizes available space by allowing different people to appropriate the same room for their own purposes. Taking the most flexible approach to space benefited an extended manorial household, whose numbers and make-up fluctuated constantly; a sanctum reserved for a single person or usage would impede the greater demands of others. Given this basic aversion to enclosure, houses logically routed traffic through rooms instead of setting aside passages dedicated to transition.

Yet with the passing of feudal society and the decline of open hospitality, the emerging nuclear family needed to rethink the utility of a single-pile house.[3] While a more intimate group might be expected to have fewer objections to a layout where rooms impinge on one another, a growing desire for privacy actually worked to the opposite effect. Circulation became a major concern as architects devised novel methods to connect and detour around rooms, as the great hall dissolved into a network of hallways. While houses aspired to screen each member of the household within a proper envelope of space, away from prying eyes, rooms themselves assumed more specialized and exclusive functions. In short, both subjects and spaces demanded a new faciality, a cohesive sense of identity that could be projected toward the exterior. Such a movement coincides with the migration of a Vitruvian and Albertian discourse of architecture into England from the mid-sixteenth century, raising questions about the subject's relation to the external and internal face of buildings. How does an Albertian concept of the facade, as explored in chapter 1, impact the discourse and practice of built space in early modern England? As the house refolds itself to push out a public face, the interior likewise adopts new kinds of facade that enclose a monadic subject. In this "architectural involution," the house remaps how a subject moves through the space of home—a space now inflected by practices of writing on multiple levels. Beyond recovering a canon of English architectural texts before the Restoration, a canon that brings architecture into the political realm, this chapter suggests that interior space assumes qualities of writing itself. The story of early modern architecture is the story of writing home.

A House for Plato

Mid-sixteenth-century England sorely needed an architectural face that could signify a coherent identity. After Henry VIII began dissolving monasteries in the late 1530s, hundreds of buildings suffered irreparable damage as the Crown seized and sold church property, often demolishing structures to plunder their construction materials. Alarmed by such wholesale "ruyne & dekay," the chaplain Thomas Starkey warned his king that "our cuntrey myght appere so to be defacyd as hyt had byn lately ouerrun wyth ennymys in tyme of warre."[4] Unlike the physical extirpation of *razed* or *plucked down,* both frequently used in this period to describe Henry's campaign of destruction,[5] Starkey's *defaced* suggests a mode of injury that despoils an architectural and thus national identity; his usage perhaps even gestures toward an iconoclastic vandalism that undresses the ornamented surface.[6] In an early English-Latin dictionary (1572), Richard Huloet notes a specifically textual aspect to defacement that involves the crossing out of words: "Dashe, or to geue a stryke with a penne, as where a strike is made through a line, at length or other wyse to deface the wryting."[7] Defacement thus implies placing something under erasure by making visible both the word and its stroke of deletion, creating "the mark of the absence of the presence."[8] For the well-traveled Starkey, who may have been "the most Italianate Englishman of his generation,"[9] the visual trauma of a defaced countryside ("appere so to be defacyd") correlates with the social injustice of transferring lands to an elite "wych haue therof no grete nede at al," a travesty that "schal much deface & gretly dymynysch the profyt of your acte."[10] Like a diminished and devalued coin, the defaced English landscape has been internally ravaged by a monarch who realigns the nexus of church, state, and property. While Starkey dares not criticize the "profyt" of Henry's war against his own country, a devastated post-Reformation England still required a social and spatial refacing to define its new structural identity.

Spurred by an inscriptional ground strewn with monastic remains like a defaced text, England embarked on an ambitious program of building that would stretch far beyond former church holdings. Such a Great Rebuilding transformed the nation's very sense of identity, not least by redesigning its most intimate spaces of habitation.[11] As George Hakewill would marvel by 1627, "whether we cast our eyes abroad into the countrey vpon the houses of Noblemen & Gentlemen, or vpon the Colleges & Schooles in the Vniversities, or vpon the dwellings of the Merchant & Artificer in the towne & citty, specially in the *Metropolis;* wee shall generally find a wonderfull great change in building within these last hundred years."[12] To fashion this "wonderfull great change," to redress the wrongs of a ruined landscape, architecture first needed to establish credibility as a design-oriented profession with intellectual moorings. John Dee's preface to *Euclid* (1570) provided an early boost to the status of architecture by placing it "among the *Artes Mathematicall.*"[13]

Anticipating that readers might find the "grosse workes" of construction "not worthy, or not mete" of elevation to the liberal arts, Dee crucially separates an architect's critical faculty from a builder's physical labor:

> the *Architect* procureth, enformeth, & directeth, the *Mechanicien,* to handworke, & the building actuall, of house, Castell, or Pallace, and is chief Iudge of the same: yet, with him selfe (as chief *Master* and *Architect,*) remaineth the Demonstratiue reason and cause, of the Mechaniciens worke.[14]

As "chief Iudge" and "chief *Master,*" architects oversee the "handworke" of a "*Mechanicien*" who merely executes a given design, who mutely follows orders. In contrast, architects engage in the headwork that furnishes "Demonstratiue reason and cause" for this manual undertaking; architecture thus becomes a discursive field of knowledge that values critical and creative problem-solving. In short, the architect should break ground intellectually, not physically. Despite the absence of an instaurational treatise like Alberti's *De re aedificatoria,* the emergence of this experimental impulse challenges the assumption that early modern England occupied a zone of perennial delay and degeneration, that "strictly speaking, England's contribution to architectural theory dates only from the beginning of the eighteenth century."[15]

Positioned as a critical interlocutor with Continental developments rather than trailing in their wake, sixteenth- and early seventeenth-century England constructed its own spatial discourse across a variety of platforms, including printed texts, manuscripts, drawings, and actual buildings. Since the same religious and political discords that defaced England also restricted travel to Italy, among other Catholic regions, English builders rarely encountered in person the Albertian facades erected abroad during this period. While a handful of major figures like John Shute, Inigo Jones, and Henry Wotton enjoyed the luxury of studying this new aesthetic firsthand, architectural exchange until the mid-seventeenth century flourished mainly through a book trade that operated along French and Flemish routes. For every artisan who crossed the Channel from the Low Countries and France to assist in refacing England, many times that number traveled virtually through imported treatises and pattern books that streamed into gentlemen's libraries.[16]

Opening a world beyond the technical advice found in Leonard Digges's *A Boke Named Tectonicon* (1556), a builder's manual reprinted seventeen times by 1656,[17] printed works by the likes of Vitruvius, Serlio, Palladio, Scamozzi, Dietterlin, and de l'Orme awakened English interest in giving architecture a discursive corpus. Indeed, the birth of a glorious Protestant nation became entwined with the birth of architecture, textually and physically. John Shute's aptly named *First and Chiefe Groundes of Architecture* (1563)—regarded as the first English treatise on the subject—broaches the question of origins by conflating biblical history with Vitruvian conjecture about how primitive societies banded together for shelter.[18] Invoking a primal knowledge "withdrawen and hidden . . . kept secret and not spoken of" during the Dark Ages,[19] Shute claims to have recovered this lost "science of Architecture" not only by searching out Latin, Italian, French, and Dutch writers, but also through his own "experience and practise, gathered by the sight of the Monumentes in Italie."[20]

Identified on the title page as a "Paynter and Archytecte," Shute attempts to model for his English readers the prototype of a new cosmopolitan architect: a researcher of foreign texts and edifices, a scholarly writer, a practical builder, and not least, an aesthete blessed with a painterly eye. A "Perfecte Architecte or Mayster of buyldings," Shute explains, clarifying the unfamiliar term *architect,* "must also be a perfect distributor of the great misteries, that he hath perceued and experymented, that playnlye and briefly he maye discurse and open demonstrations."[21] Instead of toiling at a mundane trade, Shute's magus-architect delves into mysteries to expose wondrous "depe secretes" using plain discourse and open demonstration.[22] In the first English edition of Serlio's *The First Booke of Architecture* (1611), translated indirectly from a 1549 version in Dutch, the "Architector or Workeman" must similarly master above all skills "the most secret Art of Geometrie."[23] Lucy Gent insightfully notes that Serlio's translator refashions the original "la certissima arte della Geometria" (the most certain art of Geometry) into a matter of utmost secrecy.[24] Flourishing the same cloak of concealment, Henry Wotton's *The Elements of Architecture* (1624) asserts that an architect should be "no superficiall, and floating *Artificer;* but a *Diver* into *Causes,* and into the *Mysteries of Proportion.*"[25]

In this widespread insistence on the secrecy of geometrical proportions, English architecture construes itself as a field of closed, dark knowledge that can be—with a theatrical gesture—revealed to the astonished viewer. Since rational demonstration involves display, architects who dive beyond the superficial must retrieve and re-present these profound mysteries on the built surface, whether conceived as physical or textual. As showmen of the esoteric, architects and architectural writers often borrow the incantatory language found in *libri secretorum* (books of secrets), a medieval and early modern genre predicated on revealing natural arcana for public consumption. The most popular book in this tradition, the pseudo-Aristotelian treatise *Secretum secretorum* (*The Secret of Secrets*), ranges widely over topics from politics to medicine, drawing readers into a shared arena of disclosure.[26] If Western modernity nurtures an impulse to confess hidden truths, as Michel Foucault argues, then this premodern discourse on space points to a similar cultural desire to both create and dispel shadows in knowledge, to disperse secrets across a network of scribes and translators.[27] Using the tropes of discovery that undergird a theosophical discourse, the early definers of English architecture construct an epistemology based on finding and unfolding secrets—a tactic that might be expected more from abstruse freemasons than practical masons. Indeed, such a rhetorical strategy mirrors the patter of mountebanks who peddle mysterious ointments from benches and platforms, who mount impromptu shows like the *cantimbanchi* discussed in chapter 1.[28] As street performers of a different stripe, however, architects realize buildings that stand not only as books of secrets to be pored over in reverence, but also as books of revelation that reach outward to an enraptured audience.

Adopting an erotics premised upon a continual practice of confessing interiority, the architectural body evolves a facade that can visually mark this veiling and unveiling of spatial secrets. By displaying hidden knowledge to the uninitiated through a *di-mostratio,*[29] a duplication of an enlightenment that has already occurred elsewhere, architects become purveyors (Shute's "distributor") of a cosmic interiority. In other words, architecture strives to construct microcosmic structures that resonate visually with the mathematical perfection of celestial spheres. Unlike other disciplines that ostensibly discover and divulge secrets already inherent in the world, architecture constructs its knowledge in very tangible forms that alter the landscape whose hidden truth it purports to reveal. Because architecture thus remakes the world in the course of expressing it, buildings can only imperfectly reflect an always shifting space, performing a skewed *di-mostratio* that verges into mime. Nonetheless, as the term *architect* seeps into English culture in the late sixteenth century,[30] a certain aura of mystical divination envelops the artificer whose learning, whose trafficking in transcendent ideals, allows the staging of a spatial experience akin to rapture.[31] For "euen in the priuatest workes," Wotton contends, buildings should form "a sound piece of good Art, where the *Materials* being but ordinarie stone, without any garnishment of sculpture, doe yet rauish the Beholder, (and hee knowes not how) by a secret *Harmony* in the *Proportions.*"[32] The writer George Chapman further links this musical stirring of a viewer's soul to the rhythms of metrical verse, claiming that "Ancient Poesy, and ancient Architecture, [require] to their excellence a like creating and proportionable rapture."[33] The reader of architecture thus enters a state of almost religious ecstasy when ravished by the open secret of a sublime, yet subliminal concord: a spatial poetry.

To engineer this affective resonance between the internal workings of the architectural and human corpora, architects must cultivate an aesthetic sense of proportion rather than acquire manual skills in construction. Shute thus emphasizes his visual credentials as a painter trained by the "sight of the Monumentes in Italie," while Inigo Jones first appears in the historical record as "henygo Jones, a picture maker."[34] Drawing upon an ability to compose space like a well-ordered tableau, to devise a human microcosm that thrums with divine harmony, the architect must learn to read and recreate a book of the mysterious world for an external beholder's pleasure. For Andrew Boorde, a physician and cleric who traveled widely on the Continent, a house situated in a "comodyous" setting "doth not onely satyssfye the mynde of the inhabytour, but also it doth co[m]forte and reioyseth a mannes harte to se it, specyally the pulcruse prospecte."[35] Urging architects to become picture makers who frame a beautiful "prospecte," Boorde implies that buildings serve a function beyond fulfilling the physical needs of an "inhabytour." Indeed, a good architect not only satisfies the rational mind of an insider, but also soothes and delights an outsider's heart with vistas that stretch into the distance. As the title of his treatise informs us, Boorde aspires to "*Lerne* [i.e., teach] *a man to be wyse in buyldyng of his howse*" as much for his physical health as "*for the helth of his soule.*"[36]

Architecture thus serves to uplift a person whose heart, mind, and eye fall sway to a "pulcruse prospecte." Just as George Hakewill exhorts his fellow Britons to "cast [their] eyes" upon the "wonderfull great change" wrought on their landscape, Boorde stresses the ocular sense in asserting that buildings should "be placable [pleasing] to the iyes of all men to se and to behold."[37] No one admired "the *Properties* of a well chosen *Prospect*" more than Wotton, who opted to study optics at Oxford.[38] Elevating "the *Royaltie* of *Sight*" above other means of perception, Wotton posits a rapacious gaze that renders architecture not only "placable," but also placeable:

> For as there is a *Lordship* (as it were) of the *Feete,* wherein the Master doth much ioy when he walketh about the *Line* of his owne *Possessions:* So there is a *Lordship* likewise of the *Eye* which being a raunging, and Imperious, and (I might say) an *usurping Sence,* can indure no narrow *circumscription;* but must be fedde, both with extent and varietie.[39]

Wotton contrasts two modes of sensory "Lordship" that define the master by defining his domain. For Wotton, the soaring vision of a solitary "Eye" clearly trumps the plodding motion of "Feete," which are bound not only to one another but also to the earth. Defying such "narrow *circumscription,*" the royal gaze craves both "extent and varietie" to satisfy the maw-like pupil of its ravening eye. Instead of tracing the limits of a horizontal ground, the viewer masters space by confronting and consuming surfaces unto infinity, by feeding the "usurping Sence" with optical delights.

This "Imperious" eye that conquers space could have been plucked straight from Alberti, whose personal emblem features a winged eye. Not only does Wotton's treatise praise Alberti as a "learned Searcher,"[40] but Wotton himself possessed a rare manuscript copy of *De re aedificatoria* with some of Alberti's own annotations.[41] While crediting Alberti's prowess in emending Vitruvius, who suffers from a tendency "to expresse himselfe so ill," Wotton believes that Alberti "studied more indeede to make himselfe an Author, then to illustrate his Master."[42] Since Wotton aspires to expound upon Vitruvius for English readers, he abandons further inquiry into *De re aedificatoria*'s original concepts, turning away from a Florentine hailed as "the first learned Architect, beyond the Alpes."[43] Nonetheless, Wotton reveals an intellectual debt to Alberti with references to the "*Face* of the Building," including his advice that architects check "whether the principall *Entrance* be on the middle Line of the *Front* or Face, like our *Mouthes,* whether the *Windowes,* as our *Eyes,* be set in equall number and distance on both sides, whether the *Offices* like the *Veines* in our Bodies, be vsefully distributed."[44] Wotton employs a facial analogy to express organic principles of harmony, despite never fully exploring the implications of an architecture propelled toward the exterior. In contrast, the more literal-minded Shute prescribes actual measurements for columns by posing various human figures beside and as the classical orders; bodies thus appear to petrify directly into architecture.[45] Despite a reliance on pedantic terms and lavish images of elements *all'antica,* Shute produces a folio that resembles a builder's manual, a practical guide that contrasts Wotton's attempt to devise a complete theory of building.

Neither an artist nor a builder, Wotton remains very much limited to architectural discourse in the narrow sense, confessing that "my fortune is very vnable to *exemplifie,* and *actuate* my *Speculations* in this *Art.*"[46] Wotton belongs to a new breed of hands-off architect who edifies only in his mind's eye, as Henry Hawkins's *Partheneia Sacra* (1633) explains:

> Some are Architects by hand only, and no more, who frame their buildings by roat, taking forth copyes heer and there, but can afford

> no reason at all for what they do, nor inuent ought that is worth a rush. . . . Others are Architects by booke only, and by discourses which they haue read; but they haue no hands to put in practise, and know but the Theorie only; such as they, are good for nothing, but to build a *house* for *Plato,* of Ideas, al suspending in the ayre.[47]

Moving beyond Dee's hierarchy in which an architect deploys "Demonstratiue reason and cause" to direct "the Mechaniciens worke," Hawkins designates a category of architect wholly immersed in textuality, an armchair philosopher divorced from any practical enterprise. While Vitruvius asserts that architects should combine material praxis with reasoning ("et fabrica et ratiocinatione"),[48] Hawkins parses this latter aspect not simply as design or theory, which could occur in any medium, but instead specifies written "discourses" propagated "by booke only." Such a coterie of exclusively book-bound architects would include both Wotton and Shute, two authors who leave no known legacy of built works.[49] Indeed, as an exemplary speculator and spectator of space who muses from a well-stocked library, his hands dirtied by ink rather than soil, Wotton himself plumps for a Platonic architect concerned only with "the Designement and *Idea* of the whole *Worke,* [whose] truest ambition should be to make the *Forme,* which is the nobler Part (as it were) triumph ouer the *Matter.*"[50]

Until the late seventeenth century, English architects who build piles and those who build piles of books tend to follow discrete career trajectories; although builders and builder-patrons such as Robert Smythson, Robert Stickells, Inigo Jones, Francis Willoughby, and Thomas Tresham certainly absorbed concepts from a variety of printed texts, including pattern books, they themselves never furthered a published discourse on architecture.[51] Perhaps early modern England's most tantalizing brush with producing an Albertian treatise occurs in the unpublished notebooks of Roger Pratt, a gentleman builder active in the mid-seventeenth century. Although Pratt displayed some inclination to elaborate a theory of architecture, his thirteen volumes of miscellany—comments, memoranda, and construction accounts—never coalesced into the anticipated magnum opus. Ironically, in a passage that outlines the history of architectural treatises, Pratt himself observes how numerous authors have failed to articulate a philosophy of building; coaxed to fruition, such a project would allow readers to "see how a complete body of Architecture is to be framed, *which as yet hath been done by no one of them.*"[52] Confronted by a universal inability to totalize the "body of Architecture," to place its corpus in the proper frame, Pratt's own effort to build a solid theoretical foundation could not help but fall short as well. Thus, while this section continues with a *précis* of Vitruvius and Alberti, Pratt's modern editor soon inserts this note: "*Here 13 pp. have been cut out of the note-book.*"[53] Whether they have been excised by Pratt or someone else, the unlucky loss of these thirteen pages out of thirteen notebooks, in a section immediately following his summary of *De re aedificatoria,* seems almost a facetious joke designed to underscore the desultory omissions that deface English architectural writing.

Absent a coherent discourse on architecture, a corpus finished with a smiling face, English builders must look awry to establish their own sense of spatiality. Accordingly, the first interlocutors in a Vitruvian dialogue venture into print from allied disciplines, stepping forward to deliver a brief excursus on architecture before exiting to other arenas of interest. One of the earliest attempts to grapple with Vitruvius emerges in Johannes Ferrarius's *De republica bene instituenda* (1559), a work of political philosophy translated by William Bavande. Faithfully parsing the opening section of *De architectura,* Bavande introduces an English readership to the central Vitruvian tenet that architecture

> hath twoo groundes: the frame, and deuise. The frame we call that, whiche is made by hande, a continued and frequented conceipt of practise. Deuise is that, whiche by cunnyng and reason of proporcion, can descriue and open the thinges framed.[54]

Rendering Vitruvius's *fabrica* as *frame* and *ratiocinatio* as *device,* Bavande situates architecture on joint spatial and intellectual "groundes," the same punning term chosen by Shute for the title of his treatise. Whether through writing, drawing, or mapping—all modes of inscription within the purview of the early modern *descrive*[55]—the architect unlocks secrets of the built structure with a design, a "Deuise," that "can descriue and open the thinges framed." Whereas Vitruvius more generically attributes to *ratiocinatio* the function of "demonstrare atque explicare" (to demonstrate and explain),[56] Bavande's verbs emphasize the aspects of inscribing and unfolding (the *pli* of *explicare*). Without a sound device to provide a semiotic foundation, a solid basis for the building to signify, the material "frame" remains closed, dark, illegible, faceless.[57] To unwrap an interiorized spatial meaning for the public, to shape the material ground into a device that speaks to every viewer, a Vitruvian architect employs a "cunnyng" and "reason" quite different from the pragmatism of William Cuningham's *Cosmographical Glasse,* published the same year: "he that wyll couer the roufe of his house, before he haue made the foundation, and buildyd the walles: besyde the losse of his cost, shall be thought scarse a wytty builder."[58]

Beyond knowing to build from the bottom up to avoid physical and financial collapse, a "wytty builder" by Vitruvian standards must ground himself in a discursive fluency, an ability to *descrive* articulately to stave off incoherent design. Such an investment in semiotics reappears more decisively in Dee's translation of the same passage from *De architectura:*

> Architecture, groweth of Framing, and Reasoning. &c. Reasoning, is that, which of thinges framed, with forecast, and proportion: can make demonstration, and manifest declaration.[59]

Skipping over the process of framing with a convenient "&c.," Dee focuses on how a capacity for reasoning "can make demonstration, and manifest declaration," thus imbuing architecture with a rhetorical power to elucidate the unknown to an as-yet-unknown third person. Since architecture itself stands as a declarative statement, a perpetually self-unfolding symbol, attention inevitably fastens onto the surfaces whose articulation of space makes visible this proportional harmony. While mathematical adeptness allows an architect "by measure to declare his reason," as Bavande notes, the demonstration of this spatial *decorum* still depends on expressive surfaces that

> garnishe the woorkemanship of buildyng, whereby through diligence, the cause of euery thyng maie readily bee opened. Whiche thing euery manne confesseth, maie more euidently bee shewed by Philosophie.[60]

Thus working toward the same revelatory sense of rapture, architecture and philosophy converge strikingly in early modern England on the discursive ground of political treatises like Ferrarius's *De republica bene instituenda,* a translation from the French of *Aristotles politiques, or Discourses of gouernment* (1598), and Thomas Elyot's *The Boke Named the Gouernour* (1537).[61]

As a corollary to Hawkins's observation that book architects build houses solely for Plato, political philosophy—Neoplatonic and otherwise—builds a commonwealth upon an architectural foundation. Defining a species of what Charles Taylor calls "common spaces," the meeting places that constitute building blocks of a networked public sphere,[62] the sixteenth-century theorist Jean Bodin asserts that generally accessible locales like markets, churches, walks, theaters, city walls, and open pastures bind a community as things "of citisens to be had in common among themselues."[63] In this paradigm that conceives of the public sphere as including spaces of assembly and self-definition (city walls), the facades of private dwellings become a limit-case that questions the extent of common space. After all, since the Greek *nomos* designates both law and wall, as Hannah Arendt points out, every community must be founded on both tangible and intangible edifices that enforce norms of social conduct.[64] Forming "a kind of no man's land between the public and private,"[65] these juridical and architectural boundaries distinguish not only between citizen and outsider, but also between citizen and citizen.

For Arendt, it is precisely "the boundaries between one household and the other" where external appearance most crucially enters into public signification.[66] As though echoing an Arendtian reading of *nomos,* Bavande's translation of Ferrarius notes that dwellings must be regulated by civic authority "bicause it is not so priuatly, as commonly hurtful to the comly view of a citee, by meanes of ruinous and vnperfect buildynges, defaced, whiche thing the ciuill lawe doeth prohibite vtterlie."[67] To avoid the kind of "naughtie buildyng" that defaces the common view and defiles a commonwealth,[68] private individuals must learn to build comely facades that please the public eye, to satisfy the disciplinary function of *nomos* as both law and wall. Architectural treatises serve this agenda by constructing an informed readership that reciprocally constructs the commonwealth, thus conceiving the nation as a public capable of reading—and reading about—its own spaces. In a prefatory note to "Lovers of Architecture," Serlio's translator proclaims his intent not only to enlighten other artificers, or a solitary patron, but more powerfully "to benefite the Publicke" whose ignorance of geometry "hath left us many lame Workes." To reinforce this political agenda, the translator inserts formulaic phrases at the ends of Books 1 and 2 that reiterate, like a refrain, a desire to publish "for the benefit of our English Nation, at the charges of Robert Peake."[69] An architectural discourse thus fulfills a critical public function by enabling private citizens to repair or prevent the "lame Workes" that cripple a body politic. Indeed, Alberti himself believes that facades should be decorously modest yet "as handsome as possible," since these public faces serve "as much to distinguish family and country as for any personal display."[70]

Just as facades stand together to project a coherent image of civic identity, Ferrarius staunchly advocates the right of every citizen "to bee planted in a faire builded citee: where houses be bothe artificially builded, and in rankes proporcionably matched."[71] Manfredo Tafuri claims that, for some Vitruvian commentators, architecture "not only reveals the truth of the universal harmony through its harmonic proportional structuring, but also, by extending to the city its own perspective organisation, allows a harmony which finds in the terrestrial *civitas* the concordance of the divine *civitas*."[72] Forging an aesthetic concord between geometry and sociality, Ferrarius demands that houses stand "in rankes proporcionably matched" to transform the *civitas* into a matrix of perspectival *allées,* composing rows of facades that resemble lines of smiling, similar citizens. Indeed, at this historical juncture when the architectural face becomes a form of politically charged artwork, Henri Lefebvre identifies an epistemic break in spatiality as "façades were harmonized to create perspectives; entrances and exits, doors and windows, were subordinated to façades—and hence also to perspectives."[73]

As the primary source of a facade-based spatiality, Alberti's *De re aedificatoria* leaves an early imprint upon English architectural discourse through Dee's preface to *Euclid.*[74] Lauding Alberti alongside Vitruvius as "the two most perfect *Architectes,*"[75] Dee couples the excerpt from *De architectura* mentioned earlier with *De re aedificatoria*'s key opening definition:

> The whole Feate of Architecture in buildyng, consisteth in Lineamentes, and in Framyng. And the whole power and skill of Lineamentes, tendeth to this: that the right and absolute way may be had, of Coaptying and ioyning Lines and angles: by which, the face of the buildyng or frame, may be comprehended and concluded.[76]

In propelling "the whole power and skill of Lineamentes" toward a facade created through "right and absolute" geometry, Dee introduces the notion of an architectural "face" that completes the skeletal "frame," concluding the spatial syntax of lines and angles with a visible coup de grâce. The facade thus doubly comprehends architecture by supplying a material envelope that also renders the building meaningful to a viewing subject. Yet Dee's wording leaves ambiguous whether the quasi-human face belongs intrinsically to the frame (*structura* in Alberti's original), or whether the architect imposes a mask that functions as an extrinsic ornament, an architectural appoggiatura merely contingent upon an internal harmony.

Randle Cotgrave's French-English dictionary (1611) captures the identity crisis of this unsettled architectural face, defining *façade* as "the forefront, forepart, outside, or representation of the outside, of a house."[77] In this tangle of meanings, a facade comes first and foremost in the house ("forepart") yet somehow remains "outside," detached from the frame; an even more radical break occurs when Cotgrave allows the term *façade* to indicate both a physical structure ("outside") as well as an abstract signifier ("representation of the outside"). This semantic ambiguity carries over into Cotgrave's sample translation: "*Maison qui a belle façade.* A faire, goodlie, seemelie, statelie house, or front of a house." Does the building itself embody these qualities of being goodly and seemly, or do they belong only to the house's front—or has such a distinction become useless? Do we picture this front as composed of bricks and mortar, or simply rendered on paper as lineaments? Like the mocked-up, propped-up facade in Abraham Bosse's etching of a draftsman (figure 1.1), the front here seems to stand in for the absent building as a semiotic marker, a seemly image at once inside and outside the architectural frame. Although a facade demands "the whole power and skill" of design, this most crucial element of a building also remains the most detachable, interchangeable, and ephemeral. In this sense, the facade operates as a Derridean *parergon* that "inscribes something which comes as an extra, exterior to the proper field . . . but whose transcendent exteriority comes to play, abut onto, brush against, rub, press against the limit itself and intervene in the inside only to the extent that the inside is lacking. It is lacking *in* something and it is lacking *from itself.*"[78] Likewise, the facade attracts all eyes but always seems to hover beside itself, a floating veil for an invisible frame—a floating veil that subsumes the frame. Indeed, as English architecture "tendeth" to the facade, adopting a face that supplements an otherwise sound body, the older sense of "frame" as internal structure becomes tinged with the modern sense of "frame" as purely external. In the resultant confusion between inside and outside, between natural and unnatural bodies, the very frontness of a face would be challenged by builders and theorists alike.

Pantomime Architecture

The palace of Nonsuch, planned as Henry VIII's hunting retreat in Surrey, makes evident some of the early tensions in England's move toward a facade-based architecture. Begun in 1538 though not fully complete by the king's death in 1547, Nonsuch passed through several owners before Henry Fitzalan, Earl of Arundel, undertook the finishing touches that realized the original scheme. Although dismantled in 1683, perhaps after falling into disrepair,[79] Nonsuch during its prime struck no less discerning a critic than William Camden as being of "so great sumpteousnesse and rare workemanship, that it aspireth to the very top of ostentation for shew; so as a man may thinke, that all the skill of Architecture is in

Figure 2.2. Joris Hoefnagel, drawing of Nonsuch (1568). © Trustees of the British Museum.

this one peece of worke bestowed, and heaped up together."[80] Hakewill echoes this opinion of Nonsuch as the pinnacle of building, the paragon instantiating a new tradition of English architecture:

> So as what *Sebastianus Serlius* a skilfull Architect spake of the *Pantheon* at *Rome,* may not vnfitly be applied to this pile of building, that it is *vnicum exemplar consummatae Architecturae,* the only patterne we haue of perfect Architecture.[81]

Two classic images by Joris Hoefnagel and John Speed, respectively, capture this "pile of building" as an imposing bi-level structure with crenellated parapets and octagonal corner towers, a romantic throwback steeped in the grandeur of French chateaux (figures 2.2, 2.3).[82] Yet above all else, what qualifies Nonsuch as "the very top of ostentation for shew" are the flamboyant surfaces "heaped up" with ornamental figures, an ocular surfeit that imbues its checkered face with an expression of *horror vacui.* David Howarth observes that "the external walls look like stamped and embossed leather. . . . Everything was a writhing pattern of swirling arabesques with hardly a still interval the whole length of the façade."[83] This hidebound castle has long been stamped into the cultural imaginary as the nonpareil face of Nonsuch. Yet a lesser-known painting that depicts Nonsuch from a northern perspective reveals a more austere palace, a totally different animal in terms of architectural style (figure 2.4).[84] So remote from the popular image of Nonsuch was this medieval-looking estate with plain walls—hidebound in tradition—that the painting was not properly identified until the twentieth century.

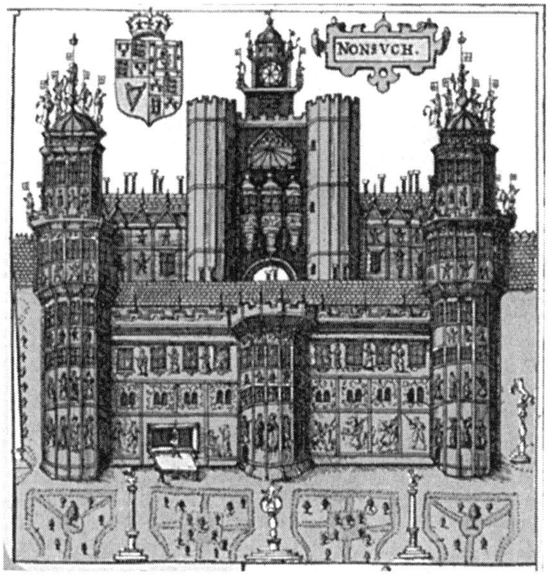

Figure 2.3. Hand-colored detail of Nonsuch from a map of Surrey in John Speed's *Theatre of the Empire of Great Britaine* (London, 1611). Engraved by Jodocus Hondius. Bridgeman Art Library.

Figure 2.4. Nonsuch from the northwest. Painting by an unknown Flemish artist (seventeenth century). Fitzwilliam Museum/Bridgeman Art Library.

Figure 2.5. Model of Nonsuch, based on plans by Martin Biddle and built by Ben Taggart. Visitors entered through the gatehouse into the northern forecourt (*top*), before passing into the inner court to the south (*bottom*). © Country Life, Image #1231863. Photo: John Crook.

These contrasting views of Nonsuch expose an aesthetic divide between the building's southern and northern halves, manifest not only on the exterior surfaces but also inside the palace's two main courtyards. Visitors to Nonsuch entered through a formal gatehouse into the northern forecourt, built of sober brick and stone; however, only those admitted to the southern court, which contained the royal lodgings, could enjoy the subsequent explosion of ornament (figure 2.5). Like the facades shown in Hoefnagel's and Speed's images, the interior walls around this southern courtyard were covered with several hundred stucco panels that were each carved into relief, perhaps colored, then framed with gilded slate.[85] In a unified scheme that included both the inward- and outward-facing walls of the southern court, these stucco panels depicted the classical gods, Roman emperors, scenes from Ovid's *Metamorphoses,* Hercules executing his labors, and the personified Liberal Arts and Virtues.[86] Thus rendering an architectural face a mosaic of human faces wrought in relief, this virtuosic display caused John Evelyn, a visitor to Nonsuch, to lament the artwork's inevitable damage outside a covered gallery.[87]

Yet an indoor placement, though practical, would make the stucco panels lose much of their semantic force. By screening on the visible exterior a panorama of desirable kingly attributes, this southern court presents itself as an emblem of Henry's power upon the political and physical landscape. Moreover, as Martin Biddle observes, the central panel among the pantheon of gods features a portrait of Henry and his young son Edward; the artistic scheme thus suggests a not-so-subtle apotheosis of the Tudor dynasty itself.[88] As "the *Royaltie* of *Sight*" feasts on the sight of royalty, Nonsuch engages what Jürgen Habermas terms the "publicity of representation" by using architecture to represent Henry's body, to advertise his virtue and virility to a subject's eye.[89] Since Nonsuch's layout suggests that spaces become more private along a southward axis of movement, visitors who finally emerge into the inner court experience a theatrical sense of revelation, of epiphany, when confronted by the spectacle of monarchic harmony suddenly unfolded in polychrome splendor. Like the dramatic opening up of a Gothic cathedral beyond the threshold, like the oculus that illuminates an English Pantheon, the staged mystery of interiority at Nonsuch nudges the architectural viewer—a "*Diver* into *Causes*"—toward the inevitable conclusion that the prime mover must be Henry and his heirs.

Nevertheless, given that Nonsuch forms "the ultimate expression of Henry VIII's quest for privacy,"[90] the inner courtyard aptly dazzles the eye with a visual excess that defers, if not repels, physical access into the royal suite. Indeed, for visitors who follow a route from the outer to inner courtyard, Nonsuch moves from a defensive mechanism founded on enclosure, a medieval stance that protects the interior with a gatehouse and crenellated parapets, to a facade-based architecture that arrests the subject with visual rapture. Thus preventing visitors from penetrating the facade by penetrating the awe-struck, ravished viewer, such a visual overload either paralyzes bodies in the courtyard as though petrifying them into columns, or else redirects bodies into circling the perimeter in endless admiration. While the outer court shields itself by raising a daunting exterior, the inner court projects an alluring public face that stands in for the private face concealed inside. Armed with bas-reliefs that flatten and literally front for Henry VIII, the southern court reduces any need for the king to show himself qua king. Instead, by crafting a material body that undergirds and mimics Henry's body natural and body politic, Nonsuch's southern court choreographs a face-to-facade encounter that precedes, frames, supplements, and even replaces any face-to-face meeting with the monarch. Thus negating the vacillation in Cotgrave's definitions of *façade,* Nonsuch elides any disparity between house and inhabitant, exterior and interior, representation and reality. Like the tooled leather covers of a lavishly bound folio, like an artificial skin that stretches over the architectural corpus, Nonsuch's facade operates as an external correlative that allows the reading of interiority in shorthand, thus forming an ideological frame around the subject of monarchical power.[91]

As a secular trinity that merges biological, political, and architectural bodies, Nonsuch's design evinces a degree of sympathy with Albertian thought. Unlike the E-shaped country houses that would later show homage to Elizabeth or oddities like Thomas Tresham's Triangular Lodge, whose proportions are based on mystical numbers, Nonsuch propels meaning toward the facialized surface rather than safeguard a hidden structural truth.[92] Indeed, Nonsuch adopts other elements of a Continental aesthetic such as the columns that delineate each bay along the southern facade, as well as the multisided towers articulated by a system of superimposed orders painted to imitate stone.[93] This introduction of classical motifs deviates so sharply from Tudor building that observers from Vasari onward have emphasized a variety of Italian and French influences on Nonsuch.[94] According to this genealogy, the stylistic divergence between the northern and southern courts serves to allegorize the difference between a northern and southern Renaissance aesthetic.

However, despite its striking innovation, an undeniably retrograde sensibility pervades the southern court's profusion of images and seeming abandon of harmonious restraint. Evelyn thus remarks upon the court's "Gotique [Gothic] fabric":[95] even without the pointed gables, timber framing, clocktower, and single-pile layout, this inner section of Nonsuch recalls a pre-Reformation penchant for gilded icons and pageantry. Like a cathedral's stained-glass windows, the stucco panels create a mythology that places Henry and Edward among the classical rather than Christian pantheon of gods and heroes. In this Pantheon that deifies an English lineage, this mundane temple devoted to the worship of political families and family politics, architecture duly pleases a mortal eye that gazes on upright surfaces rather than a divine eye that looks down, a God's-eye view that penetrates the mystery of interior structure. Neither wholly medieval nor wholly neoclassical, Nonsuch combines elements indecorously to solicit the greatest sense of wonder, staging the viewer's cathartic release upon reaching the inner court's narrative of political rightness. Architecture thus becomes a theater, a performance of itself. As Ian Dunlop remarks of Nonsuch's southern face, the overall effect is "suggestive of pantomime rather than of real fabric."[96]

The Power of Pretty Faces

Given the viewer's growing confusion between scenic reality and faked scenography, a backlash soon erupted against facades derided as purely ornamental, as visual garnish extrinsic to the structure. Indeed, despite praising Henry VIII's palaces as a "paterne" of excellent building that combines form and function, William Harrison notes how "in these daies there be manie goodlie houses" that are "rather curious to the eie like paper worke, than substantiall for continuance."[97] Informed by Palladian treatises as well as pattern books from abroad,[98] often adopting the hybrid Gothic and classical style that John Summerson terms Artisan Mannerism,[99] these "curious" facades seemed to waver between having a solid mass and being merely a sketch writ large. Just as Bosse's draftsman supports a paper facade with his constructive gaze, the desire for a viewer's approval drove the building of "lantern houses," whose exteriors featured costly sheets of glass. As the demand for thick defensive walls subsided in more peaceful times, social prestige attached to an outward-looking face with a panoply of glazed windows,[100] a modern armor that withstood the scrutiny of a public seeking a "pulcruse prospecte." As these windows gleamed with daylight and glowed with candlelight, lantern houses assumed bright and cheerful faces that conformed to Albertian ideals.

Harrison's critique of facades struck especially close to home for the courtiers and wealthy merchants who erected country piles made flimsy with glass; the most lavish of these mansions were even known as "prodigy houses." Marvelous yet somehow unnatural, perhaps even monstrous, these spatial prodigies often arose from the rubble of Henry VIII's seized monasteries. Justifying Starkey's misgivings about inequities in wealth allocation, this architectural rebirth began when parcels of formerly church-owned property came into the hands of a privileged minority, including upstart *novi homines* who translated their newly amassed piles of money into massive country piles.[101] As the most public aspect of a house, the facade inevitably assumed greater importance as a semiotic marker for those anxious to perform their status, to project their cultural refinement with a theatrical flourish—hence the embrace of a Continental aesthetic. Yet as Christy Anderson notes, these early modern facades often breached the classical *decorum* promoted in Vitruvian discourse,

Figure 2.6. Longleat, front. Photo: Mimi Yiu.

since no stable relationship obtained between the elevation (facade) and plan (layout). For example, in the work of Robert Smythson, perhaps the most prominent architect of country houses in late sixteenth- and early seventeenth-century England, "Palladio's influence remained on the 'cryptic' level of the plan, overshadowed by a native English love for fantastic ornament and chivalric details" on the exterior.[102] While a Supreme Architect peering from the heavens could admire the harmony of a building's skeleton, piercing through to a cryptic interiority that might be called a building's soul, the facade detached and descended from this Platonic ideal to delight the earthly viewer with fantasy and romance. Divorced from organic function, these frivolous motifs spurred Francis Bacon to inveigh against building for ocular rather than bodily comfort: "*Houses* are built to Liue in, and not to Looke on: Therefore let Vse bee preferred before Vniformitie; Except where both may be had."[103]

Longleat, an early Smythson house, exemplifies the pressures borne by facades that mediate between living within and looking on from without. Built upon the remains of a Carthusian priory for John Thynne, a mercer who later served as steward to the Protector Somerset, Longleat acquired an ever grander appearance over four phases of construction between 1547 and 1580.[104] Thynne spared neither expense nor effort to realize, in his final version, perhaps the most classical design that England had yet witnessed, a design that inspired many future architects (figure 2.6). Dressed in the finest Bath stone, this three-story house features expansive glass windows that cover every outward surface, creating a glinting architectural envelope visible from a great distance in the countryside. However, in a scenario that recalls Alberti's Tempio Malatestiano, Longleat's new facade was merely attached to the previous facade despite radical changes in proportion and style.[105] To achieve a perfect symmetry that pleases the external viewer, to construct a beacon of regularity upon the landscape, Thynne installed windows so poorly aligned with the height and location of rooms that some panes were eventually blocked from the inside.[106] Thus placing aesthetic uniformity before use, as Bacon feared, Longleat proffers a false transparency that disregards any correlation between interior and exterior, wrapping instead "an immense and highly decorated scarf" that conceals the scarred joints across its decidedly artificial body. Despite boasting "more glass than wall," to borrow a description often applied to Smythson's Hardwick Hall, Longleat nurtures the illusion of material transparency while neglecting structural clarity.

By elevating outward looks above finance and function, Longleat embraces a design philosophy that Bacon deplores: "Leaue the Goodly Fabrickes of Houses, for Beautie only, to the *Enchanted Pallaces* of the *Poets:* Who build them with small Cost."[107] Ironically, Bacon shares these anti-aesthetic sentiments with early modern poets who, rather than build enchanted palaces from words, praise humbler ways of dwelling now deemed passé. The genre of country-house poetry that became popular in the early seventeenth century thus reflects a cultural reaction against current practices in architecture.[108] Ben Jonson's "To Penshurst" laments the blight of mansions "built to envious show," which boast "polish'd pillars, or a roof of gold."[109] More explicitly, Andrew Marvell's "Upon Appleton House" identifies external influences as corrupting a native tradition of building: "Within this sober Frame expect/Work of no Forrain *Architect.*"[110] To produce a "sober Frame" like Appleton House, an un-Palladian villa "Where ev'ry Thing does answer Use," Marvell suggests avoiding the affected, abnormal labor of an architect:

> Who of his great Design in pain
> Did for a Model vault his Brain,
> Whose Columnes should so high be rais'd
> To arch the Brows that on them gaz'd.[111]

Gazing archly upon the columns of his classical design, this self-centered artificer models the house on his own body, which likewise changes in response to the building. Indeed, the Vitruvian builder who tries vainly "t'immure/The *Circle* in the *Quadrature*" simply distends both space and body: "where he comes the swelling Hall/Stirs, and the *Square* grows *Spherical.*"[112] In contrast to the Vitruvian man whose body naturally subtends a circle and square, the Vitruvian builder stretches a square hall with his round body; reciprocally, his round body seems to expand once inside the square hall, a space "by his *Magnitude* distrest."[113] Puffed up with false pride, with a false pregnancy that produces nothing, the architect swells as though in sympathy with the distressed space, as though his painful body suffered from piles.[114] This internal discord does not matter, however, to the "superfluously spread" builder who obsesses about the visual grandeur of surfaces, the "Marble Crust."[115] As a subject of architecture who resonates deeply with built structure, Marvell's foreign aesthete threatens to queer the face of an English populace by queering their facades—not by making their hair curl, but their brows arch.

Deriding "goodly" building as conceited and useless, this chorus of detractors quavers before a castrating architecture. Alarmed by facades whose harmony registers as an unnatural falsetto, English writers besiege these walls with pointed gibes about paper and Plato, poets and Palladio; evidently, a "goodly" appeal cannot be good, or godly, or manly. Harrison bemoans that "when our houses were builded of willow, then had we oken men; but now that our houses are come to be made of oke, our men are not onlie become willow, but a great manie through Persian delicacie crept in among vs altogither of straw, which is a sore alteration."[116] Setting up architecture as the straw man responsible for this masculine decline, Harrison implies that the early modern house enervates those who huddle behind oaken facades like willowy boys hiding behind their mothers' skirts. Just as Marvell's foreign architect creates a symbiotic bond with built space that perverts his natural body, Harrison's sapped-out householder allows the oaken frame to become his backbone, the facade his second face. As the gendering of classical orders extends to the entire building, the goodly exterior that ravishes the eye also ravishes an English sense of masculinity, now tainted by a delicate Persian effeminacy—if not sodomy—"crept in among vs."

For Harrison, the distinction between an architectural exterior and interior reflects the boundary between national identities. As he notes, it is "common in England, contrarie to the customes of all other nations . . . that many of our greatest houses haue outwardlie beene verie simple and plaine to sight, which inwardlie haue beene able to receiue a duke with his whole traine, and lodge them at their ease."[117] Indeed, "the fronts of our streets haue not beene so vniforme and orderlie builded as those of forreine cities, where . . . the vtterside of their mansions and dwellings haue oft more cost bestowed vpon them, than all the rest of the house, which are often verie simple and vneasie within."[118] While English architecture values an inward orientation, contrasting an exterior "simple and plain to sight" with a plush interior suitable for tactile dwelling, foreigners waste resources on the fancy dress of facades, aligning street fronts that parade in "vniforme and orderlie" fashion. Protestant England, by implication, should disdain such hollow pomp and pageantry to cultivate an interior richness, an inner wellspring that supplies physical and spiritual comfort.

Even Inigo Jones, that most Italianate of seventeenth-century English architects, cannot quite stomach the ornate decoration seen on foreign surfaces:

> all thes composed ornamentes, the w[hi]ch procced out of ye aboundance of dessignes and wear brought in by Mihill Angell [Michelangelo] and his followers. in my oppignion do not well in sollid Architecture and ye facciati of houses but in gardens loggis . . . & the inner partes of houses.[119]

In separating the alien notion of "facciati" from the "sollid Architecture" beneath, Jones construes the facade as a floating surface that must not be further weakened by Composite ornament, by a feminine aesthetic swirling in fertile "aboundance."[120] To reinforce "ye facciati" against Michelangelo's corrupt influence, architecture must contrive a demeanor of measured, masculine solidity:

> For as outwar[d]ly every wyse ma[n] carrieth a graviti in Publicke Places, whear there is nothing els looked for. & yt inwardly hath his Immaginacy set free, and sumtimes licentiously flying out, as nature hirseaIf dooth often tymes Stravagantly. to dellight. amase us. sumtimes moufe us to laughter. Sumtimes to contemplatio[n], and horror, So in architecture ye outward ornamentes oft to be, sollid, proporsionable according to the rulles. masculine and unaffected.[121]

In a sentence that itself explodes in the center, Jones describes an architectural body whose public masculinity conceals a passionate, churning interior linked to "nature hirseaIf." While the building's exterior should display a civilized gravitas, a restraint "looked for" in public, a secret femininity governs the private world that suddenly blossoms into visibility within Jones's sentence.

Inside this secluded interiority, which Jones specifies as the gardens, loggias, and "inner partes of houses,"[122] an imagination "set free" allows the private subject to revel in emotion and reflection. Such a realm where laughter and horror abound "Stravagantly" thus seems well suited to the riotous ornament that Jones ascribes to Michelangelo's Composite style. Yet just as the masculine facade strains to remain firmly "unaffected" by feminizing affect, the sober clauses that begin and conclude Jones's sentence barely contain the inner phrases that tumble out with fervor, that produce more emotion in the course of musing on emotion. As Jones's linear thought loses itself in the loops and whorls of a composite syntax, "Immaginacy" slides into "nature" such that either (or both) could plausibly serve as the subject of "to dellight. amase us. sumtimes moufe us to laughter. Sumtimes to contemplatio[n], and horror." Yet perhaps the most fitting subject here would be "theater" in the Aristotelian sense: a cathartic vehicle that purges excessive passions so that spectators can attain a stable and balanced "graviti" as citizens in the public sphere. Only wise men belong to these "Publicke Places," however, leaving women inside the home to enact their own dramas, to indulge their own fancies. In the process of banishing affect and affectation to a species of *hortus conclusus,* to the natural realm of gardens and the private interior of houses, Jones threshes out a binary gender on the domestic threshold.

Nevertheless, as a dreamlike space of imagination, of theatrical working through, this latent femininity threatens every surface masculinity as unresolved emotions come "licentiously flying out." Such a moment of eruption occurs in the middle of Jones's sentence, followed by a reciprocal moment of realization and shutdown; when Jones reaches the word "horror," he abruptly finishes his excursus into the feminine and wrenches his sentence back into masculine logic, completing his earlier thought. As though jolted awake simply by writing the word "horror," Jones quickly brackets the horrors of feminine license, horrified by his own slippage into an abject space without rules and decorum. Whether in rhetoric or architecture, an amorphous interiority threatens to destroy the orderly frame, to overwhelm a masculine solidity with an alluring but dangerous fluidity. If Marvell's Vitruvian builder makes the square hall into a sphere, then Jones's Vitruvian builder must similarly constrain himself and his architecture from swelling into monstrous shapes, distended by an interiority marked as both natural and excessive. For even as Jones relegates theater to a feminized interior of passions and frivolous ornament, the mask of masculine stiffness carried on the exterior proves no less a masquerade of gender,[123] a pantomime facade that performs its own desired identity in exaggerated fashion.

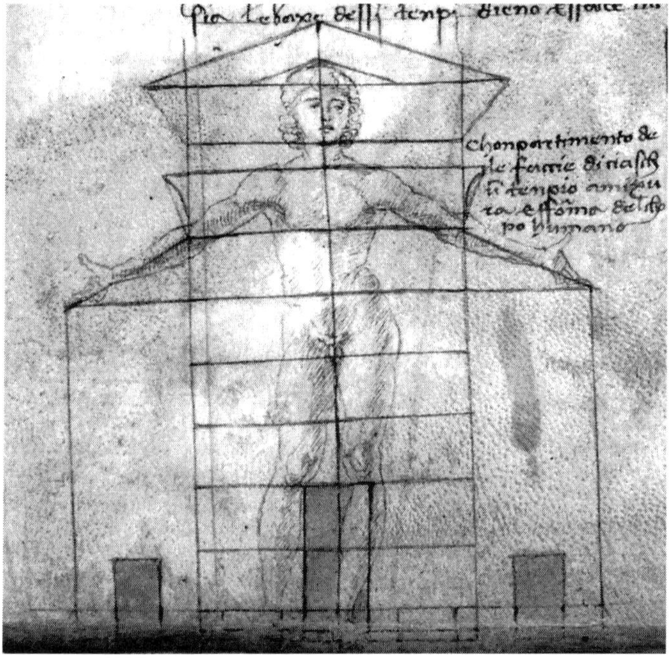

Figure 2.7. Masculine facade, from Francesco di Giorgio Martini's *Trattato di architettura* (c. 1480), 21r. Biblioteca Medicea Laurenziana, MS Ashburnham 361.

While Harrison insists on a simple exteriority that simply is, a sturdy masculinity that exists a priori without any artifice, Jones realizes that "nature" always operates in cahoots with "immaginacy" to create a theatrical subject. Just as a mime constructs an invisible wall by defining its contours through gesture, the pantomime facade must repeatedly demonstrate its own masculinity to the public, creating a perception of stability that legitimates its sovereign power, its *nomos*.[124] Such a decorous face reassures viewers that a default masculinity grounds the ideal human body, one that can "immure/The *Circle* in the *Quadrature*." Francesco di Giorgio Martini's *Trattato di architettura,* written in the fifteenth century, makes explicit this belief that a man's body should calibrate built space, since a man's body calibrates the universe; in his drawing of a church facade, an ideal masculine figure governs the proportions and contours of this sacred building in a manner that evokes the Vitruvian man (Fig. 2.7). Using this logic, a man's dwelling should mold to him like a second skin, like a natural carapace exuded from his own perfect body. Indeed, after mocking the builder who vaults his brain to contrive some absurd design, Marvell's poem observes with approval how "The low roof'd Tortoises do dwell/In cases fit of Tortoise-shell."[125]

As the fetishized object of Wotton's "*Royaltie* of *Sight,*" however, the facade inevitably assumes a feminine role for the mastering eye that consumes endlessly, collapsing the very gender protocols that an external wall should buttress. Caught between the interior and exterior, the feminine and masculine, the facade occupies a "no man's land" as both a quasi-subject that signifies the owner within and a quasi-object that receives an implied male gaze from without. According to Luce Irigaray, the strategy of miming demarcates the subject position of a woman who subversively "caricatures and deforms" a patriarchal structure from within, yet is "capable of interpreting that economy precisely because it has remained 'outside.'"[126] At once inside and outside the architectural frame, swinging freely between gender positions, the alarmingly unhinged facade resorts to a feminine mode of acting to produce the masculinity that writers from Jones to Jonson so staunchly promote. Doubtless, these men doth protest too much: facades reflect the castration anxieties of men who identify with their home, who wish their home to identify them socially. Just as "the Beasts are by their Denns exprest," as Marvell claims, men should ensure that "their Bodies measure out their Place."[127] As a result, any facade whose gender comes across as a caricature or perversion challenges not only the masculinity of buildings, but also the masculinity of bodies. As a mirror and measure of men, the facade exposes gender as a mere construct, revealing an essential lack in the organic body. After all, the facade itself often no longer upholds the building, but serves purely as an aesthetic covering, a codpiece for an always absent phallus. The fear of defacement, then, cuts deep.

Since miming creates a copy without a model, enacting a "gestural writing" on the body,[128] as Derrida suggests, any architecture that attempts to perform masculinity actually produces gender. Instead of imitating a human body to fashion a deadened other of the same, the dynamic facade shows Jones's "every wyse mann" how to construct and perform *his* gender role in public. Such an imbrication of organic and inorganic bodies calls into question Vitruvius's tenet that architecture always follows human contours. In a Vitruvian tradition, architecture either translates corporeal proportions into tangible structures through mimesis, as Francesco di Giorgio's drawing suggests, or else shapes a primitive, protective enclosure around the needs of a social body.[129] Alberti thus confirms Vitruvius in claiming that "a building is very like an animal, and that Nature must be imitated when we delineate it,"[130] while Henry Hawkins argues that architects should perform as "Mimiks of Nature":

> For what are the most iudicious Artizans, but the Mimiks of Nature? This same in our *House* is seen, comparing it with the fabrick of our natural bodies, wherin the high *Architect* of the world hath displayd such skil as euen stupifyes the human reason to enter into it.[131]

While Hawkins takes as prior "the fabrick of our natural bodies," the Platonic ideal that begets an artificial, artisanal derivative, the becoming-animal of a fabricated, unnatural architecture inevitably raises questions about the becoming-architecture of an ostensibly natural body.

For Deleuze and Guattari, the concept of becoming-animal, or indeed any kind of becoming-other, involves "neither the imitation of a subject nor the proportionality of a form," but rather an absolute deterritorialization that permits multiple potentialities to move through "*zones of proximity.*"[132] As "affect in itself,"[133] becoming-other demands a radical, ravishing openness to alterity, a surrender to an ineffable unknown whose difference "stupifyes the human reason." In contrast to the Vitruvian model of a mimetic chain that descends from organic to inorganic, imprinting cosmic proportions onto immanent material, architecture and the human reverberate with the same affective intensity as they brush against the two-way interface of a facade, performing a delicate mutual pantomime that could at any instant destroy the pretence of a dividing wall. Indeed, Wotton's "*Diver* into *Causes*" need only look in the mirror—or under the skin—to explicate the "*Mysteries of Proportion.*" In this sense, the human body provides an anatomical theater that yields to view the sacred rules of proportion, the molecular secrets of nature. Designed by an arch-architect who works in mysterious ways, the human body has always been structured as architecture, its face prefabricated as a facade.

In *Sylua Syluarum* (1627), Bacon notes the reversible character of this relationship between architectural and animal structure:

> the *Building* of *Liuing Creatures Bodies,* is like the *Building* of a *Timber-House,* where the *Walls,* and other *Parts* haue *Columnes,* and *Beames.*[134]

Bacon's analogy suggests that organic bodies are subject to the same process of building as inorganic architecture, that every corporeal element can be dismantled and reconfigured. As the absence of bodily closure allows for construction in the truest sense, the Albertian *concinnitas* that posits a foreclosed harmony of parts disarticulates into a machinic set of design possibilities.[135] Diving toward a horizon of infinite potentiality, the architectural corpus undergoes an involutionary process that Deleuze and Guattari define not only as the basis of becoming, but also as the motor of invention: "Becoming is involutionary, involution is creative."[136] While evolution involves propagation through filial bonds, involution disrupts these discrete linear relationships since "to involve is to form a block that runs its own line 'between' the terms in play and beneath assignable relations."[137] The zones of proximity that allow such creative involvement in the early modern house, as we shall see, emerge most crucially in the intimate spaces behind the facade, in the physical involution of an outward-looking architecture.

The Plot Thickens

Over the course of the sixteenth and seventeenth centuries, the fabric of English houses turned inside out with the demise of great halls and the dawn of facades. As we recall, the older paradigm of single-pile building endorses a centralized, linear ideology that permits growth through evolution. In other words, the house begins as a single-cell organism that comprises only a great hall, then expands by adding more rooms along the same axis to produce a range. At the furthest tenable limit of this linear extension, when the house cannot tolerate further stretching, the building turns around a corner to begin defining a courtyard. If needed, the house keeps turning and adding ranges until the courtyard has been enclosed; upon completing this module of a courtyard, the house may embark upon an adjoining courtyard using the same method, ad infinitum. The single-pile house thus develops by spinning a filial thread of rooms, a structure centered upon a great hall inside and a courtyard outside.

However, like the makers of tissue paper, early modern builders soon began to experiment with two-ply houses that folded an extra layer of rooms upon the first, creating a domestic space with double thickness. This "double-pile" house embraced a new density that seemed to impart substance to the aesthetic facade, thus making good the paper work of goodly faces. While a similar pressing together of rooms has been known since Norman times, mainly on constricted urban sites,[138] the rising popularity of compact houses in the late sixteenth and early seventeenth century prompted a qualitative rethinking of how interior spaces should be articulated, impelled by changes in social as well as spatial relations. Indeed, the very center of domestic life vanished from

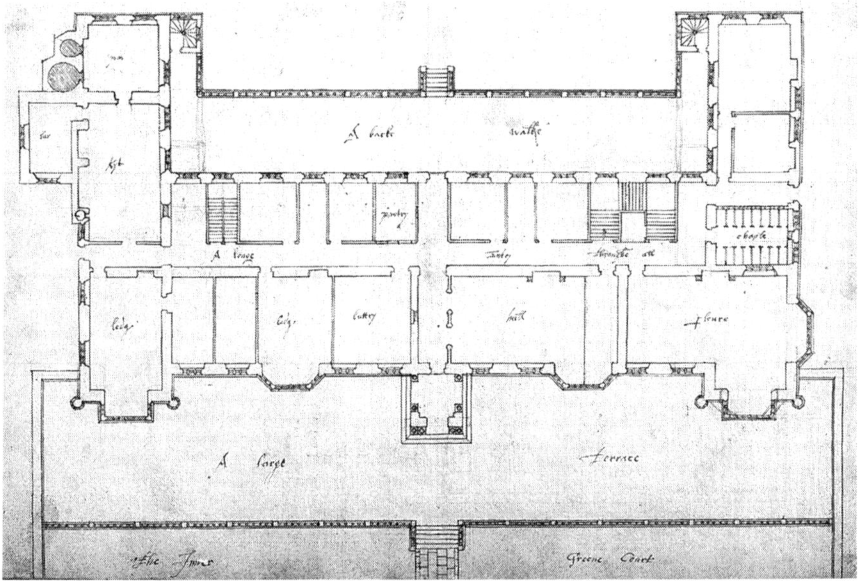

Figure 2.8. John Thorpe, Great House at Chelsea (c. 1595), T64. By courtesy of the Trustees of Sir John Soane's Museum. Photo: Ardon Bar-Hama.

sight as the great hall shrank into a mere hallway, a narrow corridor that separated one layer of rooms from another.[139] Ironically, the only modern element retained from the great hall was the screens passage that bypassed the principal area where people gathered around a hearth. Rather than assemble a household, the vestigial hallway now pushed a hollow channel through a formerly vibrant domestic heart.

In John Thorpe's Great House at Chelsea (c. 1595), the screens passage thus functions as a hallway that continues beyond the great hall and connects to a back door, which further aligns with steps that lead down from a terrace-like "backe walke" (figure 2.8). This concept of a linear passage also manifests in a lateral corridor marked "A longe entry throughe all"; where these two hallways intersect, an empty nonplace now occupies the home's center, a void that replaces a hearth. Similarly, Roger Pratt's Coleshill (c. 1650), often deemed the classic model of a double-pile, features an implied passage that extends through a parlor and reduced hall, while a lateral corridor bisects all three floors (figure 2.9). As the spatial arteries seen in these examples start to course through the double-pile, through an architectural *res* less *extensa* than *intensa,* the resultant circulatory network supplies a new structural frame, one that depends not on strong timbers but on empty space carved out between

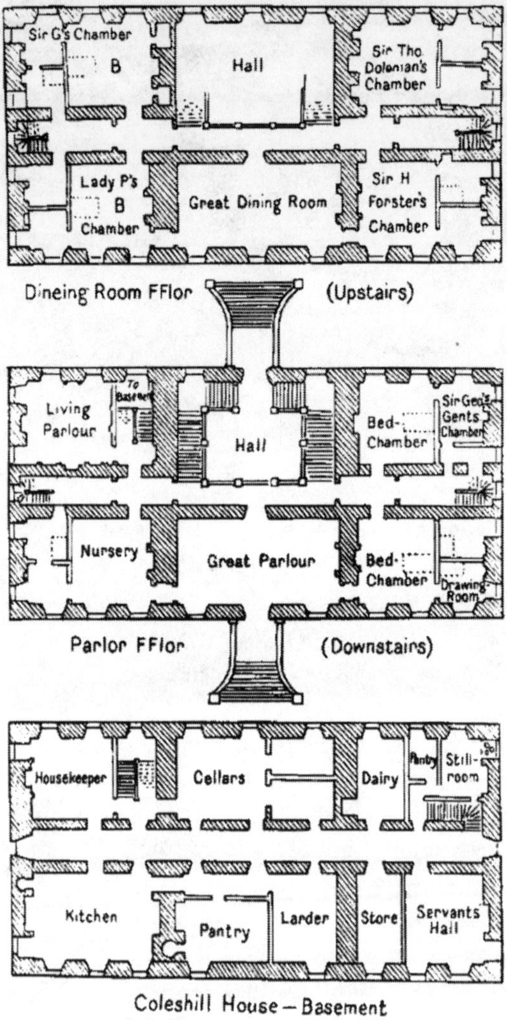

Figure 2.9. Plan of Coleshill (c. 1650). Reprinted from R. T. Gunther, *The Architecture of Sir Roger Pratt* (Oxford, 1928), 93, with permission from the heirs of Robert Theodore Gunther.

spatial layers. While the single-pile house coheres along a filial strand that knits room to room, the double-pile cinches the household together through the cord of a corridor, linking spaces that no longer open onto each other. The hallway thus replaces the cellular room as the basic domestic unit, building a house upon a hollow backbone that connects and separates.[140] By inserting a buffer that directs traffic between rooms

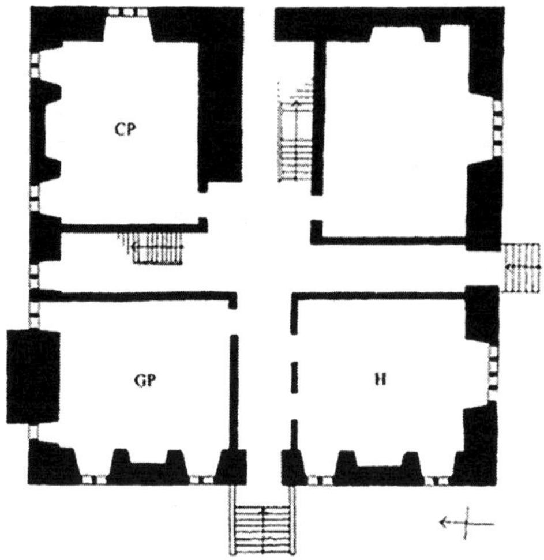

Figure 2.10. Plan of Whitehall, Shrewsbury (1578). H = Hall; GP = Great Parlor; CP = Common Parlor. Reprinted from Andor Gomme and Alison Maguire, *Design and Plan in the Country House: From Castle Donjons to Palladian Boxes* (2008), 199, with permission of Yale University Press.

instead of compelling movement through them, the early modern house undergoes a conceptual involution as a dividing space now "runs its own line 'between' the terms in play and beneath assignable relations."

While a double-pile may simply comprise two layers of rooms parted by a lateral corridor, perhaps the apotheosis of such a spatial philosophy—one that privileges transition and division—involves a double fold with two hallways that intersect at the house's center. Running both the length and breadth of a house, these corridors inscribe a perfect cross within the external frame, touching every side like the limbs of a Vitruvian man. As Andor Gomme and Alison Maguire have shown, the basic module of a square double-pile appeared early on at Whitehall, a Shrewsbury house begun in 1578 for a lawyer (figure 2.10). On the ground floor, Whitehall originally extended its screens passage through a reduced great hall to reach a back stair and door. By adding a similar passage that extends laterally through the house, Whitehall divides into four modestly sized rooms that border hallways on every inward side, thus acquiring a symmetry that hinges upon internal spaces of transition.[141] Although situated on former monastic land, Whitehall eschews the post-Reformation penchant for building houses upon the existing foundations of cloisters; this efficient recycling strategy made the courtyard model the basis of numerous homes, including prominent estates such as Longleat and Lacock Abbey (figure 2.11). In contrast, the double-pile configuration of Whitehall effects a morphological involution whereby the four ranges around a courtyard bend inward to produce a cross-hall plan (figure 2.12). Always a creative becoming rather than a simple binary inversion, this architectural involution rethinks and refolds the ground plan like origami. Yet unlike the baroque fold that demands a "severing of the façade from the inside" to seal the monad within a spatial envelope,[142] the double-pile's undulating folds profoundly involve the face and frame to undermine binary divisions between margin and center, public and private, proper and improper. Indeed, by knotting up the four corners of a courtyard house at its center, Whitehall introjects the strong defensive walls of a medieval structure to form a series of weaker "paper" facades criss-crossing the interior. Instead of defining an absolute boundary between inside and outside, a hallway's protective walls indulge and foster a nascent desire for privacy within the home, shielding room from room to create semi-enclosed wombs that nurture the early modern subject. While Mark Jarzombek rightly observes that these interior hallways constitute "a within in the within," they also supply a *without* in the within by denying full intimacy and access even inside the home.[143]

Ever quick to seize upon a novel idea, Francis Bacon notes how the double-pile affords a certain opacity as he praises the builder's choice of "a double House, without thorow Lights on the Sides, that you may have Rooms from the Sun, both for Fore-noon and After-noon."[144] Scuttling from one layer of the double-pile to another, playing hide-and-seek with sunlight, Bacon's imagined family exploits a design that avoids visual transparency to dance with nature. More insidiously, however, the density of a "double House" enables a social choreography in which subjects elude one another, biding their entrances and exits in liminal spaces that guard against direct intrusion. As the formation of a nuclear family now requires that masters separate their lives more from their servants', a double household emerges that devotes much attention to keeping a proper subjective distance. Hence, the early modern home develops not only a matrix of bypasses in the form of corridors and stairs, but also a profusion of smaller rooms such as parlors, closets, and withdrawing rooms.[145] For Roger Pratt, the architect who coins the term *double-pile,* these multiple spaces of transition function as screens around the family so that "ordinary servants may never publicly appear in passing to and fro."[146] Relegating kitchens and other service rooms to the basement to prevent "dirty servants" from offending those above, repressing bodily labor to a lower level to ensure "no noises heard, nor ill scents smelt," Pratt considers double-pile houses with "one common way in the middle

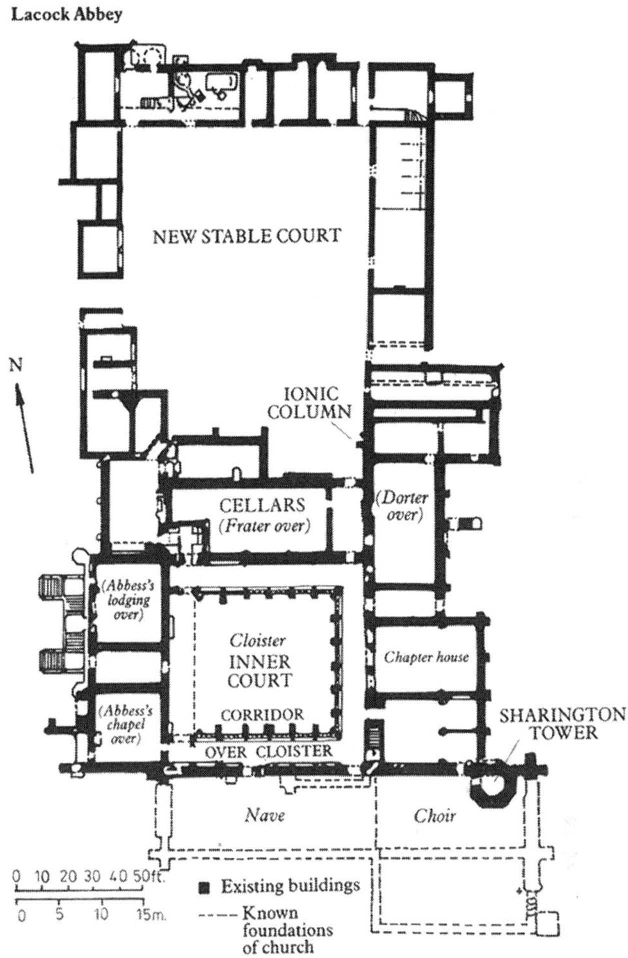

Figure 2.11. Plan of Lacock Abbey, a mid-sixteenth-century monastery conversion. The original religious functions are marked in italics while the newer domestic spaces are labeled with all-capital letters. Reprinted from Maurice Howard, *The Early Tudor House: Architecture and Politics, 1490–1550* (1987), 160, with the author's permission.

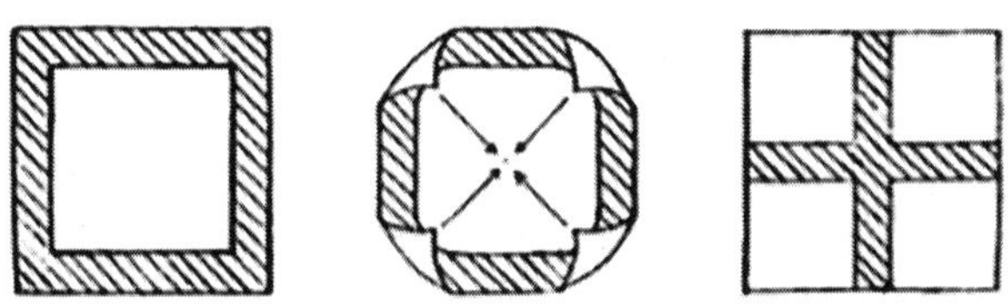

Figure 2.12. Architectural involution. Diagram: Mimi Yiu.

through the whole length of the house" as the "best forms . . . for a private man."[147]

Despite the fantasy of a facade that demarcates a clean edge between public and private, a boundary that drives performance without and releases natural affect within, the hallway creates an internal "pulcruse prospecte" that brings an existential drama within the home. While carving out a common space that replaces the great hall, the corridor offers a visual transparency that depends upon a social opacity, turning "dirty servants" into shadows forever imagined at the vanishing point of a perspectival *allée.* Indeed, since the hallway forms an improper space wedged between rooms, those walking along its route become unseen specters inside the walls, ghosts in an architectural machine designed to produce social difference. In some respects, the eye-catching pantomime impelled onto an external face deflects attention from the greater domestic theater played by a stratified household, whose silenced and disembodied members appear only as fleeting silhouettes on the paper facades of hallways. A concern with aesthetic harmony outside thus muffles the dissonance of those roaming the corridors within, tracing scripted patterns of movement. By enabling this game of musical rooms based not on proportion but mobility, the network of hallways establishes a spatial taxonomy that makes, marks, and mirrors an increasing separation between individuals, mounting a domestic scenography that masks subjects behind internalized facades-cum-faces.

Although the architectural involution that changes a courtyard to a double-pile plan comprises only a single historical trajectory among many, the adoption of transitional spaces crucially displaces what Catherine Ingraham has termed the burden of linearity,[148] dislocating the primacy of sequential ordering and unidirectional movement. The medieval great hall, like Nonsuch's inner court, enacted what Habermas calls a "publicity of representation" by assembling and displaying an extended household, often ranked in linear order (during meals, for instance). In contrast, the cross-hall's principle of unity derives from a spatial crux that disperses subjects to their proper destinations but itself forms a "no man's land," a beat, a pause in the spatial music where all identity seems to hang in suspension. Lacking all propriety, this central node functions not only as an inorganic heart that pulses with the rhythms of a circulatory network, but also as the choric womb shaped by the movement of becoming.[149] By 1690, the architect Roger North would opine that an internal courtyard did not suit "a dwelling house, that ought to have a connexion, and unity, without crossing to and fro one part to the other, thro the air, and abroad."[150] While the single-pile allows people to reach

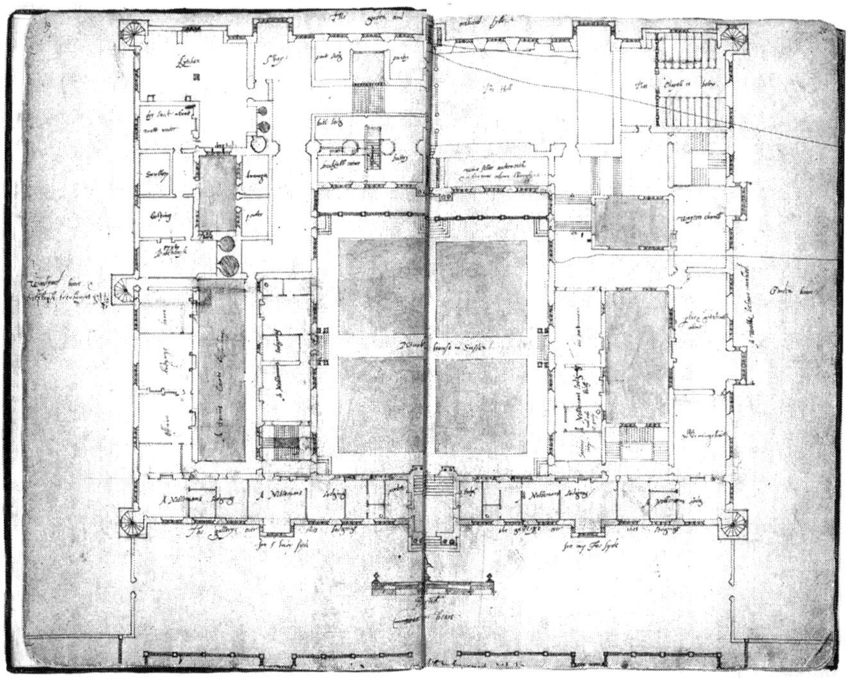

Figure 2.13. John Thorpe, central courtyard with paths that resemble cross-corridors (T19–20). By courtesy of the Trustees of Sir John Soane's Museum. Photo: Ardon Bar-Hama.

opposite wings by crossing the "empty O" of a courtyard (figure 2.13), this central space of mobility now conceals itself within the double-pile to become the intersection of a cross-hall plan.

Replying to and a re-plying of the basic courtyard module,[151] the double-pile encourages a subjective opacity and social spacing while inscribing the household upon a splintered ground. If the single-pile house may be likened to a spoken enunciation that moves forward relentlessly, a continuous expulsion of breath, then the double-pile's multiplicity of pathways enables a circuitous spatial deferral that instantiates the *writing* of architecture: the writing of architecture as a subject, the writing of the architectural subject. After all, Derrida encourages us to consider "writing as the possibility of the road and of difference, the history of writing and the history of the road, of the rupture, of the *via rupta,* of the path that is broken, beaten, *fracta.*"[152] At this moment in the late sixteenth century when the hallway insinuates itself between proper spaces to rupture the articulation of home, fracturing the architectural body from within, a *via rupta* emerges that makes dissemination and difference its central principle. Burrowing through the very walls upholding architectural structure, facing yet effacing the spaces of propriety, the hallway supplies both the instrument and scene of writing. Indeed, this space of transition exemplifies the "breaching" that Derrida ascribes to writing, a process that involves "opening up its own space, effraction, breaking of a path against resistances, rupture and irrupture *becoming a route* [*faisant route,* literally "making a route"]."[153] Building a scenic (de)tour around the house, the ever-forking corridor establishes a syntax of mobile connectivity whose subjects become legible only as spectral bodies, strewing their traces through a domestic labyrinth rather than gathering a "dirty" fullness of presence. Haunted by a transparent center that emphatically refuses to hold, the double-pile inaugurates a spatialized writing that negates the division of architects by book and by hand, constructing a house that itself figures written discourse. As Nicholas Barbon observes in his 1685 appraisal of English architecture: "almost every House is a little Book of Architecture."[154]

CHAPTER THREE

Unlocking Gertrude's Closet

O God, I could be bounded in a nutshell and count myself a king of infinite space—were it not that I have bad dreams.

—*Hamlet*

As early modern architecture began to articulate itself with a syntax akin to writing, the subject of domestic space—in both senses—reciprocally informed the narratives crafted for English theater. Becoming Vitruvian "*Diver*[s] into *Causes,*"[1] late sixteenth- and early seventeenth-century playwrights attempted to construct interior spaces with greater depth and meaning, plumbing the mental landscapes of characters while fleshing out the character of settings. Joel Fineman claims that Shakespeare occupies a special position in the history of subjectivity not least "because those characters have come subsequently to pose themselves to theoreticians of subjectivity as pressing problems to be solved."[2] Indeed, as a platform for plotting domestic fiction and friction, *Hamlet* enjoys an almost mythic status in literary scholarship for ushering in a modern subjectivity that conflates external seeming with internal being.[3] Terry Eagleton argues that "there is no heart of the mystery to be plucked out. Hamlet has no 'essence' of being whatsoever, no inner sanctum to be safeguarded: he is pure deferral and diffusion, a hollow void which offers nothing determinate to be known."[4] Similarly, noting Hamlet's "parodic and uncommitted participation" in a series of roles including prince, courtier, son, lover, and friend, Francis Barker concludes: "At the center of Hamlet, in the interior of his mystery, there is, in short, nothing."[5]

To house this miming, uncommitted hero made half-ghost by melancholy, Shakespeare designs a tragic architectonic whose heart dwells inside a closet. In the middle of Act III, at the very center of the play's action,[6] Hamlet must undertake a crucial journey from the Mousetrap to his mother's closet. Like a voyage into the heart of darkness, Hamlet's steps will soon make of him a murderer. Indeed, after Claudius's guilty reaction confirms the Ghost's tale of "murder most foul" (I.v.27), Hamlet obeys his mother's summons while ostensibly agitated enough to "drink hot blood" (III.ii.381), vowing to "speak daggers to her" (III.ii.387). Disturbed, disoriented, displaced from his proper subject position, Hamlet can only distantly admire the stoicism that defines a perfect man, a Vitruvian ideal balanced in mind rather than limb:

> Give me that man
> That is not passion's slave, and I will wear him
> In my heart's core, ay, in my heart of heart. (III.ii.71–73)

Whether Hamlet's next line—"As I do thee"—identifies or contrasts Horatio with this man "whose blood and judgment are so well commeddled" (III.ii.69), such a better person clearly remains a foreign other ("that man") to the prince. Indeed, Hamlet only dreams of installing this well-tempered man in his "heart of heart," perhaps wishing to introject a mentor who checks erratic impulses like a pacemaker. Yet in this desire to "wear" another man inside,[7] to build organic layers like Alberti's "pelt on top of clothing,"[8] the contours of Hamlet's own interior space become unstable. Can Hamlet ever locate the truest version of himself, finding "that within which passes show" (I.ii.85)? Or does his heart of heart already house another man, one who can be worn like an "inky cloak" (I.ii.77), a removable costume, a persona?

These questions acquire greater urgency as Hamlet penetrates into a physical and psychic interior, taking a journey that culminates in Gertrude's closet. But what kind of room does Hamlet walk into? Too often, the Oedipal tensions that saturate Hamlet and Gertrude's meeting have shaped the closet as surely as an architect's hand. When readers back-form a space from events that occur within, Gertrude's closet usually becomes a stiflingly feminine boudoir, or a bedchamber that makes evident the "rank sweat of an enseamed bed" (III.iv.92). Indeed, affirming a tradition that regards the closet as "synonymous with Gertrude's bedroom,"[9] countless theater and film directors signify the queen's "unweeded garden" of sexuality by displaying her marital bed during this scene (I.ii.135), even showing Hamlet and his mother romping on "the nasty sty" (III.iv.94). "Now, mother, what's the matter?" Hamlet asks (III.iv.7), punning on *mater*; "now, son, why so seedy?" we might query back. As Bernice Kliman notes, the fallacy of misplacing Gertrude's closet in her bedchamber already surfaces in Nicholas Rowe and Jacob Tonson's collected works of Shakespeare. While an engraving in their 1709 edition of *Hamlet* depicts

Figure 3.1. Louis du Guernier, frontispiece to *Hamlet* from vol. 6 of *The Works of William Shakespeare,* ed. Nicholas Rowe (London, 1714). By permission of the Folger Shakespeare Library.

Gertrude's closet as a plain room with two chairs, a revised image in their 1714 volume inserts a canopied bed that stands behind the queen (figure 3.1).[10] A persistent slippage of the closet into the bedroom thus renders Gertrude's bed too too solid, sallied, and sullied. Hamlet may picture his father merely in his "mind's eye" (I.ii.185), or as a spectral trace of armor dissolving into the night air, but Gertrude's defiled body and bed have a material presence that verges on excess—for Hamlet and for us.

Putting the closet back in the closet, so to speak, the advent of queer theory has imbued this historical space with modern overtones of a taboo, hidden sexuality.[11] Yet recasting Gertrude's closet within a psychoanalytic frame ensures that there is never a *there* there, only an architectural fantasy built from the fabric of Freudian dreams. More recently, early modern closets have emerged as secretive, gendered spaces whose inward emphasis produces a self-conscious subject. For Richard Rambuss, the prayer closet serves as a "vortex for the intensification of religious affect," creating "an interiorizing apparatus" in which a subject develops from isolated contemplation: "the door of the prayer closet opens onto an incipiently modern figuration of selfhood."[12] Yet precisely because this door remains closed to a household's prying eyes, as Alan Stewart observes, the closet arouses suspicion as a detached space infused with secrets.[13] Defining closets primarily as studies used for "knowledge-processing technologies," Stewart explores the shadowy bonds between masters and their male secretaries ("secretories" who serve as human closets for holding secrets), positing that "anxiety surrounding the locked male closet is presented to the world as sexual anxiety about the unlocked female closet."[14] Yet if female closets are construed as a screen, diversion, detour, or receptacle for discourses of male homosociality, how can we discern when allusions to women are actually about women and not covert allusions to men?[15]

Perceived as a space that assigns women to materiality and men to textuality, the closet becomes a gendering as well as interiorizing apparatus. James Knowles describes the female closet as "a site of private devotion" and "a storage space for household goods or valuables," whereas the male closet serves as "an office, muniment room, and library."[16] Likewise, Stewart quickly dismisses female closets as crammed with household rather than high-minded stuff, as domestic havens relieved by a few conduct and prayer manuals.[17] Stewart even portrays the closet of Lady Anne Clifford, the noted diarist, as a place of virtual illiteracy in relation to her husband's: "She goes to 'see the things in the closet' and to be read to, he to read."[18] Rather than discover early modern closets, as Stewart claims, this default gendering of space condemns women to enclosure, whether protecting their material goods for a lord or their immaterial souls for a Lord, while men engage in knowledge transactions that extend outside the home.[19] Even in architecture's heart of heart, the early modern closet merely reifies gender roles.

Severed from the public realm, dismissed from arenas such as politics or intellect, the female closet tucked inside an architectural body easily conflates with the private space inside women's bodies. Across

Shakespeare's canon, Georgianna Ziegler concludes, "the woman's room signifies her 'self' "—enclosed if chaste—"and the man's forced or stealthy entry of this room constitutes a rape of her private space."[20] In *Reading Shakespeare Historically,* Lisa Jardine likewise sexualizes feminine space to identify Gertrude's closet as an inner sanctum "where customarily a woman would only entertain her husband or lover."[21] From this perspective, Hamlet commits a spatial transgression by entering the closet "to encounter [his mother] as a sexualised subject," just as Gertrude violates protocol by secreting Polonius in such an intimate setting. These reciprocal breaches of socio-spatial etiquette explain Hamlet's violent reaction upon finding Polonius, an interloper from the public domain.[22] Yet despite Jardine's stated intention to perform a historical reading, her analysis shoehorns architecture into Freudian contours: "the physical spaces of intimacy in the early modern play readily lend themselves to a psychoanalytic interpretation."[23] By envisioning a closet where "intimations of erotic possibility are almost inevitable,"[24] Jardine creates a self-fulfilling prophecy in which Hamlet's meeting with his mother itself renders her unchaste. After all, if both Hamlet and Polonius succeed in entering Gertrude's closet, how could such openness not signify a most careless promiscuity, branding her a public woman in the worst possible sense? By mapping human bodies onto architecture, women's closets become nothing more than another organ to be kept enclosed, domestic, and chaste—in short, closets provide the ultimate spatial paradigm of early modern femininity.[25]

Shakespeare's *Titus Andronicus* raises questions about such a gendered approach to closets when the title character offers his ravished, mutilated daughter this consolation: "Lavinia, go with me;/I'll to thy closet and go read with thee" (III.ii.82–83).[26] If erotic intimations inevitably swirl around a son accessing his mother's closet at her request, then how do we interpret a father's willful intrusion upon the private space of his daughter, particularly a daughter who has just suffered (literally) unspeakable sexual trauma? Locked into a body violently "lopped and hewed" (II.iii.17), lacking hands and tongue to articulate what horrors she has endured, Lavinia herself occupies a closeted interiority as a muted repository of her malefactors' secrets, a discarded sexual object now hollow and wooden in shameful silence. Yet after Titus's directive to read together closes Act III, the next scene finds Lavinia emerging from her architectural, corporeal, and psychic closets with a renovated sense of herself as a subject. Inspired by Lavinia's first attempts to indicate her thoughts via bodily "signs" (IV.i.8), her uncle seizes upon the trick of using a long staff, grasped within the mouth and guided by the feet, to write on a "sandy plot" (IV.i.69). Thus shown a means to release the knowledge trapped within her mind, Lavinia can finally externalize what Hamlet calls "the table of my memory" onto a landscape tableau (I.v.98).

After watching her uncle write his own name in this plot of inscriptional space, Lavinia similarly manipulates a staff with her amputated stumps to make a prosthetic limb-tongue, anchoring this stylus within her mouth to stake a claim to her long-lost voice.[27] As Lavinia names her attackers using this strange half-speech, half-writing, she employs specifically the mode of knowledge transaction associated with her closet, breaking through imposed barriers with a communal performance of reading and writing. By transforming her body into a hybrid device of inscription to reassert her agential self, Lavinia restages her closet practices in a public arena, choosing words that ripple outward from her family to impact a wider audience. As the play soon reveals, Lavinia's accusation not only enables a rescripting of her identity beyond the strictures of abject victimhood, but also catalyzes the cathartic bloodbath that makes way for a new political regime. If her cowardly rapists believed that they had degraded her once-thriving body into a voiceless casket, consigning her to a privacy defined by a powerless, solitary privation, then Lavinia's self-refashioning into a legible instrument of retribution—aptly triggered by reading Ovid's *Metamorphoses,* evidently not just a decorative book—reminds us how closets can work *against* the sexualized enclosure of women.

In an ironic turn of the (dining) tables, her tormentors suffer the greatest defacement as subjects when Titus gags their mouths, slashes their throats, pulverizes their bones, and bakes their heads into a pie. Thus silenced, lopped, and hewn to be stuffed into culinary closets, into pastry shells known in early modern parlance as "coffins," Lavinia's rapists transform into minced meat that cannot have any interiority because it *is* pure interiority—as filler in a perverse pie, as matter for their mother's stomach. Indeed, when the villainous Tamora opens this unsavory packet of pastry, this poison-pen letter addressed specially to her, she unwittingly ingests her ground-up sons in an oral travesty of rape, granting them incestuous entrance into her body without informed consent. From Lavinia's mouth to Tamora's, from one closet to another, the policing of bodily purity depends less on an impossible enforcement of closure than a strategic circulation of knowledge. Although neither woman can escape death after their respective violations, Lavinia manages to write herself back into subjectivity from a state of utter desolation, entering again into social discourse after being written off as disposable, as mere meat to be consumed.

Opening Lavinia's closet thus emancipates a female voice that strives to effect change in the world, empowering a female pen that proves cloistering walls flimsier than lines drawn in the sand. Like Gertrude, Lavinia enters her closet to share a private moment among intimates, including men; like Anne Clifford, Lavinia employs her personal closet to read collaboratively, marking a site of textual rather than sexual intercourse.[28] An extant woman's closet from this period, likely built for Lady Anne Drury, reveals a small room covered with panels of painted emblems and mottoes that evoke the reliefs on Nonsuch's exterior. Not only do these panels suggest hours spent reading and reflecting on virtues, but their very layout makes the walls resemble the pages of an open book.[29] Negating many of the traditional distinctions between male and female closets, such an architecture of feminine interiority allots women the space not simply to figure interiority, but to possess one as well. Despite the miasma of erotic transgression blurring the critic's view, then, early modern closets cannot be deemed exclusively "female" or "male" as facilely as modern water closets with gendered signage on their doors. Here, we may usefully recall Lacan's parable about two children who glance out the window of a stopped train, trying to ascertain the station's name. Scanning the platform from seats that offer limited and opposing perspectives on the world outside, the two children dispute whether they have arrived at "Ladies" or "Gentlemen."[30]

While any journey into history inevitably neglects what lies beyond a given critical frame, resorting to a binarized system of gender to distinguish closets whose doors often remain tantalizingly closed, retaining their secrets across the distance of centuries, risks arriving at a system of arbitrary signifiers—and possibly misses seeing the bigger picture. Wiping some prurient steam off the window of hindsight, we notice an entry in Clifford's diary that details how she entered her husband's closet to peruse volumes in his library; likewise, as Lena Cowen Orlin's meticulous research has uncovered, men's closets could overflow not only with books and business papers, but also with china, linens, pewter, and plate.[31] Combing through probate inventories and other historical records to uncover a trail of shared keys, a pattern of shared access, Orlin rejects the closet as an interiorizing apparatus altogether, contending that "the Tudor closet had its genesis in the accumulation of valuable goods rather than an aspiration for personal privacy."[32]

Yet material safekeeping and subjective privacy could well coexist among the bedding—and even spare beds—found in household closets.[33] As a child, Elizabeth Isham (1609-54) stored both pantry items and prayer books in her closet, a mixture that allowed her to pluck earthly and spiritual fruit within one *hortus conclusus*. Alone in her closet, Isham would from time to time enjoy a pear stolen from the family cache, then atone for this petty crime by reading and praying in the same room.[34] Perhaps as a final penance, the adult Isham reflected upon her youthful exploits in a *Booke of Rememberance,* a memoir of some literary ambition modeled partly on Augustine's *Confessions.*[35] Isham might even have crafted her *Booke* in that very same closet, since she lived virtually her entire life in the family home. Not only does Isham's *Booke* enclose in a textual closet an account of her time spent in a spatial closet, but she also produces a material object eminently suitable for other closet libraries. Indeed, this record of personal devotion invites readers into Isham's mind and indirectly into her closet: the childless author bequeathed the manuscript to her brother's family.[36] Isham thus imagines a network of closet readers and writers from Augustine to herself and beyond; passed from one closet shelf to another, the *Booke* allows a female author to unfold her discursive heart of heart by retelling scenes of her own childhood reading, by appealing to a shared textual practice. Like Lavinia's inscription of her deepest secrets, like Clifford's intricately planned and transcribed diaries, the writing enabled by women's closets ripens, pear-like, into forms available for more public delectation.

Indeed, the early modern closet runneth over—not only into other parts of the house, but right through the streets to the print shop. From the mid-sixteenth through the seventeenth century, many authors and printers marketed their books as portable closets of knowledge that any literate person could access. United mainly by titles that invoke cabinets, treasuries, storehouses, and closets, these books enclosed a wide range of topics between their covers, as even a cursory sampling reveals: moral philosophy (Edmund Elviden, *The Closet of Counsells Conteining the Aduice of Diuers Wyse Philosophers;* 1569), cookery and physic (John Partridge, *The Treasurie of Commodious Conceits, & Hidden Secrets and May Be Called, the Huswiues Closet, of Healthfull Prouision;* 1573), religious practice (Barthélemy Batt, *The Christian Mans Closet;* 1581), natural philosophy (Thomas Tymme, *A Dialogue Philosophicall: Wherein Natures Secret Closet is Opened;* 1612), surgical remedies (Thomas Bonham, *The Chyrugians Closet;* 1630), pregnancy and plague (*A Rich Closet of Physical Secrets,* including *The Childbearer's Cabinet* and *A Preservative Against the Plague and Small Pox;* 1652), the physiology of sex (Giovanni Sinibaldi, *Rare Verities: The Cabinet of Venus Unlocked, and Her Secrets Laid Open;* 1658), and the subculture of rogues and gypsies (Richard Head, *The Canting Academy, Or, the Devil's Cabinet Opened;* 1673).[37] What secrets could remain secreted in a culture that allowed the common reader to peruse Charles I's private letters to his queen, addressed as "Dear heart," in *The Kings Cabinet Opened* (1645)?[38]

While some books in this brief catalog disclose "secrets" relevant to actual closets or, on a smaller scale, storage cabinets, most writers seem to regard the penning and opening of closets as merely a trope, a structural gambit to initiate dialogue. In this subgenre, if not more generally, early modern books define themselves as textual closets that traffic in knowledge, making visible a space where any variety of secret can be inscribed for public consumption. Like the empty frame that Alberti incises on a wooden tablet, the closet-like book outlines a blank space for discourse, providing what Charles Taylor and Jean Bodin define as a common space that unifies members of society.[39] Closets thus assume a public function as a space of discursive exchange, a ground of subjective disclosure; closets make authors and readers of those who enter. As a reusable frame that accepts and swaps out entire discourses, this closet-like book resembles the erasable writing tables that Hamlet invokes after meeting the Ghost, when the prince vows to deface his former persona by "wiping away all trivial fond records" (I.v.99) from "the table of my memory" (I.v.98).[40] Long before his meeting with Gertrude, Hamlet figures his own interiority as a space of contested writing, a rank closet of unweeded words. But cleaning the private closet of his memory proves more difficult that Hamlet expects, as both reader and writer. Trying to inscribe his father's words in his heart of heart, to keep his father's secrets, Hamlet struggles to define himself as a *Booke of Rememberance*.

Inscribing the Closet

> For God, who first writ his Law in the *Tables of our hearts;* and when our corruption had defaced them, writ it again in *Stone-tables.*
>
> —John Donne[41]

From the very first encounter with his dead father, Hamlet finds himself caught in a world of closets. Beckoning Hamlet to a "more removed ground" (I.iv.61), the Ghost seeks a platform for intimate dialogue that contrasts with a strict regime of surveillance, a constant haunting by sentinels and friends along the castle ramparts. After devising an ad hoc closet away from public scrutiny, the Ghost begins a private haunting of Hamlet with this command: "Mark me" (I.v.2). Swiftly, Hamlet signals his assent in two syllables—"I will" (I.v.2)—that mimic the Ghost's speech pattern and indeed continue the same line of pentameter. With a phrase that already echoes his father's voice, that already haunts his father's words, Hamlet enters a compact to record the Ghost's speech as a scribe, a secretary, a "secretorie" in whom secrets can be safely deposited.[42] In *The Secrete of Secretes* (1572), the pseudo-Aristotelian author counsels kings to choose "a secretarie for to write, & know thy secrets," a trusted man who "suffer none to come to the place where thy wrytinges be, and that none see them."[43] As though well trained at Wittenberg's secretarial school, Hamlet studiously transcribes the Ghost's speech onto tables both internal and external, jotting in his notebook while assuring his father and sovereign: "thy commandment all alone shall live/Within the book and volume of my brain" (I.v.102–3).[44] The Ghost thus assumes a discursive afterlife in the interior space of Hamlet's body-turned-book, revived by a filial reader who returns to a secret marked within himself, who turns his eyes inward to a closet of memory. To enjoy this gaze "all alone," however, the Ghost must dilate to occupy the entire volume of Hamlet's brain, defacing any previous inscriptions of Hamlet's self-identity.[45]

Initially, Hamlet proves a most efficient secretary who suborns his voice to his master's, who structures his interior around a master narrative. Shortly after the Ghost departs with a final "Adieu, adieu, adieu. Remember me" (I.v.91), Hamlet confirms his loyalty with a pledge:

> Now to my word.
> It is "Adieu, adieu, remember me."
> I have sworn't. (I.v.110–12)

Rather than proclaim revenge upon Claudius, Hamlet merely repeats the Ghost verbatim, electing to rewind previous dialogue instead of plotting future action.[46] Yet Hamlet's non-oath neatly performs its content as a filial secretary reads back the closing phrase of a missive, a mission newly dictated into his memory. Hamlet thus shows off his powers of recall, but only at the cost of letting the Ghost's "then" subsume his "now"; a prince of misdirection, mad only "north-north-west" (II.ii.374), Hamlet deploys a syntax that points away from himself, obscuring the "I" who swears behind the impersonal facade of "It is." Indeed, what Hamlet considers his word, his signature, proves to be the citation of another Hamlet, a spectral other. Losing his interior space to this alternate "me" who demands constant memory, Hamlet cannot help but respond as the Ghost's voice, issuing from beneath the stage, continues to demand that he "Swear" to protect their secret (I.v.157, 163, 189). Vainly shifting his ground as this awful voice emanates from various locales, Hamlet engages in a rhetorical and physical dance with the Ghost beneath his feet, impelled across the platform by a mirroring Hamlet whose presence seems "*Hic et ubique*" (I.v.164). Interpellated by the Ghost's call-and-response sequence, Hamlet inscribes his subjectivity upon the table of performative space, deepening his pledge in body and soul.

Now, then, here, there: the spaces of writing preoccupy Shakespeare's play, *Hic et ubique.*[47] Affirming Jonathan Goldberg's claim that "subjectivity is a scene of writing,"[48] Hamlet must inscribe within himself the terms of an identity newly ordained by his father. Yet Hamlet struggles to embrace his father's sacred imperative in the closeness of "here," not only in his rational precincts of his mind, but more importantly, in the organic table of his heart. Hamlet knows that his heart should pulse with a more primal sense of kinship, a muscle memory that drives him to murder, engorged with the blind passion that Laertes embodies. Just as Hamlet wishes to "wear" the ideal man "In my heart's core, ay, in my heart of heart" (III.ii.72, 73), the disconsolate prince yearns to feel the weight of his father—and his father's words—in his affective center. Indeed, the term *wear* itself evokes a passage of time that deepens the etching of letters into a stone tablet, or into obdurate flesh. Philip Sidney's *Apologie for Poetrie* (1595) suggests this usage in lauding images of noble actions that "styrreth and instructeth the mind"; "Only let *Aeneas* be worne in the tablet of your memory," Sidney advises, noting how the Trojan hero inflames the minds of readers with a desire to be worthy.[49]

While Hamlet succeeds to some degree in wearing his father's words into memory, our miming prince cannot engage his filial reflex for revenge because he *thinks* through his heart, because he cannot serve as passion's slave. Filled with "wild and whirling words" that have yet to be sorted into sense (I.v.139), Hamlet's affective interior cannot wear his father's words into a clearly incised dictum, a finished thought that spurs worthy action. As he wonders aloud to Horatio and Marcellus after the Ghost departs, "would heart of man once think it—But you'll be secret?" (I.v.125). Skittering along an associative thread from heart, to thought, to secrecy, Hamlet attempts to contain his father's secrets in what a sixteenth-century translator of Thomas à Kempis terms "the priuie closet of thine hart" (in cordis tui secretarium).[50] In the tradition of Thomas's *De imitatione Christi,* an influential book of devotion written in the fifteenth century, the heart's privy closet (*secretarium*) provides an isolated space that the subject enters to study itself, to reaffirm kinship with a holy father's spirit, to exist inside and beside itself at once: in short, the closet forms a Derridean center that both governs and eludes bodily structure. "Hold, hold, my heart," Hamlet thus exclaims while attempting to hold in, and more specifically to hold in writing, the enormity of a ghost's unquiet secrets (I.v.93).

Despite keeping the Ghost's secrets, Hamlet cannot refrain from holding onto a portion of his heart, setting aside precisely the privy closet that stages the open secret of his subjectivity. As Patricia Fumerton observes, the early modern subject "always withheld for itself a 'secret' room, cabinet, case, or other recess locked away (in full view) in one corner of the house," enabling a public gesture of withdrawal through a succession of rooms until, in a fantasy of transparency, the self unveils itself as a gift to the other.[51] Hamlet's parents model these protocols by retiring to their respective closets over several scenes and spaces: in his architectural deportment, at least, Hamlet can rightly claim himself "to the manner born" (I.iv.15). The Ghost, who nightly parades "slow and stately" in a "solemn march" (I.ii.202, 201), finally draws Hamlet away to a makeshift closet before revealing his secret identity. After this protracted, patrilineal gesture of withdrawal, Hamlet returns to the castle only to follow in his mother's footsteps to *her* closet, tracing a scenic route through Claudius's prayer room to witness the unveiling of her secret desires. Between these scenes of parental enclosure and disclosure, Hamlet wanders his home without a room to call his own, lacking a private sanctum either inside or outside the castle. Rather than define himself through physical space, Hamlet stages a retreat into his heart's "priuie closet" (Thomas à Kempis) by mounting a teasing show of madness. "Th'observ'd of all observers" more than ever before (III.i.156), a prince deprived of his public destiny to be simply, sovereignly "Denmark," Hamlet dilates his privacy as a subject with an elaborate tableau of interiority meant for display.

"Words, words, words" (II.ii.192): Hamlet opens chamber after chamber in his heart with a profuse stream of words that proffer an illusion of internal depth, of unveiling. Ironically, Hamlet's prolix madness not only prevents listeners from mapping his interiority, but also distances him from his desired identity. Instead of leaping to perform revenge, lacking even a player's "dream of passion" to unsheathe his sword (II.ii.546), Hamlet laments that he "must like a whore unpack [his] heart with words" (II.ii.581). Hamlet's jarringly material term *unpack,* more suited to a peddler than a metaphysician, construes his interiority as a cabinet filled with words made stuff, a library where divine *logos* has devolved into cheap textual objects like books and tables—even letters from a fallen king, addressed to his son's "dear heart."[52] Just as early modern books serve as closets unpacked by the wanton medium of print, by words that reveal to every customer the secrets of a private space, the closet of his heart, Hamlet fears, has become a common baggage open to all comers. Trafficking in a language as adulterated as women, "muddy-mettled" Hamlet can only "fall a-cursing like a very drab" (II.ii.562, 582), his heart crammed with words that seem meretricious, material, maternal, mad.[53] Hamlet even begins to suspect his father of being a shape-shifting "devil" who has imprinted the book of his mind not with sacred truths, but with cheap fictions (II.ii.595). Hamlet's sudden need to verify the Ghost's story—"I'll have grounds/more relative than this" (II.ii.599–600)—thus manifests his desire for a medium that is more than kin ("more relative") to justify an action less than kind, to establish Claudius's guilt through ocular rather than verbal proof. In a fallen world where secret truths must be staged for public viewing, where books serve to counter mortal forgetfulness, Hamlet suffers the "heart-ache" of a maternal flesh made word rather than a paternal word made flesh (III.i.62), of a privy closet that seems like a public market, of a *secretarium* whose center no longer holds.

Yet how should we understand this architecture of early modern interiority, figured by a *secretarium* that translators of Thomas à Kempis render first as *secretari,* then *secrete place,* and finally *closet*?[54] Would this very locus of secrecy reveal itself as "an introjected structure of intensified self-possession and sharpened devotional focus"?[55] In the fourth century C.E., Augustine would have recognized a *secretarium* as the sizable hall adjoining his basilica at Hippo, a room that served not only as a sacristy for storing ceremonial objects and ecclesiastical records—a closet in the treasury sense—but also as a place of assembly and adjudication that could house diocesan councils of several hundred people.[56] Outside of sacred precincts but with a similar emphasis on containing valuable discourse and knowledge, the term *secretarium* emerges in Roman documents from the second century C.E. to designate a special court for legal cases involving senators. Often located adjacent to municipal archives and other record-keeping buildings, the *secretarium* excluded public spectators from politically sensitive proceedings by dividing its space with a curtain (*velum*) and even physical barriers (*cancelli*).[57] According to Mary Carruthers, such a deliberate and deliberative secrecy carried over into early medieval notions of the *secretarium* as a book repository and the *secretarius* as a scribe, both enabling the conversion of fleeting memories into textual permanence; by extension, the *secretarium* could also figure an imagined mental treasury—what

Quintilian called a *secretum*—which contains a rich epistemological matrix to be perused by the mind's eye.[58]

For Petrarch, the book itself offers a printed version of the mind's storehouse, thus directly linking material and mental interiorities. In a mid-fourteenth-century Latin text known as *Secretum,* Petrarch envisions meeting a resurrected Augustine who—like *Hamlet*'s Ghost—leads him to a more secret, separated place ("in secretiorem loci partem . . . adduxit") after a warm fatherly embrace ("paternoque refovens complexu").[59] There, the poet and philosopher embark on dialogues inspired by the *Confessions*' mode of self-inquiry, reflecting critically on Petrarch's spiritual condition. Among the fictional Augustine's many pieces of advice, Petrarch confides, those sayings that "to me come closest home I have graven with more especial vividness on the tablet of my memory" (ea tamen, quibus ipse notatus sum, memorie altius impressi).[60] While these special words from his literary forefather that mark Petrarch ("quibus ipse notatus sum") are deeply impressed upon his memory ("memorie altius impressi"), the unreliable nature of such recording demands the creation of another repository to contain a discourse "so intimate and deep" (tam familiare), to prevent the architectonic of Augustine's thought from lapsing into disrepair ("dilaberetur").[61] Petrarch thus devises a little book, entitled "My Secret" ("secretum . . . meum"), which supplies a prosthetic memory to support what has already been inscribed in the mind.[62] Since a mental tome may prove fallible, ruined by the tendency to forget and confuse, Petrarch designs an external template, a platform, a blueprint that allows him to rebuild his own interiority: "all that you [the book] keep in remembrance that was spoken in secret you in secret will tell to me over again."[63] Speaking back to Petrarch in his own voice, a voice that already echoes Augustine's, this little book renews its secrets unto infinity.

Unlike closet-themed books that posit concealment to stoke curiosity, to perform a textual striptease, the uncirculated manuscript of Petrarch's *Secretum* "flee[s] the haunts of men" to inhabit a private space, carving out a nutshell of thought that refuses public reading.[64] Quite possibly, Petrarch even carried this precious book upon his person as a *vade mecum,* keeping close a tangible reminder of the secret that constitutes his innermost being, wearing an Albertian pelt (or vellum) upon his own skin. With more success than Hamlet, Petrarch revives an idealized man who reigns in his heart as a quasi-divine guide, whose relic-like book of secrets dictates the poet's choice of actions. In short, Petrarch conjures a spectral father who flees the haunts of men only to haunt a particular man, a father who comes from written sources and lives in books. Thus defining his interiority through practices of inscription, Petrarch engages in dialogue not only with an ethereal mentor who dispenses counsel, but also with a material book that serves as a stand-in body. Indeed, Petrarch constructs himself through colloquies with a little book addressed tenderly as *tu* (you), conversing with this textual quasi-subject to reconcile his current state with a spiritual ideal. Petrarch thus animates himself as a subject by reading and writing a book of the undead, by cultivating a discursive space that structures his distinctness through secrecy ("*My* Secret").

While Augustine's *Confessions* conceives the *secretum* as a tranquil patch of garden where, joined by a close friend, the future cleric ponders his own actions and ultimately receives heavenly grace, Petrarch replicates this outdoor retreat in a concealed book of secrets as well as a hidden tablet of the mind, thus connecting a network of internal places that carry traces of the mark (*notatus*).[65] By building these inscriptional grounds that mirror a physical place of withdrawal, the Petrarchan subject enacts a literally self-perpetuating exchange of secrets with a textual *secretarium,* establishing a *habitus* in which a speaking book serves as a secretary to the self, as an extra skin defining the boundary between public and private.[66] Indeed, as we shall see, the early modern subject constructs itself by enclosing a ground of inscription within the bodily temple, a secret locale connected to both the material text and a dialogic space of retirement: the closet. As English domestic architecture swallows the Augustinian *secretum,* installing a contemplative garden within that resembles an interior courtyard, the early modern closet assumes the function of allotting subjects a space to debate, inscribe, retain, and remember.

To gauge how well the English closet maps onto these older valences of *secretum* and *secretarium,* we might consider another term rendered as *closet* in *De imitatione Christi,* only here the translation pertains to an architectural rather than metaphoric site: "For commonlie thou shalt finde that in thy closet [*cella*], which thou wouldest leese [lose] abrode. The more thou vsest thy closet [*cella*], the more thou wilt like it."[67] The Latin *cella* originally indicated a Greek temple's inner sanctuary, a large central space housing a statue of the deity and serving generally as a treasury (*celare:* to hide, keep secret). This sense of containment carried over into Roman secular architecture, in which a *cella* could signify a storeroom, a domestic storefront, or simply a small room, while medieval Latin added more particular usages such as the monastic cell (*cella*), pantry (*cellarium*), and buttery (*cella vinaria*).[68] No doubt, Elizabeth Isham would feel right at home in this secret *cella* that combines household storage with solitary meditation, profane materiality with sacred asceticism. Yet as the passage from Thomas à Kempis suggests, the semantic register of *cella* always embraces mundane as well as metaphoric dimensions: the reader withdraws into both a physical and mental closet to discover a richly layered interiority that would be lost "abrode," an interiority whose almost addictive pleasures reshape the self after repeated visits. Indeed, the medieval *cella* echoes its kindred *secretarium* in figuring a storeroom of memory, as Mary Carruthers notes, thus explicating why Chaucer's storytelling Monk alludes to tragedies "Of whiche I have an hundred in my celle."[69] Given this emphasis on building an archive of recollected narratives, it seems curiously resonant that Old Hamlet's ghost speaks from the "cellarage" when repeatedly urging Hamlet and his companions to swear (I.v.159), to keep sacred and secret in their memory what they have witnessed that night. Issuing from a contained interiority beneath the stage, the Ghost's disembodied but peremptory voice reinforces the sense of a mental haunting, forcing spectators to conjure the absent father in their own mind's eye.[70]

Just as Hamlet tries to keep the tragedy of his father's death marked in his *celle,* to shelve in his internal library a volume titled *Hamlet* whose last pages remain blank, Ophelia similarly figures her mind as a closet that preserves Laertes's advice on rebuffing a prince: "'Tis in my memory lock'd/And you yourself shall keep the key of it" (I.iii.85–86). To prevent romantic tragedy, Ophelia confines her passions using the memory of her brother's words, or more precisely, using the writing-effect of his speech to protect her heart: "I shall th'*effect* of this good lesson keep/As watchman to my heart" (I.iii.45–46; emphasis added). With Laertes's words locked as a conduct manual in her mind, the effects of his words forming a chastity belt, like *cancelli,* around the privy closet of her heart, Ophelia allows her brother and later her father to shape her interiority as a *secretarium,* as both a council chamber and a treasury holding their sanctioned "prescripts" for her behavior (II.ii.142).[71] In this context, when a ghostlike Hamlet wanders unbidden into Ophelia's closet "with a look so piteous in purport/As if he had been loosed out of hell" (II.i.82–83), his intrusion must be understood as violating not only her physical space, but also the locked closet of her memory.[72]

According to a narrative unpacked from Ophelia's perturbed heart, Hamlet recently appeared in her closet "ungarter'd and down-gyved to his ankle" (II.i.80), looking ready to "speak of horrors" (II.i.84). As the prince enters her closet with surprising ease, his external dishevelment contrasts with a silence that keeps his interiority perfectly secret and enclosed. Only a "piteous and profound" sigh escapes him, seeming to "shatter all his bulk/And end his being" (III.i.94, 95–96). Whether this unstaged episode reveals Hamlet's ineffable passion or merely Ophelia's proto-mad dream of such a passion, Hamlet introduces a disorder into the domestic scene of a chaste maid sewing, disrupting the patriarchal script that structures the closet of her mind. While Ophelia will soon return his letters, primly voicing a wish to "redeliver" the textual "remembrances" of his affections (III.i.94, 93), Hamlet has already redelivered himself as a haunting remembrance of their past relationship, inserting himself as an unreadable cipher into her memory to "end his being" as a romantic interest.[73] A revenant who transgresses the architecture of Laertes's dictates, Hamlet slips across the walls of her closet, her *cella,* in a valedictory gesture of presence. Just as he seeks to erase those "trivial fond records" in himself (I.v.99), he wishes to remove himself from Ophelia's mind as he departs as a lover; a final memory to be stricken once he leaves, Hamlet rivets a backward gaze on Ophelia's face, finding a tenuous way forward "without his eyes" (II.i.98). Having thus defaced the writing-effect of old inscriptions that construe him as a young paramour, Hamlet naturally cannot remember his remembrances when Ophelia attempts to return them: "I never gave you aught" (III.i.96).

Given both parties' unusual reliance on texts and textual spaces—Hamlet enters a scene "reading on a book" (II.ii.sd), just as Ophelia reads a book while waiting to accost Hamlet "as 'twere by accident" (III.i.30)—Polonius aptly employs a textual metaphor in denying that he "had play'd the desk or table-book" in fostering their romance (II.ii.136). In other words, Polonius disclaims playing the go-between by providing a blank space of inscription, by passing messages between the lovers. Yet Polonius eagerly assumes this role in arranging the closet interview between Hamlet and Gertrude, then plotting with Claudius to secrete himself behind an arras to "o'erhear/The speech of vantage" (III.iii.32–33). By offering to transcribe Hamlet's and Gertrude's words onto the tablet of his mind, to transform their speech into remembrances, into textualized marks that represent their absent selves, Polonius executes the most vital function of a king's secretary by making himself an inscriptional ground, a desk, a table-book. Situated outside the "partial," private bond that unites a mother and child (III.iv.32), Polonius serves as an authorized organ—a scribal ear—for the "vantage" of sovereign power, defending state interests by setting up a closet-like space for depositing secrets behind a textile wall, a *velum.* Waiting there, Polonius hopes that Gertrude will "lay home to [Hamlet]" (III.iv.1), "tax him home" (III.iii.29); in short, her words must reach into her son's very heart, wearing into his psychic "home."[74]

Three scenes earlier, Claudius himself had joined Polonius to gauge Hamlet's passions from behind another screen. Believing that Hamlet's madness springs from a thwarted romance, Polonius forces Ophelia to confront the prince as though by chance. Polonius advises his monarch: "Be you and I behind an arras then,/Mark the encounter" (II.ii.163–64). Polonius thus designs a viewing platform with the ambition of "seeing unseen" another Hamlet loosed from hell (III.i.33), speaking of horrors. Indeed, as Claudius and Polonius conspire to "bestow" themselves (III.i.33) where they can "judge" Hamlet in private (III.i.34), these "lawful espials" create a secret court behind a *velum* (III.i.32). This *secretarium,* built and sealed by a royal secretary, receives its sanction to look into and judge Hamlet's interior from the sovereign presence bestowed there. In Polonius's usage of *bestow,* echoed a few lines later by Claudius (III.i.44), we glean a sense of how closets require *placing, storing,* and *giving* oneself to develop a critical mind that surveys and interprets, to acquire the powers of a subject.[75] Wrapped in a second skin, a veil, this subject conjures a place of propriety from which to mark and re-mark the world. Once *Hamlet* establishes these closet protocols in the world of Elsinore, we finally move forward with the same crew of plotters to the showdown between Gertrude and Hamlet.

Claudius's Closet

> And being therupon admonished to reflect vpon myselfe, I entred into the very inward parts of my soule, by thy conduct. . . . I entred, & discerned, with the eye of my soule. (Et inde admonitus redire ad memet ipsum, intravi in intima mea, duce te. . . . Intravi et vidi qualicumque oculo animae meae.)
>
> —Augustine[76]

Shortly after the Mousetrap scene, Rosencrantz and Guildenstern convey a request to Hamlet upon the queen's "commandment" (III.ii.308): "in most great affliction of spirit" (III.ii.303), Gertrude summons the prince to "*her* closet" (III.ii.322; emphasis added), a space that belongs to her solely and which she occupies, waiting.[77] Before reaching this sanctum of feminine property and propriety, Hamlet must depart from a room that functions like a great hall in staging theater for the household.[78] When Hamlet desires solitude in this formal place of assembly, a gentle command becomes necessary to disperse the assorted crowd: "Leave me, friends" (III.ii.378). Yet rather than trace a linear path from this public stage to a private closet, Shakespeare inserts a third space that interrupts such binary thinking. Bound for his mother's closet, Hamlet stumbles across his stepfather instead; Claudius, attempting vainly to soothe his conscience through prayer, occupies a domestic sanctuary that protects a murderer in "retirement" (III.ii.293). Turning the tables on Claudius by seeing him unseen in his most vulnerable state—spiritually undressed, spatially unshielded, and speaking openly of past horrors—Hamlet violates the implicit code of secrecy in this analogue to Gertrude's closet.

Indeed, after the Mousetrap catches his sense of guilt, a "marvellous distempered" Claudius selects this refuge to nurse a spirit more afflicted than Gertrude's (III.ii.293), a spirit that needs "light" (III.ii.263). As Scott Huelin surmises, Claudius's spiritual haven might be a closet or private chapel, both places in an aristocratic home where someone might deliver a heartfelt confession to a higher power.[79] Yet this deeply personal space also carries political overtones as Claudius discusses with Rosencrantz, Guildenstern, and Polonius the escalating "hazard" that Hamlet poses to the "terms of our estate" (III.iii.6, 5).[80] In other words, Claudius practices what James Knowles identifies as "closet government" in a secretive room that resounds with the rhetoric of sovereignty: "The heart of order and rule, the monarchical closet emerges as a central site of institutionalised brutality."[81] Given the protocols of this closet or privy chamber, this *secretarium* where political cronies initiate the most drastic measures against Hamlet, Polonius's offer to work as a domestic spy merely exposes the brutality of a regime in which all secrets belong to the sovereign.

Although textual cues remain silent on how Claudius's room connects to Gertrude's in terms of layout, Shakespeare makes these two spaces occupy adjacent scenes; in *Hamlet*'s architectonic, Claudius's prayer room always precedes his wife's closet in a linear sequence. While early modern architects separated the king's and queen's privy suites on different floors, or even different wings, Shakespeare firmly conjoins these spaces by arranging for Polonius, Hamlet, Claudius, Rosencrantz, and Guildenstern to appear in Claudius's closet before making their next entrance in Gertrude's closet.[82] Not only does the number of male visitors who matter-of-factly access Gertrude's closet militate against the notion of an erotic, gendered enclosure, but their facile passage between the two rooms shows a pattern of shared usage by an elite group at court. When Gertrude wishes to discuss Hamlet's recent activities with Claudius alone, she must dismiss Rosencrantz and Guildenstern from her closet with a request: "Bestow this place on us a little while" (IV.i.4). Just as Hamlet dispatches the Mousetrap hangers-on with an imperative,

Figure 3.2. *Coretto* from Torchiara (c. 1450–1574). Tucked into the corner of a chapel, the *coretto* presses its open sides against walls, while granting access through a door and window hinged into the carved outer surfaces. Museo delle Arti Decorative del Castello Sforzesco, Milan. Photo: Mimi Yiu.

Gertrude constructs a private space for politically sensitive revelations by discursively erecting barriers, social *cancelli,* which mobilize others to bestow her own closet upon herself. In a certain sense, the wall-like arras serves as an emblem of this flexible structure by defining a threshold *velum* between the king's and queen's privy spaces, a permeable border that allows Claudius's friends to move freely between closets in a joint effort to contain Hamlet's madness. If "man and wife is one flesh" (IV.iii.55), as Hamlet observes after calling Claudius "dear mother" (IV.iii.52), then man and wife may also form one closet, one spatial body, one piece of joint and joined property.

As the next-to-last space before Gertrude's closet, Claudius's privy room necessarily frames a discourse on looking inward that resonates against the following scene, when Hamlet launches into a harangue of his mother: "You go not till I set you up a glass/Where you may see the inmost part of you" (III.iv.18–19). By turning people's eyes inward to survey the chambers of their troubled hearts, the two closets operate as mirror images of one another, even as architectural soul mates; indeed, as Lena Orlin suggests, might Hamlet not discover both the king and queen praying in their respective spaces?[83] Such an emphasis on devotion would reflect the closet's origins as a private chapel inside medieval churches.[84] Built by wealthy patrons, these chapel closets afforded a measure of visual and spatial enclosure within the congregation, fulfilling a desire to remain apart and yet part of the whole. Purely to visualize how these chapel closets functioned, we might consider a fifteenth-century *coretto* or private room from the southern Italian town of Torchiara (figure 3.2). A two-sided structure designed for the corner of a local church, the *coretto* boasts a marquetry exterior decorated with gilded heraldic reliefs, presenting a facade eminently aware of the public's gaze. In contrast, rough-hewn planks cover an abstemious interior meant to focus thoughts inward, and upward—the structure is capped with a conical roof that evokes a steeple. After entering the closet through a door that blends almost invisibly into one wall, a wealthy patron could open the shutters of a large window built into the other wall. Since both apertures have locks on the inside, occupants control how much of the external world to admit while praying, listening to a sermon, or perhaps leaning forward on the window ledge to receive the holy sacrament. From its inception, then, the closet works to mediate conflicts between a desire to belong and a desire to be alone, articulating space to permit both private contemplation and public communion.

Chamber Music in the King's Closet

> Etymologically "theory" is derived from the Latin *theoria,* which in its turn is derived from the Greek *theaomai,* to look at something with amazement or admiration, or to contemplate with the mind's eye.
>
> —Caroline van Eck[85]

Where a closet door closes, a window opens. As the ecclesiastical closet migrates into domestic architecture, mirroring the Reformation emphasis on a direct relationship with God, the staging of a public/private divide enters the very heart of home. Perhaps most pertinent to *Hamlet* are the royal prayer closets found in Tudor palaces, rooms whose design evinces

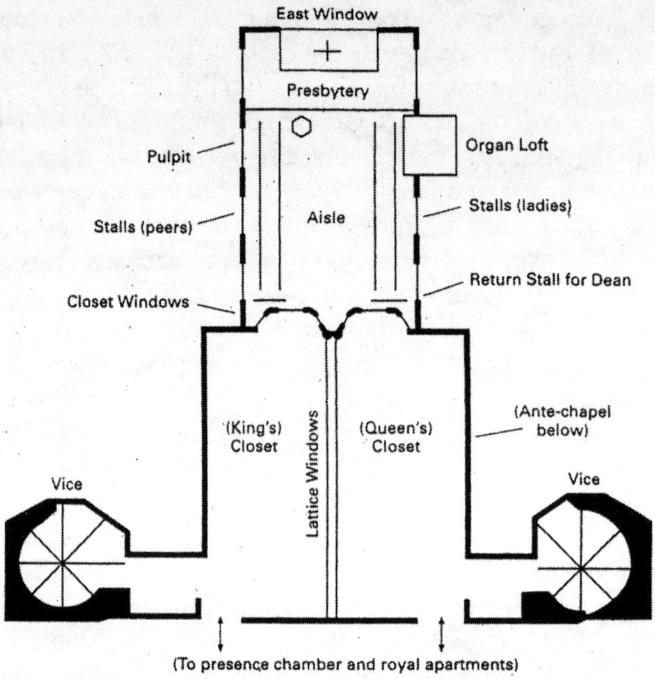

Figure 3.3. Chapel Royal at Hampton Court. Reprinted from *Sermons at Court: Politics and Religion in Elizabethan and Jacobean Preaching* (© 1998 Peter McCullough), 15, with the permission of Cambridge University Press and Peter McCullough.

the social conflicts that fractured the household. Splitting under intense pressure to conserve a space of meditation while staging functions of state, the royal closet expelled a public version of itself to the household chapel while stashing a private counterpart inside the privy lodgings. As Peter McCullough has brilliantly shown, the former type of "Great Closet" was reserved for ceremonial occasions when the sovereign, head of both church and nation, would perform religious duties before courtly observers. After processing formally along a corridor from the privy suite to the household chapel, the monarch and any selected intimates would enter a spacious closet perched on the gallery level, one story above the general congregation. Not unlike the royal box in a theater, this "Great Closet" often faced the pulpit from a prime spot at the chapel's rear, a location chosen as much to enhance personal display as to practice devotion (figure 3.3). Once seated in this enclosure, the monarch would be visible to those below—the groundlings, so to speak—through a central aperture that pierced the closet facade, such as an arched window. Nestled among the many heraldic symbols that usually adorned such a facade, the royal body became another icon to be worshipped in the chapel, an almost divine statue placed in its proper niche.[86]

Thus making interiority into theater, this visual regime allows the monarch to retain a distanced mystique while seeming available to public scrutiny; the open window suggests that even the royal soul can be examined, drawn out from a more intimate closet of the heart. Paul Hentzer, a foreign visitor to Windsor Castle during Elizabeth's reign, found this spatial openness particularly worthy of remark in his travel journal, describing the queen's chapel closet as "quite transparent, having its window of crystal."[87] Just as the *coretto*'s elite occupant forms a portrait of devotion when viewed within the window, an Albertian frame that inscribes the subject, the closet aperture describes a quasi-proscenium arch that enables an authority figure to perform a humble piety. By inserting the current embodiment of royal virtue into a built-in frame, a peephole that unlocks the chapel's visual ideology, the closet facade reaches its apotheosis in blending human and architectural faces to create a *tableau vivant*. Notably, this doubly facialized surface also makes spectators see double: the king and queen typically appeared before observers in symmetrical adjoining closets, mirror-image spaces hinged internally along a wooden screen topped with lattice windows.[88] As a transparent space divided by gender, designed to showcase the sovereign face of divine right, this platform for political image-making seems startlingly incongruous with the illicit, even incestuous sexuality attributed to Gertrude's closet, as Michael Cameron Andrews points out. Observing that Henry VIII twice undertook the holy rites of marriage in a queen's closet, once uttering his vows before twenty or so witnesses, Andrews wryly concludes that "we cannot accuse even Henry of making wedding and bedding the double business of a single room."[89]

Nevertheless, the royal closet seems perversely inclined to embrace a certain duplicity, a double-dealing that Claudius himself deems the crux of his prayer room: "like a man to double business bound,/I stand in pause" (III.iii.41–42). Such pausing and splitting emerge as key structural factors in plotting the second type of royal prayer closet, situated away from courtly drama in the monarch's privy quarters. In his extensive study of Henry VIII's residences, Simon Thurley locates this more private space within a standard "gallery-and-closet plan," which revolves around two adjacent rooms: a small chapel furnished with an altar, yoked to an even smaller oratory with a kneeling desk (figures 3.4 and 3.5).[90] Designed for the king's everyday devotions, this compact nucleus of

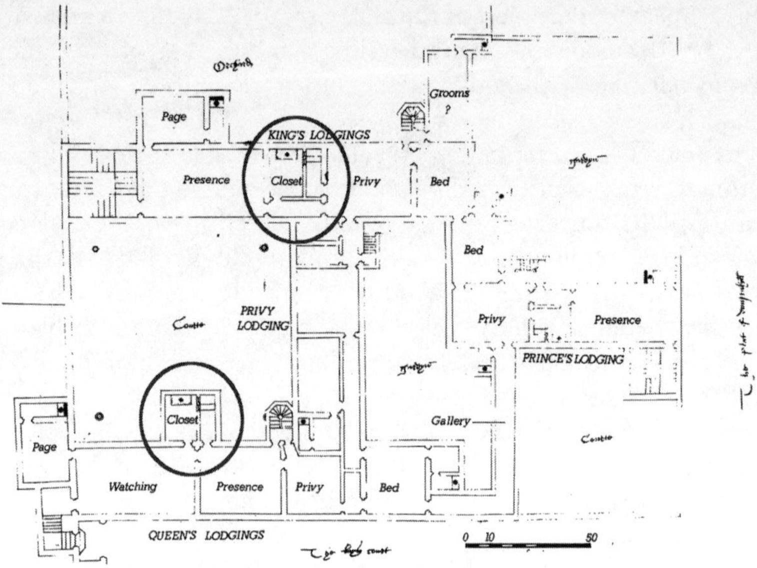

Figure 3.4. Plan of Dunstable Priory, converted into a residence for Henry VIII in the 1540s; closet-and-gallery locations circled. Labels by Simon Thurley. Reprinted from Simon Thurley, *The Royal Palaces of Tudor England: Architecture and Court Life, 1460–1547* (1993), 118. Hatfield House Archives, CPM II/22. By courtesy of Yale University Press, Simon Thurley, and the Marquess of Salisbury.

chapel and oratory occupies a central location in his privy suite, tucked between the presence chamber where official visitors might be received and the privy chamber restricted to trusted insiders.[91] Although royal suites follow a strict axis of progression from public "outward" rooms to private "inward" ones, such a single-pile trajectory breaks down at the very boundary between these two spatial categories, blocked by a doorless wall between the chapel and oratory.[92] Only a latticed or shuttered window punches through this barrier, thus permitting the king to remain largely invisible and untouchable in his oratory, while still capable of hearing services conducted in the adjacent chapel.

Absent a connecting door, however, traffic through the suite must bypass the two narrow rooms in the form of a short corridor—a "gallery"—which bridges the presence and privy chambers. Yet while most hallways increase circulation by opening into every room along their course, the gallery here provides access only to a chapel that lacks any other doorway; in contrast, the king's oratory rejects the gallery altogether by opening solely into the privy chamber. Since clergymen and

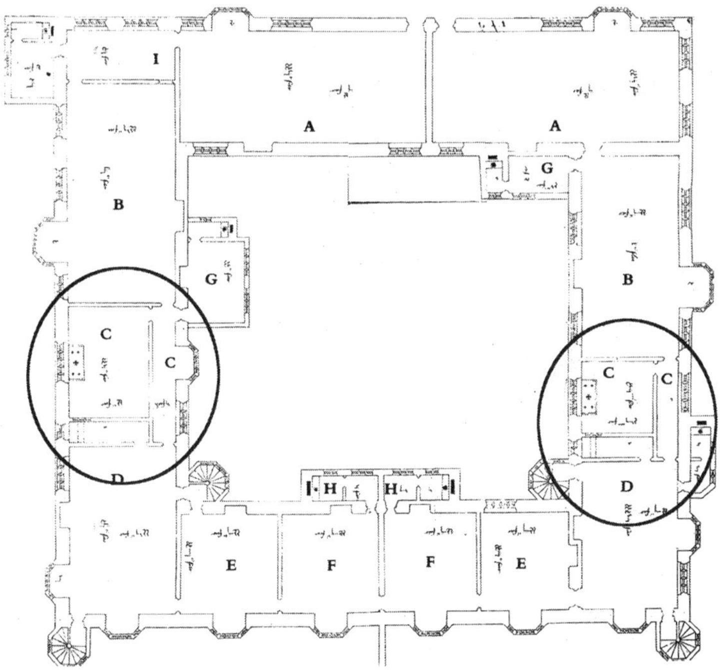

Figure 3.5. Plan of Waltham-in-the-Forest (sixteenth century), an unbuilt residence for Henry VIII; closet-and-gallery locations circled. According to Simon Thurley, the king's and queen's suites mirror each other on opposite sides of the house; both suites include a central gallery-and-closet layout (marked C and circled). A = watching chamber; B = presence chamber; C = gallery-and-closet plan; D = privy chamber; E = withdrawing chamber; F = bedchamber; G = pages' chamber; H = garderobe; I = halplace. Reprinted from Simon Thurley, *The Royal Palaces of Tudor England: Architecture and Court Life, 1460–1547* (1993), 125. Hatfield House Archives, CPM I/18. By courtesy of Yale University Press, Simon Thurley, and the Marquess of Salisbury.

their attendants were not members of the inner circle normally admitted into a king's privy chambers, such a circulatory arrangement shepherds these outsiders into the chapel almost immediately upon their entrance into the gallery. The king thus enjoys a private route into his oratory without risking public exposure.

A space to double business bound, the royal prayer closet negotiates among competing social pressures by once again splitting in half, relegating its chapel to the "outward" chambers while retaining its oratory within the "inward." Situating the closet in a central yet liminal location obviated any need, in prayer or otherwise, to forgive a clerical retinue its habitual trespasses through privy territory. At this contact zone forged between inner and outer, the gallery-and-closet plan operates not unlike a turnstile regulating access at a narrow point of entry, funneling people to destinations that match their level of security clearance, controlling visibility and movement through innovations in spatial design instead of enforced decree. As the gallery circumvents and the windowed wall punctures any binary divisions, the very heart of sovereign space abandons its hierarchical linearity to choreograph a network of entrances and exits, mounting a scenography that transforms architecture into event. Although other parts of the royal suite could vary in layout, the gallery-and-closet plan anchors every one of Henry's forty-odd residences.[93] This remarkable stability reveals the primacy of a circulatory nucleus that inscribes sanctioned paths of dissemination within the home, facilitating assembly at the complex interface of a central threshold rather than around the hearth of a great hall.

As an attention to theatricality transforms domestic architecture into a staging ground for subjectivity, for nuanced encounters with and against others, the lynchpin for this double business of public and private emerges in a transitional buffer, a spatial pause of indeterminate status that Thurley terms a "no man's land."[94] Just as the king's architectural heart of heart resorts to grafting a bypass, suturing inward and outward faces by pumping traffic through new arterial galleries, less elite domestic closets also prompted more sophisticated modes of circulation in the early modern period. Whether used for solitary introspection or material storage, secretarial business or communal reading, the enclosed closet presents a greater design challenge than a lockable, stowable piece of furniture easily integrated into the household.[95] In Robert Smythson's architectural drawings, for example, single-pile houses develop short corridors that lead past closets, studies, and other storage rooms, thus embedding discrete nodes of privacy within a system of public circulation (figures 3.6, 3.7, and 3.8).[96] Although simpler house plans treat the closet like an overgrown trunk by tucking it within a larger primary space (figures 3.7 and 3.9), or relegating it to the remotest ends of a house (figures 3.9 and 3.10), closets often sparked the most creative use of transitional spaces as builders strove to enfold multiple distinct subjects within the same domestic fabric.[97] While the royal prayer closet forms perhaps the most complex realization of this theatrical spatiality, the apotheosis of what less grandly structured households only partially achieve, the widespread adoption of corridors activates a new order of platform for staging encounters between subject and other, fostering new permutations of social performance. By inserting a crucial pause between entrance and exit, adding a *without* in the *within* even in the priviest

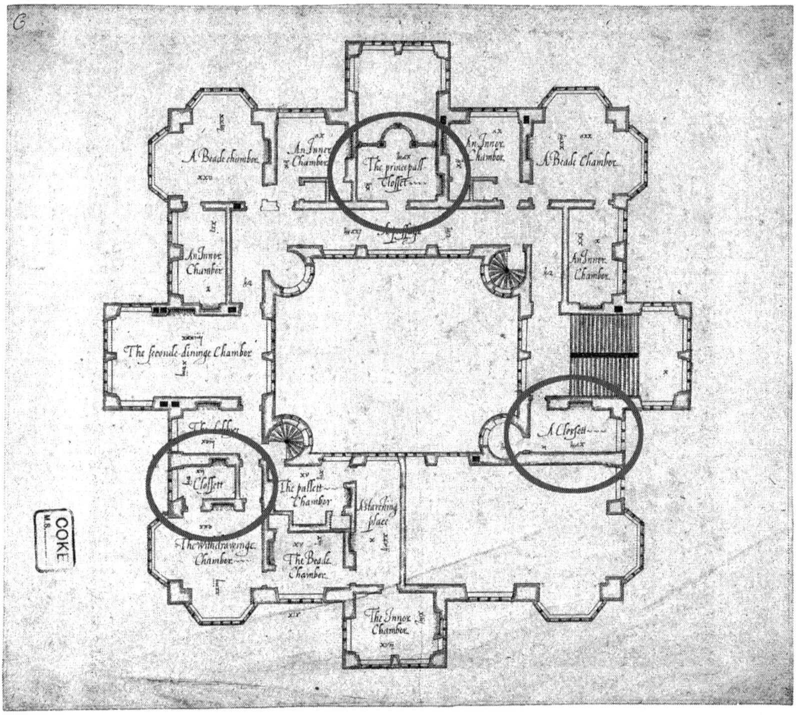

Figure 3.6. Robert Smythson, ground-floor plan of Slingsby Castle (sixteenth century). Closets are tucked inside the withdrawing room, between inner chambers, and beside stairs (all circled). RIBA Library Drawings and Archives Collection, #41598.

of suites,[98] these transitional spaces provide a "no man's land" before an inchoate self arrives at a destination, steps into a role, and becomes a full subject, a "man." For those who finally pass the threshold into a room, the buffering hallway facilitates an outward display of inwardness that Ramie Targoff identifies with Claudius's hypocritical prayer, a closet drama that "firmly aligns devotional with theatrical performance."[99]

In conceiving a third space that enables a private self to perform as a persona, this architectural model challenges the notion that modern subjectivity resides in a heart of heart, in a withdrawn interiority that Jonathan Crary associates with a camera obscura. Crary posits an epistemic shift "from the late 1500s to the end of the 1700s" in which "the structural and optical principles of the camera obscura coalesced into a dominant paradigm" that defines the subject through focused, distanced observation.[100] This visual regime survives today in pocket cameras that serve as portable, prosthetic eyes linked to an artificial memory. In the

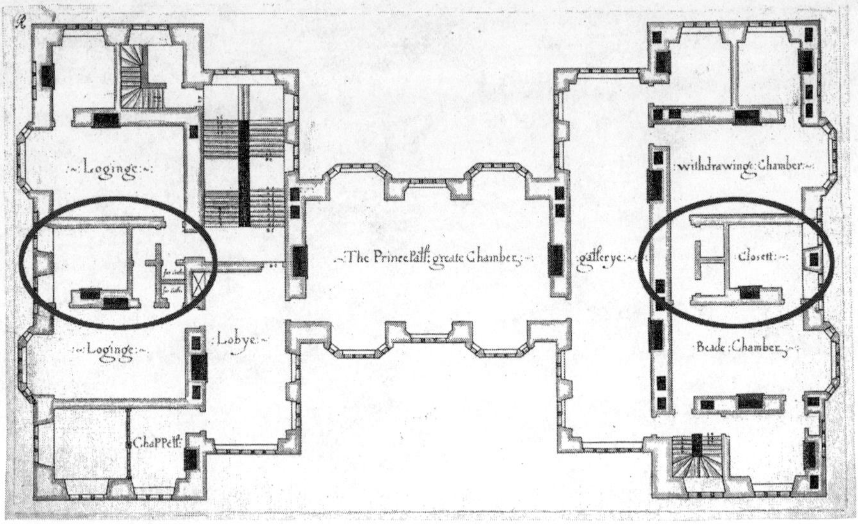

Figure 3.7. Robert Smythson, top-floor plan (sixteenth century). Symmetrical closets marked with circles. On the right, the closet is nestled between a withdrawing chamber and bedchamber, though accessible only from the latter. RIBA Library Drawings and Archives Collection, #29136.

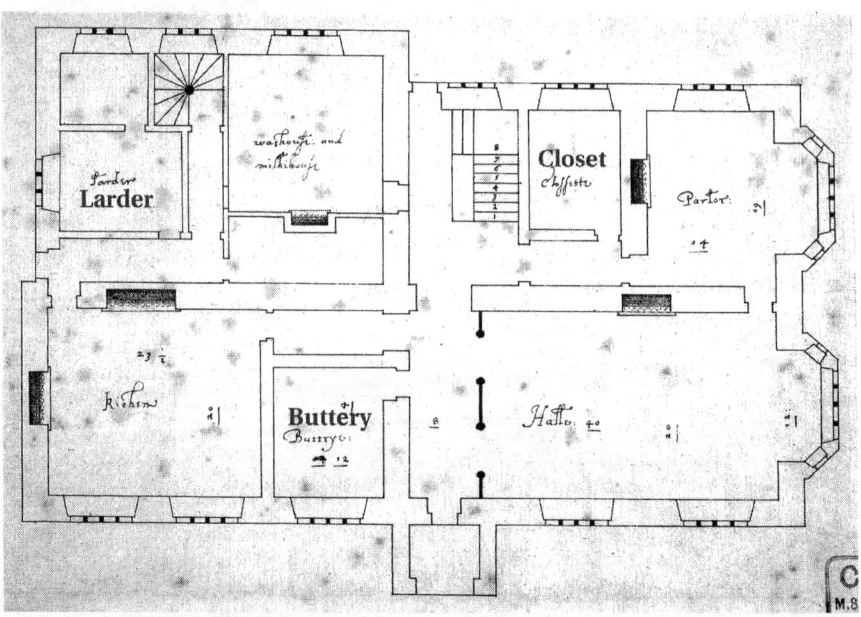

Figure 3.8. Robert Smythson, ground-floor plan (sixteenth century). Closet, larder, and buttery attach to short bypass corridors. RIBA Library Drawings and Archives Collection, #67882.

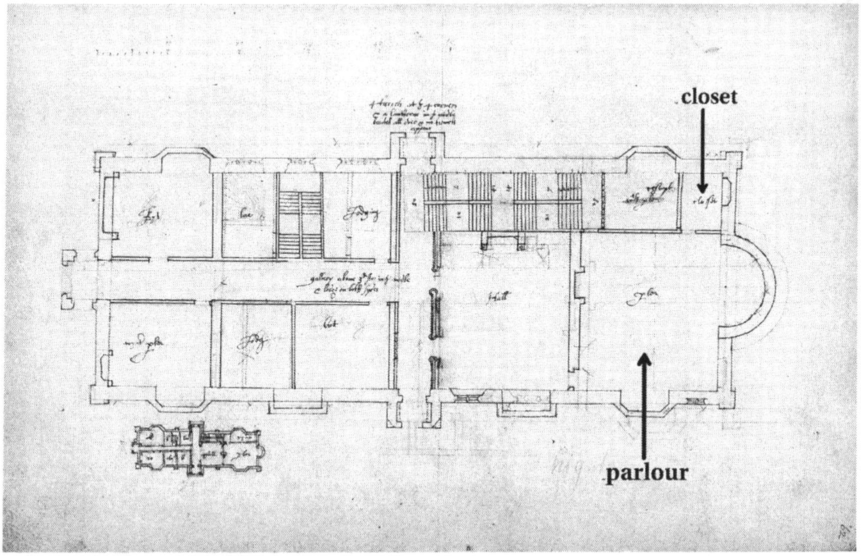

Figure 3.9. John Thorpe, ground-floor plan (late sixteenth or early seventeenth century). A small closet in the upper-right corner can be reached through a parlor. By courtesy of the Trustees of Sir John Soane's Museum. Photo: Ardon Bar-Hama.

early modern period, however, the camera obscura usually stationed viewers within an enclosed and darkened chamber, even a tent. In this spatial cell, a literal camera obscura, the outside world enters only as light through a pinhole, creating inverted images that can be projected onto a screen. Unlike an Albertian window that opens up a fictive space in depth, negating the opacity of walls to allow a visual escape unto the vanishing point, the camera obscura builds an architectural frame that separates viewers from the threat of reality, taming the world into a stream of images. This secluded *camera* for visual reflection becomes readily conflated with an enclosed closet, with a tablet-like mental space that records images, with a monad looking through a minute opening. In *An Essay Concerning Humane Understanding* (1690), for example, John Locke draws upon the workings of a camera obscura to describe how the mind serves as a passive receptacle of sensation, "not much unlike a closet wholly shut from light, with only some little opening left, to let in external visible resemblances, or *Ideas* of things without."[101]

As though unlocked from Locke's mind, Chérubin d'Orléans's *La Dioptrique Oculaire* (1671) depicts the camera obscura as a darkened study furnished with books, globes, and an armillary sphere (figure 3.11). Yet these objects that enlighten the mind actually recede into obscurity,

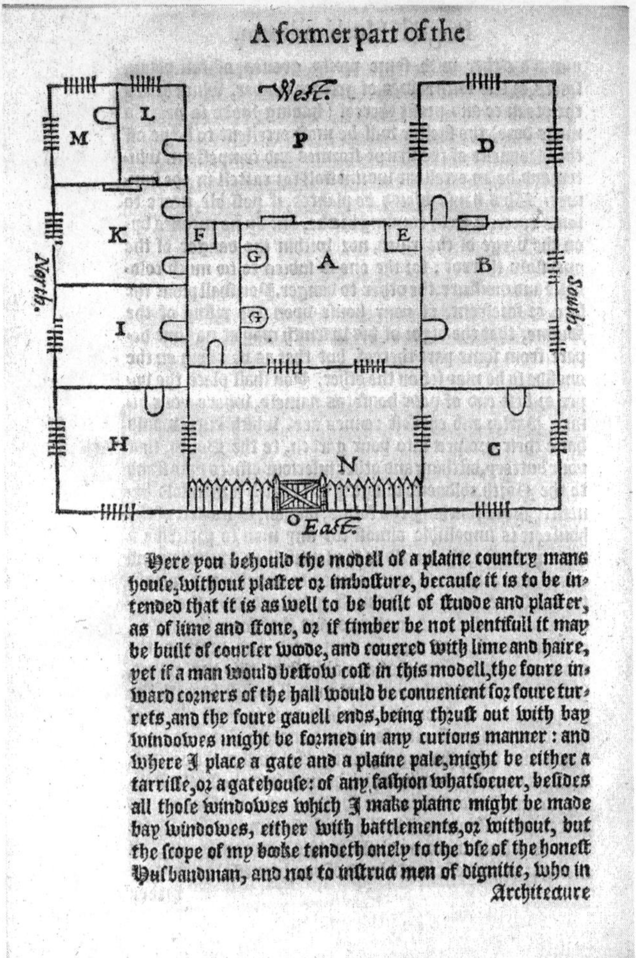

A former part of the

Here you behould the modell of a plaine countrey mans house, without plaster or imbossure, because it is to be intended that it is as well to be built of studde and plaster, as of lime and stone, or if timber be not plentifull it may be built of courser woode, and couered with lime and haire, yet if a man would bestow cost in this modell, the foure inward corners of the hall would be conuenient for foure turrets, and the foure gauell ends, being thrust out with bay windowes might be formed in any curious manner: and where I place a gate and a plaine pale, might be either a tarrisse, or a gatehouse: of any fashion whatsoeuer, besides all those windowes which I make plaine might be made bay windowes, either with battlements, or without, but the scope of my booke tendeth onely to the vse of the honest Husbandman, and not to instruct men of dignitie, who in Architecture

Figure 3.10. Plan from Gervase Markham's *The English Husbandman* (London, 1613), A4v. In this "plaine country mans house," the closet is labeled C while the dining parlor is B. Since Markham was not an architect, the rooms may not be to scale. By permission of the Folger Shakespeare Library.

relegated to dimly visible shelves across the back wall; in contrast, a brilliant shaft of light shoots across the foreground. Entering from a small aperture in the left-hand wall, this beam traverses the room before ending in a luminous circle on the right. The camera obscura thus aligns with the globe and armillary sphere as devices that represent some portion of the cosmos in a round shape. Uniquely, however, the camera obscura invites viewers to turn their backs upon the world outside, to reject peering through the aperture—only to watch images of that very same world

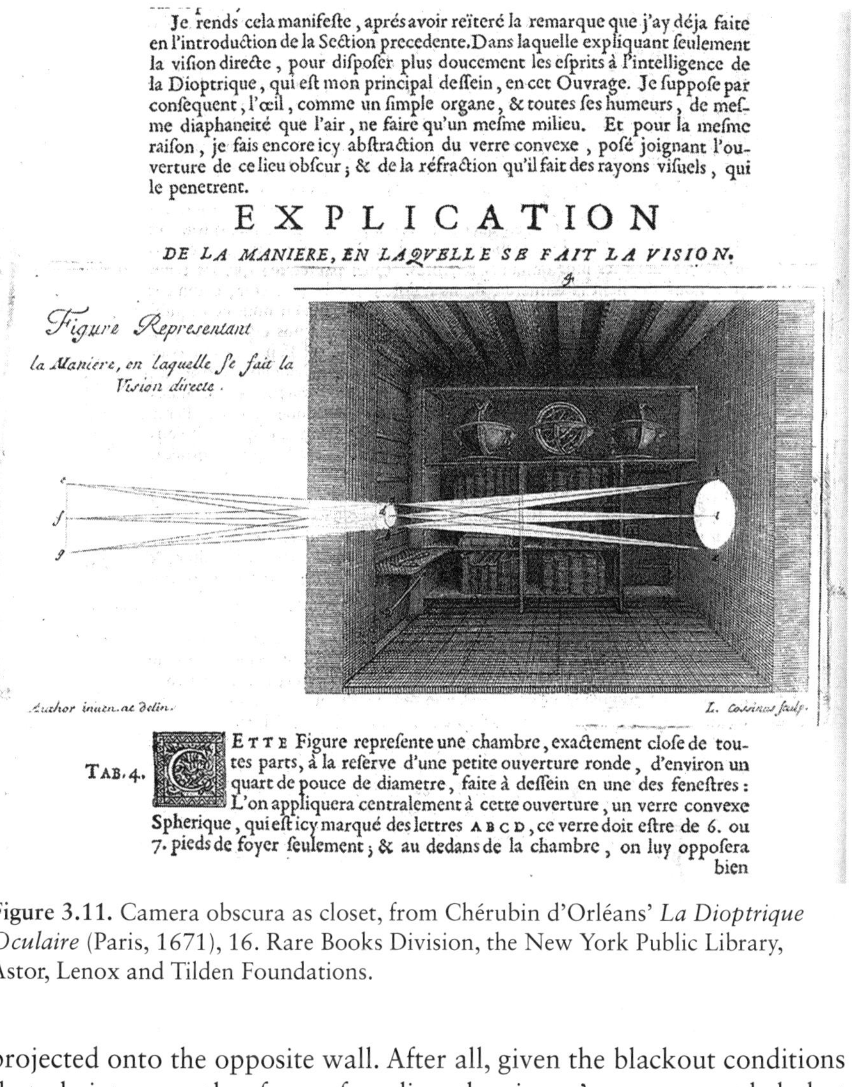

Je rends cela manifeſte, aprés avoir reïteré la remarque que j'ay déja faite en l'introduction de la Section precedente. Dans laquelle expliquant ſeulement la viſion directe, pour diſpoſer plus doucement les eſprits à l'intelligence de la Dioptrique, qui eſt mon principal deſſein, en cet Ouvrage. Je ſuppoſe par conſequent, l'œil, comme un ſimple organe, & toutes ſes humeurs, de meſme diaphaneité que l'air, ne faire qu'un meſme milieu. Et pour la meſme raiſon, je fais encore icy abſtraction du verre convexe, poſé joignant l'ouverture de ce lieu obſcur; & de la réfraction qu'il fait des rayons viſuels, qui le penetrent.

EXPLICATION

DE LA MANIERE, EN LAQVELLE SE FAIT LA VISION.

TAB. 4. CETTE Figure repreſente une chambre, exactement cloſe de toutes parts, à la reſerve d'une petite ouverture ronde, d'environ un quart de pouce de diametre, faite à deſſein en une des feneſtres: L'on appliquera centralement à cette ouverture, un verre convexe Spherique, qui eſt icy marqué des lettres A B C D, ce verre doit eſtre de 6. ou 7. pieds de foyer ſeulement; & au dedans de la chambre, on luy oppoſera bien

Figure 3.11. Camera obscura as closet, from Chérubin d'Orléans' *La Dioptrique Oculaire* (Paris, 1671), 16. Rare Books Division, the New York Public Library, Astor, Lenox and Tilden Foundations.

projected onto the opposite wall. After all, given the blackout conditions that obviate any other form of reading, the viewer's gaze cannot help but fasten onto the glowing circle that forms a "peinture naturelle" (natural painting), a *tondo* of moving images that d'Orléans claims will satisfy all ocular desires.[102] Yet this quasi-cinematic experience necessarily exposes the closet as a purpose-built optical apparatus; for images within the circle to resolve properly, the distance between the left and right walls must equal the focal length of a convex lens inserted into the aperture. Clearly, rather than retrofit an existing study, d'Orléans invents a closet that serves no function other than to model how a camera obscura works, and by analogy, how the inside of a human eye works.[103] Like Abraham

Bosse, whose etching uses built space to diagram the ocular process (figure 1.1), d'Orléans turns architect to construct a room that stages vision itself. Balancing the camera obscura's optical science against his fanciful mind's eye, d'Orléans dresses an otherwise blank cube with useless books and globes, situating what might seem a charlatan's trick in a milieu of intellectual activity.

Inviting readers into his self-designed closet, d'Orléans conjures a space that makes viewing and thinking a social event, perhaps even adding a bench along the left-hand wall to gesture toward this shared experience. Not merely a scientific instrument, as Simon During notes, the camera obscura enjoyed the greatest success in history when pressed into service for demonstrations and "delusions," spectacles that appealed to general audiences.[104] Continuing this deep-rooted praxis that "never absorbed the Cartesian and Lockean revolution in epistemology," d'Orléans performs the optical *demonstratio* that Alberti's *De pictura* disdained, reaching beyond empirical proof to transform scholarship into theater.[105] Rather than alienate a viewer from a primitive harmony with the world, as Crary posits, d'Orléans builds a camera obscura that engages the practical magic of architecture and drama. To this end, d'Orléans constructs shelves that—rather than provide actual texts for reading—function as a species of interior facade, a backdrop that frames how viewers perceive the camera obscura as a vehicle of studious contemplation. Although shrouded in an inky cloak of darkness, the spatial "heart of heart" of d'Orléans's closet never ceases to wear a public face; always ready to signify for an outsider's gaze, the closet relies on theatrical props that reinforce its identity as an interior space. Just as the camera obscura projects images onto a screen, bringing the world indoors, d'Orléans projects a carefully wrought facade onto the walls of his private closet, thus troubling the distinction between virtual and built space, between architecture and picture. In so doing, d'Orléans raises profound questions about the false interiors that we construct—in our homes, our psyches—even when we inhabit an "authentic" space that ostensibly passes show.

While reading the secrets of a camera obscura requires secreting the subject within a distanced interior, this viewer always remains embedded in a theatrical space designed for sociality. Running alongside Crary's account of a dissociated observer, not unlike a gallery that circumvents binaries, architecture proffers an alternative pathway to modernity that permits the subject to negotiate a liminal existence between interior and exterior, self and image, facade and body. Instead of a fantasy closet that remains enclosed except for a single, unchanging (pin)point of view, the royal closet's dividing wall opens a window that brings the public and private together in a spatial fold, allowing diverse people to share in rituals that define a spiritual community, a religious fold. Rejecting the notion of an absolutely exteriorized other that appears only as a mediated shadow, after the fact, the closet-and-gallery mechanism configures a spatial *camera*—as in *room*—so that players can stage an ensemble show of *son et lumière* in the present, building a complex heart whose chambers pulse with the music of social circulation. Rather than abstract the material world and its consequences for an immobile self, the risks and stakes that Claudius identifies as the "effects" of his mortal fallibility (III.iii.54), closets enfold both the physical and the spiritual in an inherently unpredictable suspension, plotting a differentially shared event whose outcome cannot be pre-scripted, or schematized with dotted lines.

In restaging Leibniz's philosophy of monads, construed as elemental, enclosed entities constituting and constituted by the cosmos, Gilles Deleuze introduces the model of a two-story baroque house to theorize just such a fold between private and public, soul and body.[106] On the lower level of this house, sensory information enters the body in a space structured by "pleats of matter"; one level above, the self-sufficient monad meditates in a windowless gloom packed with "folds of soul." Where these disparate layers meet, a floor perforated by five openings allows impulses from the five senses to flow upward into the monastic, monadic sanctum, there to resonate among the curtain-like folds lining its walls. As "the zone of inseparability that produces the crease or seam," a mediating zone that divides and connects, the porous floor constitutes a special type of fold that Deleuze calls the *Zweifalt,* after Heidegger: "not a fold in two—since every fold can only be thus—but a 'fold-of-two,' an *entre-deux,* something 'between' in the sense that a difference is being differentiated."[107] The privy closet in early modern England occupies a similar zone of inseparability at the central threshold of a royal suite, creating a double fold that differentiates the difference between inner and outer, private and public. As a linear enfilade through the apartment twists and turns at the closet-and-gallery's spatial knot, deflecting into tangents that potentially never stop differentiating, buffering, transitioning, this spinning away from full presence at once circumvents and embraces the subject in a network of spatial possibility. While Leibniz posits a hermetic monad "in which light enters only through orifices so well bent that nothing on the outside can be seen through them," a condition exemplified by "chapels and rooms where a crushing light comes from openings invisible to their very inhabitants," Deleuze's *Zweifalt* opens up this pure interiority to permit the body and soul to stage their differences across a sensory interface, punctuated by apertures that diffuse sight and sound like latticed windows.[108] Light, *camera,* action—as the closet's simple locking mechanism evolves into a turnstile that synchronizes movements and meetings, a formerly static container of space transforms into a deterritorialized map of perpetual transition. Indeed, where nodes of inflection keep deferring the final destination, we discover new vanishing points that reorient the landscape of subjectivity.

The Matter of Moles and Mothers

> within my heart I made
> Closets; and in them many a chest;
> And like a master in my trade,
> In those chests, boxes; in each box, a till
> . . . .
> We are the earth; and they,
> Like moles within us, heave, and cast about:
> And till they foot and clutch their prey,
> They never cool, much lesse give out.
> No smith can make such locks, but they have keyes:
> Closets are halls to them; and hearts, high-wayes.
>
> —George Herbert, "Confession"[109]

> Well said, old mole. Canst work i'th' earth so fast?
>
> —*Hamlet*[110]

Midway through what should be a direct, even foreclosed progression through a revenge plot, a dramatic enfilade whose object stands visibly framed from Act I, our heroic subject becomes ensnared in twinned closets: one to which he has been summoned, one that seems an ineluctable space of transition. Unable to move forward with his role as avenger, Hamlet bears the hesitation marks of an interiority plotted as a space of writing as well as a dramatic place of enunciation. As Derrida observes, writing is intrinsically bound up "with the theme of the *supplementary delay* and with the reconstitution of meaning through deferral, after a mole-like progression, after the subterranean toil of an impression."[111] Hamlet's infamous delay figures a writing subject whose whorish heart constantly unpacks language adrift in semantic promiscuity, effetely dissevered from actions and things in the real world. Wracked by "wild and whirling words" that destabilize the architecture of a subject (I.v.139),

Hamlet wanders through a maze of corridors that structure his interior space as a form of writing, his psyche inscribed by half-glimpsed traces not unlike those on Freud's mystic writing pad.[112] Thus divided from himself, perplexed and paused between destinations, Hamlet registers to critics as a self-parodic character, flushed empty by a force no less deadly than the ear-poured poison that "courses through/The natural gates and alleys" of his father's body (I.v.66–67). Tropically, to borrow Hamlet's own term (III.ii.232), the subject discovers that its inscriptional ground has been seized by a distinctly unnatural, inorganic writing that can "posset/And curd . . . the thin and wholesome blood" of a paternal *logos* (I.v.68–70). Possessed and dispossessed by a "leperous distilment" (I.v.64) that can "posset" ("possesse" in Q2), the body's circulation acquires a wondrously strange density as the aural word becomes encased in "bark'd about" flesh (I.v.71).[113] Rather than simply arrest the production of bodily meaning through death, however, this writing of interiority sends the subject into a purgatorial space constituted by haunting, a subterranean threshold that makes visible new forms of movement and being.

Permitted to roam his former kingdom yet "forbid/To tell the secrets of [his] prison-house" (I.v.13–14), the Ghost inhabits a purgatory built not of physical walls but of words. As an inmate in this secret prison-house of language, this *secretarium* of untellable tales that would "harrow up" the listener's soul (I.v.16), the Ghost assigns to Hamlet the task of writing and enacting a revenge plot that trumpets Claudius's guilt to the world. In turn, like a table-book whose waxen leaves receive the impress of his father's signet,[114] Hamlet finds his psychic tableau harrowed by the "subterranean toil" of words that he has sworn to remember: "Well said, old mole. Canst work i'th' earth so fast?" (I.v.170). In the earthy cellarage of Hamlet's mind, the "mole-like progression" of his father's spectral writing, the "eternal blazon" of narratives from beyond the grave (I.v.21), can do nothing but "heave, and cast about" like the griefs represented by George Herbert's moles, which unerringly invade the most guarded closets of the heart.[115] Aptly, as a "worthy pioner" who undermines the walls of Hamlet's memory (I.v.171), the mole-like Ghost resurfaces in the enclosed heart of Gertrude's closet, the maternal space whose corruption matters so deeply to Hamlet.

While the Ghost returns as an unresolved fragment from his son's psyche, hence visible only to Hamlet's mind's eye, another blind mole burrows into Gertrude's closet as a parody of paternal inscription, as a walking fount of malapropism, as—Polonius. Always winding up in the wrong destination linguistically and otherwise, Polonius insinuates himself behind the arras in an attempt to negate his bodily presence, enfolding himself in a dark "no man's land" to haunt Gertrude's closet from the periphery. If we take seriously Gottfried Semper's hypothesis that textiles supplied the first architectural dividers, if the popularity of linenfold paneling in Tudor England manifests just such a nostalgic desire for drapery walls,[116] then Gertrude's arras marks a primitive limit to her closet space. By slipping between a wall and a wall-like hanging, perhaps stepping into a discovery space beyond the main stage, Polonius carves out an improper, interstitial space designed to harbor a spy, a ghost, a mole, a rat. Fancying himself an éminence grise in a self-fashioned corridor of power that connects his ear to Claudius's, Polonius wraps himself within a textile to construct a windowless facade for his blinded, muted body. As a defaced specter lurking in a curtained-off *secretarium,* mapping a soundscape filtered through the reticulated screen of an arras, this "unseen good old man" contrives an auditory camera obscura to enable a detached, invisible surveillance (IV.i.12). Indeed, Bruce Smith observes how multiple dramas in this period "deploy hangings to define the space behind the curtain as a closet, cell, library, studio, or study."[117] Yet despite Polonius's desire for a monadic enclosure that allows him to absorb sensory data without bodily danger, to isolate himself as an impartial auditor (III.iii.32), the door to his imagined closet actually swings both ways. All too late, Polonius realizes that the pliable arras forms a *Zweifalt,* a zone of inseparability that enfolds him integrally into the scene. Transfixed by the point of Hamlet's rapier, punctuated by Hamlet's secretarial hand, Polonius finds that his envisioned stance of hegemonic control only entombs him within the walls. As Polonius forcibly rejoins the social fabric, the arras that once provided an effacing veil now becomes a gruesome death mask, a textile that reveals his face always to have been a fold, a hinge between interior recess and exterior action.

Where a door closes, a discovery space opens. As "well said, old mole" transforms into "How now? A rat!" (III.iv.22), Hamlet thrusts his sword through the arras expecting to find Claudius on the other side; despite striking the wrong paternal substitute, Hamlet's action suggests that his weapon could penetrate into the king's adjoining closet to rectify the previous scene's missed opportunity. Shakespeare thus creates a performative pentimento whose meaning depends on a recalled architectural sequence, demanding that spectators glance back through the memory palace of Elsinore still shimmering in their collective theatrical unconscious. In other words, Hamlet's sword-thrust activates an imagined geography that hinges two closets along the seam of an arras, a textile that supplies a permeable aural boundary not unlike a densely latticed window.[118] Indeed, Polonius occupies a spatial *entre-deux* on the margins of either closet, extending a transcriptional corridor from Gertrude to Claudius as their joint "secretorie," as a human table-book passing secrets between a usurping king and his "imperial jointress" (I.ii.9).[119] Yet while the queen authorizes the secretarial Polonius to record her present voice for her present spouse, to transmit her words to a co-regent installed in an imperially joined closet, Hamlet's arrival disrupts this political, linguistic, and spatial linearity by opening a portal to the underworld, by whetting the almost blunted inscription of Gertrude's first husband. As a secretary who not only marks his father's words but also "serves as his mother's memory,"[120] Hamlet turns Gertrude's eyes "into [her] very soul" to make legible an interiority written as a letter from the past (III.iv.89), a letter once written by a better self.

Rejecting a familiar paradigm of sexualized enclosure that depends on an absolute interiority or exteriority, Gertrude's closet engages the more complexly "penetrable stuff"—the matter—of hearts, minds, and memories (III.iv.36). By placing Gertrude in a closet, Shakespeare conjures for his early modern audience the room's strong linkage to an interiority forged through reading and writing, deliberation and communion. That is, the closet's scene of writing plays out more subtly than on the waxen surface of an "enseamed bed" (III.iv.92), an erotic table-book that has become all too commonplace; on the contrary, Hamlet must "bend [his] eye on vacancy" to visualize the absent object of his desire (III.iv.117), repeatedly conjuring "[his] uncle's bed" into being through language (III.iv.161). As the "bodiless creation" of a mind obsessed with bodies and words (III.iv.140), this ghostly furniture takes on added poignancy if Hamlet finds his mother flanked by books and papers, another Ophelia pretending to read under scrutiny, another Anne Clifford as portrayed in her "Great Picture" (figure 3.12). An enormous triptych that Clifford herself commissioned, this Great Picture captures the sitter at three stages of life, from conception to austere maturity. The final panel depicts Clifford as a black-clad matron of fifty-six years, seated in a closet where books stack up beneath her hand and spill across shelves overhead.[121] While the framed portraits of two husbands—one deceased and one estranged—hang on the wall behind Clifford, these "counterfeit presentments" remain subordinate to her own likeness in scale and position (III.iv.54). Serenely, Clifford gazes outward to claim the closet as her own space, a fitting statement for a countess who fought bitterly and waited decades before finally regaining her ancestral lands.

Might Gertrude, another widow of a certain age, present herself in a similar posture of intellect and power, down to the portraits of two

Figure 3.12. Jan van Belcamp, the "Great Picture" of Anne Clifford (1646). Abbot Hall Art Gallery/Bridgeman Art Library.

husbands? To impress upon Hamlet the severity of his misdeeds, might Gertrude select an architectural platform that bespeaks her gravitas as mother and monarch, arranging a tableau that allows her to "assume a virtue" even if she has it not (III.iv.162)? Given how she begins the meeting with a sharp rebuke—"Hamlet, thou hast thy father much offended" (III.iv.8)—perhaps we should insert here a stage direction from Ben Jonson's *The Staple of News:* "The study is open'd where she sit[s] in state" (II.v.45).[122] In other words, Hamlet walks not only into Gertrude's closet, but also into Gertrude's closet scene. For if the early modern stage derives from the "extended altar" of medieval ritual, if the arras recalls an altar cloth in a former church space, then Gertrude's closet provides a most suitable backdrop for the drama that plays out in the sanctuary of home.[123] Thus wishing precisely to cause a scene, Gertrude waits in a closet thrust onto the main stage to allow room for a deeper interiority to appear, whether this be a spy hidden in a discovery space or an even darker mole, a defect within the folds of her soul.

Indeed, just as her attempt to curtain off a private space backfires, Gertrude's attempt to unfold her son's inner space redounds upon herself. For Hamlet prizes open the enclosed garden of his mother's *secretum* to convert her soul, turning her eyes inward to connect the "black and grained spots" that narrate a sinful career (III.iv.90). Pushing verbal "daggers" into his mother's ears (III.iv.95), Hamlet seems to repeat the murder of his father, whom Claudius seized "grossly, full of bread . . . his crimes broad blown" (III.iii.80–81). Yet by incising his own pointed words on the tablet of her mind, Hamlet strives to produce a space of collective reading and writing, urging his mother to reflect upon a neglected book of self, a secret mirror writing legible only to those who introspect.[124] With this act of graffiti and grace, Hamlet entreats his mother to read the writing on her psychic wall. Yet even as Hamlet unpicks a seam to unpack her soul, Gertrude traces her gaze back only to find a vanishing point of origin, a subject position no longer tenable. A split subject caught in the (d)rift of a heart "cleft . . . in twain" (III.iv.158), Gertrude forever haunts the dark corridors of her own bifurcated desires, seeing inside herself a cracked mirror that can inscribe neither past nor present self. Left with "no life to breathe" the secret that Hamlet has just imparted (III.iv.200)—ostensibly that he is "mad in craft" (III.iv.190)—Gertrude realizes that her own interiority constitutes a prison-house of forsworn words and memories forcibly under erasure, a purgatorial closet from which she emerges time and again, mole-like, but never fully escapes.

"Bring me to the test,/And I the matter will re-word," Hamlet proclaims in defense of his status as a rational subject, telling skeptics why his words should matter (III.iv.144–45). Not just mad but also sane in craft, Hamlet recognizes that the matter of "I" inevitably comes down to a matter of words, of words that/as matter, of a *mater* made word. In this promise of a competent linguistic performance, this infinite capacity to re-word the self for future approval, the proof of a socially legible identity requires bracketing other potential iterations to achieve a coherent public face, rendering every visible subject a kind of counterfeit presentment. Yet in reworking the syntax of self through a series of breaches and bypasses whose traces inscribe a conscious landscape, Hamlet necessarily writes his subjectivity in a mole-like language of twisting inflections, constructing his interiority as a closet folded within a matrix of circulatory paths. By writing a permanent volume of self that deforms and defaces its "matter" in the very act of inscription, our melancholy prince must always serve as secretary to the spectral imperative of another Hamlet's mark in a world built from "words, words, words." Bearing the scars of a written language that marks without seeming to matter, Hamlet's twisted parody of self can never disentangle antic from authentic, miming from madness: "Writing 'under erasure' is the mark of this contortion."[125] If the Derridean subject of writing exists "as a *system* of relations between strata: the Mystic Pad, the psyche, society, the world," if the "*sociality* of writing as *drama*" attends to the interplay of selves writing themselves under erasure, of selves writing within and among other selves, then *Hamlet* reveals how early modern subjects haunt each other, literally and figuratively, in passages of transition.[125]

Chapter Four

Corpus, Chora, Crown

If *Hamlet* attempts to establish an economy of interiority that accords each persona due social and psychic spacing, how can we understand the economy of space that enables this subjective differentiation? What constitutes an inscriptional space in early modern England? Rather than provide a neutral ground upon which a subject can be inscribed and built, Western philosophy (en)genders the thinking of space from its earliest Platonic foundations. In the *Timaeus,* Plato posits a womb-like receptacle that materializes objects in the real world by holding them in a specially designated place, by wrapping them in an envelope that confers legibility; this receptacle is space, which Plato terms *chora*. Analogized to a wet nurse, midwife, and mother, the feminized chora that receives and nurtures also serves as a transitional space for the phenomenal "things that enter and leave it," the transient actors moving across a cosmic stage as shadows of unchanging ideals.[1] Poststructuralist theorists have questioned the chora's contradictory status "as being *at the interior* of philosophy" yet also mysteriously outside its logical dictates, as being strongly gendered as a maternal force yet also genderless and deforming the feminine, as the third genre (*genos*) on which Platonic cosmology rests yet also escaping genre entirely.[2] By supplying an inscriptional space for philosophy itself, as Judith Butler notes, the chora must necessarily be abjected from the processes of rational thought: "every explicit distinction takes place in an inscriptional space that the distinction itself cannot accommodate."[3]

Despite this fundamental prohibition from the realm of discursive meaning, the chora emerges as a signifying field in early modern England through the practice of chorography, a distinctive form of mapping whose very name promises to inscribe (graph) choric space. As a species of cartography that came to prominence in the mid-sixteenth century and flourished into the eighteenth century, English chorography typically blends image and text to represent places with a marked affective investment, places designed to evoke an internal resonance for both chorographer and viewer, places defined as home. Charting a series of localities with a peculiarly domestic preoccupation, chorography attempts to shore up the boundaries of an insular homeland during an era of global expansion, turning the eye inward to mark the contours of a native landscape and the narrative of a shared history. By suturing together a series of discrete chorographic views produced by knowledgeable insiders, the body of England awakens as a cohesive whole before a nation of readers, transforming a previously amorphous space into the speaking subject of mapping. Indeed, Richard Helgerson argues that this campaign to document every noteworthy feature of England endows the land with its own beguiling voice, while also granting the chorographer an authorial and authoritative identity; yet rather than openly support each other's claim to agency, these mutually constitutive selves enjoy a "mysterious and thoroughly mystified relationship."[4] Ventriloquized through a male chorographer who claims the land as his muse, the chora still performs as the inscriptional ground of a masculine nation-building, the tabula rasa capable of holding a distinctly masculine imprint of home.

With the accession of Elizabeth, however, this gendered dynamic between inscriber and inscribed necessarily takes a queer turn. While many critics stress how chorography serves as an instrument of power and property,[5] what remains occluded, mysterious, inscrutable is how an imagined feminine receptacle encloses this private estate or public state—that is, how the chora demarcates a space with material and social meaning. As a mechanism for converting an impersonal, extensive space into a landscape of signifying places (following Michel de Certeau's distinction between *space* and *place*), the Platonic chora not only confers a body upon an ethereal ideal, but also facializes space into a signifying cluster of features to address the viewer. Yet in the Cartesian project that legitimates space as chartable, in the advent of a discourse that construes architecture as rational, masculine, and professional, a certain disavowal of the Platonic chora becomes necessary to impose a masculine mask over a feminine matrix, to build upon a space that is always already built, always already gendered. To better apprehend this tension between maternal space and paternal place, between a mother who intuitively knows and a father who names by design, we might more broadly define chorography to include those crucial representations of space that implicate Elizabeth's power of inscription as a monarch and as a virginal womb. In so doing, we begin to trace how space, gender, subjectivity, and sovereignty fold into one another.

Shaking Space, Plato's Place

> If Plato had lived in our century, he might very well have chosen, not gold, but a movie screen or television screen as his analogue to a field across which ceaselessly changing non-substantial images may flicker.
>
> —Richard Mohr[6]

To begin at the beginning of this narrative, the birth before the Renaissance rebirth, we need to reconsider the spatial legacy of Plato's *Timaeus,* which defines the *chora* as the third term in a philosophical edifice. Partway into the *Timaeus,* the speaker abruptly reverses direction to discuss a time before the birth of time, an embryonic place before the Demiurge created the cosmos. In this second beginning intended to remedy a previous lacuna, to extend his narrative beyond its original origins, Plato lifts the foundation of his philosophical architectonic to expose the stakes driven into his inscriptional ground. In so doing, Plato reveals a hinge that connects the two kinds or genres already posited as constituting the universe: "one was proposed as a model, intelligible and always changeless, a second as an imitation of the model, something that possesses becoming and is visible."[7] Abruptly "marking the limit of this twofold" founded on the opposition between immutable ideals (being) and mutable bodies (becoming), Plato adds a third kind that "provides a fixed site for all things that come to be," a receptacle that grants a temporary housing for things in the physical world.[8] As Plato explains of this mediating fold, the "things that enter and leave it are imitations of those things that always are, imprinted after their likeness in a marvelous way that is hard to describe."[9] That is, as a transitional space that provisionally anchors ideals in sensible bodies, facilitating immanent copies of eternal forms, this third kind is itself "space [*chora*], which exists always and cannot be destroyed."[10] Yet unlike a Cartesian grid that extends regularly to infinity in every direction, a device that marks an impersonal location, the chora provides what Luce Irigaray calls a spatial envelope: a place that corresponds to a specific ideal and captures its essence within a cloak of visibility.[11] Both addressed to that ideal and giving it an address in the transient world, thus opening a passage between the intelligible and sensible, this choric envelope catalyzes a reverse alchemy whereby a grosser substance precipitates from the most refined and precious origin.

Since performing such a conversion requires finding the proper envelope, Plato posits a winnowing function in which the chora "sways irregularly in every direction," shaking and shaken by the elemental properties to be housed.[12] Sifted to different regions of the receptacle according to their particular traits, this jumble of primordial elements—literally, "letters" (Gr. *stoicheia*)—keeps the chora perpetually off balance, tumbling, as each letter temporarily imprints its "character" upon the matching locality.[13] In this respect, the chora behaves much like a certain separating mechanism perhaps more familiar to readers today than Plato's grain thresher: the sorting hat in the Harry Potter series, which assigns incoming students to their proper house within Hogwarts Academy. When placed on a fledging wizard's head, the venerable sorting hat announces which of four Hogwarts houses most closely resonates with the wearer's innate qualities. Following some mystified logic never divulged to anyone, this magical device unerringly reads the interiority of each initiate to divide the cohort into a new social taxonomy, reorienting the collective topography of identity into a fourfold system. In a not dissimilar process, Plato's chora distributes the four basic elements of fire, air, earth, and water to their proper places within the receptacle, "separating the kinds most unlike each other furthest apart and pushing those most like each other closest together into the same region."[14] Employing a zero-sum conservatism to sift within rather than sift out, the chora accommodates a constant rearranging of elemental letters within an enclosed frame, allowing these characters to press into a pliable receptacle-text.

Yet in this vision of an immaterial substratum, a network of inscription rather than an Aristotelian prime matter (*hyle*), Plato emphatically denies his receptacle the sorting hat's power to name, withholding from the chora any agency at all. Not only does the chora shake after passively "being set in motion," but its function as a place-holding envelope requires the stamp of an ideal, a stamp that authorizes the production of a phenomenal body.[15] To help elucidate how this mystical thresher can work without actively working, Plato compares the chora to a piece of gold cast into various shapes, a waxy substance impressed by an external schema, and the neutral base of a perfume.[16] Remaining "devoid of any of those characters [*ideai*] that it is to receive from elsewhere," the chora must keep itself perfectly bland, perfectly pure, to take an imprint without distortion; as a virginal yet completely open space that receives unconditionally, the chora must above all avoid "showing its own face as well."[17] Due to this total lack of contribution to the generative process, Plato follows the physiological theory of his time in assigning a feminine role to the chora, labeling it as nurse and mother.[18] To fill out the rest of this happily normative Platonic family, the Demiurge must imprint a paternal ideal upon the maternal chora to produce a filial body, a real chip off the old printing block.[19] As an utterly unaffected and unaffecting platform for mimetic production, a purely instrumental womb/room for rent, the chora becomes nothing more than a turnstile facilitating the passage of insensible ideals into sensible bodies, a blank but always occupied stage for others' scripts to be performed.

Textually defaced, functionally effaced, Plato's chora can be "only a receptacle for the (re)production of sameness. . . . a mirror in which the 'subject' sees himself and reproduces himself in his reflection, a shutter set up to allow the eye to frame its view."[20] Despite providing a universal home, the chora thus remains fundamentally homeless, unable to write, lacking a room of its own in Virginia Woolf's terms. Just as Lacan remarks that women cannot have the phallus because they *are* the phallus,[21] the chora cannot have a place of its own because it *is* place, or rather, it provides a space for place. Lacking either a proper name or place in this phallocentric structure, the feminized chora can never become what Irigaray calls a "place for place"—"place" in the sense of de Certeau's *lieu*—but rather holds open a space that hovers between being and becoming, between intelligibility and sensibility.[22] That is, as the prime object of exchange between two masculine extremes, the chora enables what might be called a homospatial regime, one that erases the labor of birthing, the value of providing a material and maternal home. Barred from owning space because it cannot be separated from space, the chora occupies in both gender and property relations what Marcus Doel calls a "no-man's land."[23]

Here we might recall that Cold War joke about a military ad seeking the perfect female worker: "Wanted—typist for top-secret documents. Must not be able to read." Fulfilling the desire for an illiterate, invisible conduit within a homosocial chain of command, this stereotype of a feminine secretary makes inscription legible while serving as a mindless repository of masculine secrets. Caught in a similar double bind of receiving everything yet retaining nothing, Plato's chora performs the delicate political act of occupying a "no man's land" between not knowing (purely sensible) and not acting (purely intelligible), transcribing elemental letters without plugging into a conscious linguistic network. Like an automaton relieved of any agential responsibility, a quasi-machinic extension of the typewriter, this choric secretary mutely offers up a series of blank spaces ready to receive the stamp of a signet, a signature, representing an absent other.

Such opacity to knowledge cuts both ways, however: even the eminent philosopher, expounding an intricately devised cosmogony through the guise of Timaeus, confesses to a rational aporia in sorting out how the chora sorts, unable to hold in his mind a clear imprint of how the receptacle holds. Stymied by the thinking of space, Plato abandons the realm of accepted logic to squat in "a kind of bastard reasoning," broaching via circuitous pathways a concept that "is hardly even an object of conviction."[24] So benighted is this elusive chora that philosophers must "look at it as in a dream," entering a trancelike state as though in sympathy with the aphasic secretary, unable to draw distinctions because "our dreaming state renders us incapable of waking up and stating the truth."[25] Expressing a frustration reminiscent of Freud's confrontation with female desire—"what do women want?"—Plato deviates from his usual reasoning processes to seek conjectural answers, again like Freud, in the dream world.[26] Not simply a rhetorical ploy that withholds resolution for dramatic emphasis, this logical breakdown forces the philosopher to fall back upon analogy and catachresis to create an oddly literary discourse.[27] Although Derrida rightly critiques the inadequacy of metaphor to make sense of a phenomenon outside both intelligibility and sensibility, denying this improper receptacle even a proper article in language, Plato asks readers to look awry at the chora because of its anamorphic relation to philosophy, its ability to push against the form (*morphe*) of a rational, linear patrimony. For in its apparently selfless giving of material form to an ideal, its bringing together of two opposite points in a topological fold, the chora nevertheless becomes a medium of deformation by providing the ground of an imaginary space.

To explore in further detail the mechanism of such bodily distortion, we might focus on the visual faculty to see how the chora solicits both the sensible and intelligible to establish an inscriptional ground. As we have seen in chapter 1, Alberti proposes a method for constructing perspectival space that rests on a foundational gesture of inscription (*inscribo*), an inaugural mark upon the tabula rasa of a wooden panel. That is, Alberti advises painters to draw a rectangle of sufficient size to contain the desired scene, devising a frame that serves "as an open window [*aperta finestra*] through which the subject to be painted [*historia*] is seen."[28] Within this window-receptacle that turns a blank space into a place defined by the laws of *costruzione legittima*, Alberti begins demarcating the contours of an alternative topography, designating a vanishing point on the horizon before sketching in a grid of precisely calibrated guidelines. By following these recessionary markers to place objects in the inscribed spatial container, to hold the mimetic images of ideals presumed to exist elsewhere, if only in the imagination, artists can achieve the illusion of a vivid, three-dimensional world that blossoms beyond the picture plane. For a viewer who stands transfixed opposite the vanishing point, willfully bracketing out material context to look through an artificial aperture, this choric space rewards the gaze by sorting and holding objects according to a mystical logic of place, a logic that renders images recognizable to the correctly positioned eye.

More so than the various optical devices proposed as analogues of the chora—Irigaray's mirror or camera shutter, Richard Mohr's television screen with flickering images—Alberti's *costruzione legittima* reveals how only by deforming objects into foreshortened parodies of themselves, only by disfiguring bodies into metaphoric formations, can the subjective eye perceive the truest copy of an ideal. In striving for a seamless collusion of real and represented space that conceals this distortion, single-point perspective must inscribe both a physical table (*tabella*) and a mental system of signification, what Hamlet calls the "table" of his mind (I.v.98). Visual meaning emerges when these mental and physical tables coincide at major nodes on the perspectival grid; these cruxes thus serve as Lacanian *points de capiton* (suturing knots, upholstery buttons), which stitch together a signifier and signified through metaphor.[29] Just as an upholstery button punctures and secures layers of fabric, the grid lines of a perspectival matrix anchor the illusion of coherence by preventing the matter of space from shifting internally. Yet since the dynamic cosmos remolds itself without end, the choric envelope must shake tirelessly to keep bodily letters in their rightful place, to keep the gaze from falling horrifically between the lines and rapturing the facade of realism. That is, beyond merely containing objects, the Platonic chora must serve as the receptacle for a gaze that invests and inscribes itself in an imaginary world, providing an artful lure that sutures the subject into a dream of spatial plenitude.

By securing the eye in a "stereometric cage," single-point perspective attempts to lock viewers in a kind of house arrest as they look out a window, fixed in a subject position construed as interior, domestic, philosophical.[30] After all, as Anne Freire Ashbaugh observes, Plato's *Republic* employs the term *chora* precisely to denote "the dwelling place of the philosopher and the abode of his images."[31] Yet like an Albertian *velum* that assists the painter by flattening worldly bodies onto a map, the chora must ultimately efface its own marks and *morphe* for the fictive transparency of an open window to succeed. Unveiling a facialized landscape while negating itself, the choric secretary holds its own space as the receptacle's greatest secret, keeping mum about its maternal birthing of legible spaces and subjects. Such erasure from visibility may explain Plato's initial omission of the chora from his cosmogony, an oversight that he rectifies by starting again partway into the *Timaeus;* in so doing, Plato neatly marries form and content by inscribing the receptacle within its own receptacle, by veiling even the writing of chora from readers' eyes.[32]

Charged with the essential function of making things visible to the worldly eye, the world as eye, Plato's chora offers a pictorial surface that holds a substantive imprint by constructing an immaterial system of placing, giving objects the appearance of distinctive propriety by determining the proper spacing between them. Both a threshing and fleshing machine, the receptacle provides a common ground for measuring the interstitial spaces that not only sift out diverse bodies on a horizontal plane, but also separate ideals from bodies vertically. For Elizabeth Grosz, the chora thus epitomizes the possibilities of in-between space, defining a site of contestation and transformation that "makes identities both possible and impossible."[33] In this respect, the chora behaves not unlike an illiterate secretary who reproduces only the negative spaces between letters, promoting an anamorphic anti-reading that challenges the signifying practices of inscription itself. Indeed, as a space that differentiates the difference between spaces, between genres and identities, the chora resembles a Deleuzian *Zweifalt* that introduces a double fold between the intelligible level above and the perceptible level below, a transitional space that disturbs the dualism of Leibniz's monadic edifice. By adding a threshold that threshes information from all five senses into their respective vents, constantly receiving and placing worldly elements without any apparent agency or effect, this *Zweifalt* creates a structural wrinkle inside the philosopher's dwelling, conceiving the philosopher's dwelling by conceiving a "'fold-of-two,' an *entre-deux*" that links the sensorium below to the deliberative secretarium above.[34] While a fold in two encloses, increasing density and opacity as though building walls, a fold of two opens up the fabric by extending, looking outward, inserting apertures, seams, passages in often unruly ways. As a mediating space that reveals space to always be an invested medium, the choric interface inscribes an open fold the way that Alberti inscribes an open window: through the illusion of not inscribing, of only typing, of sorting things into types using a mystical, hence feminized logic. Disguised alternately as inert matter, inactive *mater,* transcribing secretary, transparent veil, Plato's chora prompts us to question how the subjectivizing act of *inscribo* involves a facialization of space, how a "no man's land" enfolds and engenders selves whose place remains forever shaky, even illusory.

Graphic Chora

The dream of Platonic space endured a rude awakening in early modern England, however, as the personal enclosure of chora confronted the new paradigms of scientific cartography. Yet in the practice of chorography that emerged in the late sixteenth century and continued into the seventeenth, we find an inscription of local space that blends text and image, map and history, to capture a chora partial in every sense.[35] Flourishing alongside increasingly scientific methods of mapping stripped of the personal and parochial, chorography offered a paradigm for viewing home and homeland that pushed against the rise of imperialist ambitions in this period, the outward quest for conquest facilitated by a cartographic knowledge couched in universally legible code. Such a debate over space revived the classical distinction between *chora* and *topos,* between subjective perception and objective charting, between feminine and masculine. As the oldest Greek word for *place, chora* appears to be the preferred term when writers make emotional statements about space, describe sacred sites, or designate an area occupied by people, such as a local province or country.[36] In contrast, *topos* often indexes an impersonal and empirically precise location, a nameable point that corresponds roughly to the Latin *locus; topography* thus involves inscribing a collection of distinct places, separated by quantifiable intervals of *spatium.*[37] If we map these differences in discursive terms, then *topos* nominates a subject for logical demonstration, while *chora* provides an inscriptional space for human narratives, a home for affect and mystified metaphor.[38]

As the inscription of local sites implicitly marked as interior, chorography assumes a synecdochal relation to other cartographic genres. In *Cosmographia* (1553), an oft-reprinted work by the German humanist Peter Apian, a woodcut neatly captures how chorography stacks up against its more expansive cousins, geography and cosmography. Following a well-known analogy derived from Ptolemy's *Geographia* (first century C.E.), Apian's illustration compares geography to the representation of a person's head, whose shape and importance parallel the globe's in a universe thought to be Earth-centered; in contrast, chorography isolates a portion of that planetary head to depict, say, an ear or eye in extreme close-up (figure 4.1). While Ptolemy concedes the necessity of microcosmic chorography to add secondary detail, geography prepares the macrocosmic ground for such delicate in-fill by graphing the outlines of landmasses, using the most powerful mathematical techniques to calculate distances accurately.[39] If we may venture a further analogy to Apian's three units of foot-measure (figure 4.2), then the cosmographer bounds into space with an exaggerated *passus geometricus* (geometrical step), while the geographer strides confidently into the world with a *passus simplex* (simple step).[40] Lacking a phallic sword or an aggressive momentum forward, however, the feminized chorographer trails the two manly explorers with a more circumspect *gradus* (step, degree), demurely

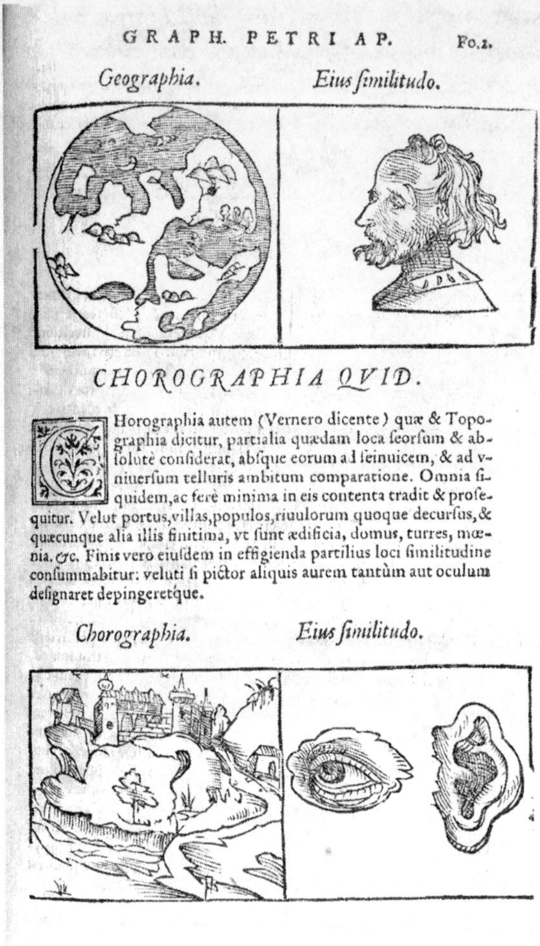

GRAPH. PETRI AP. Fo.2.

Geographia. *Eius ſimilitudo.*

CHOROGRAPHIA QVID.

Chorographia autem (Vernero dicente) quæ & Topographia dicitur, partialia quædam loca ſeorſum & abſolutè conſiderat, abſque eorum ad ſeinuicem, & ad vniuerſum telluris ambitum comparatione. Omnia ſiquidem, ac ferè minima in eis contenta tradit & proſequitur. Velut portus, villas, populos, riuulorum quoque decurſus, & quæcunque alia illis finitima, vt ſunt ædificia, domus, turres, mœnia. &c. Finis vero eiuſdem in effigienda partilius loci ſimilitudine conſummabitur: veluti ſi pictor aliquis aurem tantùm aut oculum deſignaret depingeretque.

Chorographia. *Eius ſimilitudo.*

Figure 4.1. Geography (*top*) versus chorography (*bottom*), from Peter Apian's *Cosmographia* (Antwerp, 1553), 2r. Courtesy of the Division of Rare and Manuscript Collections, Cornell University Library.

guided by the hand of geography. Instead of swashbuckling into foreign lands, the domesticated chorographer strolls within a limited area as a deeply invested insider, recording the local customs, people, and buildings that impart social meaning to any given place.

Beyond a question of scope, then, chorography departs from geography by engaging an entirely different mode of representation, aiming "to paint a true likeness, and not merely to give exact position and size. . . . Chorography needs an artist, and no one can present it rightly unless he

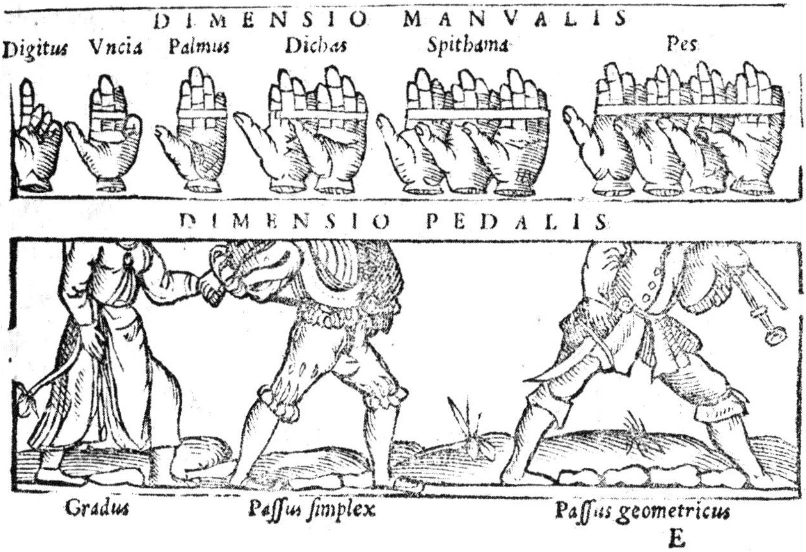

Figure 4.2. Measures by foot, from Peter Apian's *Cosmographia* (Antwerp, 1553), 15r. Courtesy of the Division of Rare and Manuscript Collections, Cornell University Library.

is an artist."[41] Apian's woodcut thus exemplifies chorography not with a map but rather a *veduta,* a city view that presents a coherent spatial entity bounded by water and walls. Translating these Ptolemaic values for an English readership, William Cuningham's *Cosmographical Glasse* (1559) affirms that "Chorographie consisteth rather in describyng the qualitie and figure, then the bignes, and quantitie of any thinge."[42] As an artistic genre that attends to the figure of space, chorography requires the skills of a portraitist who focuses on parts and provinces, a miniaturist who works with Mohr's choric television rather than the big screen. Thus striving for an intensive rather than extensive knowledge, the chorographer must capture a *genius loci* that transcends mere surface coordinates, strategically framing a chunk of landscape to reveal its affective contours, its character. While geography involves what Roman Jakobson calls a metonymic logic of spatial contiguity, charting a series of locales that simply happen to be adjoining, chorography explores the metaphor of place by delving into historical narrative and cultural particularity, establishing a necessary relation of mimesis between a chosen site and its "true likeness."[43]

In this sense, Ptolemy should assign geography to the fragment and chorography to the whole head: not only does geography operate under a metonymic regime, but its contiguities often prove to be merely

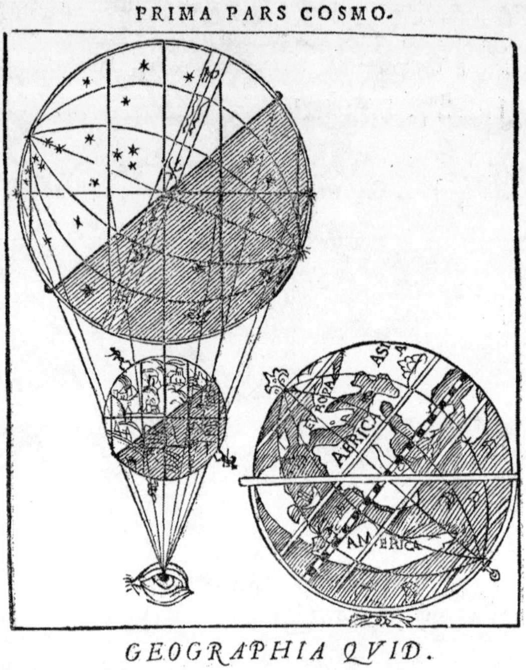

Figure 4.3. Geography (*right*) versus cosmography (*left*), from Peter Apian's *Cosmographia* (1553), 1v. Only an astrally projected eye can survey the earth and celestial sphere. Courtesy of the Division of Rare and Manuscript Collections, Cornell University Library.

imaginative extrapolations prompted by a desire to totalize space. In contrast to chorography's intimate, grounded perspective, both geography and cosmography cherish the fantasy of an omniscient eye, situated outside an earthly frame of reference (figure 4.3). Since no mortal can apprehend the entire globe, much less the universe, geographers and cosmographers must suture together discrete pieces of available empirical data, quilting a coherent map by judiciously employing *points de capiton* that batten down segments of space. For a chorographer preoccupied with excavating the cultural palimpsest of occupied spaces, however, what often anchors the local scene are the architectural landmarks that attest to a social history, the markers visible to the naked eye rather than projected from an astral perspective. Cuningham's definition of chorography thus moves from representations of "portes, Riuers[,] Hauens, Fluddes, Hilles, Mou[n]taynes" to increasingly specific pieces of architecture: "Cities, Villages, Buildinges, Fortresses, Walles, yea and euery particuler thing, in that parte conteined."[44] Likewise, while geography

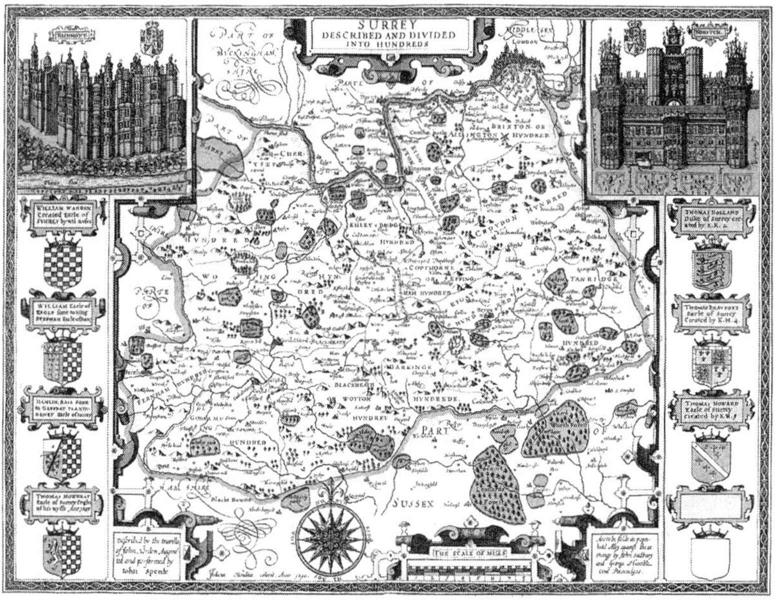

Figure 4.4. Map of Surrey, from John Speed's *Theatre of the Empire of Great Britain* (London, 1611). Engraved by Jodocus Hondius. Bridgeman Art Library.

focuses on the mountains, rivers, and seas that distinguish continents, Apian notes, chorography deals with the "aedificia, domus, turres, moenia &c." (buildings, houses, towers, walls, etc.) that display the structure of a community, thus inscribing spatial history on a human scale.[45]

Whether manifest in a *veduta,* estate map, or textual description, architecture dominates the field of vision when magnified by the intimate scope of chorography, when buildings stand above and against natural features on the landscape. Unlike the invisible lines of latitude and longitude that underpin cartography, assigning space a numerical value, architecture can forcefully identify a locale to the general public, evoking memories in some viewers, spurring wonder and desire in others. Perhaps because of this power to conjure an affective sense of place, early modern chorographers often supplement a scientific, aerial-view map with a picturesque, eye-level view of famous buildings. In John Speed's *Theatre of Great Britain* (1611), for instance, a map of Surrey includes discrete images of Richmond and Nonsuch Palaces in the upper corners, thus framing the cartographic with the scenographic (figure 4.4). Although viewed from a high vantage point, these architectural facades provide Surrey with a facial identity that contrasts with the map's intellectual,

Figure 4.5. Map of South Wales, from George Bickham's *The British Monarchy* (London, 1743). © The British Library Board, shelfmark 800.cc.17.

coded spatiality. Instead of offering a "cryptic" ground plot befitting a Palladian house, the sight of architectural marvels leaves a sensory imprint upon the table of memory, anchoring a material world within a mental inscriptional space. Indeed, if "Geographie is the imitation, and discription of the face, and picture of th'earth,"[46] then architectural faces enjoy a principal role in the smaller theater of chorography, the theater of an occupied locality.

Layering maps, pictures, and textual commentary to represent a single place, Speed's attempt to stage Britain typifies the piecemeal,

Figure 4.6. Map of Surrey, from George Bickham's *The British Monarchy* (London, 1743). © The British Library Board, shelfmark 800.cc.17.

multiplatform approach to space that defines so much of early modern cartography. Opening window upon window to break up the page, adding receptacle within receptacle to reproduce the experience of a fractured space, Speed's strategy takes the opposite tack from a later chorographic project, George Bickham's *The British Monarchy* (1743). In addition to written descriptions of every shire in England, this volume contains self-described "maps" that combine two modes of spatiality within almost every image (figures 4.5 and 4.6). The foreground of each map features an artfully composed scene of human activity, often situated against an architectural backdrop. As the viewer's gaze travels further back, however, this quaint vignette abruptly gives way to a topographical map rendered in precipitous foreshortening. For instance, Bickham's rendering of South Wales contrives an arched stone formation that separates a rustic scene in front, complete with silhouetted "natives" engaged in postcard-worthy activities, from a vertiginously slanted tableau that covers the entire breadth of Wales. Like a steeply raked stage that violates every principle of scale and perspective, this cartographic abutment yanks away the visual ground as the gaze passes through the embedded stone frame, forcing viewers to toggle between conflicting systems of representation.

While Speed's maps segment images into differing sizes and formats, Bickham's engravings forcibly clamp disparate views together to attempt a semblance of uniform perspective, strategically placing architectural elements to conceal any awkward breaks in the middle. In Bickham's map of Surrey, unlike Speed's, pleasure boaters near the front appear capable of rowing blithely uphill to the coast, albeit only after crashing through the miniature bridge to Westminster. By suturing over the disjunction between a *veduta*-like foreground and an almost vertical map beyond, Bickham's chorographic project assimilates all perspectives into a Frankenstein body of misaligned parts, aspiring to a holistic dreamscape visible simultaneously in plan, section, and elevation. At the same time, by jarring viewers into an awareness of spatial representation, Bickham raises questions about the epistemology that undergirds mapping. Rather than construe space as a theater to be imprinted by human action, Bickham positions mapping itself front and center as the subject of theater, using architecture as a proscenium arch to stage one built space within another. Indeed, for the map beyond the chorographic frame to signify, the gaze must sweep past the slow-moving figures in the foreground, leaving behind the slow pace of everyday life to slingshot upward across broad swaths of Britain. Hastening from a *gradus* to a *passus geometricus,* this parabolic journey of visual acceleration tries to preserve the intimacy of immersion in homely life while soaring above the homeland as an eagle-eyed observer. In other words, Bickham wants to have his country and his countryside too.

As chorographies themselves circulated among a popular audience, their physical migration into a range of households enabled many otherwise homebound to indulge in armchair travel, giving a virtual face to Britain for readers facing the challenge of forging a cohesive national identity. After all, William Cuningham advises that depictions of space "deliuereth vs from greate and continuall trauailes. For in à pleasaunte house, or warme study, she sheweth vs the [w]hole face of all th' Earthe."[47] By indulging a vicarious thrill from sojourns around the theater of Great Britain, chorography affords a sort of closet drama to spur a collective imagination of place, encouraging a nascent sense of nationhood rooted in a commonwealth of regions. Indeed, such readers in a "warme study" may well assume the mantle of chorographer in due course.

For William Harrison, producing his comprehensive *Description of England* required no more than a mental *passus*: "I sayled about my country within the compasse of my study."[48] Like books that market themselves as open closets, as discussed in chapter 3, this early modern chorography arose from the knowledge transactions of an enclosed study. Although sailing dangerously close to producing mere commonplace books, derivative vessels blown along by the stale breath of commentary, early modern chorographers also transformed a taste for antiquarian research into voyages across a physical landscape. In the theater of chorography, a genre more interested in Surrey than Surinam, travels through textual authority created and reinforced a desire for personal "trauailes" through a certain locality, for a domestic drama shared with fellow countrymen. The closet thus opened directly onto the nation of England and indirectly onto an emergent Great Britain, a spatial body pieced together from disparate fragments.

Publish or Perish, Early Modern Style

Such an intertwining of received knowledge and firsthand observation defines the career of John Leland, an antiquarian whose famous *Itinerary* inspired and informed several generations of chorographers. Under Henry VIII's auspices, Leland undertook years of travel to study various regions of England and Wales, amassing an archive of notes so prodigious that, as legend goes, the futility of sorting them for publication drove him into a fatal "frenesy."[49] Leland had originally accepted the king's commission in 1533 to "serche and peruse" the books held by monasteries and colleges, but the upheavals of Reformation soon prompted him to assume a more proactive role in conserving, if not acquiring, these same texts.[50] Alarmed by his country's "desidiousness and negligence" following the first Act of Suppression, passed in 1536, Leland warns the king's chief minister about Germans who "send dayly young Scholars hither, that spoileth them [books], and cutteth them out of Libraries, returning home and putting them abroad as Monuments of their own Country."[51] Alongside the architectural defacement wrought by the dissolution of monasteries, this bibliographic defacement deprives Britain not only of its material texts, but also of its authorial heritage, its "publyque wealthe."[52] When pirated editions masquerade under foreign imprints, "depopulating" libraries while veiling the true identity of authors, the "Monuments" of Britain's textual landscape suffer as much devastation as its pillaged monastic ruins.[53]

Yet for Leland, this "dayly" invasion of scholarly scofflaws, of Germanic vandals sacking Britain, merely draws attention to the more fundamental problem of native authors lost to the collective memory, not least "for lacke of empryntynge of such workes as laye secretely in corners."[54] Reminding his sovereign "how great a numbre of excellent godlye wyttes and wryters . . . hath bene in thys your regyon," Leland reached beyond his original cataloging mission to chronicle the lives of English authors from Roman times to the present, embarking on his own four-volume monument to the literary achievements of his nation.[55] Yet the more that Leland discovered of Britain through this antiquarian research, wending his way from library to library, the more that the subjective journey itself became important:

> after that I had perpended the honest and profytable studyes of these hystoryographers, I was totallye enflamed wyth a loue, to se throughlye all those partes of thys your opulent and ample realme, that I hadde redde of in the aforsayd wryters.[56]

Impassioned by the words of "hystoryographers" to see for himself, Leland rechanneled his energies from a textual to topographical survey, from metaphorical history to metonymic space, from belated writing to present image.

In this chorographic transition from the intelligible world of books to the sensible environment, Leland dedicated six years (or more) to searching and perusing the secrets of every corner in Britain, inscribing memories in his mind to supplement the monuments left by his literary precursors. That is, Leland decided to pursue the physical monuments whose specters haunt the textual monuments of his research, aiming to complete the cycle by transforming his imprinted memories back into a material work of "empryntynge." Leland thus describes his project with a catalog of landmarks found by his mastering gaze, moving in Ptolemaic fashion from natural elements (capes, bays, rivers, lakes, mountains, etc.) to architectural structures: "cyties, burges, castels, pryncypall manor places, monasteryes, and colleges." Remapping these spatial features as a series of monuments to be reviewed in his mind's eye, Leland boasts,

"I haue seane them, and noted in so doynge a whole worlde of thynges verye memorable."[57] As a correlate to this chorographical text that already furnishes a "pycturinge out of the vniuersall worlde," Leland also promises his luxury-loving sovereign to inscribe "thys your worlde and impery of Englande . . . in a quadrate table of syluer."[58]

Yet even as he saturates the choric ground of his mind with "verye memorable" images to transcribe later onto linguistic and visual tables, Leland inevitably confronts more troubling memories embedded in what Jennifer Summit calls a desacralized landscape, a post-Reformation realm where secular itineraries replace the pilgrimages now banned by law.[59] Forced to decipher a Book of the World that painfully evinces its loss of transcendent meaning, Leland must give face and form to a nation pockmarked by "monasteryes" whose defacement he remembers all too well. As Summit demonstrates, Leland's manuscript avoids any mention of the Reformation that might upset his court patrons, framing the dissolution of monasteries as simply a history of property exchange.[60] In recasting the violent disruption of Reformation as a Great Rebuilding, as the conversion of religious sites into secular homes, Leland attempts to bracket out the cultural politics of dispossession by nominalizing the landscape, by addressing a topography of named possessions and possessors, "a whole worlde of thynges" in "thys your opulent and ample realme." Despite this editorial act of suppression that places the Reformation under erasure, leaving a catastrophic event lurking between the lines and within the living memory of readers, Leland's sins of omission indicate his keen awareness of a metaphorical historicity playing out against a backdrop of ruins, of monastic revenants brought back to life, but not truly domesticated, as the architectural undead.

"In the ruin," Walter Benjamin observes, "history has merged physically into the setting."[61] Epitomized by a sacred edifice reduced to picturesque rubble, a symbol of eternity devolved into an artistic motif to be arranged in a tableau, Benjamin's ruin figures a baroque aesthetic that spatializes time as a constellation of fragments, transforming the metaphoric progression of history into the metonymic scenography of a *Trauerspiel,* a German drama of mourning. Such a spatialized history eludes Leland, however, as he struggles to separate a chronicle of people from a chorography of "regyon," as the sacred ruins around him evoke a trauma too recent to be narrated safely. Leland's silences thus eloquently express his own ambivalent role within a mourning drama that cannot be plotted to a meaningful closure, to a cathartic rebirth that clears the ground for a holy continuity. Wandering in this unframed theater of becoming, Leland attempts to stand apart as a witness spared from disaster, a monument testifying to the possibility of survival despite tragedy, the possibility of rebuilding, rewriting—until even he, the seemingly untouched, becomes touched by a madness that leaves his mind in ruins, his manuscript in fragments.

What the archive cannot speak in its content, it demonstrates through form; the story that Leland cannot tell in words, he writes through the defacing of his own bodily temple, the dissolution of his own interior cell. Far from being a neutral ground of inscription for "a multitude of thinges here named," a sifter of metonymic *copia* into their proper chorographic places, Leland finds himself holding a mirror to the land as an unintentional self-portrait of space.[62] As Jacques Derrida observes: "Ruin is the self-portrait, this face looked at in the face as the memory of itself, what *remains* or *returns* as a specter from the moment one first looks at oneself and a figuration is eclipsed. . . . For one can just as well read the pictures of ruins as the figures of a portrait, indeed, of a self-portrait."[63] Looking into a quadrate table of silver to plot the "portiture" of Britain, Leland finds only his own face inscribed in the reflective surface, his own self-portrait superimposed onto the contours of a nation beyond figuration, beyond facialization.[64] Most notably for a precarious British identity always in fragments, an archipelagic realm always coming undone, the illusion of a "[w]hole" face reveals itself as only a hole face already in ruins, as an abyssal ground rent asunder by the black hole of subjective memory.

Perambulate and Publish

Thirty years after Leland unveiled his prospectus to Henry VIII, William Lambarde embraced the spatial fragment to produce *A Perambulation of Kent* (1576), likely the first published work of English chorography.[65] Though envisioned as merely one segment of a "Topographicall Dictionarie" that organizes Britain by alphabetical entries, *Perambulation* was released to the public when Lambarde decided that "the matter was by our diligent trauaile growne (as me thought) to a conuenient Masse."[66] Following in Leland's footsteps by dividing Britain into shires, Lambarde confined the initial survey to his home county of Kent, searching out monuments of antiquarian knowledge that might "lie hidden in olde bookes hoorded up in corners."[67] Though a London-born lawyer associated with Lincoln's Inn, Lambarde inherited a manor in Kent from his father, held various administrative positions in the county, and eventually settled there around 1570 upon marrying the first of three Kentish wives. A draft manuscript of Lambarde's book started perambulating around Kent later that year, though only upon publication would the work reach a wide enough readership to justify Lambarde's claim to be a "*xenagogus,*" or guide to outsiders.[68] Perhaps due to this initial circulation within a local coterie, or perhaps due to his own preference for textual exploration, Lambarde failed to include a map of the region until the second edition of 1596; instead, the 1576 volume contains a map of the Anglo-Saxon heptarchy that establishes Kent's place in a broader historical picture.

Balancing the intellectual curiosity of an outsider against the authoritative knowledge of an insider, Lambarde's first-person narrative foregrounds his critical judgment in sifting through "olde bookes" and other credible sources, quarrying the best evidence relating to the region's historical, etymological, religious, legal, and physical features. Yet *Perambulation*'s structure remains firmly anchored in geography: every section bears the rubric of a new place name, usually a place of habitation, as the book traces an inwardly spiraling trajectory around each of the shire's two dioceses. Though undoubtedly familiar with some of these places through personal experience, Lambarde probably never traveled physically along the route described textually. Instead, aiming for an "enterlacing" of spatial and temporal modes,[69] Lambarde attempts to recount a history gleaned from textual sources while ranging spatially across an English shire. Although an opening chapter provides an overview of Kent from Roman times to the present, the main portion of the book features a variety of historical figures who appear desultorily to populate anecdotes "perteining to some peculiar places," to perform vignettes in the theater of a locality.[70] In short, Lambarde deploys a syntagmatic logic to connect topoi according to their spatial contiguity, while opening a window in each section to allow a vista in paradigmatic depth, a vista that exposes the strata of otherwise invisible narratives inscribed into the bedrock.

Turning away from a medieval notion of itinerary that often involves a sacred journey, a pilgrimage with a definite telos, Lambarde's perambulation outlines the figure of a choric place, tracing an inward-turning gyre that looks to some nebulous origin in space and time, an origin that situates the *habitus* of a community. In contrast to the modern valorization of visuality that Henry Wotton calls a lordship of the eye, "raunging, and Imperious . . . an *usurping Sence,* [which] can indure no narrow *circumscription,*" Lambarde chooses instead to engage in an older, more restrictive lordship of the foot, walking mentally around a region marked as a proper home, as property.[71] Quite aptly, then, Lambarde arranged to publish his work through one Thomas Wotton, Henry's father, a fellow lawyer with a country seat not far away in Boughton Malherbe. Armed with a somewhat parochial notion of publishing, the elder Wotton contributed a book introduction that addresses a remarkably homogeneous readership comprised of "his Countriemen, the Gentlemen of the Countie of Kent."[72] Indeed, decades after Leland's *Itinerary* proved such a ruinous project, Lambarde writes from and for the perspective of a landed gentleman to construct a stable landscape that mirrors himself. His narrative thus projects an Anglican triumphalist history upon the rubble of dissolved monasteries—some of which have been rebuilt as estates for the class of self-fashioning gentry to which he belongs.[73]

Ironically, Lambarde deplores how his country has been too thoroughly scrubbed of its former altars to idolatry, leaving no monument to make legible its former sins to forgetful viewers. While Leland the antiquarian scrambled to rescue books as monasteries collapsed, Lambarde the lawyer wishes to retain forensic evidence that could prove the justness of Henry VIII's verdict against Catholicism, seeking material traces in the Book of the World to support his own interpretive framework. Citing the prescience of a certain Bishop Theophilus of Alexandria, who would "reserue undefaced that part of eche Idol which was most grosse & filthie," Lambarde regrets the loss of signifying ruins that could be arranged to form a pictorial field, bringing shards of past and present into dialogue upon a common stage.[74] With such a constellation of desacralized, carefully deconstructed ruins dotting the country, scarring the body of Britain to keep a "fresh memorie" of the Reformation for future generations, present-day recusants would have "wanted [i.e., lacked] the faces" to deny an Anglican narrative of their past corruption.[75]

Unlike a "raunging, and Imperious" eye that issues outward to conquer a panoramic view, the perambulating subject wishes to define a choric locality using the historical fragments along its route, building an already ruined picture of place that shifts and dissolves with every step. Because "the Inwardes of each place may best be knowen by such as reside therein," Lambarde urges other scholars to create textual perambulations of their native shires, so that "by ioyning our Pennes, and conferring our labours (as it were, *ex symbolo*) we might at the last by the union of our many partes and papers compact one whole and perfect bodie and booke of our English Topographie."[76] Equating parts and papers, bodies and books, Lambarde's exhortation—not to arms, but to pens—underscores the necessity of a collective spatial imagination that makes Britain signify. The nation must be written and underwritten by a network of monadic subjects whose perspective remains embedded in their own home regions. In this semiotic project that transcends dialect and regionalism, a cadre of implicitly male chorographers labors in union to create "one whole and perfect bodie and booke," shaping a cohesive body of Britain that resonates in the consciousness of readers.

Lambarde's proposed "Topographicall Dictionarie" of Britain would never come to fruition, preemptively ruined by the publication of William Camden's magisterial *Britannia* (1586). Combining research derived from books and from multiple forays across the country, Camden's *Britannia* awakes a nation to its own coherent identity by enacting the textual equivalent of a Great Rebuilding, feeding a seemingly insatiable demand among readers with multiple editions first in Latin, then English:

> Si qui verò sint, qui in vrbe sua hospites, in patria sua peregrini, & cognitione semper pueri esse velint, sibi per me placeant, sibi dormiant, non ego illis haec conscribo, non illis vigilo. (If there are those who are strangers in their own cities and foreigners in their own countries, who wish to be always children in thinking, I say let them please themselves, let them sleep; I do not write this for them, nor do I keep awake for them.)[77]

Motivated by "the common love of our common mother our natiue Country," Camden finds in Britain a feminized choric space that provides a fertile ground for the birth of a nation; he builds a true empire that adds Scotland and Ireland to Leland's original purview of England and Wales.[78] Although even this most totalizing of chorographies recognizes its limitations, defending its editorial choices against detractors who point to omissions and errors, Camden builds on the fragments of his predecessors to conclude a provisional construction of Britain, holding together a spatial body made whole and perfect if only by the force of imagination.

On the frontispiece of *Britannia* (1600), engraved by William Rogers (figure 4.7), a large central ellipse displays all the disparate parts of this body for the public's "raunging, and Imperious" gaze, framing a prostrate subject of mapping designed to "allure the eies by pleasant portraiture."[79] As the reader's astral eye roams across a geographic portrait of Britain, a choric place defined by an oval border that seems to protect Camden's dream of nation-building, this visual perambulation inscribes and animates a facialized landscape that contrasts with the actual woman's face depicted in a cartouche above. Indeed, a personified Britannia, drawn from Roman iconography, perches on a rock high above a picturesque scene, an insular and iconic fragment of antiquity

Figure 4.7. Frontispiece to William Camden's *Britannia* (London, 1600). Engraved by William Rogers. By permission of the Folger Shakespeare Library.

borne dreamlike from the past, hurtling forward into the early modern consciousness despite the figure's still posture. Yet Camden's Britannia no longer exists as a province in subjection to the Roman Empire, but has rather become a subject mapping itself as a growing empire, as a textual topos feverishly revised, enlarged, translated, illustrated, and marketed to an ever-growing public. In this double portrait of place that literally hinges upon the unstable title and signifier, "Britannia," the viewer's gaze must oscillate between two faces of a nation still being imagined, suspended in a semiotic matrix between two modes of conceiving home. Appropriately, Rogers's frontispiece positions the name *Britannia* as a transitional space impinging on multiple parts, an interface between past and present rather than a singular immobile center.

Motherland

That a chorographic enterprise should resonate across multiple registers in the late sixteenth century indicates not merely the divergent methods of visualizing space, or the print technologies that allowed a critical mass of readers to constitute themselves as a community. More cogently, Britain assumed a peculiarly gendered political identity as the domain of Elizabeth I. Casting herself as a Virgin Queen married to her country and the mother of her subjects, Elizabeth reinforced this persona of chaste femininity through a series of similar portraits, produced from the late 1570s through the mid-1580s, that associate her body with a sieve and with Vesta, the Roman goddess of hearth and home.[80] As Petrarch relates in *The Triumph of Chastity,* a Vestal virgin named Tuccia refuted accusations of sexual incontinence by carrying water in a sieve, walking from the Tiber River to her temple without losing a drop.[81] Of the many emblems that Elizabeth employed to manifest her interiority, to perform her desired attributes, Camden notes that she "most commonly [chose] a Sive without a Motte, for her words, *VIDEO, TACEO,* and *SEMPER EADEM,* which shee as truely and constantly performed."[82] That is, the sieve visually represents the queen's textual mottoes of "Video, taceo" (I see, I keep silent) and "Semper eadem" (Always the same). In these qualities of muted knowledge and immutable persistence, Elizabeth's sieve-like body recalls Plato's description of the chora as a receptacle that silently disperses and contains, providing a space of inscription that never changes its nature.

While it would be untenable to claim that Elizabeth's iconography deliberately references Plato, an intriguingly similar logic undergirds how both sieves engender place and place the engendered body. By plotting these two motifs in the same constellation of ideas rather than along a timeline, by spatializing history in the same way that Elizabeth drapes herself in the relics of a Vestal Virgin, we might better see how the space of a sieve constitutes a (w)hole face. Extending Derrida's insight that the chora "anachronizes being," this atemporal critique—using what some might term queer temporality—enables the subject to emerge as a spatialized becoming, a constant threshing out of identity that rearranges fragments upon a stage.[83] As Elizabeth figures herself as an eternally chaste womb for producing and holding the identities of her subjects, this true and constant performance of purity legitimates her political authority upon actual spaces and bodies.[84] In the queen's attempt to birth a nation *ex symbolo,* to incarnate the image of Britannia, achieving a coherent face of empire depends on the paradox of a womb both maternally filled and virginally empty, a womb that provides a single receptacle to enclose a multitude of regions. As a porous sieve becomes the face of Britain's national chastity, at once dangerously riddled with holes and keeping a disparate empire whole, the mapping of this

Figure 4.8. Quentin Metsys the Younger, Siena sieve portrait (c. 1583). Pinacoteca Nazionale, Siena. Alinari/Bridgeman Art Library.

inherently feminine, political space assumes the form of an early modern chorography.

Devoted to the intimate probing of a single bodily part, to the portrait of a locale invested with human meaning, chorography promotes an alternative modality of space that challenges the universalist ambitions of cartography. Using a feminine dream logic that questions the Cartesian ideal of transparent legibility, chorography proves eminently suitable for charting an interior space whose contours can never be verified through public demonstration. As a fantasy of interior purity, Elizabeth's virginity—made visible by a sieve that works miracles—justifies an ideology of global expansion that might otherwise seem rapacious and promiscuous. In the "Siena Portrait," painted by Quentin Metsys the Younger around 1583 (figure 4.8),[85] Elizabeth delicately grasps a sieve in front of her billowing skirts to propel the notion of her chastity to the utmost foreground, using this external symbol of her womb to demarcate "the point of transition" between herself and viewers.[86] Just as her whitened face presents an idealized mask that conceals and perfects what lurks beneath, the blank sieve provides a twofold screen for Elizabeth's

Figure 4.9. George Gower, Plimpton sieve portrait (1579). By permission of the Folger Shakespeare Library.

womb: the object not only blocks our gaze of her body, but also projects an emblem of her interiority upon a contrasting background.

We discover a more explicit linkage to Elizabeth's womb in a 1579 painting by George Gower, perhaps the earliest template for this genre of sieve portrait (figure 4.9).[87] Gower connects his sieve to the queen's crimson skirts with a short ribbon, which fastens upon an oddly navel-like node with a central indent. As Deanne Williams observes, this white ribbon attaches to Elizabeth's dress with a knot that resembles a "little pearl," a feminine correlate to the Henrician codpiece.[88] Like an umbilical cord that issues from a mock navel, the ribbon extrudes a womb-like double to mirror Elizabeth's imputed chastity within, deflecting a close survey of her body by offering an iconic fragment displaced to the side. Thus standing beside herself, Elizabeth mimes the process of labor by birthing an idealized version of her interiority *ex symbolo,* by opening herself virtually. Not unlike the ropes of pearls that signify and multiply her chastity, the sieve—the largest pearl of all—tethers the queen to her own virginal treasure.

As a surrogate womb with its inner face turned outward, revealing its untainted emptiness, the sieve that Elizabeth takes in hand also takes her by the hand, leading her forward to meet the public gaze with tangible evidence of her purity. Yet the Gower portrait extends this axis beyond the queen's body to reveal a shadowy globe in the corner, a circular entity that echoes the sieve in shape and size, an exterior world in contrast to the interior womb. Planted between these two objects to define a rough line of symmetry, Elizabeth's body marks a plane of reflection—or perhaps an open window—through which the globe and sieve encounter each other as specular doubles. Any distinction between subject and object collapses as the microcosmic sieve resonates with the macrocosmic globe, as a principle of metaphoric resemblance ensures a Ptolemaic harmony between these inner and outer spheres. Anchored upon an actual womb that remains invisible, the occluded nucleus of an Elizabethan cosmos, the geometry of Gower's painting invites our eyes to travel backward from the sieve, following a route that extends along the queen's girdle to a globe that might as well be tethered to her back. As our gaze slides back and forth along this imaginary line, the formally twinned sieve and globe function as balanced offshoots of Elizabeth's womb, stabilizing a trinity of virginal spaces that reinforce the legitimacy of a distinctly gendered empire. As Gower's visual syntax suggests: where chaste virtue leads the way, can a morally pure imperialism linger far behind?

For a viewer who looks upward from a suitably humble position at Elizabeth's feet, occupying the implied terminus of this diagonal as it extends through the picture plane, the painting's ocular itinerary of empire makes access to the globe contingent upon a royal body and its resonant, radiating womb. Like the secular equivalent of a Mariological intercessor, the stoic and statuesque Elizabeth furnishes an outward-facing womb to birth viewers as British subjects in the world, providing an authorizing interface between a domestic public and the globe beyond. Holding her feminine interiority rather than a phallic sword, the queen threshes out her microcosmic subjects by mapping them within a choric system of space, producing bodies as well-aligned in geopolitics as the Vitruvian man perfectly subtends geometry. The sieve portraits thus allow Elizabeth—a woman entering her late forties with dimming prospects of marriage—to reframe her maternal potential as a globalizing womb for her country, an inscriptional space where Britannia inducts her subjects onto a world stage.[89] Such a strategic turning away from personal fertility becomes even clearer in the Siena Portrait, which departs from other sieve paintings by adding a sharp recession on the right that looks into a lengthy, lofty arcade. Choosing to render only this particular feature in the technique of single-point perspective, rarely employed among English court artists at the time, Metsys punches through the background gloom to reveal a brightly lighted corridor populated by a procession of male figures, including a courtier identified as Christopher Hatton, his young page, and several guards brandishing halberds. Dressed in jaunty colors that complement the terracotta-hued columns, this aristocratic *enfilé* streams through a realistic space toward the fathomless, tenebrous foreground occupied by Elizabeth, tracing a line that visually continues along the queen's girdle to a point marking her biological womb.

Although Roy Strong implicates Hatton as a proponent of empire who financed expeditions abroad, the dashing, dancing nobleman also enjoyed a considerable reputation as one of Elizabeth's favorites, and hence a perennial implied suitor.[90] Remaining single even after another stalwart, Robert Dudley, finally married in 1578, the ever-hopeful Hatton bankrupted himself building one magnificent estate after another, trying vainly to entice his queen to visit. As though to highlight the futility of these aspirations, the Siena Portrait relegates Hatton to a spatial fragment tenuously adjoined to the main allegorical stage, thwarting his advance toward Elizabeth's womb by delineating clear formal contrasts between the two regions. Indeed, while Hatton's presence suggests his involvement in the painting's commission, hence decreasing the possibility that Metsys intended any mockery, the spatial composition segregates him in a manner that, ironically, happens to mirror his social predicament. Beyond stationing armed guards and possibly an elderly chaperone at the threshold, Metsys establishes an aesthetic dichotomy that confines Hatton to a distant realm of luminous color rather than somber darkness, worldly movement rather than mystical stasis, courtly protocol rather than interior solitude, masculine verticality rather than feminine roundness.[91] Boxed within tightly spaced columns and a phalanx of retainers, Hatton cannot escape a fantastically soaring arcade reminiscent more of his own grandiose ambitions in architecture than his frugal sovereign's—even in art, Elizabeth will never look upon or enter his domain.

In contrast to the immanent world of courtly bodies glimpsed through this perspectival window, the painting unfolds a dreamlike space in front that displays the transcendent power of Elizabeth's choric fecundity. While Hatton inscribes a trajectory that approaches but never arrives at the royal womb, Metsys literally undercuts this biological determinism with an alternate route that travels beneath, but not quite parallel to, the first diagonal. As in the Gower portrait, this second track connects the formally paired objects of the sieve and globe, suggesting an imperial chain of chastity that stretches from Rome to Britain. By doubling the lines of recession, Metsys makes available a more subversive passage to fertility that proceeds from a womb both public and prosthetic, displaced and displayed. Just as the queen's pearl necklace forms a secondary loop to the side, her ectopic womb moves outside its designated topos of a private, feminine interiority, recasting itself as an instrument of performative chastity to underwrite an empire.[92] Indeed, muting the political maelstrom over her ability to produce an heir, Elizabeth wears a severe black dress that renders her body a depthless void, donning a costume that both mourns and liberates her from sexuality. To represent a woman who precisely could not separate her internal physicality from her external power, the painting establishes a tension between dual lines of recession that resolves only at some imaginary point of convergence outside the frame, some vanishing point of infinite plenitude where Elizabeth can finally have everything.

This difficult negotiation between the queen's two wombs—one natural, one political—assumes a monumental stature on the ornamented pillar to Elizabeth's right. In a series of incised roundels aligned in three rows, Metsys draws upon Virgil's *Aeneid* to depict the tragic affair between Aeneas and Dido, a woman often linked to Elizabeth: not only was Dido the queen of Carthage, but her alternate name was Elissa.[93] Departing from earlier sources that portray Dido as a paragon of chastity, Virgil recounts her all-consuming infatuation with Aeneas, the Trojan hero chosen by gods to found a great empire in Rome. When Aeneas finally sails from Carthage to fulfill his imperial destiny, a forlorn Dido stabs herself with his sword before setting her body ablaze in a funeral pyre. Aeneas watches the smoke ascend from the harbor, but never returns. To access this poignant lesson on the price of empire, the Siena Portrait demands that viewers navigate through the roundels to discover the correct sequence, tracing an epic journey that actually begins with the bottom layer.[94] Yoking these metonymic fragments into a coherent narrative, viewers mentally smooth over the lacunae between vignettes as though spooling through cinematic frames, mapping the *Aeneid*'s story onto each architectural story. Rising ever higher in the quest to follow Aeneas's exploits, the viewer's gaze performs the very gesture of imperial foundation, plotting the narrative as a triumphal ascent rather than romantic downfall.

Although the viewer's gaze thus builds an empire beside Aeneas, roundel by roundel, the pillar's iconography proves to be anything but linear. As Deanne Williams notes, the painting's allegory of Elizabeth forces viewers to discern, sieve-like, among a "dizzyingly unstable set of identities": the Aeneas who sacrifices love to assume his political role, the Virgilian Dido who immolates herself in immoderate passion, and the pre-Virgilian Dido who commits suicide to preserve her chastity.[95] To thresh out Elizabeth's proper role among these three characters, the erudite viewer must not only scrutinize the picture currently before the gaze but also recollect images in the mind's eye, reflecting upon the Dido abjected from Virgil's account. Does Elizabeth resemble Aeneas in striding forward to imperial glory while leaving behind the foolish Elissa, the amorous persona associated with Hatton and the gaudy trappings of court? Or does Elizabeth resemble Dido as the virtuous, female ruler of an empire that threatens the domination of Rome? Without a clear antecedent on whom the queen can be modeled, the neatly sutured chain of roundels necessarily comes undone, as ghostly shards of other Didos and other Carthages churn through Virgil's otherwise sedimented epic. Though inscribed on the globe across from the pillar, the motto "Tutto vedo e molto mancha" (I see all but much is missing) may well describe the viewer who cannot distinguish the roundels for the revenants seeping through the cracks, the obscuring plumes of smoke that represent the displaced and disembodied Didos.

Constantly deflected from a linear route in mapping the pillar's allegorical minefield, the viewer endlessly reconfigures a matrix of scenes both seen and unseen, stepping outside Aeneas's footprints to deconstruct the architecture of classical authority. As an inscriptional space that should consolidate Elizabeth's imperial claims, the pillar instead dissolves textual certainty into the associative, fragmentary logic of dreams. Despite uniting the masculine verticals of the background with the feminine roundness of the foreground, despite an amber-and-black scheme that echoes Elizabeth's sieve and dress, the pillar cannot synthesize the painting's motifs into a coherent architectonic. Suffering from a certain erectile dysfunction, the pillar cannot uphold a central *point de capiton* that keeps the semantic fabric from shifting. Such an inability to found a secure empire of signs derives from a certain evasiveness that Derrida observes in the chora itself. As Plato's third genre, the chora oscillates not between two poles but between "two types of oscillation: the double exclusion (*neither/nor*) and the participation (*both this and that*)."[96] In one sense, the pillar cannot be wholly understood by either a metonymic narrative that orders events by spatial contiguity or a metaphoric paradigm that allows two incompatible Didos to haunt the same place; the pillar always engages the logic of both metaphor and metonym. To embrace the pre-Virgilian Dido whose chastity mirrors Elizabeth's, viewers must place under erasure the Virgilian Dido before their eyes, sacrificing (yet again) the bodily presence of a bawdy Dido to serve the rhetoric of empire. However, defacing Virgil's Dido cannot prevent a triangulated oscillation that destabilizes a simple virgin/whore dichotomy, as viewers imagine Elizabeth as both Dido and Aeneas, neither this Dido nor that, neither Aeneas nor Dido, both this Dido and that.

Just as Shakespeare's Gertrude confronts the counterfeit presentments of two brothers, only to reflect upon her own spotted soul, Metsys's Elizabeth confronts images of Dido and Aeneas only to expose the abyssal ground within herself. A third space caught between relations of *neither/nor* and *both/and,* Elizabeth's body flutters within a logical ménage à trois while threshing out the imprint of potential identities. In the slippage between "Video, taceo"—what Camden cites as the queen's motto—and the Siena Portrait's "Tutto vedo e molto mancha," Elizabeth's already muted voice (*taceo*) may be counted among the missing (*molto mancha*), since what she embodies cannot be shaped into a linear narrative. With a womb both political and natural, yet neither political nor natural, Elizabeth becomes a chimera of gender and genre in the effort to conceive an immaculate empire, to picture an imperial project without a spotted soul. As Elizabeth stands among fragments that stage an encounter between past and present, the allegory of Britannia can no longer be mapped in a diachronic column as one man's itinerary, as a closed circuit of perambulation.

Indeed, while the imperial column reminds viewers of the mythical Brutus, a supposed descendant of Aeneas who settled England in prehistory, the success of a British New Troy depends crucially upon a globe that stands in radiance on Elizabeth's other side, bearing a promise of future prosperity. An emblem of spatialized history, of simultaneity, the globe inscribes a network that expands in every direction at once, whether through sailing vessels or *ex symbolo.* Metsys even situates the globe over the lacuna between foreground and background; like the choric womb, the globe thus forms a *Zweifalt,* "a 'fold-of-two,' an *entre-deux,* something 'between' in the sense that a difference is being differentiated."[97] That is, the globe mediates between the choric space of eternity and the Cartesian space of modernity, posing a turnstile between different spatialities while making these differences visible as difference. This global womb surfaces more clearly in Crispijn de Passe's 1592 engraving of Elizabeth, which places the royal orb that symbolizes her rule before a central site on her body (figure 4.10). Adorned with jeweled bands that form a T-shape, this royal orb evokes the schema of medieval T-O maps that divide the earth (O) into three segments (T), one for each known continent. Although offset by a phallic scepter held in the queen's

Figure 4.10. Crispijn de Passe, engraving of Elizabeth (1592). © Victoria and Albert Museum, London.

other hand, just as Metsys locates a pillar across from the globe, Elizabeth's royal orb collapses the world and womb into a single entity under a Christian cross. To capture the power assured by her sacred womb, the caption below names her as the ruler over an empire that comprises England, France, Ireland, and Virginia.

An even more ambitious dream of feminine interiority emerges in John Case's *Sphaera Civitatis* (1588), a political treatise that counters Aristotle's *Politics* to endorse the authority (*imperium*) of women.[98] Castigating the medieval *De faeminarum secretis* (*On the Secrets of Women*), a treatise that locates women's vices mainly in the womb, Case argues that women should have sovereignty as creatures free (*libera*) by nature, capable of intellect and virtue.[99] Such a woman may be seen in the woodcut that prefaces Case's text (figure 4.11): this image represents Elizabeth as ruler over the *sphaera civitatis* (literally, "sphere of state"). Her bodily presence remains the greatest secret as drapery engulfs her torso, while a diagram of the Ptolemaic universe obscures anything below. Anchored upon a nucleus marked "Iustitia Immobilis" ("Immovable Justice"), this cosmos includes seven inner circles that match each of

Figure 4.11. Woodcut of Elizabeth, from John Case's *Sphaera Civitatis* (Oxford, 1588), verso of the title page. By permission of the Folger Shakespeare Library.

the seven planets with a quality needed to govern well. The eighth and ninth rings are reserved for the Star Chamber and Elizabeth herself, since both have public offices that should encompass all the virtues of the circles within. Positing the immovable rightness of Britain as a model of geopolitical harmony, Case's diagram presses against the chaste female body to secure a proper inscriptional space, hence conflating the national and global, the domestic and imperial. By transposing human spheres of power onto a cosmological schema, the woodcut naturalizes Elizabeth's seemingly unnatural rule as a female monarch, supporting the notion of a woman's *imperium*.

While Elizabeth's famous rallying speech at Tilbury, delivered the same year in which Case published *Sphaera Civitatis,* invests her authority as monarch in having a king's heart and stomach, Case's woodcut suggests that such power actually resides in a queen's womb. As Kaara Peterson observes, this illustration bears a strong formal resemblance to the sieve portraits that foreground Elizabeth's chastity, except that here a uterine cosmos displaces her entire lower body.[100] Dwarfed by this distended uterus, Elizabeth functions less as the head of her *sphaera civitatis,* as the lettering on either side of her ruff implies, than as a pregnant sieve-womb that sprouts rings of political concordance from a navel-like center.[101] Tom Conley draws our attention to how the navel, a bodily fragment "freighted with cartographic and literary meanings," figures not only the birthplace of space, but also "the site of a ruptured attachment to the world."[102] For example, medieval *mappaemundi* often represent Jerusalem as a geographic navel that centers a T-O map, providing a Christian point of orientation that makes visible the world's attachment to and break from its divine creator. Yet the navel in Case's woodcut marks a point of rupture from the maternal queen as a cosmos both presses against and bursts from her body, a womb gone wild.

Although the outer circle proclaims her imperial title, thus making the *sphaera civitatis* emphatically hers, does Elizabeth truly hold this Ptolemaic orb in hand? Forced to embrace her femininity as something outside herself and larger than life, Elizabeth stands behind the very object that defines her power as a woman, occupying an ambiguous subject position in relation to her own monstrous womb.[103] On the one hand, the textile sphere that cloaks Elizabeth suggests a body natural that echoes the *sphaera civitas* of the body politic; yet these formal resonances also suggest that an irregular feminine sphere must be imprinted and refined by a masculine geometry, contrasting the architecture of textile folds with the floating, yet perfectly structured world of a womb. Footless and pregnant, the queen unveils her public-private womb with a posture that evokes the type of illustration found in anatomy manuals, some of which depict women peeling open their stomachs to expose their uteruses (figure 4.12). Flaunting her feminine interiority as a fetishized accessory not unlike the Henrician codpiece, Elizabeth remains in thrall to a conceptual double bind that makes her have and be her womb at the same time. Swollen as a receptacle for the world, Elizabeth works as a prime mover who places without herself having a place, a choric center abjected from the system of (re)production.

As a womb that embraces the paradox of a (w)hole face, serving as both the public facade of a *civitas* and the private space behind a navel, the cosmos that Elizabeth carries before her performs the same kind of miracle as a sieve that carries water. Indeed, by linking women with a magic sieve, early modern culture attempts to stave off the radically porous body that, for Gilles Deleuze, bears witness to a social and psychic trauma, a breakdown in making sense of a distinct subject: "Body-sieve,

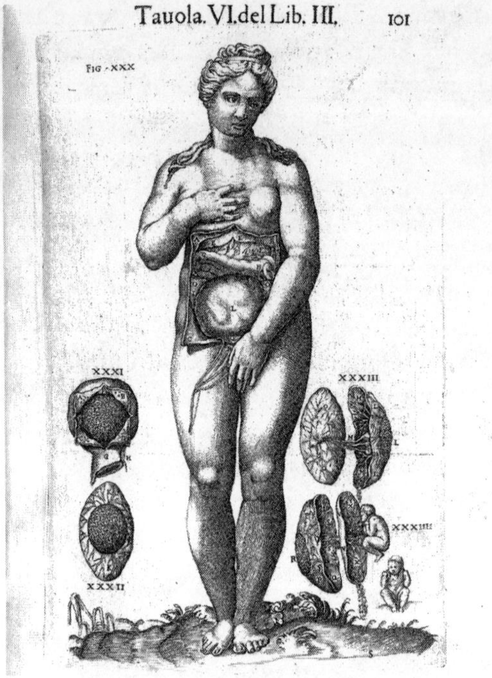

Figure 4.12. Female interiority unveiled, from Juan Valverde de Amusco's *Anatomia del Corporo Humano* (Rome, 1560), 101. A similar image appears in Helkiah Crooke's *Mikrokosmographia* (London, 1615), which draws on Valverde's work. By courtesy of the U.S. National Library of Medicine.

fragmented body, and dissociated body—these are the three primary dimensions of the schizophrenic body."[104] Unable to remain bounded by skin, the schizophrenic body all too easily opens its interior closet to become one with space, a condition not unlike Leland's "frenesy." Collapsing the border that divides subject from object, self from world, a schizophrenic loses the ability to sustain the logic of a Platonic, Ptolemaic system that abhors holes. Nowhere does this schizoid conflation of body with space appear more explicitly than in a 1598 Dutch engraving often called "Elizabeth as Europa" (figure 4.13).[105] In this personified map of Europe, a sword-waving queen defines the outlines of a continent, her Amazonian body forming a ground of inscription that also underwrites the coherence of Europe. Devolving into pure space below the waist, this ruined female body fulfills the dream logic of chora: having and being a porous womb that births, yet still contains a host of named topoi, of nation-states. In thus facializing space, albeit with a schizophrenic twist, this allegory of feminine power dissolves a linear imprinting into

Figure 4.13. Elizabeth as Europa (1598). Ashmolean Museum/The Art Archive at Art Resource, NY.

a diffuse interpenetration, a becoming-space of the body.[106] After all, the Greek Europa was herself a mythical princess transformed into a marker of place.

Yet as Jodi Mikalachki contends, political space in early modern England underwent a paradigm shift "from Mater Terra to the Artificial Man": the medieval ideology of a fertile and nurturing motherland, exploited to the fullest under Elizabeth, eventually lost ground when Hobbes's model of patriarchal sovereignty emerged in the mid-seventeenth century.[107] In contrast to the sacrificial woman whose maternal body unifies space, the title page to Thomas Hobbes's *Leviathan* (1651) portrays British statehood as an Artificial Man looming over the horizon, a singular masculine authority literally formed by his obediently aligned masculine subjects, their unseen faces turned like sunflowers toward his own (figure 4.14). Not only does this monarch frame

Figure 4.14. The Artificial Man: Title page of Thomas Hobbes's *Leviathan* (London, 1651). © Trustees of the British Museum.

himself with a sword and crosier—old boys' clubs that put a roof over his head, in every sense—but his body also stands erect *on* the earth. That is, where Elizabeth's nether regions fritter away into nations, Hobbes's Leviathan stamps the unmatched power of the state upon a prostrate land: *Non est potestas super terram quae comparetur ei,* proclaims the Latin motto above him (from Job 41:24, "There is no power on earth which can be compared to him"). While offering a coherent face to what Hobbes saw as a defaced, dispersed landscape after the Civil War, this sovereign figure also rises above the ground in a way that resembles a built structure, a true Artificial Man. Just as the steepled churches watch over rows of small, identical houses in the foreground, an idyllic scene that fulfills what chapter 2 showed as Johannes Ferrarius and Jean Bodin's vision of civic harmony, the masculine ruler stands like a tower that both guards his territory and is his territory. With each little man a stone that shores up this monument to power, this Vitruvian building turned perfect body, Hobbes sacrifices individual difference to render the skin of Britain a uniform facade, plugging the body-sieve of state with subjects who must stand in object-like, faceless solidarity. Yet as the

Leviathan gathers subjects into a collection of stony hearts, of defaced bodies, what happens to the "Matter, Forme, and Power of a Commonwealth" that Hobbes's subtitle claims to define? From Plato's *mater* to stony matter, from ideal to immanent form, the British *civitas* suffers a crisis of spatial gender that deforms the nation into an *epicoene* Britain/Britannia, a body whose interior essence cannot be mapped. As we shall see in chapter 5, however, the theater offers a transitional space of inscription that allows dreams of home to shimmer briefly, mapping—or miming—the ideal subject that Britain can wear inside its heart of heart.

Chapter Five

Making the Difference in Jonson's *Epicoene*

Stepping Awry

Something is rotten in the state of *epicoene.* Derived from the Latin *epicoenus,* which combines the Greek *epi* ("above, near, around") and *koinos* ("common"), the adjective *epicoene* originally described a gendered noun that could denote a referent of either sex. As Ben Jonson remarks in *The English Grammar* (1640), there is a gender known as "the *Promiscuous,* or *Epicene,* which understands both kinds: especially, when we cannot make the difference."[1] That is, the ambiguity of an *epicoene* noun arises mainly from the speaker's inability to determine gender, not from the actual bodily traits of the referent; for example, a speaker may describe a group of animals using a noun of one gender, even though the animals may belong to more than one gender, or to another gender altogether. Although such a distinction does not usually obtain in English, which has abandoned categories of grammatical gender, this otherwise archaic word blossomed in early seventeenth-century usage by expanding its semantic domain from the linguistic to the material, from describing words to describing things. Yet *epicoene* did not simply become more determinate when applied to physical bodies rather than abstract signifiers. On the contrary, this "promiscuous" term embraced an even broader range of non-normative gender conditions such as androgyny, hermaphroditism, and effeminacy.[2] Instead of fixing a noun's gender within an arbitrary linguistic paradigm, *epicoene* could now register a spectrum of gender logics including absence, excess, and crossing over. As a third genre that oscillates between double exclusion (*neither/nor*) and double participation (*both/and*), the uncertain states of *epicoene* inscribe a conceptual space in early modern England that literary theorists might call *queer.*

Yet if *epicoene* by definition thus hovers above, near, or around the common ground as something not quite seen, not quite seemly, then Jonson's comedy *Epicoene, or The Silent Woman* (1609) effects a kind of reversal by putting queerness front and center on the London stage.[3] Basing his drama upon the notion of deviance, Jonson constructs a queer architectonic that focuses on the marriage of a silent woman and a cranky old bachelor named Morose, who cannot tolerate any noise. After disowning his nephew Dauphine, Morose has searched arduously—but ardorlessly—for a spouse able to produce a new heir without making too much sound. Plotting a delicious revenge, Dauphine tricks his uncle into marrying a specially trained and disguised boy, a seemingly meek virgin who changes into a vociferous shrew right after the wedding vows. Morose's travesty of a marriage finally dissolves when the bride unveils her true gender, hence showing the nuptial contract to be founded on a mistake "*in primo gradu*" ("in the highest degree"; V.iv.209).[4] In this acerbic comedy that ends not in marriage, but rather one of the most festive and welcomed annulments in Jacobean drama,[5] gender categories themselves become nullified as bodies prove their performative basis *in primo gradu.*

As Edward Partridge points out, the play's gender confusion does not confine itself to the cross-dressed silent woman, since "nearly everyone in the play is epicene in some way."[6] Yet this epidemic of *epicoene* characters shows no diagnostic symptoms except for a generally perceived sense of deviance, indicating an imbalance more social than humoral. As Partridge himself concludes after surveying the Oxford English Dictionary's sample citations: "the main point about all seventeenth century uses of *epicene* is that they suggested the abnormal no man's land (and no woman's land, too) between the normal male and the normal female."[7] Like a revenant circling in perpetual limbo, this spatial metaphor of the "no man's land" appears yet again to mark a certain aporia, an unthinkable impasse in the binary system of gender. Facing a similar logical problem in the *Timaeus,* Plato bridges the lacuna between ideals and bodies by detouring into a third space, a third type (*genos*) that he names the chora. As we saw in chapter 4, the chora provides a feminine ground of inscription, a constantly sifting womb that engenders place. Beyond a mere coincidence of rhetoric, a chance meeting in the corridor while heading to the men's or ladies' room, the "no man's land" of *epicoene* forms both a third gender (*genos*) and a third space. While the previous two chapters focused on feminine subjects and spaces, often deformed into silenced and sexualized enclosures, this chapter examines the masculine subject who builds, speaks, and legislates, yet succumbs to utter humiliation as the *epicoene* outcast of a new social order.

As a mechanism for threshing out legible bodies, the queer space of *epicoene* becomes dominant in Jacobean London during a moment of transition when, from Jonson's viewpoint, every interior seems deviant and every center seems corrupted, performed. While *epicoene* occupies a transitional space in the mapping of gender, *Epicoene* inhabits a cityscape born queer: for the first time in his canon, Jonson explicitly marks "The Scene LONDON" at the outset.[8] Jonson's attempt to define the topography of gender thus coincides with a mapping of his hometown, London, whose social and spatial identity changed greatly over the playwright's lifetime. Between 1500 and 1700, London shifted from being an insular capital to being the leading European metropolis, gaining stature as an economic center fueled by global trade. As immigration from the provinces and abroad caused a massive population boom, early modern London underwent a version of the Great Rebuilding, expanding far outside its ancient defensive walls; inevitably, such a rapid increase in urban density and suburban growth tested the city's sense of coherence.[9] Rising from this remapping of the known world in England and overseas, a remapping that inevitably undermined the normative grid of *koinos, Epicoene* shows an anxiety over the precarious ground upon which the drama itself stands: namely, the London that no longer settles into a stable backdrop.

As the first English play to immerse itself entirely in the milieu of polite London society,[10] *Epicoene* charts the mores of gentry and would-be gentry who reside in the fast-developing, fashionable region between the court at Westminster and the City proper to the east. In this domestic comedy situated in the dubious, possibly diseased corpus of a Jacobean city, the interiors of homes and subjects become conflated as bodily spaces. Architecturally, *Epicoene*'s action moves steadily inward from scenes that occur within a handful of domestic interiors and around their thresholds, to scenes exclusively within Morose's house from III. ii onward. *Epicoene* further restricts its focus to several adjacent streets where characters easily walk to one another's homes, staging a narrative that perambulates around a specific neighborhood.[11] Despite alluding to a wide range of locales around London, despite a broad reference to "The Scene LONDON," *Epicoene* frames a *veduta* that offers an in-depth exploration of a very limited spatial field. If we recall Apian's scalar contrast between geography and chorography (figure 4.1), then Jonson isolates only a small portion of London's corpus in his attempt to represent an intimate, affective place with a history. From Apian's menu of bodily parts, we might choose an ear—given Morose's affliction—to signify Jonson's staging of chorography, his inscribing and alienating of spaces familiar to an audience of Londoners. Strolling through London streets from one household to the next, *Epicoene* takes an inward journey that always returns home to the theater.

Indeed, as Frances Teague observes, *Epicoene* makes a self-reflexive gesture toward the space where the comedy was initially performed: the indoor theater of Whitefriars, whose viewers would appreciate Jonson's numerous, pointed allusions to the surrounding area.[12] Likely established in the refectory of a Carmelite priory suppressed during the Reformation, the Whitefriars theater formed an enclosed playing space evocative more of domestic great halls than of sizable outdoor theaters like the Globe, where even Gertrude's closet appeared in daylight conditions with spectators crowded around a thrust stage.[13] In contrast, the candlelit indoor theaters that arose in the late sixteenth century—fittingly called "private houses"—filled a smaller auditorium with patrons who could afford higher ticket prices. As a monastic conversion into a "private house," the Whitefriars theater seems an ironic place to stage the townhouse of a confirmed bachelor who yearns to withdraw from the world, to enjoy an isolated silence mocked by everyone as unnatural; such a retiring person might have felt perfectly at home when the "private house" functioned as a priory. Although the building now houses a secular public, as Teague notes, the theater's unusually intimate dimensions would amplify the trumpets, drums, and loud voices introduced as a device to annoy Morose.[14] Thus aurally assaulted in close, if not cloistered quarters, audiences necessarily develop an empathy with the otherwise unlikeable misanthrope, sharing his abhorrence of noise simply because their home in the theater mimics his.

While Mary Bly usefully points out the touristic voyeurism of audiences who entered the liberty of Whitefriars merely to gawp at spectacles in the theater and prostitutes on the street, Jonson's Prologue blunts such geographic and social distinctions by welcoming all comers to his theatrical "feast," promising to satisfy his guests with delicacies "populare" but not "far fet" (Prologue 26, 6, 21).[15] Ever the genial host, Jonson furnishes an ample board for his customers on the boards of his stage, dishing out some tidbits suitable for aristocrats, "Some for your waiting wench, and citie-wires [merchant wives],/Some for your men, and daughters of *White-Friars*" (Prologue 23–24). Hailing a broad cross-section of society, Jonson develops an extended culinary analogy that reminds spectators of their playhouse's former usage as a refectory. The Prologue's framing device thus conjures a homely atmosphere while ingraining a sense of place, interpellating viewers who sit down to consume the comedy as locavores, themselves not "far fet," united for the time being as sons and daughters of Whitefriars. Despite this gesture toward effacing social difference to forge a common spatial identity, the Prologue's allusion to "your men, and daughters of *White-Friars*" instantly muddies gender, class, and place by invoking not only serving men and Whitefriars prostitutes ("your men" taken as a structural parallel to "your waiting wench"), but also the local pimps, johns, and catamites in the auditorium (the comma thus providing a comic beat that deceives the audience into construing "serving-men" before the speaker reveals the full descriptor, "your men of Whitefriars").[16] More subversively, this phrase succinctly describes the *epicoene* company of boy actors who now inhabit the Whitefriars theater, whose trade requires that they exploit the fraught space of the comma as not quite men, not quite daughters.[17]

As this boys' troupe prepares to stage an *epicoene* woman, a true daughter of Whitefriars, the Prologue's locution echoes in playgoers' minds as something of a rhetorical joke—but at whose expense? On the one hand, the punch line "daughters of *White-Friars*" winkingly implies that even the daintiest "ladies" seated in the audience may really be ladies of the night (Prologue 22), especially if we construe "men" broadly to include all male viewers—hence making "daughters of *White-Friars*" an umbrella rubric for all female viewers. But the phrase also confounds expectations that the Prologue will contrast two social classes with the same gender, thus mirroring the previous line's setting of "waiting wench" against "citie-wires." Rather than balance "men" (taken as "serving-men") against a second masculine group, Jonson inserts the Whitefriars "daughters" into a poetic context that forces the auditor to reverse gender assumptions, to perform the same type of about-face that attends the final unmasking of Epicoene. Those who laugh at the Prologue's joke thus necessarily laugh at and among themselves, unsettled by the ambivalent marking of bodies everywhere around them. No longer can social divisions be strictly maintained at the common table of theater; no longer can *epicoene* actors who cross gender and class boundaries be held apart from an *epicoene* audience, seated in a dimly lighted hall that resembles the interior of a private house, whose own differences cannot easily be made out.

Since the "Whitefriars Theatre, where *Epicoene* itself was playing, was part of the developing town" west of the City walls, the segregation of theatrical districts and *epicoene* activities in marginalized, walled-off liberties became increasingly difficult.[18] As indoor theaters like the Blackfriars and Whitefriars arose in pockets of space tucked inside a metropolis, the monastic cloisters that formerly provided a sacred inner sanctum now become places where gendered facades prove false to their interiors. Like vestigial organs awakened to new purpose, these indoor theaters challenge the identity of London from within; as the defensive walls of antiquity become more porous and irrelevant, as a globalized city turns its face outward, the corpus of London undergoes an involution that forces inhabitants to consider how difference can be constructed. Refolding the interface between sensible and intelligible, proper and performed, Jonson's play thus raises a crucial question: What marks the space of *epicoene,* and the scene of *Epicoene?* How do we make difference, and how do we make it out?

Choric and Choral Space

As a bricklayer's stepson who briefly took up the trade himself in the 1590s, Jonson often equates the craft of writing with the craft of building, the plotting of narrative with the plotting of architecture.[19] In Jonson's commonplace book, published as *Timber: Or, Discoveries Made Upon Men and Matter* (1641), we discover this musing on linguistic structure:

> The congruent, and harmonious fitting of parts in a sentence, hath almost the fastning, and force of knitting, and connexion as in stones well squar'd, which will rise strong a great way without mortar.[20]

Although Thomas Rymer snipes how "it is lamentable that *Ben. Johnson,* his Stone and his Tymber, however otherwise of value, must lye a miserable heap of ruins, for want of Architecture, or some Son of *Vitruvius,* to joyn them together,"[21] the fragmented nature of Jonson's *Timber* provides a felicitous model for conceiving theater as an *epicoene* space to be contested, a space valuable precisely for its unbuilt openness. To begin *Timber,* Jonson briefly explains in Latin his conceit that a commonplace book resembles a wood, or *sylva,* which provides the raw material of things and thoughts (*rerum et sententiarum*). Like a vibrant forest of "timber-trees" not yet felled for lumber, like a sylvan ecosystem diversified into multiple species (*multiplici materia et varietate in iis contenta*), the commonplace book stands not as a ruin defaced but rather a frame pre-faced, a pre-built landscape of unlimited potential. Jonson's word for this living timber—ὕλη (*hyle*)—recalls Aristotle's usage of this term to denote prime matter, that ineffable substance constituting all things; what the philosopher calls "wood" in the absence of a better word, the poet and playwright claims as the material for books, for miscellanies that the ancients called *sylva*. As Jonson begins to build from this timber, cutting and stacking cords to form a stage, a platform, the narratives imprinted on this *hyle* raise questions about the essential stuff that knits together "*Men and Matter,*" things and thought. What remains at home, at heart, despite any external alteration?

The early modern stage offers Jonson the chance to dissect the process of building a subject, pre-face and post-face. In plotting these interior spaces of psyche and home, Jonson utilizes not only the masonry skills inherited from his stepfather, but also the intellectual tools supplied by another father figure: William Camden, his beloved teacher at the Westminster School and the author of *Britannia.* If Jonson's practical training affords him insight into building very tangible spaces, then his education under Camden frames that experience within the liberal arts, perhaps even within emergent genres of mapping. As the previous chapter argued, Camden's *Britannia* attempts to discover a semiotic basis that unifies an empire in fragments, thus pushing a nascent sense of nationhood over the symbolic threshold. Camden awakens his fellow Britons to the historical and cultural meanings embedded beneath their feet; for Camden, only a child or dreamer would experience space as a semiotic virgin territory. Urging readers to construct a nation in their minds and, ultimately, with their hands, *Britannia* holds a mirror up to British subjects who must suture themselves together like the "harmonious fitting of parts in a sentence," like the bodies that pour into and produce the space of Hobbes's Leviathan.

In *Epicoene,* however, Jonson proves more skeptical about this desire for spatial and social coherence, probing satirically into the stuff (*hyle*) that comprises the immutable hearts of men and women. In the figure of Morose, Jonson creates a paternal icon of resistance to London's evolving identity, an urban hermit whose hatred of noise supplies a pretext for living in the most enclosed, artificial house. As Clerimont's page exclaims, "hee hath chosen a street to lie in, so narrow at both ends, that it will receiue no coaches, nor carts, nor any of these common noises" (I.i.167–69). Yet even this exclusive hideaway, secreted between turnstiles that restrict traffic, cannot prevent the "common noises" of London from coming inside the radius of Morose's hearing. On the one hand, Morose's aversion to noise has acquired such notoriety that pranksters outdo themselves to cause the most clamor outside his house. For example, Clerimont's page "entreated a Beare-ward [i.e., bear-baiter], one day, to come downe with the dogs of some four parishes that way" (I.i.173–74); another time, the same boy "practis'd on him, one night, like the Bell-man" until Morose scares him away with a sword (I.i.164). Yet what Morose considers most unbearable are the sounds that indicate a thriving community outside his domain, the sounds that Londoners hold in common. Thus, Morose objects to church bells that regularly interpellate a spiritual fold, calling disparate social groups into communion. A vicious cycle ensues when Morose responds to these auditory stresses with classic fight-or-flight actions that further erode social contact. Church bells prompt strategic retreats to the country on holiday eves and Saturdays; the Beare-ward has "his head made a most bleeding spectacle to the multitude" (I.i.176–77), while a marching fencer has his drum "most tragically run through" (I.i.178–79).

Yet since current outbreaks of plague keep Morose from fleeing London, as he had done "i' the Queenes time" (I.i.181), he decides upon a novel solution to preserve his delicate hearing: Morose assumes the function of an architect. In an early modern instance of disability planning that accounts for a "disease" widely mocked as "ridiculous" (I.i.148),[22] Morose noise-proofs his residence by "deuis[ing] a roome, with double walls, and treble seelings; the windores close shut, and calk'd: and there he lives by candlelight" (I.i.184–85). An old-fashioned *senex* to a fault, Morose seems to eschew the trend for glass windows by caulking his shutters closed, hiding in candlelight behind defensive "wind-doors" that deflect both sound and gaze.[23] Locked in this closet par excellence, lacking an architectural face that looks upon the world, Morose finally achieves a measure of security in a house that shows his phallic power of creation, a house that defines his contours as a subject. These reinforced borders remain constantly under attack, however, since every little sound that London creates threatens to penetrate Morose's kingdom of silence. Tellingly, in one of these moments of sonic intrusion, Morose performs his masculinity by threatening a noisemaker—a "wind-fucker" (I.iv.79)—with a "huge long naked sword in both his hands" (IV.iii.3).[24]

As Lorna Hutson rightly observes, the "metaphorics of the male body" concern above all "the definition of spaces of inaccessibility, of interpretative opacity, of nonpenetrability."[25] Thus, when Morose expects a visitor to his house, an intrusion that figures as "nearly a rape," his servant Mute embarks on fetishistic rituals to lessen the impact of this aural invasion.[26] Perhaps fearing an assault similar to Old Hamlet's poisoning through the porches of his ears, Morose confirms that Mute has "fastened on a thicke quilt, or flock-bed, on the out-side of the dore" (II.i.10–11), checked the "quilting of the staires" for adequate muffling

(II.i.27), and oiled every lock and hinge to prevent the tiniest squeak. Protecting his welfare by preparing his house, Morose treats built space as a bodily prosthesis, as an anti-hearing aid. In effect, Morose transforms his dwelling into a giant lubricated condom for social intercourse, shielding his architectural phallus by reinforcing the dangerous places of transition (doors, stairs, hinges).[27] Ironically, to smooth over the seams where a hermetic enclosure proves most fallible, Morose provides visitors with a house key to facilitate their noiseless entry, turning them into silent ghosts who enter his closet without leaving a trace. Clearly, opening this inner sanctum to outsiders worries Morose less than the disabling of their bodies; Morose takes every measure to forestall others from marking their presence, thus keeping a sonic tabula rasa for his own voice.

Such a fixation on insular purity carries over when Morose essays outside on business matters. To fortify himself against the aural shocks of London, Morose rebuilds his body as a walking closet that expresses the same will to power inscribed on his house. Indeed, Morose first appears in our mind's eye as a social misfit, an odd duck with odder plumage, when the gallant Truewit recalls seeing him around London wearing "a huge turbant of night-caps on his head, buckled over his eares" (I.i.144–45). Strikingly, Truewit describes Morose after a debate over the propriety of women who disguise and display their bodies through cosmetics, apparel, and other forms of artifice. While Clerimont deplores the "peec'd beautie" of a matron's "autumnall face" (I.i.85), Truewit counsels women to "practice any art" that cultivates their beauty, comparing female bodies to "a delicate garden" enclosed not for chastity but for periodic cosmetic repairs (I.i.105). Following on the (no doubt shapely) heels of this discussion, Morose registers as yet another feminine persona who fusses to extremes over his/her public appearance, a body-conscious misanthrope who dresses to most spectacular effect. Although Morose styles himself for isolation by crafting a "peec'd" ugliness, this calculated making of difference transforms him into a monstrous cynosure, a "prodigie" whose fantastical tower of nightcaps enjoys landmark status on the London scene (I.ii.3).

Yet beyond swaddling his ears in a quasi-architectural bulwark of silence, Morose also insulates himself socially by behaving as "a stiff peece of formalitie" (I.i.144), belying his pliable headgear with a wall of flinty-faced reserve. Just as quilted doors police the boundaries of Morose's home, this double layer of repulsion enfolds his rigid formality within a textile shell, a portable *vade mecum* that seals and conceals his vulnerable body to survive its ventures abroad. Ensconced in what

Figure 5.1. Frontispiece to William Lithgow's *The Totall Discourse* (London, 1632). By permission of the Folger Shakespeare Library.

Truewit characterizes as a makeshift turban, Morose adopts a peculiar costume that aligns this homebound misanthrope with a discourse of exotic travel. Such a discourse includes not only visibly marked foreigners in England but also locals who sojourn overseas, returning with anecdotes of cultures both alluring and daunting to most London audiences. For example, the Scottish adventurer William Lithgow, who in 1609 started trekking on foot across Islamic regions, portrays himself on the frontispiece to one of his travel narratives, *The Totall Discourse* (1632), wearing a "Turkish *suite*" complete with turban, cape, and walking staff (figure 5.1).[28] Rather than conquer the world with such a bold *passus geometricus,* however, Morose huddles behind a reinforced exterior to barricade himself against his own city's aural/anal penetrations, to quarantine himself against London's aural/anal plague. Desperate to transform himself into a walled enclosure, a masculine *hortus conclusus,* this *epicoene* "caricature of the centered self" succumbs to eccentric anxieties that alienate him from family, society, and even his own body.[29] As a monk in his mobile cell, a nut in his nutshell of privacy, the eminently unnatural Morose vibrates in discord with his surroundings, thus forming the perfect sonic counterpart to a silent woman. To dampen any harsh realities that emerge in the daytime, realities dismissed as mere noise, Morose swathes himself in multiple nightcaps to remain safely in his own "waking dreames" (IV.vii.42), using the stage of London to perform his difference to the hilt—or rather, to the turban.[30]

In plotting a counternarrative to urbanization through what Barbara Sebek wittily calls "turbanization," Morose maps out an alternative realm that engages critically with London's social, economic, and geographic changes.[31] Marked by a distinctly Anglicized turban that blends elements of home and away, domestic and foreign, Morose creates an oriental self-image that renders him inscrutably remote in public, but stiflingly autocratic in private. As we discover in Act II when Morose finally appears in person, a Turkish model of absolutism motivates his desire for complete silence:

> The *Turke,* in this diuine discipline, is admirable, exceeding all the potentates of the earth; still waited on by mutes; and all his commands so executed . . . an exquisite art! and I am heartily asham'd, and angrie often-times, that the Princes of *Christendome,* should suffer a *Barbarian,* to transcend 'hem in so high a point of felicitie. I will practise it, hereafter. (II.i.29–38)

Since Morose considers all discourses but his own "harsh, impertinent, and irksome" (II.i.4–5), he forces his servants to respond only through bodily signs such as bows or nods, reducing them to the status of prelinguistic infants so as to preserve his tenuous superiority. Morose's insistence on pure and hermetic spaces thus reveals itself as a power play, an assertion that the master's house must be built only for the master's voice, the master *logos.*[32] Yet in pledging allegiance to a "diuine discipline" opposed to Christendom, Morose reveals himself as already penetrated by "Barbarian" values, his orifices all too susceptible to what the common ground of early modern England—the *koinos*—counted as profane noise. Enthralled with the fluid movements of "an exquisite art," a rhetoric that recalls the discussion of women's false adornment, Morose inevitably feminizes himself as an oriental other whose politics can be dismissed as mere theater, as a frivolous dumb-show lacking substance.[33] His porosity to noise thus exposes an even deeper weakness in mind and body than initially thought. Aiming to "practise" the Turkish art of despotism just as Clerimont's boy "practis'd" a trick (I.i.164), Morose inhabits an *epicoene* space that seems both overly masculine for seizing boundless authority and overly feminine for being physical, vulnerable, private, and irrational.[34]

Morose thus embodies the paradox of an insider so closeted in his home that he becomes the ultimate outsider, a misanthrope so disengaged from common noises and the common scene that he assumes a status not fully British, not fully human. By "turning Turk" in relation to his environs, his chora, Morose elects to remain a stranger in his own city, as Camden would say, enjoying the dream of his oriental empire within the artificially bounded nation of his home, giving Britannia a dark twin in London's heart of heart. Extending his scope beyond a Prospero-like wielding of language over his dehumanized servants, Morose embarks on a series of political maneuvers to secure his exotic isle from aural siege, negotiating "diuers treaties with the Fish-wives, and Orenge-women; and articles propounded between them" (I.i.150–51), ensuring that the "Waights [musicians] of the citie haue a pension of him, not to come neere that ward" (I.i.162–63). As what Gail Kern Paster memorably terms "a city planner in reverse" and a "bad architect" akin to Milton's Satan, who thinks the mind is its own place, Morose drafts the laws of a self-made liberty where "common noises" do not apply, where his cloistered cell stands as a theater directed by a white Turk rather than a Whitefriar.[35] Wearing a turban of nightcaps as distinctive as a friar's cloak, Morose initiates a self-centered cult whose disciples adhere to a monastic silence within the reach of his voice, within his sphere of influence. Morose thus mocks the dream of a Vitruvian Man whose corporeal symmetry echoes a cosmic harmony; on the contrary, this diabolical empire builder possesses a body so out of sync with the spatial cadences around him that even caulking and padding cannot remedy the disjunction.

As a dystopian ruler whose servants cannot even curse like Caliban, as a backward planner whose noise ordinances involve bribing others to stay clear, Morose stands opposite the figure of Amphion, the miraculous city-builder from Greek mythology. A sovereign of ancient Thebes, Amphion played such enchanting lyre music that stones flocked to the sound; charmed, these stones formed into buildings founded on the same lyrical cadences. Amphion thus produced an instant community based on a melody with the power to move stones, a community whose perfect regularity can be attributed only to magic. In his rhetoric handbook *The Arte of English Poesie* (1589), George Puttenham recasts this urban pied-piper story for English readers by drawing a further parallel with language: "Amphion builded up cities, and reared walles with the stones that came in heapes to the sound of his harpe, figuring thereby the mollifying of hard and stonie hearts by his sweete and eloquent perswasion."[36] By equating the stones that construct tangible surfaces with the "stonie hearts" that structure human interiority, Puttenham implies that cities require not only a solid frame of architecture but also a frame of softened hearts fitted together, a social architectonic:[37] in some ways, Puttenham's vision resembles a utopian reading of Hobbes's Artificial Man, which unites subjects into a single body described by a sovereign's absolutist contours.[38] In this choral spatiality that assembles rather than a choric spatiality that disperses, every voice must submit to a scripted harmony, a shared rhetoric, to produce an immaculate urban birth without conflict or discord. These are the common noises that Morose abhors and avoids most in a Satanic attempt to create himself as a subject with unbowed knee; in both chronology and concept, then, Amphion precedes that more famous king of Thebes, Oedipus.

Jonson took an interest in Puttenham's fable of urban origin, as his personal copy of the handbook attests.[39] In the section on Amphion and Orpheus, Jonson has not only underlined this short passage but also drawn an asterisk and vertical line in the margin. While Jonson's *Timber* describes textual building in terms of architecture, Puttenham reverses and extends this analogy to envision an ideal urban space founded on concordant, balanced rhetoric. Just as well-crafted prose connects words without mortar, Amphionic stones construct perfect cities that adhere to the same musical template. In *Epicoene,* however, Jonson satirizes this choral harmony in Morose's overbearing voice and dissonance with others, parodying Amphion with the portrait of a bad architect who dampens the social pulse with quilting, a bad urban planner who blockades rather than eases the rhythm of traffic. Indeed, if the premise of *Epicoene* assumes that a silent woman constitutes an oxymoron, a social impossibility, then Morose's dictatorial man presents an equally absurd counterpart who ruins London's ambition to an inclusive Amphionic harmony, who quivers with such insecurity that he caulks himself into a closet with too much mortar. Sealed into this envelope of space addressed to and from himself, Morose withdraws from spatial and social circulation to shelter inside an artificial womb, rejecting both sexual creation as a childless bachelor and discursive creation as a silencing monologist. Exercising a phallic authority to construct a maternal chora, Morose reduces others to an infantile state to bestow upon himself the luxury of inhabiting a womb-like, wrapped-up home without noise.

Thus, Morose perversely decides to marry as a backlash against the progeny of others, retaliating against perceived abuses of production: the passing of his fortune to Dauphine, his sister's offspring, and the derogatory rumors about himself being circulated around London. Conflating these two instances of (de)generation, Morose accuses Dauphine and his friends of being "authors of all the ridiculous acts, and moniments are told of him" (I.ii.9), taking umbrage at the *epicoene* speech acts that subvert his master discourse.[40] When Morose threatens to punish this unauthorized circulation by awakening his own faculty of procreation, Truewit identifies the perfect counterattack in advising Dauphine to become "the author of more" (I.ii.11). Truewit envisions printing a false almanac that scrambles temporal order, hence drawing an unwitting Morose into London's most deafening event: the annual coronation day ordnance that, like church bells, sonically unites a community of subjects under a supreme architect, the British sovereign. Repelled by noise-based rituals of solidarity, whether these involve festive assembly or pernicious rumor, Morose attempts to deface the social contract by designing an alternative family. To castrate Dauphine financially and socially, Morose intends to rewrite the future, to reorder time, by producing a new successor to his anti-British empire. The conflict between Morose and Dauphine thus becomes a struggle over the power of authorship, specifically the power to inscribe someone's identity in society, to produce writing that combats other writing.

Ironically, Morose wishes to transgress the current social paradigm through marriage and children, a perfectly normative agenda except for a misanthrope. Although this marital venture requires admitting an outsider, Morose intends to mitigate any collateral damage by imprinting upon the choric receptacle of a silent woman, by cloning himself upon a passive space of inscription. In this oddly Platonic scheme, the desired woman serves merely as a transparent interface that enables a property exchange between father and junior, reduced to a muted womb that retains Morose's authorial imprint without agency. As the dumb secretary who performs a dumb-show of transcription in his closet, as the invisible mortar that holds together an imbalanced patriarchal edifice, this model wife makes possible a homospatial exchange that allows the eldest son to assume his father's place in the social matrix. With a peruke and some powder, however, Dauphine queers this patrilineal exchange of place by conjuring a silent woman who fulfills Morose's dream perfectly—too perfectly. If Morose's desire for a silent woman enforces traditional gender roles, Dauphine's prank questions whether such a feminine ideal exists outside a masculine script, outside of masculine fantasy.

Morose's agent has combed "all ouer *England,* to harken him out a dumbe woman" able to bear children (I.ii.24–25), yet the requisite specimen who "spends but sixe words a day" has actually been "lodg'd i' the next street to him" (I.ii.30; I.ii.28–29). Striking much too close to home in both space and gender, this uncanny woman challenges Morose's ability to transform others into dumb-shows for his pleasure. As James Mardock observes, "the obvious cultural context suggested by the disguised boy is theatrical cross-dressing. . . . Dauphine's scheme is thus based specifically on the practices of English theater."[41] Indeed, Dauphine learns the "exquisite art" of drama from his kinsman and fellow dramaturge, Morose. Just as Morose teaches his servant Mute to gesture silently, Dauphine spends months training Epicoene to nod and curtsy like a female Mute, to perform a feminized subordination; each master hopes to assert his masculine power through theater. Preempting Truewit's advice to be "the author of more" (I.ii.11), Dauphine has already been raising a boy at "great charges" (V.iv.206), creating a queer family that aspires to produce not children but child actors, fusing Morose's silent woman and expected son into the same malleable body. Just as the Greek artist Zeuxis wins a contest of skill when his rival Parrhasios attempts to unveil Zeuxis's painting, only to realize that the curtain itself is painted, Dauphine stakes his authorial reputation on Morose's inability to recognize the *order* of illusion embodied by Epicoene. Not merely a shrew disguised as a silent woman, Epicoene suggests that gender itself comprises nothing more than a coached performance, a painted curtain without interior content, a facade that replaces any need for a *there* there.

In this "fashioning of Epicoene," Adam Zucker notes, "a seemingly abstract form of knowledge is made (in)to matter as out of the obscure grammatical term 'epicoene.'"[42] While the "grosser" female body usually figures materiality (Aristotle's *hyle*), Dauphine exposes the matter of femininity as an ephemeral imprint shared between men on a specifically masculine ground. As theater precipitates gender as binary difference, bundling any remainder under the rubric *epicoene,* femininity merely provides a facade that concludes the default masculine body and preserves the lineaments of patriarchy. Such an architectonic of gender underlies the Prologue's allusion to "men, and daughters of *White-Friars*" (24), which implies that women must always perform as offspring created by men, as daughters who are deprived of matter and *mater,* as second-order men. After all, women cannot *have* matter because they *are* matter. Jonson shrewdly mines this stereotype of women to prank those audience members who, like Morose, accept Epicoene at face value as either a silent or shrill woman, never querying her miming of femininity itself. Yet anyone familiar with early modern staging has always known that Epicoene held a boy actor within, though this awareness must usually be suppressed for theatrical illusion to succeed. With the "unfair" trick that Epicoene proves to be exactly what viewers have known all along, Jonson overturns assumptions of what counts as gender in a particular social context, forcing viewers to reassess their eagerness to suspend a cognitive dissonance, to suture over the cracks of a "peec'd beauty" when seated in a theater, a liberty, a place of exception.[43] Such a logic of self-deception cannot hold when all the world's a stage, when every body may be *epicoene*.

To expose the notion that women derive from Adam's rib as Dauphine's fib—and the playwright's own—Jonson creates a satirical realm where the false notes of theater queer even the innermost spaces of bodies and homes. As Dauphine moves toward a climactic showdown with his uncle, mounting an elaborate set piece that culminates in Epicoene's unveiling, what should register as an astounding revelation of artifice comes across as merely the latest theatrical gesture. Shattering the dream of an Amphionic harmony, Jonson affirms Morose's fear of a chaotic, discordant cosmos where anything goes. Indeed, once Epicoene arrives in Morose's house, married in a suitably quiet ceremony, the domestic order so carefully maintained by a potentate dissolves into utter cacophony. Like a Pandora's box opened, Morose's closet becomes a great hall as hordes of uninvited guests—neighbors—descend upon his house to furnish and enjoy a wedding banquet, to initiate him into an unwanted, local sociality.[44] Thus realizing the feast promised to the Whitefriars audience by the Prologue, this banquet transforms a cloistered residence into the common space of a refectory and theater as Morose soon finds drama served to him, willing or not. In the most explicit signal that Morose's house has become a playhouse, Truewit takes charge of this domestic space to mount a "*tragi-comœdy*" intended to humiliate two gulls, John Daw and Amorous La-Foole (IV.v.31).

Echoing Dauphine's plan to deceive his uncle through theater, Truewit gives the boastful Daw and La-Foole their just deserts by exposing their "effeminate" cowardice, while casting Dauphine as the heroic avenger. After convincing Daw, then La-Foole, that the other man wishes to cause him bodily harm, Truewit directs the two victims into separate "studies" (IV.v.30), located behind doors on either side of the Whitefriars stage; meanwhile, Clerimont and Dauphine watch from the central discovery space as "the *chorus* behind the arras" (IV.v.33–34). While viewers formerly had to suspend their disbelief to accept the stage as Morose's home, Truewit remaps this cognitive illusion to turn Morose's home back into a stage, marked explicitly with a chorus inside a discovery space.[45] Just as Epicoene must ultimately be seen as a fictional boy actor who has been playing a fictional woman who has been played by an actual boy actor, Jonson challenges the Whitefriars audience to perceive a fictional stage projected upon a fictional character's house projected upon an actual Whitefriars stage. But how do we see the fictional boy actor not as the actual boy actor? How do we see the fictional stage not as the actual stage? Like the *epicoene* body of Epicoene, the *epicoene* body of space created in this scene oscillates in our mind's eye between different architectural types, forming a choric "no man's land" that intercedes between an otherwise direct cloning, or a crystalline reflection. Just as an *epicoene* body materializes as both masculine and feminine, but also neither masculine nor feminine, an *epicoene* space can appear as both home and stage, but also neither home nor stage.

Likewise, Daw and La-Foole's retreat to their studies recalls Morose's escape to a specially enclosed room to avoid a violent aural penetration, a fearful response that itself emasculates. After Epicoene disdains performing a "coacted, vnnatural dumbness" after the wedding (III.iv.54), Morose decides to create even more distance from the ensuing ruckus by hiding in his attic, as Dauphine explains:

> Hee has got on his whole nest of night-caps, and lock'd himselfe vp, i' the top o' the house, as high, as euer he can climbe from the noise. I peep'd in at a crany, and saw him sitting ouer a crosse-beame o' the roofe, like him o' the sadlers horse in *Fleetstreet,* vp-right. (IV.i.21–25)

Not quite a knight riding off into the sunset with his damsel, less an Amadis de Gaule than Don Quixote (IV.i.56–57), batty old Morose roosts within his "nest of night-caps" while mounted on a crossbeam to nowhere, his architecture failing to deliver him from a shrew. Just as Truewit had previously compared women to the painted statues of Love and Charity flanking Aldgate (I.i.122–25), Dauphine frames this image of Morose in terms of a model horse and rider posted outside a saddlery, taming a suspect Turkishness into a well-known shop sign found on bustling Fleet Street, just a few blocks from the Whitefriars theater. Thus reduced to a wooden pantomime of humanity not unlike the ideal woman, who should remain "as silent as Signes" (IV.iv.173), Morose appears in the public's mind not as an exotic contaminant but rather a muted symbol of commodity, his heretical empire against common noises absorbed into the chatter of London's consumerism.

Demoted from a potentate of radical alterity to just another husband who has "sold [his] liberty to a distaffe" (III.iv.57–58), Morose gradually surrenders his identity to a process of domestication and disintegration, assuming the "coacted, vnnatural dumbness" that Epicoene disavows (III.iv.54). Yet before Morose's subjective fragments can be reunited and resignified by Dauphine in Act V, before this outcast undergoes a social rebirth, Jonson refracts the story of Morose through the subplot with Daw and La-Foole, similarly trapped in their respective closets. As Truewit produces this tragicomic play-within-a-play, viewers witness an alternative outcome to Morose's own narrative, not least because the talkative Jack Daw and the absurd romantic Amorous La-Foole embody different aspects of dictatorial, henpecked Morose. Just as Morose yearns to "redeem [his marriage] with the loss of an eye . . . a hand, or any other member" (IV.iv.8–9), Daw and La-Foole eagerly offer to sacrifice body parts to assuage the other's putative anger; Daw would even chop off his left arm rather than bear arms in an honorable duel. After Truewit negotiates with both victims to ascertain what punishment they would endure, Dauphine arrives as a masked, silent avenger who metes out the contracted penalty: "There's a carpet i' the next roome, put it on, with this scarfe ouer thy face, and a cushion o' thy head" (IV.v.256–57). Dauphine thus seizes upon Morose's furnishings to parody his uncle's pseudo-oriental garb, putting on a cushion like a turban and wrapping a possibly Turkish carpet around his shoulders. As he proceeds to give Daw a round of kicks and La-Foole a series of nose tweaks, Dauphine displaces his anger toward Morose onto two hapless substitutes, while dressed in a costume that mocks his uncle's pretensions. Yet echoing Morose's devolution from Turkish ruler to saddler's model, this disguise no longer carries an explicitly foreign charge; instead, Dauphine shows viewers how such an illusion of otherness can be improvised from common household materials, demystifying how architectural fragments construct a facade of difference. Like the theatrical "cates" promised to the Whitefriars audience, Dauphine's sartorial bricolage exposes Morose's exoticism as a commodity, as purchased goods and labor that may not be "far fet," but simply "deare-bought" for public consumption (Prologue 20, 21).

In the splintering of Morose into aspects of Dauphine, Daw, and La-Foole, Jonson suggests that simple techniques of staging can refold the borders of a subject, enacting interior design in every sense. As Morose discovers with horror, the most intimate spaces of home prove to be nothing more than a theater of contingent roles, a provisional site where material forces shape marriage and mutability, voice and power. Thus, Truewit points out that Morose's dream of finding a mute wife has been rendered moot by the theatrical nature of Jacobean culture, especially the pervasiveness of spectacle that perverts women into promiscuous, *epicoene* creatures:

> Alas,
> sir, doe you euer thinke to find a chaste wife, in these times? now?
> when there are so many masques, plaies, puritane preachings,

> mad-folkes, and other strange sights to be seene daily, priuate and publique? (II.ii.32–36)

In these fallen days of "strange sights," presumably including "mad-folkes" like Morose himself, theater permeates both interior and exterior spaces, queering public and private spaces alike—queering the division between any of these spaces. By dulling a person's ability to recognize gender norms, to delineate where ego separates from alter ego, these *epicoene* spaces negate the concept of identity as a chaste enclosure imprinted by a single patriarchal figure. In Jacobean London, a repeated dalliance with theater has defiled the purity of female spectators, penetrated through the eyes and ears, while a chaste wife exists merely as a character in a comedy, a "strange sight" known from dreams of bygone days. Only during this utopian Golden Age, Truewit suggests, were gender roles a matter of intrinsic propriety rather than alienable property, interior fixity rather than external platforms reworked at will, with licentious abandon.

In a society where people *have* rather than *are* a certain gender, however, Morose enters a doubly queer marriage that involves two impossible wives: a silent woman and a male bride, both parodies of women scripted by Dauphine. By playing on Morose's perverse desire for an orientally submissive woman who speaks no evil, sees no theater, and hears no voice but his own, Dauphine crafts a silent, bespoke spouse to enact a homosocial exchange that Morose thinks is marriage, but that his nephew knows to be theater. By soliciting a boy rather than a girl to piece together the perfect woman, Dauphine reveals the *epicoene* impact of living in Jacobean London, and hence Jacobean theater; immersed in an acting tradition that assumes a male default body, Dauphine never doubts the premise that theater should be written by men and for men. In David Henry Hwang's play *M. Butterfly,* a cross-dressed opera singer—given the Jonsonian name of Song—provides the rationale that "only a man knows how a woman is supposed to act."[46] As a male performer who exploits precisely this slippage between knowing and being a woman, Song dismisses women themselves as automata inhabiting a dream state without any self-recognition, as choric voids unaware of the master script driving their actions. Within such a patriarchal system of thought, men alone possess the knowledge and power to construct a female simulacrum that behaves as women should, thus staging the other as a seductive fantasy of the same. Extending this logic, Dauphine succeeds in creating the perfect woman by miming the desires of men, by producing a feminine copy without an original. Showing an impressive capacity to play matchmaker with theater, always flirting with performance, Dauphine proves himself his uncle's true heir and alter ego.

While Morose dispatches an agent to search far and wide for a compatible silent woman, to discover his Virginia, Dauphine knows that such exotic merchandise cannot be procured from travel to distant lands, but rather from domestic manufacture by canny sellers of dreams. Turning away from a pilgrimage that extends outward in search of a mystical goal, Dauphine surveys his uncle's psychic landscape to build the perfect woman as negative space, filling Morose's every lack—hence, the aptness of a woman lodged in the next street over, whose space forms the inverse of Morose's. Engaged in a species of theatrical chorography, Dauphine translates Morose's local topography of desire into an embodied performance. In contrast, Jonson relegates scientific cartography to the dilettante blundering of Daw, who carries sketching equipment everywhere to "draw maps of euery place, and person" (V.i.20–21). His name already marking him as only half the man of Dauphine, Daw relies on "his squire [square], his compasses, his brasse pens, and black-lead" to measure the world's contours (V.i.19–20), especially those "of his mistris, mistris Epicoene (V.i.25). Yet as Daw soon realizes, his surface mapping of Epicoene cannot possibly capture her interiority, his instruments failing to calculate the subtle vectors of gender and identity. Despite affirming before witnesses that both he and La-Foole "haue knowne [Morose's] bride" (V.iv.112), Daw has evidently not "found out her latitude," sexually or otherwise (V.i.26). For this failure to master a feminized space, for making vows that mistake gender *in primo gradu,* Daw and La-Foole share Morose's destiny of a social castration, deprived of their manhood for their inability to penetrate the intricacies of staging gender.

For both places and persons, the growth of an *epicoene* culture renders futile a mapping that regards the visible surface as related to interior truth, as an index to corporeal soundness. Where once the facade merely traced the outline of interior space, misgivings about these structural relations now throw the social architectonic into doubt. The upsurge of bad architects who aspire to construct their own cosmos, their own bodies, means a collective loss of faith in an Amphionic community ruled by similarity, by stone-like authenticity. As Michel Foucault remarks of baroque culture in the early seventeenth century: "The age of resemblance is drawing to a close. It is leaving behind it nothing but games."[47] As the chora shakes bodies out with a roll of dice, identities must be regarded as ongoing construction projects, as facades that stand in for an absent interior, as painted curtains that celebrate artifice as artifice, as theater without reality. Coherence emerges only when viewers surrender to an illusory picture that proffers a dream of endless depth, accepting the limited window of perspectival vision as equivalent to a cosmic eye:

> We, as subjects that see, cannot unlike God, separate ourselves completely from the diverse, actual world. This is because the self that gazes upon an object is itself a diverse, opaque presence full of distorting noise. The transparent cone that has been isolated from the infinitely pleated, diverse world is enveloped by the opacity of the self which gazes from the vortex and the opacity of that part of the world that the cone has ignored. One might almost say that transparency is a chance product born of these opaque pleats.[48]

Within this enclosed optical cone that provides an illusion of distortion-free transparency, the monad enjoys an Amphionic harmony in which orthogonal lines converge to a single point. Just as the Vitruvian man subtends a circle and square with his body, the ideal eye (or ear) inscribes a perfect cone that ignores both the common noises of society and the private noises of an always imperfect, opaque, lacking body. Despite the truism that Renaissance architecture takes musical proportions as its highest ordering principle—as shown by Palladio's fugal structure or Alberti's harmonic ratios[49]—these Amphionic structures actually function as artificial closets that exclude an opaque world of common noises. Morose's crazy house of silence, then, reflects a darker critique of musical building by making audible the ringing hollowness behind an ever-smiling facade, the desperate padding and caulking needed to maintain a harmonic surface. Even though the subject who enters such a closet leaves behind common noises to meditate, to enjoy a secure home, the distortions inherent in both the world and the psyche inevitably threaten to shatter this concordant, isolated realm.

Cuckoo for the City

> Because "*I*" am not I, I *am* not, I am not *one*.
>
> —Luce Irigaray[50]

Recent studies of *Epicoene* have linked the early modern city to how Jonson depicts the status of women. In particular, critics point to the "Collegiate women" who establish homes away from their husbands, enabling them to consume material goods and sexualized male bodies with equal voracity.[51] Karen Newman observes that Jonson directs such mocking and misogynist laughter against these subversive models of femininity since "the talking woman represents the city *and* what in large part motivated the growth of the city—mercantilism and colonial expansion."[52] When Morose decides to open his empire to acquire a silent woman, he inevitably admits this city whose artificial constructions speak in discordant tones, a tower of Babel built upon injurious feminine noises and thus distinctly not well squared. Since Morose in some respects marries the city of London, the wife admitted will always already prove herself a shrew. This parallel between woman and city emerges most clearly when Truewit tries to dissuade Morose from marriage by comparing such a strategy to various forms of suicide:

> Marry, your friends do wonder, sir, the Thames being so near, wherein you may drown so handsomely; or London Bridge, at a low fall . . . or, such a delicate steeple in the town, as Bow, to vault from; or from a braver height, as Paul's. (II.ii.20–25)

As Leo Salingar notes, Truewit adopts the "tone of a tourists' guide to the sights of London," choosing spectacular modes of suicide that "confer the greatest *eclat.*"[53] Not only does Truewit compare Morose's marriage to a performance of death on the London scaffold, a public staging of his literal downfall from major architectural landmarks, but this equating of woman and city turns London into a femme fatale whose features lure Morose from his hermetic cell, a gendered body whose siren call means death on the stones of an un-Amphionic city. Instead of diving into the mysteries of proportion, then, Morose the bad architect and worse husband finds himself diving off facades that appear beautifully harmonious, but prove to be rotten to the core; whether coronation ordnance, church bells, or parish steeples, the urban infrastructure perpetually attempts to trick Morose into joining a lethally mind-numbing community, a Circean matrix that leads to endless waking dreams, a castrating city that charms in superficially dulcet tones.

By thus conflating anxieties about the changing nature of London with the changing nature of women, in particular the new roles available to women in this urban economy, the *mater terra* of olden days becomes an artificial woman who boasts a treacherous "peec'd beauty." Perhaps the most striking figure of this unnatural talking woman emerges in Jonson's caricature of Mrs. Otter, a wealthy china merchant who benefits directly from global trade. An upwardly mobile denizen of London—not unlike those seated in the Whitefriars audience—Mrs. Otter dominates and maintains her husband while enjoying a visible presence in the public sphere. Indeed, Mrs. Otter's body displays her status as a self-made woman, as her not-nearly-silent-enough husband observes:

> All her teeth were made i'the Blackfriars, both her eyebrows i'the Strand, and her hair in Silver Street. Every part o'the town owns a piece of her. . . . She takes herself asunder still when she goes to bed, into some twenty boxes, and about next day noon is put together again, like a great German clock: and so comes forth, and rings a tedious larum to the whole house, and then is quiet again for an hour, but for her quarters. (IV.ii.82–89)

Like a surgeon, Mrs. Otter constructs her anatomy by reaching inside the urban corpus to extract the desired consumer goods, thus mapping her body parts onto local shopping areas (figure 4.12). For Mrs. Otter and her cohort, Daw's agenda to "draw maps of euery place, and person" seems perfectly rational (V.i.20–21). While Amphion makes stones assemble with music, Mrs. Otter exerts the force of global cash flow to collate pieces of her body, to design a facade that passes muster under public scrutiny. As Otter's blazon indicates, this artificial woman can exhibit her insider knowledge of London by making a spectacle of herself, by inscribing the city's trade secrets upon her public body.

Standing at the confluence of London's commerce and technology (figure 5.2), Mrs. Otter opens her closet to reveal a cyborg woman, a woman who knows how a woman should be and buys the needed parts. Yet as Otter's description suggests, this damsel locked in a clock tower may be no damsel at all, for if she can "take herself asunder into some twenty boxes," then what remains? What horrific body lurks behind the architectural casing that encloses her secrets, the painted curtain that may conceal nothing but its own illusion? While Epicoene eventually discards her facade to reveal a default male, Mrs. Otter seems to break down into nothing at all once her parts have been neatly stowed away in twenty boxes, twenty wombs from which she is reborn daily, "put together again" by unseen, un-Amphionic forces. Speaking in a clockwork voice that emanates from her inner workings, rather than a womb, Mrs. Otter replaces Amphion's mythic harmony with a steady rhythmic alarm that regulates domestic order. Like the bellman's cries and church ringing that so annoy Morose, Mrs. Otter's clockwork language appeals to a like-minded circle of London gentry and gentrifying merchants—like those in the Whitefriars theater. Indeed, as a talking woman, she

Figure 5.2. The Artificial Woman: Martin Engelbrecht, *L'Horlogère* (c. 1735). Bibliothèque des Arts Décoratifs, Paris. Archives Charmet/Bridgeman Art Library.

belongs in *epicoene* spaces like Whitefriars between traditional centers of City and court.

Extending Morose's reliance on architecture as prosthetic, Mrs. Otter constructs a half-furniture, half-machine carapace that seems to cannibalize her very interiority. If Morose appears to Truewit as "a stiff peece of formalitie," then Mrs. Otter's clockwork body stands as the stiffest piece in London: all form and no content, being a phallus and having it too. Not only does Mrs. Otter eclipse her husband's power, but she also owns the body that she inhabits and animates. Indeed, this female Vitruvius builds a commodified facade that signifies to an early capitalist public, displaying a manufactured identity as legible as a clock face, as audible as a watchman crying the hours. Mrs. Otter thus rejects Morose's candlelit domesticity to thrive in the bustle of daytime commerce, declaring that she would do "any thing but . . . dreame o' the city" (III.ii.66). According to Mrs. Otter, these nighttime dreams presage the imminent damage of her clothing or other goods, thus dashing the social-climbing hopes of her daytime persona.[54]

Like Morose, however, she seems unable to leave the city that so afflicts her:

> CLERIMONT: I would not dwell in the citie, and 'twere so fatall to mee.
>
> MRS. OTTER: Yes sir, but I doe take advise of my doctor, to dreame of it as little, as I can. (III.ii.79–82)

Just as Morose's aversion to noise implicitly derives from an imbalance in humors, Mrs. Otter's dreams are seen as a medical ailment rather than a symptom of urban disorder. Although Truewit earlier deplored London's ability to corrupt, those who take measures to block the noises and dreams of such toxic environs are mocked as *epicoene,* branded as "Turkish" (Morose) and "German" (Mrs. Otter), even dehumanized and denatured. Seeping into interior spaces through every nook and cranny, every bodily orifice, "fatall" London clasps its victims in a thrilling, killing thrall during their moments of greatest weakness. After all, despite taking advice to control her dream activity, Mrs. Otter must submit to proleptic nightmares that subvert her clockwork temporality and consumerist achievement. Ceding both economic and metronomic control, yielding the conscious power of inscription, Mrs. Otter finds her interior space penetrated by ghostly portents that, *Hamlet*-like, reveal to her London's horrors. At the same time, this dream-rape underscores her own mechanical infertility, her inability to produce anything more than spoken time; even her own body must be produced by others from twenty womb-like boxes. In the darkest hours of the night—finally defaced, disassembled, and phallically dispossessed—Mrs. Otter reduces to her primordial stuff as a choric void for urban dreams.

Mrs. Otter's evacuated maternity, perhaps linked to her desire for a dreamless futurity, challenges the humanist model of femininity posited in William Austin's *Haec Homo,* a proto-feminist treatise that engages with England's *querelle des femmes.* Published in 1637 but likely written around 1620, *Haec Homo* responds to the gender issues raised by two pamphlets from that earlier year, *Hic Mulier* (*The Mannish Woman*) and *Haec Vir* (*The Womanish Man*). Following the authors of these satirical texts, Austin devises an *epicoene* title in Latin that conjoins a definite article of one gender with a noun of another: the feminine article *haec* (the) modifies the masculine noun *homo* (man). Yet while *Hic Mulier* and *Haec Vir* focus on how apparel defines gender roles, *Haec Homo* makes the deeper claim that men and women share "*one figure;* made by *one workman*" as well as "the same reasonable soule."[55] Given this common humanity, Austin proposes the usage of *homo* as a category that indexes both genders. To impress upon readers how the same proportions "are expressible in the *body of Woman* and *man, equally,*"[56] Austin includes

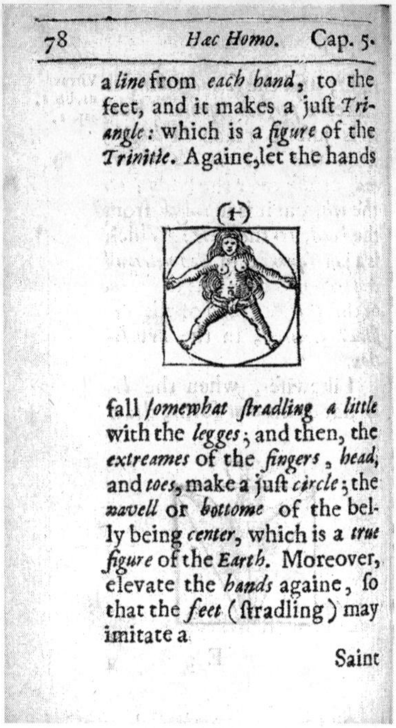

78 *Hæc Homo.* Cap. 5.

a *line* from *each hand*, to the feet, and it makes a juſt *Triangle:* which is a *figure* of the *Trinitie.* Againe, let the hands

fall *ſomewhat ſtradling a little* with the *legges*; and then, the *extreames* of the *fingers*, *head*, and *toes*, make a juſt *circle*; the *navell* or *bottome* of the belly being *center*, which is a *true figure* of the *Earth.* Moreover, elevate the *hands* againe, ſo that the *feet* (ſtradling) may imitate a

Saint

Figure 5.3. Vitruvian woman, from William Austin's *Haec Homo* (London, 1637), 78. By permission of the Folger Shakespeare Library.

four small woodcuts that measure a woman's body against various geometric shapes, thus proving the intrinsic harmony of her framing. Indeed, the divine workman has designed a woman's bodily contours to subtend a circle and square, much like the Vitruvian man's (figure 5.3). Despite this figural parity between the sexes, differences emerge internally since the "*faire . . . aedifice*" of every female "must containe *another house* within her, with an *unruly* ghest, and all *provision* necessarie for him."[57] Forced into a double-pile formation by the sheer prospect of pregnancy, a woman's interiority subdivides into multiple layers of rooms to accommodate a "ghest," both a temporary guest soon to leave her womb and a ghost that always haunts the feminine body as its structuring center.

Ruled by this unruly homunculus, the female receptacle must harbor a miniature "him" of indeterminate gender, the pronoun *him* signaling a neutral usage held over from Old English; that is, following Jonson's definition in *The English Grammar,* Austin employs an *epicoene* pronoun because he cannot make the difference of an unseen fetus.[58] By splitting the feminine subject to enfold an *I* for an *I,* an *I* within an *I,* the womb provides a *homo* space that suspends distinctions between masculine and feminine, self and other, both/and and neither/nor. Yet beyond affirming Irigaray's claim that a woman can never be simply one, Austin's female edifice holds open a choric third space for a third genre (*genos*) not yet a twinkle in the parent's *I* (or eye), an *epicoene* gender not yet forced into a binary. As a choric space both inside a woman and yet apart from her as the house of another, the womb provides a transitional space that attempts to domesticate the exotic, the *epicoene,* while gestating the very concept of gender. Such is the architecture of femininity. Even within a *homo* framework that equalizes gender by mandating a single body and soul, a single monadic viewpoint, women figure differently from men as a site of doubled interiority, as a duplicitous housing that envelops and buffers a faceless subject within an otherwise empty center of potentiality. Formally hardwired to furnish a circuit of private rooms through which an inchoate subject must pass and define itself against, the female edifice displays qualities that, in chapter 2, we associated with spaces that are structured as writing rather than as verbal enunciation. Acting reflexively as the housing for a house, the female body provides not merely a ground for inscription but rather a model for writing as a form of interior spacing, as the primal scene of an *epicoene* pregnancy.

While Epicoene follows a homosocial script to birth the default masculine body hiding within, Mrs. Otter challenges a uterine paradigm of reproduction by converting her interior space into a womb that produces time as *chronos,* churning out a linear progression of points.[59] As a piece of clockwork housing who transforms her house into a giant clock calibrated by her alarms, constructing a domain resonant with the overtones of her voice, the cuckoo Mrs. Otter exchanges the traditionally limited space allotted a chaste wife for the forward propulsion of modernity, occupying an *epicoene* position between spatial simultaneity and temporal continuity, metonymy and metaphor, being and becoming. Never quite fully built and always coming undone, Mrs. Otter embodies that interval between when "the silent woman" constitutes the norm and when the phrase becomes nostalgically ironic, an oxymoron. Mrs. Otter thus stands in this *epicoene* culture as the beacon of a hollowed-out subjectivity, her mechanical heart softened only by the rhetoric of commerce, her call to community a spiritually empty marker of time. Nonetheless, Mrs. Otter's artificial femininity escapes the punishment meted out to Morose, the artificially masculine pretender to an alternative sociality demonized as barbaric. Castigated for his misanthropic indulgence in an impossible dream logic, in the fantasy of a choric reproduction with no material consequences, no inscriptional trace, Morose undergoes a sham divorce proceeding that socially castrates him, forcing him to publicly admit impotence as grounds for voiding his marriage: "I am no man" (V.iv.44).

As Morose finds his dream world annulled by the voices of others,[60] as his carefully enclosed home becomes a stage for the taming of a male shrew, his torturous divorce evokes Shylock's forced conversion to Christianity in the trial scene of Shakespeare's *Merchant of Venice*. Dislodged from his self-image as oriental potentate to inhabit the communally designated role of eunuch, Morose experiences a social downfall comparable to the modes of suicide proposed by Truewit, cut down to size by an intrusive, insatiable London community seeking its own pound of flesh. As this marauding mob takes up Morose's earlier offer to cut off his own "member" (IV.iv.9), at least metaphorically, the hapless misanthrope finds himself transformed from paternal imprint to passive conduit, providing merely a choric space of inscription for his nephew's *epicoene* plot of succession. As Judith Butler notes of the chora, Plato employs the term *eilephen* to indicate what the chora must not perform as a vehicle of pure receptivity; while most translators render *eilephen* as "to assume a form," Butler points out that the verb can also mean "to take or have a wife" or "of a woman to conceive."[61] Barred from either taking a wife or conceiving, Morose suddenly becomes aware of his own queer subject position in the interstices of gender, his own unresolved haunting of the transitional passage between masculinity and femininity. Yet rather than rush to manifest his masculine authority as before, menacing away usurpers with a "huge long naked sword in both his hands" (IV.iii.3), a deflated Morose proclaims his willingness to "seale . . . to a blanke" contract with Dauphine in exchange for divorcing Epicoene (V.iv.190–91); eventually, Morose agrees to bequeath everything to his nephew. By making himself an unconditional "blanke" ground for Dauphine to dictate the terms of their future relationship, Morose relinquishes control of his identity to become a formless receptacle, yielding his architectural and economic phallus to "seale" a new monogamy with his nephew.

Unable to articulate his own subjective framework, to *conceive* himself, this would-be Turk wordlessly leaves the stage upon Dauphine's command, banished from society as another Mute, recast as the silent woman in an *epicoene* partnership. Exiting through one of the side doors that once connected—memorably—to those private studies where Daw and La-Foole found their inner mettle tested, the socially tweaked and kicked Morose "may goe in and rest" undisturbed until his death, as Dauphine cruelly remarks, "which I care not how soone it come" (V.iv.215, 217). Morose's retreat to a more private room demands that he "goe in" to a house by going offstage, thus entering an unseen space marked for "no man," a perfect nonplace behind the *frons scenae* for a defaced "blanke." Enabled by the feminine nested structure of a house now thoroughly divested of its phallic power, Morose withdraws to a womb-like interiority to recuperate his dismembered self, potentially to write himself back into being. Will Morose successfully resurrect himself just as Mrs. Otter collects herself from fragments scattered among twenty boxes, or will this fine and private space truly prove to be his grave? Suspended as a silent cipher just beyond the common ground of *koinos*, an *epicoene* subject of indeterminate gender and form, Morose raises uneasy questions about how such a malcontent dissenter, an icon of times past and cultures far away, can be reintegrated into the commonwealth of common noises. If Morose can unman himself with a simple phrase, undone by that very voice in which he so delighted, then might he not reconstruct his identity with a counteractive word? If Morose can sign away his power and property, then might he not regain at least a semblance of propriety with a countersignature, one that reads and responds to the text of his former self?[62]

In the play's closing lines, Truewit suggests one possible method to bring such a pariah back into the fold, informing the audience that "now Morose is gone in, clap your hands./It may be that noise will cure him, at least please him" (V.iv.252–53). What cures an untenable aversion to noise is the applause designed to please an *actor*'s ear, enjoining a defeated pariah who has slinked offstage, out of sight and out of lines, to mount a jubilant comeback as a player.[63] Transcending the formal limits of a comedy that Jonson calls a "dumbe peece,"[64] the player who responds to his plaudits thus heeds a summons to assembly as plangent as church bells, accepting the interpellation of a London community whose common noise resounds heartily within an indoor playhouse.[65] Like Epicoene and Hwang's Song, Morose repairs a social rupture by enacting a figurative striptease to reveal a default actor's body, a *homo* body (in Austin's sense) defined by its ability to house a queer space of performance. Having exorcized a deviant interiority behind closed doors, thus leaving the unlovable in the spatial "within," the player returns as a fully socialized subject before the public eye, offering a legible countersignature to the Morose who uncannily inhabits the same skin. By permitting this specter only periodic release from its prison-house to roam the stage, the player reframes a deeply rooted misanthropy as a mask chosen from his closet of *personae*, converting pathology into mere performance: after all, only an actor knows how a subject should behave. In thus refolding interiority as an external facade, Morose enacts a dramatic rehabilitation that allows the barred subject to emerge from a gestational exile, a social death, to build a public home in the theatrical "private house": after all, only a playhouse reveals how a home should operate.

Asking spectators yet again to reclaim Morose's house as the White-friars theater, to perceive actors as actors, *Epicoene* makes visible the stagecraft that allows not only a "dumbe peece" of space to accrue meaning in diverse ways, but also a "dumbe peece" of flesh to perform as desired—including those watching Jonson's play. For how could such an extended meta-theatrical joke neglect those ostensibly "dumbe peece[s]" whom Truewit exhorts to applaud, to render bodily obeisance to Morose just like Mute? While such an overture may induce clapping, heckling, or merely silence, Truewit co-opts these actions into a shared epilogue that extends Jonson's script, asking viewers to imagine and produce the scene of Morose's return. Truewit thus binds every viewer to a social contract that entails finishing *Epicoene*'s project of community- and subject-building. Just as Morose once arranged "diuers treaties" with merchants and musicians to behave in a certain manner (I.i.150), Truewit suborns the audience into an open-ended contract to perform in response to—and with—the players, sealing a "blanke" compact that potentially extends beyond the playhouse. Thus conscripted into countersigning Jonson's text, audience members become truly the "men, and daughters of *White-Friars*" (Prologue 24), the progeny and propagators of a theatricality that cannot make the difference between actor and viewer, subject and object. Yet rather than debase spectators as clueless gulls, kicked in a private joke, *Epicoene* shows vividly how these feminized "dumbe" pieces can achieve the final laugh if they unlock the secrets of theater, speak from subject positions outside a master script, and dumbfound others. Indeed, for playgoers who must soon "goe in" to their own private houses, Jonson's refusal to enclose the subject may well inspire an inward look at the theater closeted in their own hearts—the most exotic, *epicoene* space of all.

Chapter Six

Writing Home

Inside Samuel van Hoogstraten's Perspective Box

When you first enter Samuel van Hoogstraten's house, a narrow boxy affair, the interior seems the very picture of domestic life, Dutch-style. A broom leans casually near the corner of one room, while several cloaks hang from a wooden rack mounted on the wall. Solidly middle-class taste prevails in the paintings, mirrors, prints, and maps that adorn every room visible. Although a solidly middle-class family does not emerge to welcome you, they have sent a canine delegate: a brown-and-white spaniel that meets your gaze steadily while perched on the fancy tiled floor, a warm body on a cold surface. Such homely touches abound in the salon where you have been left to your own devices, though your arrival has long been expected. A small comb and strand of pearls, draped across the crimson seat of a chair, suggest a woman's recent presence. Another chair stands forlornly askew in the room's center, a large cushion propped against its front legs. These markers of human activity invite guests to imagine any number of possible narratives, to conceive a static house as a domestic stage briefly deserted by its household players. At this point, however, only the spaniel could attest to any recent drama—and the silent dog refuses to disclose any secrets.

To make sense of such a domestic still life, you soon begin looking beyond the salon for clues, tracking down more pieces of Hoogstraten's puzzle. Thus reading his interiority by roaming through his house, plotting the spaces of his personal drama, you discover a layout typical of bourgeois (*burgerlijk*) residences from the seventeenth century; among the rooms are a front hall (*voorhuis*) that faces the street, a bedroom, a sitting room or two, a large salon (*zaal*) at the center, and a kitchen that connects to a rear courtyard.[1] In a discreet survey of these rooms, you observe with relief that you are not alone in the house, though no one seems aware of your presence. One bedroom contains a woman fast asleep in a four-poster bed, the covers drawn up to her chin, while the *voorhuis* reveals another woman reading in the corner, her chair raised on a small platform that keeps her feet off the cold stone floor. Lost in the logic of other worlds, absorbed in dreams and letters, these women may count themselves the queens of infinite space, to borrow a phrase from *Hamlet.* Bounded by the confines of a four-poster or platform, however, the women's bodies appear within a visual and spatial frame that evokes Antonello's portrait of Saint Jerome, discussed in the introduction. Just as Antonello locates Jerome's closet beyond a stone aperture, forcing viewers to penetrate multiple layers of space, your access to these women requires gazing through doorways that outline even smaller enclosures. Placed upon these mini-stages, the women perform their privacy in the feminine equivalent of Jerome's closet, offering their bodies for public display while mentally detached from that very realm. Bed curtains thus draw back to reveal the sleeper's face, while sunlight passes through the many windows and doorways to wash across every room.

Unlike the heavily glazed "lantern houses" of early modern England, however, these apertures do not look outward to greet the visitor with a pleasing, balanced facade. On the contrary, the house's various openings serve only to enhance your view of, from, and through the interior. Although you see a house that consists of a pure inside, a house that neglects even to fashion an exterior face, such a monadic space still provides for the outside world. Indeed, as your eyes probe into distant recesses of the house, you notice a strange man whose face presses against the front window, looking from the street into the *voorhuis.* Could this nosy intruder be family, friend, or foe? You strain to discern more visual detail, but with the bright sun against his back, the dark-hatted and dark-cloaked figure appears indistinct, a mere silhouette. Ominous scenarios come to mind as his shadowy form, a specter of the public sphere, looms just behind the reading woman. Will this bearer of masculine exteriority intrude upon her chaste, domestic enclosure? Will his visual access to her space turn physical? While the woman seems oblivious to his proximity, his threat to her privacy, you soon realize that his sightline clears a path to *your* salon. Just as you see him through an enfilade of doorways and windows, he sees you framed by the same openings, albeit in reverse sequence. As your gazes interlock along a single axis, this voyeur who looks back from the vanishing point stands as your alter ego, a dark other forever held outside the home, lurking at the furthest limit of vision and knowledge: "this thing of darkness I acknowledge mine," you must admit. Yet if such an *unheimlich* peeper somehow breaches the sanctity of Hoogstraten's home, might *you* be violating the same protocols? Might your mirroring double question the propriety of your own presence, your own roving eye?

Unsettled by this jarring thought, you step back to review your place in the scheme of things, to affirm your subject position. In so doing, you suddenly become aware that you too are standing outside the walls, peering into the salon through a small aperture. Somehow, you have succumbed to an illusion that made you believe yourself at the very heart of Hoogstraten's home. Now wiser, you figure out why an eerie calm pervades the house, why the spaniel—like Conan Doyle's Hound of the Baskervilles—makes no sound in your presence. This domestic mystery can be solved when you identify Hoogstraten's boxy house not as a house, but a box (figures 6.1 to 6.4). A seventeenth-century artist known for his interest in optics, Hoogstraten has created nothing so predictable as a dollhouse or architectural model, a shrunken house. Instead, taking a wooden box about the size of a small trunk,[2] Hoogstraten has removed one panel (front) while painting the other surfaces inside with scenes of a domestic interior, rendered in a virtuoso display of linear perspective.[3] The demure women that you have been ogling turn out to be painted ladies by the strictest definition: ladies painted expressly for your viewing pleasure. Likewise, wielding smoke and mirrors with Sherlockian cunning, Hoogstraten has created a mutely immobile spaniel with a few strokes of his brush.

A semi-architectural, semi-artistic artifact, Hoogstraten's project invites a playful response even while raising serious questions about the writing of space and subjectivity. This staged house thus allows us to reflect on the themes that *Architectural Involutions* has explored, to review the diverse strands of an argument now drawing to a conclusion. Chapter 1 traced the advent of Alberti's facade in both theory and practice, attending to the spatial relations that arise when a facialized building returns the viewer's gaze. Chapter 2 followed this quasi-human facade into England, building a local discourse about architecture from a range of sources including political treatises. While English writers expressed concern that this foreign, aesthetic surface feminized the home, turning a functional building into spectacle, theater actually invaded the interiors of these houses through an "architectural involution" that folded mini-facades around individual rooms. As hallways became the structuring principle of domestic space, thus dispersing rather than assembling members of a household, the layout acquires a structure more akin to writing than speech. The semiotics of architecture thus switches into a different modality as movement through the house inscribes meaning, as subjects negotiate an identity that signifies with the density of writing.

Figure 6.1. Samuel van Hoogstraten's perspective box (c. 1655–60). © National Gallery, London/Art Resource, NY.

Figure 6.2. Left panel of perspective box. © National Gallery, London/Art Resource, NY.

Figure 6.3. Right panel of perspective box, with a man framed in the window behind a reading woman. © National Gallery, London/Art Resource, NY.

Figure 6.4. Back panel of perspective box. © National Gallery, London/Art Resource, NY.

Moving into theater proper, chapter 3 studied the most often cited prototype of an early modern subject: Hamlet. To explore *Hamlet*'s "heart of heart," we traced how gender and power inflect the closet's private space, thus allowing a monadic subject to perform interiority. Chapter 4 probed more deeply into these issues of gender and power by looking back to Plato's concept of space as chora, a womb-like ground of inscription. Born of this Platonic lineage, early modern chorography attempts to define Britain as a feminized, interior landscape most strikingly linked to Elizabeth's virginal womb. Finally, chapter 5 returned to the theater to consider the queer space of a masculine subject in Jacobean London; mounted in an indoor playhouse, *Epicoene* combines actual and imagined space to question how an interiority emerges from performance.

Just as Jonson's comedy stages a chorography that charts the mores of a local region, Hoogstraten's box seduces viewers with a familiar mise-en-scène, asking viewers to survey a bourgeois home rigged like a piece of theater. Engaging viewers in a game of discovery, Hoogstraten pushes the limits of projective geometry to devise a unique experiment in the construction of interiority. While most painters schooled in *costruzione legittima* are content to achieve the illusion of spatial depth on a level surface, Hoogstraten creates a literal showcase for perspective by spreading a domestic scene over five planes that form right angles to one another. By painting new contours that negate the existing corners and edges, Hoogstraten rejects the easy solution of painting a miniature house whose illusory structure mimics its physical container.[4] Thus working against the grain of his wooden box, confident that his artistic prowess can overcome any material constraints, Hoogstraten "combines both real and suggested space" to present a coherent visual matrix.[5] Unlike pictures on two-dimensional surfaces, which deceive the mind into seeing a wholly absent depth, perspective boxes transform one three-dimensional space into another so that viewers cannot discern where physical space ends and feigned space begins. As a result, the artist who devises a perspective box must serve as both painter and architect, merging simulated and actual space into a unified schema.

To prepare the ground for his optical trickery, Hoogstraten first maps the house's central salon onto the main void within the box. He designs the side panels to resemble interior walls, while painting black-and-white tiles on the bottom panel to imitate a stone floor. For viewers who look into the box from its open front side, however, this trompe l'oeil house appears oddly unsettled in its own skin, its spatial body out of joint. The floor tiles seem to run amok as they spill over onto the left and back panels, where the salon walls ought to be. While the checked pattern never changes, the square tiles distend into more oblong shapes as they march up the vertical panels; the effect resembles an Albertian *pavimentum* tilted to an absurd degree. Similarly, on the right panel, imaginary architecture collides against material structure as the salon wall climbs onto the top panel (the "ceiling") and stretches partway across the back. Since all the overflow sections appear distorted like a carnival fun house, Hoogstraten's interior alternates between regions of skewed and legible space.

Yet these optical hiccups vanish when the viewer finally moves away from a full-frontal stare to adopt more discreet, oblique tactics. Near the front edge of both the left and right panels, Hoogstraten has drilled a peephole that directs the viewer's gaze toward the opposite, interior corner. Such a diagonal sightline maximizes the focal distance to enable the most drawn-out progress into the interior. Like a visitor to Nonsuch who passes courtyard after courtyard, the viewer here sweeps across the domestic stage by peering through real space (the box) into illusory space (the perspectival image). By locking viewers into the ideal subject position, each peephole allows the fullest extension of depth while smoothing the distorted patches into a seamless inner world. For example, the wooden chair that stands in the middle of Hoogstraten's salon has actually been painted over three planes that meet at a corner. Seen from the front, the chair resembles a cubist sculpture, splayed oddly across the back, left, and bottom panels; seen from the right peephole, however, the chair seems perfectly upright. Rather than confine the chair to a single, distant panel in classic Albertian style, Hoogstraten negotiates a complex geometry to render the object larger and more immediate to viewers. As a result, the peephole not only secures viewers in the stereometric cage of *costruzione legittima,* but also projects them inside a domestic scene that seems life-size.[6]

Mad in craft, Hoogstraten deforms the image to furnish a secret pleasure when viewers discover the proper subject position, then claim a realistic interior depth as their reward. This type of optical illusion—known as anamorphosis—applies linear perspective with a twist; though incoherent when viewed normally, anamorphic images suddenly make sense from an unusual angle or with a special device. To solve Hoogstraten's spatial coding, viewers submit to a peephole that re-forms the fractured architectural body and realigns its Albertian lineaments. Yet to transform a dark void into home, the viewer's desire to see a domestic space must negate the box's actual size and shape. Beyond fixing the body in place, each peephole limits the field of vision to prevent any contrast with an external scale, to preserve a hermetic fantasy of home. Tumbling headlong into Wonderland through a peephole, viewers privilege their ocular senses to inhabit a self-referential world that denies any intrusion of external reality. Hoogstraten thus closets the gaze to promote an absolute belief in his cult of the interior. Building a home upon the structure of a cloister, Hoogstraten constructs a self-sufficient monad with its own viewpoint on the world—a world of its own making.

As a machine that turns eyes inward for a brief time, that inscribes a domestic tableau on the tablets of his viewers' minds, the perspective box offers a platform that generates novel angles upon the topos of home. Both skewed and straight, Hoogstraten's interior enfolds viewers into a secret, closet-like space, which then unfolds to infinity: in this sense, Hoogstraten subverts the notion of home through a process of spatial, visual, and psychic involution. Indeed, to surprise viewers with a world that seems to burst from its trunk-like container, the external surface no longer signifies anything of interior space. Such a baroque severing of the facade recalls the evolution of early modern closets from locked chests, from the Italian *cassone* and similar caskets found across Europe. The perspective box, "half painting and half furniture,"[7] reminds viewers to guard a treasure that is interiority itself, but also reveals this interiority to be a construct, a contorted illusion. In the extant handful of Dutch perspective "cases" (*perspectijfkas* or *perspectyfkas*),[8] the desire to unlock a closed space emerges clearly, since peepholes reveal either a church or household interior—the two sites also linked to closets. For Lacan, anamorphosis developed in the early modern period as an attempt to recover "the sacred emptiness of architecture," the central void that organized built space before the advent of linear perspective.[9] The Dutch boxes reinforce this theory of a mystical interior meant to inspire wonder, since viewers discover a hidden locale sanctified as the most interior of interior spaces, whether religious or domestic. The sacred void that cannot be seen head-on, linked to the blinding truth of the *objet petit a,* must always be viewed awry.[10] For viewers who embark on ocular journeys into this sacred void, the process of mapping such a closet—an affective, local, womb-like chora—necessarily produces them as subjects.

The Threshold of Performance

The perspective box thus constructs an indoor theater that confines the gaze within a choric space, a darkened container that imprints upon the mind a narrative of domestic interiority. Like a proscenium arch that frames the stage as an aesthetic object,[11] a stage that suspends normal disbelief, the panels of the perspective box comprise an Albertian border that defines a three-dimensional ground of inscription. Yet by checking the viewer's body at a material threshold, thus setting up the ideal viewing platform, Hoogstraten does not so much exclude the outside world as embrace the symbiosis of physical and illusory space. From trompe l'oeil to anamorphosis, Hoogstraten constantly experiments with techniques that produce visual plenitude by drawing upon architectural context; such an impulse may even derive from his reading of Alberti's treatises, *De pictura* and *De re aedificatoria,* in tandem.[12] Perhaps the most striking instance of Hoogstraten's desire to construct an indoor theater can be found in his *Perspective from a Threshold* (1662), a painting with telling parallels to the perspective box (figure 6.5). Created during the artist's sojourn in England from 1662 to 1667, *Threshold* was designed for the London home of Thomas Povey, a politician who lived near Lincoln's Inn Fields. For viewers of Hoogstraten's perspective box, *Threshold*'s scene of a domestic interior recycles many familiar motifs: a black-and-white floor, a rustic broom that leans against the wall, a curious dog that looks out toward the spectator. *Threshold* likewise aligns a series of rooms whose doorways form an enfilade, thus drawing the gaze along an optical tunnel to the utmost depth.

Yet this illusory space of perspective, no matter how skillfully achieved, still requires architecture to provide a visual scaffolding. In a diary entry dated January 26, 1663, Samuel Pepys records his delight upon viewing the artwork in Povey's home:

> But above all things, I do the most admire his piece of perspective especially, he opening me the closet door and there I saw there is nothing but only a plain picture on the wall.[13]

Although no evidence survives to indicate whether Hoogstraten designed the painting for this specific closet, *Threshold*'s proportions (264 × 136.5 cm) correspond roughly with the outline of a doorway. The painting would thus have maximum impact if placed directly across from a door, but distant enough to co-opt the closet space into extending the illusion of a corridor. Indeed, the painting's size and content seem ideally planned to exploit the contrast between a small, enclosed closet and the wondrous portal thrown open by *costruzione legittima.* Like a backdrop rendered in single-point perspective, Hoogstraten's painting transforms an otherwise empty closet into a theater, allowing viewers the secret pleasure of unveiling interior space. As Celeste Brusati observes, Hoogstraten's

Figure 6.5. Samuel van Hoogstraten, *Perspective from a Threshold* (1662). Dyrham Park, UK. National Trust Photo Library/Art Resource, NY.

"painted conceit hinged, quite literally, on Povey's gesture" of revelation.[14] A bon vivant who loved to entertain, a patron of the arts whom John Evelyn calls "a nice contriver of all elegancies," Povey enjoyed the ritual of showing visitors this "piece of perspective in his closett in the low parler."[15] As an after-dinner trick, a dumb-show, Povey would offer his guests a peek into his private space, thus making his interiority the object of desire in a literal parlor game.[16]

For Povey, as for Gertrude in *Hamlet,* the closet serves a social function by enabling interiority to be shared and staged. Quite clearly, the empty closet does not traffic in solitary pursuits, but rather the kind of social cachet that results from an elegantly contrived intimacy. Instead of using the closet to enlarge his own interior space—physical, mental, spiritual—Povey chooses to have interiority on hand as a public commodity, as capital that boosts his reputation about town. In short, Povey *has* rather than *is* an interiority in the Lacanian sense. Yet this reified interiority only appears to yield itself to common possession; even as Povey opens the door as though raising a stage curtain, spectators find themselves arrested at the threshold, stymied as an Albertian veil descends at the border that divides interior from exterior. Since viewers must stand transfixed at the threshold to activate the fullest perspectival effect, this veil also renders the closet space off-limits in terms of physical access, creating a "no man's land" where even a single footfall would spoil the fine illusion. A social and visual contract thus prevents visitors from entering Povey's inner sanctum, ensuring that his closet remains chastely inviolate. Between the threshold at which viewers stand and the threshold that Hoogstraten paints as a framing device, Povey's home attempts to protect the sacred void of architecture.

As private enclosure and painted extension become mutually dependent, a visitor who enters Povey's closet disrupts not only the concept of a bounded interior space within his home, but also the vision of a coherent exterior world that stretches to infinity. Instead of punching out an Albertian window that supplements actual space, *Threshold* subordinates the closet into serving as a colossal peephole, a device that orients the viewer's gaze. Thus rendered a Derridean *parergon* that surrounds and supports the artwork, an architectural frame that houses the lineaments of perspective, the closet's physical space loses its claim to being the original that a painting mimics ad infinitum. Reduced to being the runway that allows Hoogstraten's perspective to take flight, built space begins to waver in the mind like a mirage, a mere simulacrum of itself. Policing a mimetic binary proves especially fraught because Hoogstraten's aperture opens inward rather than outward: *Threshold* depicts a series of rooms that draw the gaze ever deeper into interior space, finally dissolving into a haze at the vanishing point. Promising a liberating openness while burrowing into an unattainable heart, *Threshold* belies Povey's apparently generous invitation into his private space. Neither the closet nor the painting allows more than a simulation of intimacy, leaving interior space a mere specter on the distant horizon. In contrast to Morose's desperate attempt to cordon off his London home, Povey forestalls any incursion upon his privacy by astounding and arresting the visitor's gaze, thus setting boundaries tacitly even as he abolishes them with a flourish.

By turning his private closet into a public showcase, Povey constructs a life-size perspective box that deforms the very idea of interior space.

Povey's closet reveals more clearly how the perspective box responds to a philosophical legacy that unites architecture and visuality, pushing the notions of facade and perspective to their logical extremes. It should come as no surprise, then, that Alberti himself has often been cited as an originator of the peepshow (a more generic term for any visual device that involves looking into a box). An anonymous fifteenth-century biography claims that the father of single-point perspective

> produced works unheard-of in this art of painting and unbelievable to spectators, which he displayed in a small enclosed box through a tiny hole. . . . He called these things *demonstrations.* (opera ex ipsa arte pingendi efficit inaudita, et spectatoribus incredibilia, quae quidem parva in capsa conclusa pusillum per foramen ostenderet. . . . Has res *demonstrationes* appellabat.)[17]

In this *capsa conclusa* (enclosed box), Albertian painting offers a counterpart to the Albertian building concluded with a facade. Indeed, by staging optical illusions "unbelievable to spectators," Alberti performs the "demonstrations" missing from his *De pictura,* the treatise on perspective that refuses to provide any diagrams, figures, or other means of proof. While the peepshow ensnares viewers into looking inward, closeting them in a darkened space of wonder, Alberti requites this sacrifice by punching out a window using linear perspective. Marvelous sights beguile the viewer inside this enclosed space: "tall mountains, vast provinces, a huge sweep of encircling sea, and at the same time, a long vista of distant regions so remote that the viewer's eyesight failed."[18] Such a panoramic landscape underscores how, for Alberti, interiority serves as the precondition of a fantastic, far-reaching exteriority limited only by the failure of mortal eyesight.

As Roger Hinks notes, the "peepshow box is only a camera obscura in reverse."[19] By making a pinhole that allows a stream of images to enter a darkened room, where a viewer awaits, a camera obscura transforms the external world into intangible, unpredictable ephemera. In contrast, Alberti's peepshow situates a viewer outside a small aperture looking inward, but mitigates this ocular constraint by staging a false, fixed exteriority that surpasses reality. Taking this process further, the perspective box rejects the exterior altogether to reveal a perfectly banal interior, a sanctum made sacred by its mundane intimacy. While the camera obscura values a singular mind that reflects on a mediated world, an interior self that muses upon an exterior made distant, the perspective box relegates the viewer to a powerless location outside the *camera,* peering into a space that has itself been tainted as image. A spatial involution marks the shift between these optical devices, since the perspective box deems interiority rather than exteriority the object of desire, boxed up like a present for an inward gaze. Foreclosed by the parameters of built and unbuilt space, this interiority becomes visible with the kind of repeated, strategic unveiling that Povey enacts; interiority thus emerges as a social, performative construct. Indeed, furnished with a one-sided *Threshold* that moves only inward, Povey's closet allows a painting to hijack a space often meant for self-scrutiny, thus inverting a camera obscura model of the Cartesian *cogito.* In contrast to the monad that looks outward from an enclosed space, the perspective box questions the stability of this internal point of origin, and thus of the sacred void that organizes the architecture of a subject.

That the perspective box represents a version of interior selfhood becomes evident when we consider the exterior of Hoogstraten's work. While Povey's closet might possibly succeed in obscuring any sense of an outside, being tucked within a parlor and accessed by a door, the smaller perspective box must expose a God's-eye view of its exterior to anyone who approaches. Yet rather than devise an architectural facade, or merely leave the exterior blank, Hoogstraten elects to confront viewers with "a self-representation of the maker."[20] Each panel along the sides and back contains an emblem, with both motto and image, that justifies an artistic career: "Gloriae Causa" (For the Sake of Glory), "Lucri Causa" (For the Sake of Money), and "Amoris Causa" (For the Sake of Love).[21] Coupled with these mottoes are vignettes that feature a male artist at work, though his face remains carefully averted from viewers. Despite this attempt to deface the artist, his visible traits accord with those found in Hoogstraten's self-portraits; the emblems thus apply to someone just like Hoogstraten, if not actually Hoogstraten. In blazoning this artistic credo on the surface of his own creation, Hoogstraten marks the body of his perspective box with his raison d'être as painter. As Hoogstraten defines his artistic territory upon the perimeter of his spatial territory, the faceless artist becomes the facade of his own home.

Hoogstraten thus projects outside the artistic principles that he cherishes most deeply, the innermost motives that underlie every professional venture. Inscribing onto the spatial envelope the contents of Hoogstraten's interior, these emblems outline the ground of his artistic philosophy before viewers discover his final viewpoint—and handiwork—through the peepholes. Seen through this frame of

Figure 6.6. Bottom panel of perspective box. Note the letter on the anamorphic chair at bottom left. © National Gallery, London/Art Resource, NY.

self-identity, the domestic scene inside the box assumes a more personal character; even though no avatar of the artist steps forward to claim this interior stage, Hoogstraten *has,* in a sense, opened his closet space with as much authority as Povey.[22] Scattered among the rooms are subtle clues that affirm Hoogstraten's claim to this house: a portrait hanging on the salon wall bears the Hoogstraten family crest, a stained-glass window in the bedroom embeds a coat of arms that belongs to his wife's family, and most suggestive of all, an envelope casually dropped on a chair names Hoogstraten as the recipient (figure 6.6).[23]

While Hoogstraten declares his public identity on the external panels using Latin-filled banderoles, his writing on the interior takes a suitably intimate form, namely, an inward-folded envelope inscribed in French. Letters in this period were simply folded, sealed, and addressed on the outside, thus making envelopes the obverse of their written content. Like a textual closet that hails a proper subject, the early modern letter reveals its secrets to readers who unlock the interior with a gesture of inversion, a spatial unfolding. Yet Hoogstraten's letter, forever unopenable, must project its interior meaning onto the exterior as a public signifier. When used by painters in this way to insert a message into their work, letters usually credit the artist or identify the sitter.[24] Hoogstraten's envelope follows this tradition by placing the artist's signature discreetly near the margins of the artwork, thus making his name an alternate center from which creative activity emanates. Yet since Hoogstraten inscribes his own address on the envelope, the artist's name also becomes inextricably yoked to the artist's home, to the very object depicted. Situated among the other personal signifiers, Hoogstraten's self-addressed letter defines the anamorphic interior as a lived-in domestic realm, a household rather than a mere house. Indeed, while Hoogstraten's surname and family emblems indicate temporal descent, even to the point of being rooted in place as an architectural fixture, the letter suggests motion across space; Hoogstraten stakes his claim to selfhood where these two modes of travel converge in the perspective box.

However, just as the external surfaces present an artist both faceless and like Hoogstraten, sporting emblems both prosaic and personal, the internal surfaces gesture toward and away from the artist's own home. Despite all the special touches legible mainly to insiders, the perspective box likely does not replicate Hoogstraten's actual residence in miniature, not least because *pentimenti* reveal his efforts to rework the floor plan.[25] With furnished rooms that resemble those found in countless other Dutch genre paintings,[26] Hoogstraten's domestic scene adheres to convention in every aspect of decor, thus allowing a tricky anamorphic image to register in viewers' minds as a typical household. Despite a *burgerlijk* interior that seems not to merit a second glance, the perspective box should never be treated as merely an exemplar of realism, as a trompe l'oeil painting that blends smoothly into its context.[27] On the contrary, Hoogstraten demands that viewers adopt an eccentric vision of domesticity, skewing gazes toward back corners and spilling content across material borders. Rather than muddle the line between painting and *parergon,* Hoogstraten integrates structure and ornament by painting on a wooden frame whose disassembly renders the artwork illegible. Like a self-addressed envelope that always circulates back to the sender, Hoogstraten's box cannot survive being unfolded except by the admiring gaze; ultimately, the artist closes the door on his home, his void. Firmly molded into right angles to enable a perfectly slanted gaze, donning a *burgerlijk* anonymity spiked with veiled hints at identity, Hoogstraten's box teases the viewer with an interior that defies a singular logic.

In this spirit of paradox, Hoogstraten performs an architectural involution that places the facade inside, folding the house inward so that painted interiors, in Albertian terms, "comprehend and conclude" a perspectival space. If architecture devises a facade to conclude the building's internal lineaments, the perspective box concludes its external frame to safeguard the lineaments of perspective within; Hoogstraten thus draws the viewer's gaze inward to unfold and explicate another concept of an external face, one that exists on the inside. Indeed, unlike external facades that stretch a cosmetic skin over an ungainly structure, Hoogstraten's internal facades efface themselves to dissemble a transparent depth. Squeezed out of the woodwork to create a painted veneer, this interior depth must be flattened into submission and fractured into anamorphic shapes. While a normal house constructs an outward facade that greets the public, the perspective box wears a mask that hides the drawbacks of its internal body, glossing over awkward joints and using optical tricks to enlarge its heart. Only with this decorous, introjected covering can the perspective box signify a cohesive architectural identity, presenting to viewers an illusion of wholeness, of normalcy: in short, the perspective box functions as a closet that attempts to negate itself, to conceal its queer bodily frame.

Such a circuit of duplicity arises in part from the double-peephole scheme, unique among surviving examples of the Dutch *perspectyfkas.* As Brusati observes, Hoogstraten basically combines two simpler, triangular models of *perspectyfkas* to achieve a single rectangle.[28] A triangular *perspectyfkas* features a peephole drilled into the middle of one side, which channels the gaze into a corner directly across; however, the painter uses anamorphic distortion to "flatten" this corner, so that viewers perceive a larger interior shaped like a rectangle. Working on the same principle, each of Hoogstraten's peepholes directs the gaze toward the opposite back corner, which also vanishes under the new spatial schema dictated by anamorphosis. This double-peephole device creates two fields of vision that overlap in the center, while requiring viewers to move around in physical space to access the interior fully. For Svetlana Alpers, the perspective box manifests a typically Dutch impulse toward mapping, a descriptive mode that consists of "various views adding up to make a single world."[29] Yet the box's two views refuse to cohere into a single body, a single architectural corpus. Instead, Hoogstraten prohibits any dialectical resolution of opposed perspectives, ruining the dream of opening infinite windows into the same monadic structure.

This inability to aggregate a coherent space becomes evident if viewers attempt to sketch a ground plan for the house. Despite the orderly geometry implied by the enfilades and checkered floor, the house can never be reconstructed outside the anamorphic box.[30] On a basic level, certain regions of the house remain beyond our knowledge because Hoogstraten has partially occluded them from either peephole, or omitted them from his composition. Although these spaces extend beyond the reach of the artist's worldview, beyond representation, a graver problem arises in the very center of the salon where the two halves of the box meet. Viewers might expect a strong central fulcrum to anchor the two views, especially since the box's physical structure exhibits a high degree of symmetry: the peepholes are situated almost exactly across from one another,[31] while their respective anamorphoses cover an equal amount of surface on the panels. Yet even though Hoogstraten merges two identical triangles to construct his rectangular space, the peepholes do not function as mirror images of each other. That is, instead of planting viewers in the middle of a room, then offering the illusion of looking in either direction, Hoogstraten severs the two views in scale and angle. Peering into the right peephole, viewers seem to occupy a position quite remote from the opposite wall, while their gazes are directed toward the far corner of the salon (which coincides with the far corner of the box). From the left peephole, however, viewers seem much closer to the opposite wall, while their gazes now focus on the center of the salon wall (which again coincides with the far corner of the box—the salon wall extends across the back panel to offset this enlarged scale). As viewers move from one peephole to the other, they jump from being very close to being very distant, from looking into the salon's corner to facing the wall squarely.

Hoogstraten clearly wishes to project a matrix of space without obvious lacunae, yet the interior views are designed to unhinge the sense of balance instilled by the box's own structure. Because of these internal disparities, Hoogstraten must suture together a room with two disjunct faces, packing a visually lozenge-shaped space within a perfectly right-angled box. Wherever possible, Hoogstraten includes features that appear coherent from either peephole; despite his best efforts, however, a fault line traverses the center of this Janus-faced interior, forcing Hoogstraten to place a cushion and round mat onto the floor where he cannot reconcile the pattern of square tiles (figure 6.4). Like his twentieth-century compatriot, M. C. Escher, Hoogstraten conjures architectural illusions that seem plausible locally, but crumble when spatial discordances appear within the same frame of reference. Thus, to protect the viewer from looking through the missing front panel, hence stumbling upon a landscape scarred by mismatched spatial logics, Hoogstraten likely covered the opening with a sheet of oiled paper.[32] Such a translucent screen would block the prohibited angle of vision but still provide enough light for viewers shunted off to either peephole. Unlike Holbein's *Ambassadors,* which offers a second, secret perspective embedded within the normative frontal view, Hoogstraten's box permits nothing but sidelong gazes limited to a partial space, a veiled field of vision. Secrecy becomes the norm within the home—even the center must be covered up, as though to cushion the blow when viewers catch sight of a spatial fissure.

The Secret Spaces of the Self

> The secret was invented by society.
>
> —Gilles Deleuze and Félix Guattari[33]

In *A Thousand Plateaus,* Deleuze and Guattari define the secret as "a content that has hidden its form in favor of a simple container."[34] By rejecting a facade that signifies a domestic interior, Hoogstraten's box seems to materialize this concept of secrecy, building a generic container for the wondrous content within. After all, viewers who accept using the peepholes must also embrace the role of a voyeur, pressing their eyes against the boundary of someone else's home. Yet just as *Threshold* draws upon the space of Povey's closet, Hoogstraten's box deploys the material parameters of its medium to reinforce a specific artistic theme. As viewers walk around to the opposite side of the box, they *expect* the new peephole to reveal the opposite side of a house, just as they expect the interior views to match the box's rectangular space. While a triangular perspective box contains the secret of a rectangular illusory space, Hoogstraten reinforces the connection between exterior and interior in his double-peephole schema; although the viewer's apparent location changes from peephole to peephole, the salon's proportions follow those of the box, albeit on a larger scale. Thus using a wooden frame to nudge viewers into a certain frame of mind, to think inside the box, Hoogstraten builds upon viewers' own spatial memory to enhance his illusion. Having just encircled a rectangular structure, viewers recreate this sacred void in their minds as they look through the peephole.

While the process of discovery plays a crucial role in the game of anamorphosis, the secrecy of Hoogstraten's box reaches beyond physical space into the psyche. Indeed, the central rift that splits the house also splits the subject of single-point perspective. Since each peephole must be accessed in sequence, at distinct temporal and spatial points, Hoogstraten's box demands that viewers double around the box in an incessant effort to catch up with their phantom alter ego.[35] For Hoogstraten, home requires yielding the certainty of place for an endless game of relay, an endless process of coming home that never quite reaches the desired interior. Just as the artist must function as both sender and receiver of his self-addressed letter, a letter both written by him and writing him into existence as an artist, the viewer must similarly produce a coherent sense of identity through endless circulation, attempting to reconcile one end of the room with the other while never quite resolving the problem of an absent center. Such visual pivoting evokes the process of cinematic suture, which likewise responds to a viewer who abruptly discovers the frame that encloses each image, hence shattering the needed suspension of disbelief.[36] An existential crisis plagues the viewer for whom the projected world now seems like a cheap sleight of hand, controlled and framed by some invisible mastermind; in short, the camera's eye seems to replace instead of enhance the viewer's own eye. For directors anxious to dispel these doubts, one popular solution involves a shot/reverse-shot sequence in which the camera angle rotates 180 degrees, or slightly less, thus showing viewers a complete and accessible world that conceals nothing behind the scenes. Hoogstraten's perspective box makes a similar gesture toward openness by offering a reverse view through the house, thus allaying suspicions that a master artist has made a broken home seem whole through deceit.

Ironically, what triggers this necessity for a reverse view is the same thing that enables a perspectival suture: the opposite peephole. Although Hoogstraten directs the gaze as deeply into rear corners as possible, the moment inevitably arises when viewers look straight across the wooden box and encounter an inexplicable void in the field of vision, a puncture wound marring an otherwise meticulously detailed world. Chancing upon the peephole's optical frame and frame-up, viewers experience a sudden loss of power and identity in a home that no longer seems familiar, a home that estranges them from their interpellated subject positions. Just as a frontal view of the box destroys the anamorphic illusion of cohesion, a frontal view of the opposite peephole shatters any comforting sense of plenitude and centrality in the home, forcing viewers to start thinking outside the box. Indeed, the other who waits behind the opposite peephole, a specular double who must always hover unseen, defines a new vanishing point where a horrific reality just might erupt into Hoogstraten's simulacrum of bourgeois life.

Rather than radiate order and propriety,[37] as one critic believes, Hoogstraten's box searches for a proper center from which to radiate, a single vanishing point that can anchor his illusory world. As Fred Leeman observes, the term *anamorphosis,* composed of the Greek *ana* (again) and *morphe* (shape), "indicates that the spectator must play a part and re-form the picture himself."[38] Going further, Hoogstraten's perspective box requires that viewers not only re-form and suture two disjunct views, but also continually re-form and suture their own deformed subjectivities. Indeed, since these interiors have themselves become pictures for introspection, peepshows for the mind's eye, viewers must assume multiple subject positions to make sense of a complex world that exists both within and without. Always denied access to some part of themselves, viewing subjects become agents in their mobile quest to recover an alternative depth in their space and bodies. Nevertheless, unable to look themselves in the eye, viewers inevitably leave something of their subjectivity in the transitional spaces between strategic points of access to the matrix.

As we saw in chapter 1, Deleuze and Guattari's notion of faciality juxtaposes a white wall of signification against a black hole of subjectivity. By creating "the wall of the signifier, the frame or screen,"[39] the face presents a legible surface imbued with social meaning, thus finding a home for itself in the world. Likewise, Hoogstraten's interior facades construct a screen of *burgherlijk* comfort that viewers instantly recognize, placating the gaze with familiar images. Yet by opening an unexpected breach in the faciality of Hoogstraten's interior, the opposite peephole constitutes a black hole of subjectivity that threatens this illusion of domestic coherence. In contrast to an Albertian window that looks outward to an infinite, mappable distance, the black hole opens inward to reveal the subjective eye lurking behind every signifying face. Manifest only as a small aperture that pierces the facade of public order, this unsocialized, unfacialized self always threatens to burst through its domesticated veneer. Indeed, the sacred void that primitive architecture safeguards, a void that Plato names *chora,* may well be the sanctity of a primitive self without semiotic order; in this sense, the black hole of subjectivity preserves a chora that recalls Kristeva's notion of a presymbolic self. While Hoogstraten attempts to contain this uninitiated self through the box's architecture, the peepholes that induct the eye into a facial semiotics also exert a chaotic force upon his illusory space. Like the skull that occupies the central foreground in Holbein's *Ambassadors,* the opposite peephole both completes the picture's meaning and confronts the viewing subject with a vision of its own demise, rupturing a stable image of home and self. The viewer's only possible role in this domestic scene is to provide a hole, an absence—a ghost that even the dog fails to bark at.

Just as Jonson's Morose offers to "seale . . . to a blanke" contract with his nephew to regain his social position (V.iv.190–91), Hoogstraten's viewer must agree to be reduced to a blank void for entry into his world, paying a form of subjective blackmail for the security of domestic accord. This implicit contract might not even be fully understood by viewers were the opposite peephole not to obtrude, shifting the gaze from a distant vanishing point to an all-too-near gash in the fabric of vision. The second peephole alerts viewers that what has appeared so normative and transparent has been a slanted, superficial illusion all along. While Hoogstraten deforms the material box using tricks of perspective, the peephole deforms his internal facades by pointing to the material conditions that nullify an illusory world; in this respect, as deformation pushes against deformation, one species of anamorphosis leads to another. By drawing attention to the legerdemain involved in constructing a visible home, the opposite peephole functions as a mirror that implicates viewers who thought themselves safely ensconced behind a panel as voyeurs, as theatergoers separated by a fourth wall. Now caught in the midst of seeing, these viewers must look inward to consider the mechanisms that construct and deconstruct their own faces, their own peepholes. After all, every viewer stationed at a peephole assumes a mask of interior space, of domestic calm, for the opposite viewer—though this mask cannot be seen by the original person. As viewers come to realize the public mask imposed upon them, leaving only a dark hole to mark the private subject left behind, the opposite peephole assumes the function of an *objet petit a* in moving viewers to search out its secrets, propelling viewers in a futile quest for wholeness. Is there actually someone lurking behind the opposite peephole? Or is that someone always already yourself? The ground falls away as the cushion and round mat no longer suffice in disguising the fissure that divides the salon, the fissure that threatens to divide the viewing subject. In response, viewers can only walk around this scene of horror—to the other peephole that so distracts and disturbs. As the symbolic order of Hoogstraten's anamorphoses dissolves with a peephole that reveals the material frame, viewers enact a kind of suture upon their own faces by looking back at themselves from the opposite side.

Curtain

> The real seems to have been more real at home.
>
> —Richard Helgerson[40]

To correct the queerness of Hoogstraten's anamorphic home, viewers can only inscribe an endless loop that institutes a spatial remedy for a visual breakdown. Since the home no longer offers a center that holds, viewers carve out an external corridor to bridge an internal crevice, building a bypass for a broken heart. Stepping awry from Hoogstraten's interior, viewers attempt to regain equilibrium by sending themselves into perpetual transition, recentering the home through a kind of spatial anamorphosis. Detouring from the long enfilades depicted within, viewers regard architecture less as a facialized perspective than as embodied movement, shifting from perfect coherence to patchwork construction. While Alberti's peepshow immobilizes the viewer in a frontal position, forcing the eye to look straight ahead, Hoogstraten's perspective box requires a circuitous movement that considers not only depth in front, but also depth behind. By combining Povey's staging of the space within and cinematic suture's staging of the space behind, Hoogstraten's perspective box attempts to extend the principles of *costruzione legittima* in all directions, creating an illusion of spatial fullness even as the viewer remains partial, never quite capable of taking all the discrete viewing positions at once, never quite capable of actually coming home.

Indeed, rather than lock the viewer into gazing through an imaginary Albertian window, Hoogstraten renders this stable position the only prohibited view. The house's main window remains a mere gesture: Hoogstraten paints the shadow of a mullion and transom upon the left salon wall, while adding various shading effects to suggest that light streams in through the front panel. The translucent screen that covers this opening thus becomes an ersatz window, as Hoogstraten co-opts an actual light source into his illusory house. As a result, viewers at either peephole must stand beside rather than before a window, looking away from this aperture into distant corners. Yet beyond merely injecting another touch of realism, a conceit to disguise a missing wall, Hoogstraten seizes this pretext of a simulated window to insert a curtain that blocks one peephole from seeing the other. A thin strip of wood, painted to mimic a billowing swath of brocade, once slotted into a groove adjacent to the front edge (figure 6.7). Clearly, every stage must have its curtain: this "fold of curtain" not only frames the false opening as a window, but also obscures the opposite peephole from view.[41] Just as a sheet of oiled paper seals off the frontal view, a piece of window dressing interposes between peepholes to forestall the disaster of coming eye to eye with the other. Partly material, partly visual fakery, this non-Albertian veil attempts to prevent indecorous gazes while enhancing the sense of voyeurism. After all, like Polonius hiding behind the arras, every viewer aspires to be secreted behind a curtain in someone else's closet, spying on an intimate scene from an invisible position of privilege and power. But while Polonius was killed for his literal and figurative blindness, never emerging from his darkened recess behind the arras, viewers are doomed to an eternal vigilance, a Sisyphean encounter and reencounter with a wound that marks their place, an accusing eye that never closes. For the curtain that should suture over the opposing peephole has long since vanished, leaving viewers to ponder unto infinity their own state of unveiled nakedness.

It seems curiously appropriate that both the translucent paper and trompe l'oeil curtain have not survived, leaving only scarring traces upon the denuded architectural body. As these ghostly marks recount the futile efforts to build a seamless enclosure, a contained matrix of space without an outside, viewers realize that Hoogstraten's various curtaining devices have always been a deforming illusion, a theater prop, a veil to avoid dealing with bare reality. Instead, the staging of home demands a certain asymmetry that makes the system dynamic, ensuring that even self-addressed letters circulate in perpetuity, always in transition between a sender and receiver never found in their proper subject positions. Like the delicate fold of curtain that holds in place a coherent worldview, the letter that writes us into being must constantly be refolded to stave off a dark blot that appears when least expected, thus rendering illegible the neatly inscribed address. As though to demonstrate the precarious nature of identity, Hoogstraten's own letter displays a public face made cryptic by flaking paint and faded letters, reading something like: "A Monsieur/Mons. S. de Hoogstraten/a/. . . drecht" (figure 6.7). One of the most deteriorated elements of the perspective box, this address manifests both a strange hiccup in its salutation (Monsieur/Mons.) as well as a fragmented location (the final letters of the artist's birthplace, Dordrecht). Even as Hoogstraten writes his name and hometown in his own hand, what should be the most secure affirmation of his identity falters, stutters, and fades away into ambiguity. Like the box itself, Hoogstraten's self-addressed letter underscores how a subject remains both doubled and incomplete, reduced to an inscription that remains visually irresolvable, a facade that promises and withholds an interior.

Yet beyond the uncertain forces of entropy, Hoogstraten actually builds into his world the viewer's inability to make sense of his letter, making the very marker of his authority into an illegible void. Hoogstraten places the letter on a chair in the box's front left corner, almost directly below the left peephole—a virtual blind spot in the field of vision. An obscure white splotch on the margins when seen from the right peephole, the envelope comes into clearer focus only if viewers look straight down from the left peephole. Given such an extreme viewing angle, however, the words on Hoogstraten's envelope become too small

Figure 6.7. Detail of the self-addressed letter. The vertical notch for the artificial curtain appears at the top left, adjacent to the edge. © National Gallery, London/Art Resource, NY.

and blurred to read without great straining; even viewers who know in advance what he has written find it almost impossible to make out the inscription.[42] Hoogstraten thus renders his artistic signature a secret for others to discover and decode, tucking his letter into a fold of space that does not fully belong to either peephole. By devising an object too remote to be read from one peephole and too close to be read from the other, Hoogstraten makes viewers acutely conscious of the perspective box's limitations as an optical device. Indeed, while viewers once pressed their eyes against the peephole, trying to suture themselves into an illusory home, achieving a feasible viewing angle for the letter requires abandoning this dream of total immersion. Instead, searching for the optimal position by shifting their bodies, raising their eyes slightly above the left peephole to attain a steeper angle, viewers inevitably become aware of Hoogstraten's artificial and restrictive framing of the visible world.

All these problems disappear, however, if viewers simply leave both peepholes to look through the missing front panel; in earlier times, perhaps viewers lifted a corner of the oiled-paper screen to peek into the corner. While such a tactic destroys the anamorphic schema that makes the house coherent, Hoogstraten's writing suddenly resolves into distinct letters of readable size, turning the envelope into an oasis of legibility amid an otherwise warped landscape. Seeing the artist's signature thus means seeing the artist's genius, as viewers realize how skillfully

Hoogstraten creates order from a jumble of distorted objects. This peek "behind the scenes" not only reveals the scaffold that underpins Hoogstraten's illusion, but also suggests how the subject resists being suborned into such deception. That is, while other parts of the house are carefully mapped onto a grid, Hoogstraten has written his name and address across the envelope in what seems like a freehand script, unfettered by anamorphic calculations. Perhaps this more casual approach to writing accounts for the repeated "Monsieur/Mons.," as well as the awkward visibility from either peephole. By opening up a black hole of subjectivity amid a polished screen of meaning, the tattered letter stages a conflict between alternate modes of reading and writing space.

Like the book that unlocks Antonello's *St. Jerome,* Hoogstraten's letter draws the gaze toward a secret ground of inscription, calling out to viewers: "Mark me." Despite leaving its raison d'être right on the surface, this ex-centric text remains illegible unless viewers decide to violate the protocols of single-point perspective. Since no amount of reverse-angle framing can render the envelope perfectly accessible, viewers must interrupt their circuit between peepholes to assume a taboo position, sacrificing illusory depth for the pleasure of reading across a surface. Viewers thus choose to unmoor their previous system of place-making to uncover a letter hidden in plain sight, a letter that defines a kernel of closed space, a closet. For Hoogstraten, then, writing home entails leaving that home in ruins, fracturing a cohesive screen to promote an illicit, triangulated view. While any self-addressed letter returns to a self-made-other, a self that looks with fresh eyes from one moment to the next, from one position to the next, Hoogstraten's letter demands a more radical shift that orients the world around a resistant subject, an alternate center of meaning. Rather than unfold the wonder of boundless space, Hoogstraten ultimately arrests the viewer with the promise of a message from a spectral other, a promise to reveal the in-folded secrets of an absent self. Once lured to a place of no return, however, viewers can never go home again; sullied by a forbidden act of voyeurism, of improper access, viewers become complicit in Hoogstraten's anamorphic secret.

As Deleuze and Guattari observe, "the perception of the secret must necessarily be secret itself: the voyeur, the blackmailer, the author of anonymous letters are no less secretive than what they are in a position to disclose."[43] A visitor who never manages to arrive at the house, a viewer who disdains being viewed, the voyeur holds himself tightly enclosed as a secret, a letter with no legible content. Given how the letter functions to disrupt the viewer's sense of stability, the dark-hatted voyeur who lurks behind the seated woman takes on another cast. Perhaps the scene of reading that catches his interest does not occur right before his eyes in the *voorhuis,* but rather on the opposite side of the house: the voyeur watches as you, the hapless viewer, struggle to read the letter from behind the peephole. Could this dark-hatted voyeur even be an avatar of the artist, waiting to see how viewers resolve the dilemma posed by his letter? Hanging around to witness the reception of his work, his signature, the voyeur-artist welcomes viewers into a shared knowledge of his creative powers, lifting the curtain on the illusion that he construes as home. Regardless of his identity, however, the voyeur figures an externality that remains visible within the interior, captured by a system of perspective that provides for such an "outside" presence. But what status do *you* occupy within this system as a viewer? Where will you stand in relation to the interior of another—or indeed your own interior? In contrast to Alberti's peepshow, Hoogstraten's box conceives the most distant exteriority as the most deeply folded inward; what remains most alien is not the stranger in the street, but the letter that has ostensibly come home. As Hoogstraten's heart of heart, this letter reminds the viewer that interior space remains opaque in spite of a desire to facialize the world, to hollow out the home. Yet at the same time, this heart may also be pure illusion.

NOTES

Introduction

EPIGRAPH: Raphael Holinshed, *Chronicles,* 2nd ed. (1587), vol. 1, ch. 11, p. 45.

1. The *Oxford English Dictionary* cites the earliest attestation of *architecture* as the title of John Shute's *The First and Chief Grounds of Architecture* (1563). (All citations of the *Oxford English Dictionary* [*OED*] refer to *OED Online,* last updated March 2013, Oxford University Press, http://www.oed.com.) However, the *Early English Books Online* database finds two earlier instances that cite *architecture* as a term "Englished" from Latin: Richard Eden's translation of Peter Martyr (Pietro Martire d'Anghiera), *The Decades of the Newe Worlde* (London, 1555), 284, and William Bavande's translation of *A Woorke of Ioannes Ferrarius Montanus, Touchynge the Good Orderynge of a Common Weale* (London, 1559), 90v. Bavande's text, discussed in chapter 2, mentions *architecture* only in relation to Vitruvius's title. Shute's book thus remains seminal for defining *architecture* in depth and shifting the word into English use.

2. Michel de Certeau, *The Practice of Everyday Life,* trans. Steven Rendall (Berkeley: University of California Press, 1984), 117.

3. Robert Weimann, *Shakespeare and the Popular Tradition in the Theater: Studies in the Social Dimension of Dramatic Form and Function,* ed. Robert Schwartz (Baltimore: Johns Hopkins University Press, 1978), 80. I do not follow Weimann's distinction between "platform" (flat playing area) and "scaffold" (built stages such as double-decker pageant wagons). Erika Lin maps Weimann's *locus/platea* binary onto modes of theatricality; see "Performance Practice and Theatrical Privilege: Rethinking Weimann's Concepts of *Locus* and *Platea,*" *New Theatre Quarterly* 22, no. 3 (2006): 283–98. Ric Knowles relates *locus/platea* to Michel de Certeau's strategy/tactic; see review of *Author's Pen and Actor's Voice: Playing and Writing in Shakespeare's Theatre,* by Robert Weimann, ed. Helen Higbee and William West, *Early Theatre* 8, no. 1 (2005): 146.

4. Weimann, *Shakespeare and the Popular Tradition,* 76.

5. Ibid., 74.

6. Vitruvius, *On Architecture,* trans. Frank Granger (London: William Heinemann, 1931), 1:6–7.

7. The first English edition of *De architectura,* a 1692 abridged version translated from French, defines architecture purely as theory and practice with no mention of signification. See Abel Boyer (?), *An Abridgment of the Architecture of Vitruvius* (London, 1692), 24. William Newton's 1771 edition,

which also renders *ratiocinatione* as "in theory" and *fabrica* as "in practice," keeps the passage on signification without gloss. Instead, his footnote makes architecture intellectual by noting that practice includes only the knowledge of practical matters, not manual labor; see Vitruvius, *The Architecture of M. Vitruvius Pollio,* vol. 1., trans. and ed. William Newton (London, 1771), 2. Compare Henry Turner's claim that *ratiocinatio* involves an "enacted knowing," while Vitruvian semiotics requires praxis; see *The English Renaissance Stage: Geometry, Poetics, and the Practical Spatial Arts, 1580–1630* (Oxford: Oxford University Press, 2006), 256.

8. For a comparison between Epicurean and Stoic linguistics, see Ingrid D. Rowland's edition of Vitruvius, *Ten Books on Architecture,* with commentary by Thomas Noble Howe, Ingrid D. Rowland, and Michael J. Dewar (Cambridge: Cambridge University Press, 1999), 135. Indra Kagis McEwen links Vitruvius's signifier and signified to Stoic language theory; see *Vitruvius: Writing the Body of Architecture* (Cambridge, Mass.: MIT Press, 2003), esp. 74.

9. See Vitruvius, *Ten Books,* 135; McEwen, *Vitruvius,* 76.

10. Vitruvius, *On Architecture,* 1:6–7.

11. McEwen associates the signified with the Greek *lekton* and the Latin *res* (*Vitruvius,* 77). While Rowland defines the signified as the "actual object of discussion" (*Ten Books,* 135), Vitruvius's diction clearly avoids a slippage between the thing and the thing proposed.

12. Vitruvius, *On Architecture,* 1:6–7.

13. Henri Lefebvre, *The Production of Space,* trans. Donald Nicholson-Smith (Oxford: Basil Blackwell, 1991), 36.

14. Lefebvre, *Production of Space,* 42.

15. Geoffrey Broadbent, "A Plain Man's Guide to the Theory of Signs," in *Theorizing a New Agenda for Architecture: An Anthology of Architectural Theory, 1965–95,* ed. Kate Nesbitt (New York: Princeton Architectural Press, 1996), 36.

16. Martin Kemp describes perspective as a stereometric cage in *The Science of Art: Optical Themes in Western Art from Brunelleschi to Seurat* (New Haven: Yale University Press, 1990), 34.

17. Vaughan Hart, "'Paper Palaces' from Alberti to Scamozzi," in *Paper Palaces: The Rise of the Renaissance Architectural Treatise,* ed. Vaughan Hart and Peter Hicks (New Haven: Yale University Press, 1998), 1–32. See also Mark Girouard's chapter on "Speaking Buildings," in *Elizabethan Architecture: Its Rise and Fall, 1540–1640* (New Haven: Yale University Press, 2009), 217–54.

18. Mary McLeod, "'Other' Spaces and 'Others,'" in *The Sex of Architecture,* ed. Diana Agrest, Patricia Conway, and Leslie Kanes Weisman (New York: Harry N. Abrams, 1996), 20.

19. Turner, *English Renaissance Stage,* 2.

20. Ibid., 21.

21. Alison Findlay, *Playing Spaces in Early Modern Women's Drama* (Cambridge: Cambridge University Press, 2006), 21.

22. Ibid., 21.

Chapter One

1. Latour has expanded on his theory of quasi-subjects and quasi-objects in multiple publications, most notably *We Have Never Been Modern,* trans. Catherine Porter (Cambridge, Mass.: Harvard University Press, 1993).

2. Michel Serres, *The Parasite,* trans. Lawrence R. Schehr (Baltimore: Johns Hopkins University Press, 1982), 225.

3. Friedrich Nietzsche, *Beyond Good and Evil,* trans. Marion Faber (Oxford: Oxford University Press, 1998), 68. Aphorism 146.

4. Alberto Pérez-Gómez and Louise Pelletier relate this illustration to optics in *Architectural Representation and the Perspective Hinge* (Cambridge, Mass.: MIT Press, 1997), 110.

5. Abraham Bosse, *Traité des manières de dessiner les ordres de l'architecture antique* (Paris, 1664), I.

6. Ibid.

7. For seventeenth-century definitions of *arresté* (modern French *arrêté,* from the verb *arrêter*), see Abel Boyer, *The Royal Dictionary* (London, 1699): "Arresté, *S. M.* (resolution prise dans une Compagnie) *Resolution, Agreement*" and "Un Arresté de compte, *an Account agreed upon*"; also, "Arrester les yeux . . . sur quelque chose . . . *to fix one's Eyes . . . upon a thing.*" Compare Guy Miege, *The Great French Dictionary* (1688): "Arrêté. A thing agreed upon."

8. See chapter 1 in Jean Baudrillard, *Simulacra and Simulation,* trans. Sheila Faria Glaser (Ann Arbor: University of Michigan Press, 1994).

9. Louis Althusser, *Lenin and Philosophy and Other Essays,* trans. Ben Brewster (New York: Monthly Review, 2001), 118.

10. Bosse, *Traité des manières de dessiner les ordres de l'architecture antique,* XLI.

11. Martin Kemp, *The Science of Art: Optical Themes in Western Art from Brunelleschi to Seurat* (New Haven: Yale University Press, 1990), 34.

12. Slavoj Žižek, *Looking Awry: An Introduction to Jacques Lacan Through Popular Culture* (Cambridge, Mass.: MIT Press, 1991), ix, 114. Žižek links the blot to Jacques Lacan's *objet petit a,* the impossible object of desire that only a distorted, subjective gaze can perceive.

13. Vitruvius, *On Architecture,* trans. Frank Granger (London: William Heinemann, 1931), 1:9, 1:21. All subsequent references to Vitruvius derive from this translation.

14. Henri Lefebvre, *The Production of Space,* trans. Donald Nicholson-Smith (Oxford: Blackwell, 1991), 41.

15. Martin Jay gives a historical and theoretical overview of how Cartesian perspectivalism became the dominant visual paradigm of Western culture; see "Scopic Regimes of Modernity," in *Vision and Visuality,* ed. Hal Foster (Seattle: Bay Press, 1988), 3–23. Compare Chris Jenks, "The Centrality of the Eye in Western Culture: An Introduction," in *Visual Culture,* ed. Chris Jenks (New York: Routledge, 1995), 1–25. William M. Ivins Jr. hyperbolically claims that the past five hundred years of European art "has been little more than the story of the slow diffusion of his [Alberti's] ideas"; see *Art and Geometry: A Study in Space Intuitions* (Cambridge, Mass.: Harvard University Press, 1946),

81. James Elkins disputes whether linear perspective was ever a dominant paradigm during the Renaissance, in part because of fragmented knowledge and the persistence of other workshop methods; see both "Renaissance Perspectives," *Journal of the History of Ideas* 53, no. 2 (1992): 209–30, and *The Poetics of Perspective* (Ithaca: Cornell University Press, 1994). Patricia Lee Rubin similarly warns against seeing *De pictura* as a painter's manual, noting its limited circulation; see *Images and Identity in Fifteenth-Century Florence* (New Haven: Yale University Press, 2007), 95–96.

16. Erwin Panofsky, *Perspective as Symbolic Form,* ed. Christopher S. Wood (New York: Zone Books, 1991).

17. The first printed edition of Vitruvius followed hard on Alberti's heels in 1486.

18. Anne Friedberg, *The Virtual Window: From Alberti to Microsoft* (Cambridge, Mass.: MIT Press, 2006). Mark Jarzombek examines how Alberti constructs a literary identity across his oeuvre; see *On Leon Baptista Alberti: His Literary and Aesthetic Theories* (Cambridge, Mass.: MIT Press, 1989).

19. Hans-Karl Lücke, *Alberti Index: Leon Battista Alberti, "De re aedificatoria," Florenz 1485; Index verborum* (Munich: Prestel, 1975).

20. Leon Battista Alberti, *On Painting and On Sculpture: The Latin Texts of "De Pictura" and "De Statua,"* ed. Cecil Grayson (London: Phaidon, 1972), 38–39. All references to *De pictura* come from this bilingual edition.

21. Joseph Masheck, "Alberti's 'Window': Art-Historiographic Notes on an Antimodernist Misprision," *Art Journal* 50, no. 1 (1991): 36. Although perspectival rules apply to any two-dimensional surface, including flexible ones, the painters addressed by Alberti still worked primarily on rigid surfaces like walls, detached wooden panels, altarpieces, and furniture. In Book III, Alberti warns against painting on "very small panels [*minimis tabellis*]" (101). In Book VII of *De re aedificatoria,* Alberti states a preference for "detached painted panels rather than pictures applied directly to the walls" (220).

22. Alberti, *On Painting,* 49.

23. For more on perspective versus *perspicere* (to see clearly), see Claudio Guillen's "On the Concept and Metaphor of Perspective," in *Comparatists at Work: Studies in Comparative Literature,* ed. Stephen G. Nichols Jr. and Richard B. Vowles (Waltham, Mass.: Blaisdell Publishing, 1968), 28–90. Thomas Frangenberg notes that Alberti never uses the term *prospettiva;* see *Der Betrachter, Studien zur florentinischen Kunstliterature des 16 Jahrunderts* (Berlin: Gebr. Mann, 1990), 29. Cited in Thomas Puttfarken, *The Discovery of Pictorial Composition: Theories of Visual Order in Painting, 1400–1800* (New Haven: Yale University Press, 2000), 70. John White gives a classic history of perspective in *Birth and Rebirth of Pictorial Space* (London: Faber and Faber, 1957); see also David C. Lindberg, *Theories of Vision from Al-Kindi to Kepler* (Chicago: University of Chicago Press, 1981), 147–77.

24. Alberti, *On Painting,* 36–37. See also Jack M. Greenstein, "On Alberti's 'Sign': Vision and Composition in Quattrocento Painting," *Art Bulletin* 79, no. 4 (1997): 669–98.

25. Alberti, *On Painting,* 54–55.

26. Roland Barthes, *Camera Lucida: Reflections on Photography,* trans. Richard Howard (New York: Hill and Wang, 1981), 26–27.

27. Alberti, *On Painting,* 40–41; repeated at 42–43.

28. Puttfarken, *Discovery of Pictorial Composition,* 72. Alberti deliberately skirts the debate over whether rays enter into or emanate from the eye; see *On Painting,* 41. The idea of an *axis visualis* traces back to Euclid's *Optics* (c. 300 B.C.E.).

29. Alberti, *On Painting,* 57. There is debate whether Alberti used a distance point, or whether this concept derives from northern Renaissance figures such as Jean Pelerin and Vignola.

30. Jacques Lacan, *The Four Fundamental Concepts of Psychoanalysis: The Seminar of Jacques Lacan Book XI,* trans. Alan Sheridan (New York: W. W. Norton, 1981), 86.

31. Kaja Silverman, following Lacan, suggests that Alberti wishes to "plac[e] the spectator *outside* the spectacle, in a position of detached mastery," but ultimately fails; see *Male Subjectivity at the Margins* (New York: Routledge, 1992), 146. Yet *De pictura* underscores how deeply enmeshed the viewer must be in the perspectival architecture. While Silverman argues that the accord between the vanishing point and the geometric point of the viewer's eye "encourages a further deconstruction of the Albertian paradigm" (146), this relation is in fact *built into* Alberti's definition of the centric point.

32. Alberti, *On Painting,* 67, 55.

33. Alberti, *On Painting,* 49.

34. Gilles Deleuze and Félix Guattari understand perspective as a reterritorialization of lines of flight; see *A Thousand Plateaus: Capitalism and Schizophrenia,* trans. Brian Massumi (Minneapolis: University of Minnesota Press, 1987), 329.

35. David Summers, *Vision, Reflection, and Desire in Western Painting* (Chapel Hill: University of North Carolina Press, 2007), 61. Summers notes that Alberti leaves behind the *speculum animatum* when *De pictura* is translated into Tuscan and dedicated to Brunelleschi.

36. John Donne, "The Ecstacy," lines 7–8.

37. Ibid., 55.

38. Catherine Belsey similarly claims that both the spectator and painted surface can be thought of as "the fourth wall of the three-sided box of space which is a perspective picture"; see "Making Space: Perspective Vision and the Lacanian Real," *Textual Practice* 16, no. 1 (2002): 46.

39. Alberti, *On Painting,* 73, 103, 39, 103.

40. Ibid., 101. Alberti also contrasts the *historia* with a "colossus" (73) and discourages the use of small panels (101).

41. Ibid., 81.

42. Ibid., 83.

43. The parallel syntax stems from the original Latin: "*et quae illi cum spectantibus et quae inter se picti exquentur.*" Alberti, *On Painting,* 80–82.

44. Moshe Barasch similarly notes a conflict between the temporal motion of *historia* and the spatial immobility of linear perspective; see *The Language of Art: Studies in Interpretation* (New York: NYU Press, 1997), 247.

45. Alhazen produced his Arabic text near the end of the eleventh century, but many Latin translations and commentaries have existed from the twelfth century onward. Thomas Frangenberg situates the legacy of Alhazen's "glance" and "scrutiny" not in Alberti, but in later fifteenth-century perspective treatises; see "The Image and the Moving Eye: Jean Pélerin (Viator) to Guidobaldo del Monte," *Journal of the Warburg and Courtauld Institutes* 49 (1986): 150–71.

46. Norman Bryson, "The Gaze and the Glance," in *Vision and Painting: The Logic of the Gaze* (London: Macmillan, 1983), 93. Compare Edward S. Casey's positing of the gaze and glance as "the two great modes of human looking" in *The World at a Glance* (Bloomington: Indiana University Press, 2007), 132 and *passim.*

47. Alberti, *On Painting,* 69.

48. Ibid.

49. Friedberg sees the veil as encoding information like a bitmap (*Virtual Window,* 39).

50. Alberti, *On Painting,* 69.

51. Alberti, *On Painting,* 57–59. Mark Wigley notes how Alberti's "strategy of masking the mask" prevents art from questioning its own status; see Mark Wigley, "Untitled: The Housing of Gender," in *Sexuality and Space,* ed. Beatriz Colomina (New York: Princeton Architectural Press, 1992), 380.

52. Alberti, *On Painting,* 37, 59, 57–59. It is generally accepted that the Latin edition of *De pictura* (1435) addresses a more learned readership, while the Tuscan edition (1436) targets mainly artists. Samuel Y. Edgerton Jr. characterizes Alberti's tone as that of an "earthy craftsman"; see *The Renaissance Rediscovery of Linear Perspective* (New York: Basic Books, 1975), 82. In contrast, J. V. Field argues that Alberti addresses patrons rather than practitioners; see *The Invention of Infinity: Mathematics and Art in the Renaissance* (Oxford: Oxford University Press, 1997), 25.

53. Alberti, *On Painting,* 55–56.

54. Vitruvius, *On Architecture,* 1:6–7.

55. Alberti, *On Painting,* 59. Clark Hulse also notes this "peculiarly double rhetorical stance" in *De pictura,* though he goes on to argue, quite traditionally, that Alberti uses this doubled voice "to demonstrate that painting has all the characteristics of a liberal art"; see *The Rule of Art: Literature and Painting in the Renaissance* (Chicago: University of Chicago Press, 1990), 47–76, esp. 55–56. I would contend that what Alberti is able to *avoid* demonstrating through this strategy of a doubled voice drives, in large part, his later architectural projects.

56. Piero della Francesca, *De prospectiva pingendi* (late fifteenth century). Elkins, among others, speculates that this treatise may contain the demonstrations that Alberti referenced as sharing with friends; see "Piero della Francesca and the Renaissance Proof of Linear Perspective," *Art Bulletin* 69, no. 2 (1987): 220–30.

57. Leon Battista Alberti, *On the Art of Building in Ten Books,* trans. Joseph Rykwert, Neil Leach, and Robert Tavernor (Cambridge, Mass.: MIT Press, 1988), 7. I cite the Latin version from the Italian edition of *L'Architettura,*

trans. Paolo Portoghesi (Milan: Edizioni Il Polifilo, 1966), 19. All Latin references of *De re aedificatoria* come from this edition.

58. From Italian *faccia, facciata* and French *face, façade*. David Friedman traces the term *facciata* to a 1340 Sienese building contract; see "Palaces and the Street in Late-Medieval and Renaissance Italy," in *Urban Landscapes: International Perspectives*, ed. J. W. R. Whitehand and P. J. Larkham (London: Routledge, 1992), 93–97. The first theoretical elaboration of the facade, however, still belongs to Alberti.

59. In keeping with Alberti's definition, I use *facade* broadly to mean all visible exterior surfaces, not just the front.

60. Alberti, *On Painting*, 36–37.

61. Carol Herselle Krinsky tracks Vitruvian manuscripts across medieval Europe; see "Seventy-Eight Vitruvius Manuscripts," *Journal of the Warburg and Courtauld Institutes* 30 (1967): 36–70. The oldest extant copy of *De architectura* may have been brought by monks from Italy to England in the eighth century (British Library, Harleian 2767).

62. Françoise Choay sees *De re aedificatoria* as the "instaurational text" of the Renaissance, in contrast to Vitruvius's less structurally coherent work; see *The Rule and the Model: On the Theory of Architecture and Urbanism*, ed. Denise Bratton (Cambridge, Mass.: MIT Press, 1990). Richard Krautheimer similarly contends that Vitruvius writes a manual for craftsmen, whereas Alberti offers a conceptual program; see "Alberti and Vitruvius," in *Studies in Early Christian, Medieval, and Renaissance Art* (New York: NYU Press, 1969), 323–30.

63. Choay, *Rule and the Model*, 66–67.

64. Book VI, Prologue. Alberti, *Art of Building*, 154. This Prologue to Book VI famously criticizes Vitruvius's language, incoherence, and lack of refinement.

65. Ibid.

66. Ibid.

67. While Friedman notes that Vitruvius and Alberti both use *frons* to indicate the front of a building, he cites only one usage of *facies* from *De re aedificatoria* (from Book IV, chapter 5), and observes that the term *facciata* was not available to Alberti's Latin discourse.

68. All four references come from Book II. The first three are from the prologue, paragraphs 1 and 4, while the fourth is from chapter 8, paragraph 8. See *Vitruve "De architectura" Concordance*, pt. 1, ed. L. Callebat, P. Bouet, Ph. Fleury, and M. Zuinghedau (Hildesheim: Olms-Weidmann, 1984), 417.

69. See Javier Fresnillo Nuñez, *Leon Battista Alberti "De re aedificatoria": A Lemmatized Concordance*, pt. 1 (Hildesheim: Olms-Weidmann, 1996), 675. Charles Burroughs traces some early usages of the face/facade in Italian architectural discourse and mentions Alberti's use of *facies;* see "The Building's Face and the Herculean Paradigm: Agendas and Agency in Roman Renaissance Architecture," *RES: Anthropology and Aesthetics* 23 (1993): 7–30.

70. Alberti, *Art of Building*, 295–96. Book IX.2.

71. Vitruvius, *On Architecture*, 1:75. Book II, Preface.

72. Lacan, *Four Fundamental Concepts*, 96.

73. Vitruvius, *On Architecture*, 1:161. Book III.1.

74. While not entirely flat, the Vitruvian man's bodily perfection derives mainly from relations of height and width rather than depth. In *De architectura,* the only measurement in depth concerns the length of a foot; in Leonardo's sketch, however, even this foot is turned sideways for easy comparison with other body parts.

75. Ibid., 1:27.

76. Alberti, *Art of Building,* 302. Book IX.5.

77. Ibid.

78. Deleuze and Guattari, *Thousand Plateaus,* 168.

79. Ibid. Andrew Ballantyne refers to Alberti's Santa Maria Novella and Palazzo Rucellai as examples of facialized facades; see *Deleuze and Guattari for Architects* (London: Routledge, 2007), 74–75.

80. Deleuze and Guattari, *Thousand Plateaus,* 172.

81. Though critics speculate about Alberti's role in earlier projects, there is no reliable evidence.

82. Alberti likely began work on the Tempio in 1453; see Charles Hope, "The Early History of the Tempio Malatestiano," *Journal of the Warburg and Courtauld Institutes* 55 (1992): 94.

83. For a summary of views on the relation of Alberti's theory and practice, see Hanno-Walter Kruft, *A History of Architectural Theory from Vitruvius to the Present,* trans. Ronald Taylor, Elsie Callander, and Anthony Wood (New York: Princeton Architectural Press, 1994), 49. See also Joseph Rykwert, "Theory as Rhetoric: Leon Battista Alberti in Theory and in Practice," in *Paper Palaces: The Rise of the Renaissance Architectural Treatise,* ed. Vaughan Hart and Peter Hicks (New Haven: Yale University Press, 1998), esp. 33.

84. Krautheimer, "Alberti and Vitruvius," 326.

85. Mark Jarzombeck explores the rhetoric of Alberti's humanist self-identification; see *On Leon Baptista Alberti: His Literary and Aesthetic Theories* (Cambridge, Mass.: MIT Press, 1989). Other accounts of Alberti's humanism include Cecil Grayson, *Studi su Leon Battista Alberti,* ed. Paola Claut (Mantua: Leo S. Olschki, 1998), 129–48; and Anthony Grafton, *Leon Battista Alberti: Master Builder of the Italian Renaissance* (New York: Hill and Wang, 2000), esp. 31–70.

86. Alberti likely continued to revise the treatise after presenting it in 1452; parts of the final treatise seem to reference his work in Rimini. As Rudolf Wittkower concludes after surveying Alberti's four major church facades, these surfaces "must be regarded as an intellectual and artistic achievement of supreme importance"; see *Architectural Principles in the Age of Humanism* (New York: Random House, 1962), 56.

87. Alberti's self-portrait medal in the National Gallery (Washington, D.C.) bears the inscription "LBAP," believed to stand for "Leon Battista Alberti Pictor."

88. The church became important to the Malatesta family when the first Lord of Rimini was buried there in 1312; see Robert Tavernor, *On Alberti and the Art of Building* (New Haven: Yale University Press, 1998), 49. Mary Hollingsworth argues that Sigismondo "had gone out of his way to emphasize the Christian context"; see "Art Patronage in Renaissance Urbino, Pesaro, and

Rimini," in *The Court Cities of Northern Italy: Milan, Parma, Piacenza, Mantua, Ferrara, Bologna, Urbino, Pesaro, and Rimini,* ed. Charles M. Rosenberg (Cambridge: Cambridge University Press, 2010), 331. In my view, the Christian symbols are overshadowed by a wealth of secular images, especially those related to the Malatesta family.

89. Scholars dispute whether the chapels and niches were meant for funerary purposes. Helen Ettlinger reviews the relevant primary documents in "The Sepulchre on the Facade: A Re-Evaluation of Sigismondo Malatesta's Rebuilding of San Francesco in Rimini," *Journal of the Warburg and Courtauld Institutes* 53 (1990): 133–43. Joscelyn Godwin proposes a Neoplatonic reading of the iconography found in the chapels; *The Pagan Dream of the Renaissance* (Grand Rapids: Phanes, 2002), esp. 39–45.

90. Pius II, *Commentaries,* ed. Margaret Meserve and Marcello Simonetta, vol. 1 (Cambridge, Mass.: Harvard University Press, 2003), 329.

91. Just as the Arch of Augustus frames the pilgrimage route of the via Flaminia, Charles Burroughs sees the Tempio as "a framing device for a Christian Via Flaminia"; see *From Signs to Design: Environmental Process and Reform in Early Renaissance Rome* (Cambridge, Mass.: MIT Press, 1990), 213.

92. *The Lives of the Artists,* trans. Julia Conaway Bondanella and Peter Bondanella (Oxford: Oxford University Press, 1991), 180. Vasari's term *templum,* rendered in this translation as *church,* emphasizes Alberti's radical evocation of Greek temples in a Christian space.

93. The Tempio's building history is contentious and convoluted. Charles Hope excavates the building's formative stages in "The Early History of the Tempio Malatestiano," *Journal of the Warburg and Courtauld Institutes* 55 (1992): 51–154. For Italian readers, the most thorough history and analysis can be found in Massimo Bulgarelli's chapter "L'architettura," in *Il Tempio Malatestiano a Rimini,* ed. Antonio Paolucci, vol. 1 (Modena: Franco Cosimo Panini, 2010), 49–121. See also chapter 6 in Tavernor, *On Alberti.*

94. Compare Jarzombek's claim that Alberti wishes to avoid infecting San Francesco with a secular Malatesta facade (*On Leon Baptista Alberti,* 173).

95. From a letter dated November 18, 1454, now at the Pierpont Morgan Library. See Cecil Grayson, *An Autograph Letter from Leon Battista Alberti to Matteo de' Pasti* (New York: Pierpont Morgan Library, 1957), 17–20. See also Hope, "Early History," 150; and Tavernor, *On Alberti,* 59–61.

96. "*Prestantissimo viro Matheo de' Pasti et caetera amico dulcissimo*"; Grayson, *Autograph,* 19.

97. Alberti, *Art of Building,* 156. Book VI.2.

98. Compare Girolamo Mancini's claim that Alberti tries to unite old and new by aligning his arches with the Gothic windows ("Da vero maestro l'architetto collegò l'antica alla nuova costruzione. Per esempio ciascuna cappella ha due finestre situate in guisa che gli archi del rivestimento esterno non impediscono punto il passaggio all luce"); see *Vita di Leon Battista Alberti,* 2nd ed. (Florence: G. Carnesecchi, 1911), 317.

99. From the letter to Matteo de' Pasti, cited above. Wittkower's *Architectural Principles* relates Pythagorean musical intervals to Alberti's architectural

proportions. Manfredo Tafuri, however, notes the conflicting theories of spatial harmony in Renaissance architecture and writing; see "Discordant Harmony from Alberti to Zuccari," *Architectural Design* 49 (1979): 36–44. More recent scholarship by Christine Smith and Tim Anstey points to Alberti's modification of musical theory to offset real-world limitations; Anstey reads these discordances across the surface rather than in depth. See Christine Smith, *Architecture in the Culture of Early Humanism: Ethics, Aesthetics, and Eloquence, 1400–1470* (New York: Oxford University Press, 1992); T. A. Anstey, "Fictive Harmonies: Music and the Tempio Malatestiano," *RES: Anthropology and Aesthetics* 36 (1999): 187–204.

100. Canto 9.

101. Alina A. Payne, *The Architectural Treatise in the Italian Renaissance: Architectural Invention, Ornament, and Literary Culture* (Cambridge: Cambridge University Press, 1999), 74.

102. Wittkower, *Architectural Principles,* 38.

103. Alberto G. Cassani, "Per foramina obductae personae: Una fonte inedita per la facciata del tempio Malatestiano," *Albertiana* 5 (2002): 75, 76. The two relevant passages are "Cosí è per lo staordinario concetto di *concinnitas,* che non è affatto una banale armonia, ma il simbolo stesso della difficile consonanza tra elementi che *per loro natura* sarebbero in conflitto" and "stonature lasciate bene in vista dall'Alberti, tra gli archi del fianco, per *pietas* o per sadismo." In contrast, Godwin believes that Alberti's perfect forms "speak for themselves" (*Pagan Dream,* 40).

104. Alberti, *Art of Building,* 180. Book VI.12.

105. Ibid.

106. See Wittkower's *Architectural Principles* for more detailed analysis. I use the term *column* broadly to indicate the various types of vertical supports (engaged or detached, square or round, etc.) that Alberti places in this genre of "false opening."

107. Curiously, the Leoni translation of 1755—the first translation of *De re aedificatoria* into English—omits this analogy of pelt over clothing.

108. Gottfried Semper, *The Four Elements of Architecture and Other Writings,* trans. Harry Francis Mallgrave and Wolfgang Herrmann (Cambridge: Cambridge University Press, 1989), 104.

109. Ibid., 104.

110. Alberti, *Art of Building,* 180. Book VI.12.

111. Ibid., 164. Book VI.5.

112. Ibid., 175–77. Book VI.9.

113. See Mark Wigley, "Untitled: The Housing of Gender," in *Sexuality and Space* (New York: Princeton Architectural Press, 1992), esp. 354ff.

114. Alberti, *Art of Building,* 174. Book VI.9.

115. Pier Giorgio Pasini discusses the sightlines of the front, lower facade in "La facciata 'prospettica' dell Tempio Malatestiano," *Romagna: Arte e Storia* 1, no. 2 (1981): 21–34. Virtually every image of the Tempio that appears in Alberti criticism employs these strategic viewing angles. In Carlo Fossati's monograph, an engraving of Alberti's side arcade eliminates de' Pasti's

walls altogether, indulging a fantasy of cohesion by leaving a shadowy recess between arches; see *Le Temple de Malateste de Rimini: Architecture de Leon Baptiste Alberti de Florence* (Fuligno, 1794).

116. Charles Burroughs suggests that the side sarcophagi create a "street of tombs, implying a processional reading of successive tombs" as viewers walk beside the church before entering; see *From Signs to Design,* 213.

117. Alberti describes every represented object as a type of body: "We must now speak of the other property of a surface, which, if I might put it this way, is like a skin [*cutis*] stretched over the whole extent [*dorsum,* "back"] of the surface" (*On Painting,* 39). These contours of an object are what the veil must translate for the painterly eye (ibid., 69).

118. See chapter 4 for a fuller explanation of *chora* as defined in Plato's *Timaeus.*

119. Alberti's work on Santa Maria Novella likely began around 1456.

120. The family behind the original facade won a lawsuit to preserve its design (Tavernor, *On Alberti,* 103).

121. For more on Alberti's possible changes, see Franco Borsi, *Leon Battista Alberti: The Complete Works,* trans. Rudolf G. Carpanini (London: Faber and Faber, 1989), 61–74, and Phyllis Williams Lehmann, "Alberti and Antiquity: Additional Observations," *Art Bulletin* 70, no. 3 (1988): 388–400.

122. See Wittkower, *Architectural Principles,* 45; also Lehmann, "Alberti and Antiquity."

123. Charles Burroughs, calling Alberti "an architect of facades," names the Palazzo Rucellai as the most important building in establishing a tradition of secular facade architecture. Yet Burroughs attributes this status to the social and political impact of Rucellai's house, not Alberti's formal innovations; see Burroughs, "Building's Face," 9–10.

124. Burroughs notes that Rucellai "observed tradition by remodeling an ancestral site," thus deepening local memory despite the new facade; see *The Italian Renaissance Palace Façade: Structures of Authority, Surfaces of Sense* (Cambridge: Cambridge University Press, 2002), 102. For more on the site's development, see Brenda Preyer, "The Rucellai Palace," in *Giovanni Rucellai ed il suo zibaldone II: A Florentine Patrician and His Palace* (London: Warburg Institute, 1981), 155–228. Though dated by critics from the late 1440s to early 1460s, Alberti's facade likely groups with other Rucellai projects executed in the 1450s.

125. Howard Saalman dismisses the interior while praising Alberti's facade as "the most significant statement of this theme in the Quattrocento"; see "Tommaso Spinelli, Michelozzo, Manetti, and Rossellino," *Journal of the Society of Architectural Historians* 25, no. 3 (1966): 161.

126. Most historians accept Vasari's attribution of the facade to Alberti. However, Charles Randall Mack argues for Bernardo Rossellino as architect in "The Rucellai Palace: Some New Proposals," *Art Bulletin* 56, no. 4 (1974): 517–29, as does Kurt W. Forster in "The Palazzo Rucellai and Questions of Typology in the Development of Renaissance Buildings," *Art Bulletin* 58, no. 1 (1976): 109–13. Saalman argues that Rossellino built the facade as Alberti's

proxy; see review of *Giovanni Rucellai ed il suo zibaldone, II: A Florentine Patrician and His Palace*, ed. F. W. Kent et al., *Journal of the Society of Architectural Historians* 47, no. 1 (1988): 82–90.

127. Saalman even invents a scenario where Cosimo de' Medici advises his future in-law Rucellai to hire Alberti (review of *Giovanni Rucellai,* 89). Tavernor, in contrast, sees Rucellai's choice of architect as rejecting Medici influence.

128. Based on the *opus reticulatum* brickwork discussed in *De re aedificatoria* (II.10) and illustrated by Cosimo Bartoli's woodcut illustration. See Alberti, *Art of Building,* 52–53.

129. Situated at a forty-five-degree bend along the via Larga, a major Florentine street, the Palazzo Medici "seems to turn its face to the visitor"; see Friedman, "Palaces and the Street," 103–4.

130. Tavernor, *On Alberti,* 89.

131. Ibid., 85.

132. Aptly, Vitruvius discusses these site-based optical illusions in the book on private houses (VI.2); see *On Architecture,* 2:21. The more famous section on optical adjustments in temple columns and entablatures is in III.3; see *On Architecture,* 1:177–81.

133. Yvonne Elet, "Seats of Power: The Outdoor Benches of Early Modern Florence," *Journal of the Society of Architectural Historians* 61, no. 4 (2002): 453 and passim. I thank Rosa Salzburg for referring me to this essay. As Elet notes, the Palazzo Rucellai's benches provide a base for the facade rather than the whole building, thus deepening a schism between the architectural body and face (457). For more on facade benches, see F. W. Kent, "Palaces, Politics and Society in Fifteenth-Century Florence," *I Tatti Studies: Essays in the Renaissance* 2 (1987): 60.

134. Compare Umberto Eco's concept of an "open work" designed for public appropriation; see *The Open Work,* trans. Anna Cancogni (Cambridge, Mass.: Harvard University Press, 1989).

135. As discussed in my introduction, Michel de Certeau defines *lieu* and *espace* in *The Practice of Everyday Life,* trans. Steven Rendall (Berkeley: University of California Press, 1984), 117–18.

136. As Dale Kent notes, benches in piazzas and on palazzo facades served as informal stages for street performers such as *cantimbanchi;* see *Cosimo de' Medici and the Florentine Renaissance: The Patron's Oeuvre* (New Haven: Yale University Press, 2000), 43–46, 407n27.

137. Friedman, "Palaces and the Street," 94.

138. Bryson, *Vision and Painting,* 121.

139. Alberti, *Art of Building,* 295. Book IX.2.

140. Ibid., 296. Book IX.2.

141. Ibid., 106. Book IV.5. Alberti notes that, besides making the city seem larger, these nonlinear roads provide "great benefit in terms of appearance and practical convenience."

142. Ibid., 106. Book IV.5.

143. Ibid., 314. Book IX.9.

Chapter Two

1. For example, John Norden's *The Surueyors Dialogue* (London, 1607) compares the pile to St. Paul's steeple: "If this loftie Pyle bee not equalized by the estate and reuenewes of the builder, it is as if Paules steeple should serue Pancras Church for a Belfry" (84). In Milton's *Paradise Lost,* the fallen angels build an "ascending pile" at Pandemonium (Book I, line 722).

2. For more on medieval great halls, see Maurice Barley, *Houses and History* (London: Faber and Faber, 1986); Olive Cook, *The English House Through Seven Centuries* (Woodstock, N.Y.: Overlook Press, 1968); Margaret Wood, *The English Mediaeval House* (London: Studio Editions, 1965).

3. For more on the changing family in early modern England, see Lawrence Stone's classic *The Family, Sex and Marriage in England, 1500–1800* (New York: Harper & Row, 1977).

4. Sidney J. Herrtage, ed., *England in the Reign of King Henry the Eighth, Part I,* Early English Text Society, Extra Series 32 (London: N. Trübner & Co., 1878), lviii.

5. Howard Colvin cites "deface" and "plucked down" as the two main descriptors of Henry's violence; see "Recycling the Monasteries: Demolition and Reuse by the Tudor Government, 1536–47," in *Essays in English Architectural History* (New Haven: Yale University Press, 1999), 52–66. As Colvin's examples show, the two terms are sometimes used in tandem to indicate different types of damage.

6. Unlike *plucked down, defaced* is commonly used with abstract nouns in early modern English to indicate a social defilement, defiance, and effacement; thus Philip Sidney's *Apologie for Poetrie* (1595) describes the scorn that defaces poetic achievement in modern times (B2r). Richard Huloet's English-Latin dictionary (1572) parses the term *deface* as both to "brynge out of estimation the acte of others" and to erase or deform ("deformare") writing (M5r).

7. See Huloet's entry for "Dashe" (M3r). In this sense of disfiguring texts, Huloet links *deface* to *cancel* (G3r) and *enterlyne* (P7v); the former means to cross out, while the latter indicates a revision or tampering between lines (cognates are L. *interlinere,* Fr. *effacer*). Compare definition 3 of the verb *deface* in *OED:* "to blot out, obliterate, efface (writing, marks)." Like a defaced reputation or authority, this textual defacement obscures and defiles words without removing them.

8. See Gayatri Spivak's "Translator's Preface" to Jacques Derrida, *Of Grammatology* (Baltimore: Johns Hopkins University Press, 1974), viii. Derrida's term "sous rature" (under erasure) draws on Martin Heidegger's work.

9. Thomas F. Mayer, *Thomas Starkey and the Commonweal: Humanist Politics and Religion in the Reign of Henry VIII* (Cambridge: Cambridge University Press, 1989), 3.

10. Sidney J. Herrtage, ed., *England in the Reign of King Henry the Eighth,* lviii.

11. W. G. Hoskins identifies the Great Rebuilding as a period of intense construction; see "The Rebuilding of Rural England, 1570–1640," *Past and Present,* no. 4 (1953): 44–59. See also Colin Platt, *The Great Rebuildings of*

Tudor and Stuart England: Revolutions in Architectural Taste (London: UCL Press, 1994); Peter Borsay, *The English Urban Renaissance: Culture and Society on the Provincial Town* (Oxford: Clarendon Press, 1989), esp. 47–49.

12. George Hakewill, *An Apologie or Declaration of the Power and Providence of God in the Government of the World* (Oxford, 1627), 249.

13. John Dee, preface to *The Elements of Geometrie of the Most Auncient Philosopher Euclide of Megara* (London, 1570), D3r. For the relationship of English architecture and mathematics, see J. A. Bennett, "Architecture and Mathematical Practice in England, 1550–1650," in *English Architecture Public and Private,* ed. John Bold and Edward Chaney (London: Hambledon, 1993), 22–30.

14. Dee, preface to *Elements of Geometrie,* D3r.

15. Hanno-Walter Kruft, *A History of Architectural Theory from Vitruvius to the Present,* trans. Ronald Taylor, Elsie Callander, and Anthony Wood (New York: Princeton Architectural Press, 1994), 229. Kruft does, however, caution against overlooking earlier English writers. Recent anthologies attempt to recover these texts; see *British Architectural Theory, 1540–1750: An Anthology of Texts,* ed. Caroline Van Eck and Christy Anderson (Aldershot: Ashgate, 2003), and *British Architectural Books and Writers, 1556–1785,* ed. Eileen Harris with Nicholas Savage (Cambridge: Cambridge University Press, 1990).

16. Accounts of how Continental treatises influenced English architecture include Simon Thurley, *The Royal Palaces of Tudor England: Architecture and Court Life, 1460–1547* (New Haven: Yale University Press, 1993), 88–98; Christy Anderson, "Learning to Read Architecture in the English Renaissance," in *Albion's Classicism: Britain and the Visual Arts, 1550–1650,* ed. Lucy Gent (New Haven: Yale University Press, 1995), 239–86; and Malcolm Airs, *The Making of the English Country House, 1500–1640* (London: Architectural Press, 1975), 25–28. Lucy Gent's appendix catalogs the books on art, architecture, and perspective found in English libraries of this period; see *Picture and Poetry, 1560–1620* (Leamington Spa: James Hall, 1981), 66–86.

17. Harris and Savage, *British Architectural Books,* 313–14.

18. John Shute, *The First and Chiefe Groundes of Architecture* (London: 1563), B2r.

19. Ibid., B2v.

20. Ibid., B2r, A2r. While Shute toured Italy with his patron, the book draws mainly from Serlio. See Vaughan Hart, "From Virgin to Courtesan in Early English Vitruvian Books," in *Paper Palaces: The Rise of the Renaissance Architectural Treatise,* ed. Vaughan Hart and Peter Hicks (New Haven: Yale University Press, 1998), 297–318; Platt, *Great Rebuildings,* 103; Mario Carpo, *Architecture in the Age of Printing: Orality, Writing, Typography, and Printed Images in the History of Architectural Theory,* trans. Sarah Benson (Cambridge, Mass.: MIT Press, 2001), 103.

21. Shute, *First and Chiefe Groundes,* B2v.

22. Ibid., A2v.

23. Sebastiano Serlio, *Five Books of Architecture,* trans. Robert Peake [?] (London, 1611), B1r. In his 1629 *Sermons,* Lancelot Andrewes mocks

Caiaphas as "a very *Vitruvius,* such a Workman" (439). Thomas Elyot's dictionary, *Bibliotheca Eliotae* (1542) defines an *architector* or *architectus* as "a diuiser of buildynge, or a maister of the warkes" (D6v).

24. Gent calls this mistranslation "a measure of his distinctively English attitude"; see "'The Rash Gazer': Economies of Vision in Britain, 1550–1660," in *Albion's Classicism: The Visual Arts in Britain, 1550–1660,* ed. Lucy Gent (New Haven: Yale University Press, 1995), 384. Since the English edition derives from Pieter van Aelst's Dutch translation, first published in 1539 with a second edition in 1549, the slippage seems to occur when the translator renders "sekerste" (from *zeker,* Dutch for *certain,* plus the superlative suffix *-ste*) as "most secret." The English translation is not completely wrong, however, since the preface from Serlio's 1545 French-Italian edition claims that his first book concerns "des Secretz de Geometrie" (AA3r).

25. Henry Wotton, *The Elements of Architecture* (London, 1624), 55.

26. For more on this genre, see William Eamon, *Science and the Secrets of Nature: Books of Secrets in Medieval and Early Modern Culture* (Princeton: Princeton University Press, 1994), and Steven J. Williams, *The Secret of Secrets: The Scholarly Career of a Pseudo-Aristotelian Text in the Latin Middle Ages* (Ann Arbor: University of Michigan Press, 2003). The popular *Secretum secretorum* was translated into English numerous times in this period; see *"Secretum Secretorum": Nine English Versions,* ed. M. A. Manzalaoui, Early English Text Society No. 276 (Oxford: Oxford University Press, 1977).

27. See Michel Foucault, *The History of Sexuality,* vol. 1, *An Introduction* (New York: Vintage, 1990). In *Covert Operations: The Medieval Uses of Secrecy* (Philadelphia: University of Pennsylvania Press, 1999), Karma Lochrie critiques Foucault in relation to medieval secrecy and sexuality (12–55), while discussing the *Secretum secretorum* as a feminine secret from the East (esp. 98–118).

28. For more on *libri secretorum* and mountebanks, see Eamon, *Science and the Secrets of Nature,* 235–50.

29. Hubert Damisch, *The Origin of Perspective,* trans. John Goodman (Cambridge, Mass.: MIT Press, 1994), 94. The *di-mostratio* (double showing) refers originally to the necessity of using two mirrors to reflect an object without reversal. Damisch later associates this concept with that which escapes perspectival representation, such as the sky in Brunelleschi's experiment—which could not be painted but only reflected with a mirror. Damisch finally links *di-mostratio* to the creation of a subject who looks at others looking back, who relies on a "relay mechanism, a subsequent scansion" to construe him/herself (126).

30. For more on the origins of English architects, see John Wilton-Ely, "The Rise of the Professional Architect in England," in *The Architect: Chapters in the History of the Profession,* ed. Spiro Kostof (Berkeley: University of California Press, 2000), 180–208.

31. Christy Anderson notes that the instability of wonder distinguishes English architecture from the fixed order of classical tradition ("Learning to Read," 268).

32. Wotton, *Elements of Architecture,* 21 (misnumbered, should be 12). Likewise, Alberti claims that "within the form and figure of a building there resides some natural excellence and perfection that excites the mind and is immediately recognized by it" (*Art of Building,* 302; IX.5). Compare Wotton's definition of *eurythmia* as a concordance of dimensions that "taketh euery *Beholder,* by the secret power of *Proportion*" (*Elements of Architecture,* 119).

33. From Chapman's dedication to Inigo Jones in *The Divine Poem of Musaeus* (London, 1616); discussed in William A. McClung, *The Architecture of Paradise: Survivals of Eden and Jerusalem* (Berkeley: University of California Press, 1983), 93.

34. Historical Manuscripts Commission, *The Manuscripts of His Grace, the Duke of Rutland, K. G., Preserved at Belvoir Castle,* vol. 4 (London: H. M. Stationery Office, 1905), 446.

35. Andrew Boorde, *The Boke for to Lerne a Man to be Wyse in Buyldyng of His Howse for the Helth of Body and to Holde Quyetnes for the Helth of His Soule, and Body* (London, 1540[?]), A3v. Paula Henderson notes a trend to approach houses through gardens and forecourts; see *The Tudor House and Garden: Architecture and Landscape in the Sixteenth and Early Seventeenth Centuries* (New Haven: Yale University Press, 2005). Lucy Gent examines early modern ways of looking at architecture; see "The Rash Gazer," 377–93.

36. Boorde even suggests that "yf the herte and mynde be not pleased nature doth abhorre. And yf nature do abhorre, mortyfycacion of the Vytall and anymall and spyrytuall powers do consequently folowe" (*Boke for to Lerne a Man,* A3v). Maurice Howard links architecture to medical books, intertwining the roles of architect and physician; see "The Ideal House and Healthy Life: The Origins of Architectural Theory in England," in *Les traités d'architecture de la Renaissance,* ed. Jean Guillaume (Paris: Picard, 1988), 425–35.

37. Boorde, *Boke for to Lerne a Man,* A3v.

38. Wotton, *Elements of Architecture,* 4. Izaak Walton claims that Wotton studied optics for his M.A.; see "The Life of Sir Henry Wotton," in *Reliquiae Wottonianae* (London, 1651), b4v.

39. Wotton, *Elements of Architecture,* 4.

40. Ibid., 53.

41. See Alberti, *Art of Building,* xviii. This volume, now at Eton College, once belonged to the humanist and diplomat Bernardo Bembo.

42. Wotton, *Elements of Architecture,* "Preface."

43. Ibid.

44. Ibid., 21, 117. See also his discussion of Palladio and sculpture on the building's exterior (101). Roy Eriksen locates the "pervasive" influence of Alberti in Wotton's rationalist approach to building; see *The Building in the Text: Alberti to Shakespeare and Milton* (University Park: Pennsylvania State University Press, 2001), 16.

45. Shute conflates what Charles Burroughs calls *anthropometric* and *anthropomorphic* readings of Vitruvius; see *The Italian Renaissance Palace Façade: Structures of Authority, Surfaces of Sense* (Cambridge: Cambridge University Press, 2002), 31. Vaughan Hart traces how female bodies are

analogized to columns in English architectural treatises ("From Virgin to Courtesan," 297–318). Compare Joseph Rykwert's relation of bodies to the orders, *The Dancing Column: On Order in Architecture* (Cambridge, Mass.: MIT Press, 1996), esp. chapter 2's discussion of Shute.

46. Wotton, *Elements of Architecture,* "Preface."

47. Henry Hawkins, *Partheneia Sacra* (Rouen, 1633), 166–67.

48. Vitruvius, *On Architecture,* trans. Frank Granger, 2 vols. (London: William Heinemann, 1931), 1:7.

49. Shute has been speculatively linked to building projects initiated by his patron, John Dudley, the Duke of Northumberland, though no definitive evidence exists. See W. Douglas Simpson's "Dudley Castle, the Renaissance Buildings," *Archaeological Journal* 101 (1944): 119–25; also Maurice Howard, "The Ideal House and Healthy Life: The Origins of Architectural Theory in England," in *Les Traités d'Architecture de la Renaissance: Actes du Colloque Tenu à Tours du 1er au 11 juillet 1981,* ed. Jean Guillaume (Paris: Picard, 1988), 425–33.

50. Wotton, *Elements of Architecture,* 21 (misnumbered, should be 12).

51. John Summerson discusses Stickell's knowledge of Serlio, "Vitruvius and all those authors" in "Three Elizabethan Architects," *Bulletin of the John Rylands Library* 40, no. 1 (1957): 218–20, 227. Mark Girouard traces the Continental sources in Smythson's "Library and Books"; see *Robert Smythson and the Elizabethan Country House* (New Haven: Yale University Press, 1983), 15. For more on Jones's library, see John Newman's "Inigo Jones's Architectural Education Before 1614," *Architectural History* 35 (1992): 18–50; also, chapter 3 of Christy Anderson, *Inigo Jones and the Classical Tradition* (Cambridge: Cambridge University Press, 2007). Anderson notes the influence of Palladio's "user-friendly" volume in "Palladio in England: The Dominance of the Classical in a Foreign Land," in *Palladio and Northern Europe: Books, Travellers, Architects* (Milan: Skira, 1999), 123. Alice T. Friedman marks the extensive architectural library of Wollaton's owner, Francis Willoughby; see *House and Household in Elizabethan England: Wollaton Hall and the Willoughby Family* (Chicago: University of Chicago Press, 1989), 29–33. Tresham's library is documented in Gent's *Picture and Poetry.*

52. Pratt, *Architecture of Sir Roger Pratt,* 284. For more on Pratt's reading, see Kimberley Skelton, "Reading as a Gentleman and an Architect: Sir Roger Pratt's Library," *Transactions of the Ancient Monuments Society* 53 (2009): 15–50.

53. Pratt, *Architecture of Sir Roger Pratt,* 285.

54. Johannes Ferrarius, *A Woorke of Ioannes Ferrarius Montanus, Touchynge the Good Orderynge of a Common Weale,* trans. William Bavande (London, 1559), 91r. Bavande's usage of "cunnyng" and "deuise" echoes Thomas Elyot's definition of *architectura* as "the counnynge of [or] diuysynge of buildynge" (*Bibliotheca Eliotae,* D6v).

55. Bavande also stresses the skill of painting so that an architect "shall thereby be able by picture, to descriue vnto you the plotte of any piece of woorke" (Ferrarius, *Common Weale,* 91r).

56. Vitruvius: "Ratiocinatio autem est, quae res fabricatas sollertiae ac rationis proportione demonstrare atque explicare potest" (*On Architecture,* 1:6).

57. Rayna Kalas usefully defines early modern *framing* as "any act of bringing matter into presence in conformity with a design or pattern"; see *Frame, Glass, Verse: The Technology of Poetic Invention in the English Renaissance* (Ithaca: Cornell University Press, 2007), 54.

58. William Cuningham, *The Cosmographical Glasse Conteinyng the Pleasant Principles of Cosmographie, Geographie, Hydrographie, or Nauigation* (London, 1559), 5 (B3r).

59. Dee, preface to *Elements of Geometrie,* D3r.

60. Ferrarius, *Common Weale,* 91r.

61. Compare Michel Foucault's claim that architecture was important to eighteenth-century political treatises, but not earlier texts like Jean Bodin's; see "Space, Knowledge, Power," trans. Christian Hubert, reprinted in *Architecture Theory Since 1968,* ed. Michael Hays (Cambridge, Mass.: MIT Press, 2000), 428–39.

62. Charles Taylor, *A Secular Age* (Cambridge, Mass.: Harvard University Press, 2007), 186–87.

63. Jean Bodin, *The Six Bookes of a Commonweale,* trans. Richard Knolles (London, 1606), 11. While stressing that a commonwealth's buildings should not be confused with the commonwealth itself, Bodin notes that common spaces are essential for any political regime.

64. Hannah Arendt, *The Human Condition* (Chicago: University of Chicago Press, 1958), 63–64. For more on definitions of *nomos,* including in terms of musical harmony, see Carl Schmitt, *The* Nomos *of the Earth: In the International Law of Jus Publicum Europaeum,* trans. G. L. Ulmen (New York: Telos Press, 2006), 67–79.

65. Arendt, *Human Condition,* 63. Compare Giorgio Agamben's relation of *nomos* to sovereignty, most notably in *Homo Sacer: Sovereign Power and Bare Life,* trans. Daniel Heller-Roazen (Stanford: Stanford University Press, 1998).

66. Arendt, *Human Condition,* 63.

67. Ferrarius, *Common Weale,* 91v.

68. Ibid.

69. As the tags become shorter in later books, the reference to an English nation disappears.

70. Alberti, *Art of Building,* 292.

71. Ferrarius, *Common Weale,* 91v.

72. Manfredo Tafuri, "Discordant Harmony from Alberti to Zuccari," *Architectural Design* 49 (1979): 41.

73. Henri Lefebvre, *The Production of Space,* trans. Donald Nicholson-Smith (Oxford: Basil Blackwell, 1991), 47.

74. Harrison's 1577 edition of *Description of England* lists only "olde Vitrunius, and Serlo" as exemplars of architectural writers, while the 1587 edition adds "Leo Baptista" to this group; see Airs, *Making of the English Country House,* 26, 43n18.

75. Dee, preface to *Elements of Geometrie,* D3r.

76. Ibid. Frances Yates examines Dee, the Hermetic tradition, and architecture in *Theatre of the World* (Chicago: University of Chicago Press, 1969).

77. Randle Cotgrave, *A Dictionarie of the French and English Tongues* (London, 1611), Nn1v. Thomas Blount repeats this definition, sans example, in *Glossographia* (London, 1656), which the *OED* cites as the first attested usage.

78. Jacques Derrida, *The Truth in Painting,* trans. Geoff Bennington and Ian McLeod (Chicago: University of Chicago Press, 1987), 56.

79. For more on Nonsuch's material history, see Martin Biddle's *Nonsuch: The Material Culture of a Noble Restoration Household* (Oxford: Oxbow, 2005).

80. William Camden, *Britain, or A Chorographicall Description of the Most Flourishing Kingdomes, England, Scotland, and Ireland, and the Ilands Adjoyning, Out of the Depth of Antiquitie* (London, 1610), 287 (out of order; between pages 298 and 302). Camden's assessment is repeated in Hakewill (*Apologie,* 248–49).

81. Hakewill, *Apologie,* 249.

82. John Summerson calls Nonsuch "a deliberate attempt to emulate" François I's chateau at Chambord; see Summerson, *Architecture in Britain, 1530–1830,* 9th ed. (New Haven: Yale University Press, 1993), 33–34. Martin Biddle claims that Henry VIII was "keeping abreast of developments both stylistic and iconographic" at Fontainebleau; see "The Stuccoes of Nonsuch," *Burlington Magazine* 126, no. 976 (1984): 412.

83. David Howarth, *Images of Rule: Art and Politics in the English Renaissance, 1485–1649* (Berkeley: University of California Press, 1997), 18.

84. A similar view of Nonsuch appears in Henry Danckerts's painting, owned by the Epsom and Ewell Borough Council. Martin Biddle details Nonsuch's pictorial sources in "The Gardens of Nonsuch: Sources and Dating," *Garden History* 27, no. 1 (1999): 145–57. In *De re aedificatoria,* Alberti compares the building to an animal; see VI.3, VII.5 (Alberti, *Art of Building,* 158, 199).

85. Hoefnagel's watercolor seems to show painted panels, although John Dent insists that the reliefs were white. Among seventeenth-century visitors, John Evelyn vaguely describes "pictures," while Samuel Pepys reports flat painted panels in the style of Rubens or Holbein. For more on the debate, see John Dent, *The Quest for Nonsuch* (London: Hutcheson & Co., 1962), 95–96; Howard Colvin, ed., *The History of the King's Works,* vol. 4 (London: H. M. Stationery Office, 1962), 199; Cloudesley S. Willis, *A Short History of Ewell and Nonsuch* (Epsom: Pullinger, 1932), 66; Ian Dunlop, "Nonsuch Palace," *Connoisseur* 128 (1951): 115. For more on Nonsuch's stucco material, see Claire Gapper, "What Is 'Stucco'? English Interpretations of an Italian Term," *Architectural History* 42 (1999): 333–43, esp. 336–37.

86. Biddle, "Stuccoes," 412.

87. See the entry for January 3, 1666, in *The Diary of John Evelyn,* vol. 3, ed. E. S. de Beer (Oxford: Clarendon Press, 1955), 427.

88. Biddle, "Stuccoes," 417.

89. Jürgen Habermas, *The Structural Transformation of the Public Sphere: An Inquiry into a Category of Bourgeois Society,* trans. Thomas Burger and Frederic Lawrence (Cambridge, Mass.: MIT Press, 1989), 7 and passim.

90. Simon Thurley, *The Royal Palaces of Tudor England: Architecture and Court Life, 1460–1547* (New Haven: Yale University Press, 1993), 63.

91. This usage of Nonsuch as the king's substitute echoes how Louis Marin analyzes Versailles and Louis XIV; see "Classical, Baroque: Versailles, or The Architecture of the Prince," *Yale French Studies,* no. 80 (1991): 167–82.

92. For more on emblems in Elizabethan architecture, see Mark Girouard, *Robert Smythson,* 24–28; also John Summerson, *Architecture in Britain,* 72–74.

93. Biddle, "Stuccoes," 412.

94. Vasari attributes Nonsuch's design to Antonio Toto del Nunziata, who became Serjeant Painter to Henry VIII in 1543/4; see Dent, *Quest for Nonsuch,* 50. Martin Biddle credits Nicholas Bellin with the stucco reliefs; see "Nicholas Bellin of Modena," *Journal of the British Archaeological Association,* 3rd ser., 29 (1966): 106–21. Indeed, records show that Bellin carved the slate; see Colvin, ed., *History of the King's Works,* 194–95. John of Padua, named "Devizer of the King's Buildings" in 1544, may also be involved; see Ian Dunlop, "Nonsuch Palace," *Connoisseur* 128 (1951): 113–15, 127.

95. Evelyn, *Diary,* 427. Mark Girouard calls Nonsuch "barbarous" in style (*Robert Smythson,* 3).

96. Ian Dunlop, "Nonsuch Palace," 113.

97. Raphael Holinshed, *Chronicles* (London, 1587), 195. Compare a later section on quarries where Harrison remarks how stone is now commonly used for building, so that "timber frames are supposed to be not much better than paper worke, of little continuance, and least continuance of all" (234). William Harrison's "The Description of England" forms the first part of Holinshed's *Chronicles;* the first edition of 1577 was followed by a revised edition in 1587. Unless otherwise specified, all citations are from the 1587 edition, whose spelling and pagination are more regular.

98. While Palladio's English influence peaked during the eighteenth century, he inspired seventeenth-century architects like Inigo Jones. See Rudolf Wittkower, *Palladio and Palladianism* (New York: G. Braziller, 1974); Robert Tavernor, *Palladio and Palladianism* (London: Thames and Hudson, 1991); Christy Anderson, "Palladio in England: The Dominance of the Classical in a Foreign Land," in *Palladio and Northern Europe: Books, Travellers, Architects* (Milan: Skira, 1999).

99. Summerson, *Architecture in Britain,* 142–56.

100. For more on glass and sixteenth-century building, see Platt, *Great Rebuildings,* 15–20; Eleanor Godfrey, *The History of English Glassmaking, 1560–1640* (Oxford: Clarendon Press, 1975), esp. 200–215.

101. For more on monastic conversions, see Summerson, *Architecture in Britain,* 37; Colvin, "Recycling the Monasteries"; Maurice Howard, *The Early Tudor Country House: Architecture and Politics, 1490–1550* (London: George Philip, 1987), 136–62.

102. Anderson, "Palladio in England," 123. She refers specifically to Wollaton.

103. Essay XLV; see Francis Bacon, *The Essayes or Counsels, Ciuill and Morall, of Francis Lo. Verulam, Viscount St. Alban* (London, 1625), 257.

104. Timothy Mowl, in contrast, regards Longleat as "a glass palace . . . more native English than Classical"; see *Elizabethan and Jacobean Style* (London: Phaidon Press, 1993), 84. For Longleat's building history, see Girouard, *Robert Smythson,* 40–65; for a social history, see David Burnett, *Longleat: The Story of an English Country House* (London: Collins, 1978).

105. Girouard, *Robert Smythson,* 49. Girouard observes that disjunctions between the third and fourth facades are still apparent along the roofline and at certain windows. Similarly, Burnett notes that "the classical façade was thrown out of balance by the apparently haphazard positioning of eight pepper-pot domes . . . amidst the gables and guttering," while "a line of grotesque stone dogs on the balustrade . . . look down into the inner courtyards" (*Longleat,* 35).

106. Girouard, *Robert Smythson,* 54.

107. Bacon, *Essays,* 257.

108. Recent studies that relate country house poetry to social and architectural history include Michael McKeon, *The Secret History of Domesticity: Public, Private, and the Division of Knowledge* (Baltimore: Johns Hopkins University Press, 2005), 419–22; Kari Boyd McBride, *Country House Discourse in Early Modern England: A Cultural Study of Landscape and Legitimacy* (Aldershot: Ashgate, 2001); Alastair Fowler, *The Country House Poem: A Cabinet of Seventeenth-Century Estate Poems and Related Items* (Edinburgh: Edinburgh University Press, 1994); and Don Wayne, *Penshurst: The Semiotics of Place and the Poetics of History* (Madison: University of Wisconsin Press, 1984).

109. Ben Jonson, *Workes* (London, 1616), 819 (lines 1, 3). The poem was written around 1612. Don Wayne speculates that Jonson sees Longleat as a contrast to Penshurst (*Penshurst,* 93, 96).

110. Andrew Marvell, *Miscellaneous Poems* (London, 1681), 76 (lines 1–2). "Upon Appleton House" was likely written c. 1651. Rosalie Colie contrasts the foreign builder with an English frame "secreted to hold its master, who was, in fact, its architect"; see *"My Ecchoing Song": Andrew Marvell's Poetry of Criticism* (Princeton: Princeton University Press, 1970), 228.

111. Marvell, *Poems,* 78 (lines 62), 76 (lines 5–8).

112. Ibid., 77 (lines 45–46, 51–52).

113. Ibid., 78 (line 53).

114. For Leonard Barkan, these lines exemplify Alberti's "psychological tradition," which emphasizes human responses to architecture; see *Nature's Work of Art: The Human Body as Image of the World* (New Haven: Yale University Press, 1975), 147–48.

115. Marvell, *Poems,* 76 (lines 17, 21).

116. Holinshed, *Chronicles,* 212. In a marginal note here, Harrison explains that "Desire of much wealth and ease abateth manhood, and ouerthroweth a manlie courage."

117. Ibid., 187.

118. Ibid.

119. From the January 20, 1614, entry in Jones's Roman sketchbook, now at Chatsworth. I have given Edward Chaney's transcription from his two-volume *Inigo Jones's "Roman Sketchbook"* (London: Roxburghe Club, 2006); the transcribed entry in vol. 1 (167–68) corresponds to Fol. 76r in vol. 2. John Peacock offers a differing transcription and analysis in *The Stage Designs of Inigo Jones: The European Context* (Cambridge: Cambridge University Press, 1995), 232.

120. The Composite order combines the womanly Ionic and the girlish Corinthian.

121. Chaney, ed., *Roman Sketchbook,* 1:168. The "periods" in mid-sentence are ink dots rather than punctuation marks. Gordon Higgott notes that Jones echoes Vasari; see "'Varying with Reason': Inigo Jones's Theory of Design," *Architectural History* 35 (1992): 58.

122. Paula Henderson notes the early modern rise of a garden facade and Italian-style loggia that formed a "perfect intermediary between the house and garden" (*Tudor House and Garden,* 214).

123. I draw on Joan Riviere's notion of masquerade as a performance that produces gender identity; see "Womanliness as a Masquerade," *International Journal of Psycho-Analysis* 10 (1929): 303–13. Compare Stephen Heath, "Joan Riviere and the Masquerade," in *Formations of Fantasy,* ed. Victor Burgin, James Donald, and Cora Kaplan (London: Methuen, 1986), 45–61; Judith Butler, *Gender Trouble: Feminism and the Subversion of Identity* (New York: Routledge, 1990), esp. 43–57.

124. Hilary Robinson discusses the mime artist's importance to Irigaray in *Reading Art, Reading Irigaray: The Politics of Art by Women* (London: I. B. Taurus, 2006), esp. 31.

125. Marvell, *Poems,* 76 (lines 13–14).

126. Luce Irigaray, *This Sex Which Is Not One,* trans. Catherine Porter and Carolyn Burke (Ithaca: Cornell University Press, 1985), 137, 152. For more on miming in French theory, see Timothy Murray, ed., *Mimesis, Masochism, and Mime: The Politics of Theatricality in Contemporary French Thought* (Ann Arbor: University of Michigan Press, 1997).

127. Marvell, *Poems,* 76 (lines 11, 16).

128. Jacques Derrida, *Dissemination,* trans. Barbara Johnson (Chicago: University of Chicago Press, 1981), 195.

129. Rudolf Wittkower's *Architectural Principles in the Age of Humanism* gives a classic account of the microcosm/macrocosm theory in the Renaissance; see also Barkan, *Nature's Work,* esp. chapter 3. Conversely, Marco Frascari claims that the desire for anthropomorphic spaces creates monsters that inhabit interstices; see *Monsters of Architecture: Anthropomorphism in Architectural Theory* (Savage, Md.: Rowman and Littlefield, 1991).

130. Alberti, *Art of Building,* 301; Book IX.5. Catherine Ingraham's *Architecture, Animal, Human: The Asymmetric Condition* (New York: Routledge, 2006) theorizes how biology relates to technology from the Renaissance onward. For a historical review of the building-animal analogy, see Philip

Steadman, *The Evolution of Designs: Biological Analogy in Architecture and the Applied Arts,* rev. ed. (New York: Routledge, 2008), esp. chapter 2.

131. Hawkins, *Partheneia Sacra,* 168.

132. Gilles Deleuze and Félix Guattari, *A Thousand Plateaus: Capitalism and Schizophrenia,* trans. Brian Massumi (Minneapolis: University of Minnesota Press, 1987), 272 and 273. Deleuze and Guattari develop the notion of becoming-animal in *Kafka: Toward a Minor Literature,* trans. Dana Polan (Minneapolis: University of Minnesota Press, 1986).

133. Deleuze and Guattari, *Thousand Plateaus,* 259.

134. Francis Bacon, *Sylua Syluarum* (London, 1627), 193.

135. Alberti defines *concinnitas* thus: "every body consists entirely of parts that are fixed and individual; if these are removed, enlarged, reduced, or transferred somewhere inappropriate, the very composition will be spoiled that gives the body its seemly appearance" (*Art of Building,* 302; IX.5).

136. Deleuze and Guattari, *Thousand Plateaus,* 238.

137. Ibid., 239.

138. Andor Gomme and Alison Maguire, *Design and Plan in the Country House: From Castle Donjons to Palladian Boxes* (New Haven: Yale University Press, 2008), 96. Mark Girouard points to some late-medieval compact plans with small or no courtyards, which were later filled in with a hall (*Robert Smythson,* 56).

139. Nicholas Cooper notes a through-passage that arises from aligning a centered front door with the great hall and main stair; see *Houses of the Gentry, 1480–1680* (New Haven: Yale University Press, 1999), 275–89. Andor Gomme traces the emergence of vestibules or hallways in a group of late sixteenth-century houses built for those who eschewed a great hall for entertaining; see "Halls into Vestibules," in *The Renaissance Villa in Britain, 1500–1700,* ed. Malcolm Airs and Geoffrey Tyack (Reading: Spire, 2007), 38–63, as well as his work with Alison Maguire in *Design and Plan in the Country House.*

140. Maurice Howard cites three types of medieval corridors: the wooden "pentice" propped against the outside of a range, a freestanding, covered corridor linking different buildings within a complex, and "alleys" in gardens (*Early Tudor Country House,* 88). Notably, these early instances situate the corridor as something added on, secondary, and outdoors; in contrast, the double-pile makes the corridor its internal organizing frame.

141. Gomme and Maguire, *Design and Plan,* 199–201.

142. Gilles Deleuze, *The Fold: Leibniz and the Baroque,* trans. Tom Conley (Minneapolis: University of Minnesota Press, 1993), 28.

143. Mark Jarzombek, "Corridor Spaces," *Critical Inquiry* 36, no. 4 (2010): 746. Although Jarzombek traces the term *corridor* only to the eighteenth century, I use *hallway* and *corridor* without distinction to indicate transitional passages.

144. Bacon, *Essays,* 121.

145. For more on the changing role of parlors, see Mark Girouard, *Life in the English Country House: A Social and Architectural History* (New Haven: Yale University Press, 1978), 58–59, 102–4; J. T. Cliffe, *The World of the*

Country House in Seventeenth-Century England (New Haven: Yale University Press, 1999), 28–29; Platt, *Great Rebuildings,* 36–37; Summerson, *Architecture in Britain,* 85. For servants' halls and the distancing of servants, see Girouard, *Life,* 136–43; Platt, *Great Rebuildings,* esp. 99; Cooper, *Houses of the Gentry,* esp. 11.

146. Roger Pratt, *The Architecture of Sir Roger Pratt, Charles II's Commissioner for the Rebuilding of London After the Great Fire,* ed. R. T. Gunther (Oxford: R. T. Gunther, 1928), 64.

147. Ibid., 27, 62.

148. Catherine Ingraham, *Architecture and the Burdens of Linearity* (New Haven: Yale University Press, 1998).

149. Compare Julia Kristeva's concept of chora as a "rhythmic space" marked by "vocal or kinetic rhythm"; see *Revolution in Poetic Language,* trans. Margaret Waller (New York: Columbia University Press, 1984), 26. While I do not follow Kristeva's idiosyncratic usage of *chora* to name a semiotic phase that precedes the symbolic, I draw upon her notion of a non-thetic chora that produces subjectivity, but is always regulated by social constraints such as family structure.

150. Roger North, *Of Building: Roger North's Writings on Architecture,* ed. Howard Colvin and John Newman (Oxford: Clarendon Press, 1981), 32.

151. The two modes of building are not exclusive. For example, Howard cites the open arcade around a monastic courtyard as one of the earliest uses of a corridor; this feature was often retained when monasteries converted into homes and college buildings (*Early Tudor Country House,* 90–95).

152. Jacques Derrida, *Of Grammatology,* trans. Gayatri Chakravorty Spivak (Baltimore: Johns Hopkins University Press, 1974), 107.

153. Jacques Derrida, *Writing and Difference,* trans. Alan Bass (London: Routledge, 1978), 268.

154. Nicholas Barbon, *An Apology for the Builder, or, A Discourse Shewing the Cause and Effects of the Increase of Building* (London, 1685), 3. Barbon refers specifically to the sophistication of London's houses.

Chapter Three

EPIGRAPH: *Hamlet* II.ii.254–56. All *Hamlet* references are to the Arden edition by Harold Jenkins (London: Routledge, 1982).

1. Henry Wotton, *The Elements of Architecture* (London, 1624), 55.

2. Joel Fineman, *Shakespeare's Perjured Eye: The Invention of Poetic Subjectivity in the Sonnets* (Berkeley: University of California Press, 1986), 46.

3. For Francis Barker, "a separation has already opened up between the inner reality of the subject, living itself, as 'that within that passes show,' and an inauthentic exterior"; see *The Tremulous Private Body: Essays on Subjection* (Ann Arbor: University of Michigan Press, 1995), 31. Similarly, Katharine Eisaman Maus explores the conflict between "an unexpressed interior and a theatricalized exterior"; see *Inwardness and Theater in the English Renaissance* (Chicago: University of Chicago Press, 1995), 2. Catherine Belsey posits this interiority as a construct of liberal humanists in the late seventeenth

century; see *The Subject of Tragedy: Identity and Difference in Renaissance Drama* (London: Methuen, 1985). Jonathan Dollimore's *Radical Tragedy: Religion, Ideology, and Power in the Drama of Shakespeare and His Contemporaries* (Chicago: Chicago University Press, 1984) labels this interiority a retrospective projection caused by essentialist humanism. Elizabeth Hanson marks an epistemic shift that construes early modern subjects as secrets to be discovered; see *Discovering the Subject in Renaissance England* (Cambridge: Cambridge University Press, 1998). In contrast, Margreta de Grazia sees Hamlet more as "the roustabout clown of medieval folk tradition than . . . the introspective consciousness acclaimed by the modern period"; see *"Hamlet" Without Hamlet* (Cambridge: Cambridge University Press, 2007), 9.

4. Terry Eagleton, *William Shakespeare* (Oxford: Blackwell, 1986), 72.

5. Barker, *Tremulous Private Body,* 32, 33. David Aers critiques early modernists who overlook the inwardness evinced by medieval nondramatic texts, particularly those following an Augustinian tradition; see "A Whisper in the Ear of Early Modernists, or Reflections on Literary Critics Writing the 'History of the Subject,'" in *Culture and History, 1350–1600: Essays on English Communities, Identities and Writing,* ed. David Aers (Detroit: Wayne State Press, 1992), 177–202. However, Aers fails to recognize that both Belsey and Dollimore trace the development of a *dramatic* subjectivity, more specifically a *tragic* subjectivity.

6. Keith Brown notes a Mannerist double center in which the closet scene forms the "numerological" center as the tenth of nineteen scenes, while the Mousetrap scene forms its "strategic" core; see "'Form and Cause Conjoin'd': *Hamlet* and Shakespeare's Workshop," *Shakespeare Survey* 26 (1973): 11–20. Bridging the two scenes, Hamlet's walk thus comprises the play's heart of heart.

7. Compare Claudius telling Laertes, "you must put me in your heart for friend" (IV.vii.2). More generally, the *OED* cites this usage as definition 8a, "To carry about with one in one's heart, mind, or memory." As discussed later in this chapter, there may also be echoes of etching or inscribing from the sense of "wearing into" stone.

8. Leon Battista Alberti, *On the Art of Building in Ten Books,* trans. Joseph Rykwert, Neil Leach, and Robert Tavernor (Cambridge, Mass.: MIT Press, 1988), 180. See chapter 1 for more on this passage.

9. Jerry Brotton, "Ways of Seeing *Hamlet,*" in *Hamlet: New Critical Essays,* ed. Arthur F. Kinney (New York: Routledge, 2002), 164.

10. Bernice Kliman, "The Bed in *Hamlet*'s Closet Scene: Rowe 1709 and 1714," *Shakespeare Newsletter* 43 (1993): 8–9. See also Alan Young, *Hamlet and the Visual Arts, 1709–1900* (Newark: University of Delaware Press, 2002), esp. 18–25.

11. The key work on the erotics of closet spaces remains Eve Kosofsky Sedgwick's *Epistemology of the Closet* (Berkeley: University of California Press, 1990).

12. Richard Rambuss, *Closet Devotions* (Durham: Duke University Press, 1998), 8, 105. Similarly, for Catherine Richardson, the closet "facilitates the

intensification of experience" and "magnifies the significance of physical presence"; see *Shakespeare and Material Culture* (Oxford: Oxford University Press, 2011), 114, 126. For more on how devotional reading practices change from medieval to early modern, see Jennifer Bryan, *Looking Inward: Devotional Reading and the Private Self in Late Medieval England* (Philadelphia: University of Pennsylvania Press, 2007), esp. 12–13 on closets.

13. Alan Stewart, "The Early Modern Closet Discovered," *Representations,* no. 50 (1995): 76–100; a version of this essay forms the last chapter of Stewart's *Close Readers: Humanism and Sodomy in Early Modern England* (Princeton: Princeton University Press, 1997).

14. Stewart, "Early Modern Closet," 89. Lisa Jardine and William Sherman coin the term "knowledge transactions" to describe the scholarly work done in masculine studies; see "Pragmatic Readers: Knowledge Transactions and Scholarly Services in Late Elizabethan England," in *Religion, Culture, and Society in Early Modern Britain: Essays in Honour of Patrick Collinson,* ed. Anthony Fletcher and Peter Roberts (Cambridge: Cambridge University Press, 1994), 102–24. For a book-length study on secretaries and letters, see Jonathan Goldberg's *Writing Matter: From the Hands of the English Renaissance* (Stanford: Stanford University Press, 1990). The primary Renaissance source remains Angel Day's *The English Secretary* (2nd ed., 1599), a letter-writing manual by a male secretary.

15. For example, when *The Closet of the Eminently Learned Sir Kenelme Digbie Kt Opened* (1669) reveals only household information, Stewart reads this as an evasion that substitutes the lesser secrets of a female closet. But can an archive of recipes and medicinal remedies be excluded from the realm of masculine "knowledge-processing technologies," especially since Digby's son and male secretary published the volume?

16. James Knowles, "'Infinite Riches in a Little Room': Marlowe and the Aesthetics of the Closet," in *Renaissance Configurations: Voices/Bodies/Spaces, 1580–1690,* ed. Gordon McMullan (Houndmills: Macmillan, 1998), 9. Alberti's treatise, *Della Famiglia,* advocates keeping masculine closets off-limits to women, whose own private spaces were secreted in the house's furthest reaches. See Mark Wigley, "Untitled: The Housing of Gender," in *Sexuality and Space,* ed. Beatriz Colomina (New York: Princeton Architectural Press, 1992), 327–89; Stephanie Jed, *Chaste Thinking: The Rape of Lucretia and the Birth of Humanism* (Bloomington: Indiana University Press, 1989).

17. Stewart, "Early Modern Closet," 82–83, 87. Recent scholarship, however, shows the political dimensions of household miscellanies. See Laura Lunger Knoppers, "Opening the Queen's Closet: Henrietta Maria, Elizabeth Cromwell, and the Politics of Cookery," *Renaissance Quarterly* 60, no. 2 (2007): 464–99; and Wendy Wall, *Staging Domesticity: Household Work and English Identity in Early Modern Drama* (Cambridge: Cambridge University Press, 2002), esp. 18–58. Stewart's only allusions to the closets of powerful females are drawn from fiction (88–89); even the closets of Queen Elizabeth's secretaries of state are described as male domains whose papers are handed down among men (only a footnote mentions the queen in passing).

18. Ibid., 82. Clifford's book deals with the Turkish government, however—hardly a light romance. Ronald Huebert notes that Clifford refers to her closet as "the closet" while her husband's is "his closet," concluding that his ownership is "secure and specific" while hers seems "by accident or convenience"; see "The Gendering of Privacy," *Seventeenth Century* 16, no. 1 (2001): 41. Stewart's and Huebert's suggestion that Clifford was less capable of silent, independent reading than her husband seems unlikely. As Aaron Kunin observes, Clifford was a writer and antiquarian while her husband—Richard Sackville, the third Earl of Dorset—was a notorious rake without any known scholarly tendencies; see "From the Desk of Anne Clifford," *ELH* 71, no. 3 (2004): 587–608, esp. 590. Kunin further notes the class privilege of employing a servant or secretary to read (604). Kate Chedgzoy affirms that Clifford "was at ease in a cultural world where oral, manuscript and print modes all co-existed and interacted"; see *Women's Writing in the British Atlantic World: Memory, Place, and History, 1550–1700* (Cambridge: Cambridge University Press, 2007), 18.

19. Marta Straznicky astutely notes that a man withdraws into his closet as "an extension of his role as public and political being, while for a woman the same gesture can be seen to comply with patriarchal restrictions on her sphere of activity"; see *Privacy, Playreading, and Women's Closet Drama, 1550–1700* (Cambridge: Cambridge University Press, 2004), 116.

20. Georgianna Ziegler, "My Lady's Chamber: Female Space, Female Chastity in Shakespeare," *Textual Practice* 4, no. 1 (1990): 73. She thus regards Hamlet as "committing a kind of mental rape" when chastising Gertrude in her closet (86). Compare John Harington's comic epigram in which a husband reproaches his wife for sitting with her legs apart and thus leaving her cabinet open ("Of a Ladyes Cabinet," in *Alcilia* [London, 1613], no page number); discussed by Arthur Marotti, *Manuscript, Print, and the English Renaissance Lyric* (Ithaca: Cornell University Press, 1995), 141–42.

21. Lisa Jardine, *Reading Shakespeare Historically* (London: Routledge, 1996), 151; compare de Grazia, Hamlet *Without Hamlet,* 102.

22. Jardine, *Reading Shakespeare,* 151.

23. Ibid., 153.

24. Ibid., 151.

25. Compare Peter Stallybrass's argument for enclosed female bodies in "Patriarchal Territories: The Body Enclosed," in *Rewriting the Renaissance: The Discourse of Sexual Difference in Early Modern Europe,* ed. Margaret W. Ferguson, Maureen Quilligan, and Nancy J. Vickers (Chicago: University of Chicago Press, 1986), 123–42.

26. William Shakespeare, *Titus Andronicus,* ed. Jonathan Bate (London: Arden Shakespeare, 1995), 210. As in *Hamlet,* this recourse to the closet provides a key turning point in the play while bridging Acts III and IV.

27. Daryl W. Palmer, noting that acts of reading link Act III to IV, posits Lavinia as "a reader, who like most martyrs, can only escape meaningless violence by writing herself"; see "Histories of Violence and the Writer's Hand: Foxe's *Actes and Monuments* and Shakespeare's *Titus Andronicus,*"

in *Reading and Writing in Shakespeare,* ed. David M. Bergeron (Cranbury, N.J.: Associated University Presses, 1996), 107. Compare Jonathan Goldberg's claim that this "scene of reading had virtually re-enacted the rape (for the character seizes the book [Ovid] that seizes her), and writing is its violent perpetuation"; see *Voice Terminal Echo: Postmodernism and English Renaissance Texts* (New York: Methuen, 1986), 82.

28. Clifford's secretaries included George Sedgwick and a Mr. Marsh. For more on women's employment of male secretaries, see Julie Crawford, "Women's Secretaries," in *Queer Renaissance Historiography: Backward Gaze,* ed. Stephen Guy-Bray, Vin Nardizzi, and Will Stockton (Aldershot: Ashgate, 2009), 111; also James Daybell, "Female Literacy and the Social Conventions of Women's Letter-Writing in England, 1540–1603," in *Early Modern Women's Letter Writing, 1450–1700,* ed. James Daybell (Houndmills: Palgrave, 2001), 59–76.

29. See Bruce R. Smith, *The Key of Green: Passion and Perception in Renaissance Culture* (Chicago: University of Chicago Press, 2009), 144–45. Smith notes that the couch, chair, and stools listed in a 1655 inventory suggest intimate conversation (22). See also Norman K. Farmer Jr.'s "Lady Drury's Oratory: The Painted Closet from Hawstead Hall," in *Poets and the Visual Arts in Renaissance England* (Austin: University of Texas Press, 1984), 77–105.

30. Jacques Lacan, "The Instance of the Letter in the Unconscious, or Reason Since Freud," in *Ecrits: A Selection,* trans. Bruce Fink (New York: W. W. Norton, 2002), 138–68, esp. 143.

31. For more on Clifford entering her husband's closet, see Sasha Roberts, "Shakespeare 'Creepes into the Womens Closets About Bedtime': Women Reading in a Room of Their Own," in *Renaissance Configurations: Voices/Bodies/Spaces, 1580–1690,* ed. Gordon McMullan (Houndmills: Macmillan, 1998), 35–36. Roberts also cautions that "gender distinctions in the use of the closet were, however, subject to considerable local variation in different households" (35). Lena Cowen Orlin explores the material conditions of early modern closets in *Locating Privacy in Tudor London* (Oxford: Oxford University Press, 2007), esp. 302–4. Compare Orlin's related essay, "Gertrude's Closet," *Shakespeare Jahrbuch* 134 (1998): esp. 59–61.

32. Orlin, *Locating Privacy,* 299. Orlin points to shared keys (306) and shared access (312–16).

33. Ibid., 316.

34. Erica Longfellow, "Public, Private, and the Household in Early Seventeenth-Century England," *Journal of British Studies* 45, no. 2 (2006): 321.

35. Isham produced two manuscripts: a diary covering thirty-two years and a confessional autobiography in fair copy. For more on these works, see Elizabeth Clarke and Erica Longfellow, "'[E]xamine My Life': Writing the Self in the Early Seventeenth Century," in *Constructing Elizabeth Isham, 1609–1654,* http://www2.warwick.ac.uk/fac/arts/ren/projects/isham/texts.

36. Isham makes her bequest in the margins (2r); see the *Constructing Elizabeth Isham* website for an online edition. Isham's text recalls the maternal

advice books that invoke closets to authorize women's writing; see Kristen Poole, "'The Fittest Closet for All Goodness': Authorial Strategies of Jacobean Mothers' Manuals," *SEL, 1500–1900* 35 (1995): 69–88, esp. 80. Whether or not Isham altered her history to parallel Augustine's, her narrative strives for believable realism; the pear/prayer episode thus reflects *plausible* closet practices within her social circle.

37. For more on this analogy of closets to books, see Cecile M. Jagodzinski, *Privacy and Print: Reading and Writing in Seventeenth-Century England* (Charlottesville: University of Virginia Press, 1999), 15–17.

38. Michael McKeon details the politics behind *The Kings Cabinet Opened;* see *The Secret History of Domesticity: Public, Private, and the Division of Knowledge* (Baltimore: Johns Hopkins University Press, 2005), 482–87.

39. See chapter 2 for more on common or public spaces.

40. I use *deface* to mean not only to remove a childish persona, but also "To blot out, obliterate, efface (writing, marks)" (*OED* definition 3). For more on memory and table-books, see Peter Stallybrass, Roger Chartier, J. Franklin Mowery, and Heather Wolfe, "Hamlet's Tables and the Technologies of Writing in Renaissance England," *Shakespeare Quarterly* 55, no. 4 (2004): 379–419. Compare Alan Stewart's discussion of Hamlet's writing as a technology of remembrance; see *Shakespeare's Letters* (Oxford: Oxford University Press, 2008), esp. 279–87. For early modern links between memory and notebooks, see Richard Yeo, "Notebooks as Memory Aids: Precepts and Practices in Early Modern England," *Memory Studies* 1, no. 1 (2008): 115–36.

41. John Donne, "Essay 1," in *Essays in Divinity* (London, 1651), 12

42. Compare Daniel Sibony's reading of the mark as related to Hamlet's drive to write so as to forget; see "Hamlet: A Writing-Effect," *Yale French Studies,* nos. 55–56 (1977): 68–69 and passim.

43. Anthony Kitson [?], *The Secrete of Secretes* (London, 1572), 34. Earlier published versions of this treatise, known in Latin as the *Secretum secretorum,* include John Lydgate's *This Present Boke called the Gouernaunce of Kynges and Pryncles]* (London, 1511) and a 1528 edition printed by Robert Copland. See chapter 2 for more on this "book of secrets" tradition.

44. Where Hamlet exclaims, "My tables. Meet it is I set it down" (I.v.107), modern stage directions often demand some gesture of writing, though no such direction appears in Q1, Q2, or the First Folio. Charlotte Scott believes that Hamlet does not write anything precisely to distinguish an internal book of truth from an external book of words; see *Shakespeare and the Idea of the Book* (Oxford: Oxford University Press, 2007), 133. Compare Francis Goyet's claim that Hamlet's mind is a master *fichier* to which notes from the table-books are transferred; see "Hamlet, étudiant du XVIe siècle," *Poétique,* no. 113 (1998): 5. Yet Stewart notes that table-books on the early modern stage often signal "fashionable gullery" (*Shakespeare's Letters,* 284).

45. My usage of *dilate* draws upon Patricia Parker's linkage of this term to both *delation* (secret narrative, accusation) and the opening of female bodies; see esp. *Shakespeare from the Margins: Language, Culture, Context* (Chicago: University of Chicago Press, 1996), 229–30, 237–40.

46. As Stephen Greenblatt notes, the Ghost constitutes "a kind of embodied memory" whose desire to be remembered derails revenge; see *Hamlet in Purgatory* (Princeton: Princeton University Press, 2002), 212.

47. Even Claudius becomes a subject of inscription in this scene, giving a foretaste of the Mousetrap. After writing in his tablet "That one may smile, and smile, and be a villain" (I.v.108), Hamlet declares: "So, uncle, there you are" (I.v.110). Claudius has been positioned *there* as a subject—a villain—in Hamlet's writing.

48. Jonathan Goldberg, "Hamlet's Hand," *Shakespeare Quarterly* 39, no. 3 (1988): 311. Compare P. K. Ayers's claim that both *Hamlet* and Hamlet are "anomalous scribal commentators on the print culture that surrounds them"; see "Reading, Writing, and *Hamlet*," *Shakespeare Quarterly* 44, no. 4 (1993): 438. Patricia Parker sees *Hamlet*'s network of writing as a historically specific mode of knowledge bound up with state power; see *Shakespeare from the Margins,* esp. chapters 5 and 7. Philip Armstrong links Hamlet's memory to early modern forms of writing, tablets, and Freud's mystic writing pad; see *Shakespeare in Psychoanalysis* (New York: Routledge, 2001), esp. 147–55. Likewise, Richard Halpern explores how Hamlet's Oedipal desires are both inscribed and effaced on Freud's mystic writing pad; see *Shakespeare Among the Moderns* (Ithaca: Cornell University Press, 1997), 227–88.

49. Philip Sidney, *An Apologie for Poetrie* (London, 1595), G1r. Cited also in the *OED* entry for *wear,* definition 8a.

50. Thomas Rogers, *Of the Imitation of Christ* (London, 1580): "So oughtest thou to enter into the priuie closet of thine hart" (208). Compare Matthew 6:6. An early translation of Augustine's *Confessions* also urged readers to find this inner bodily space: "and what *place* is there in me, that so my God may come into me" (et quis locus est in me quo veniat in me deus meus?); *The Confessions of the Incomparable Doctour S. Augustine,* trans. Tobie Matthew (St. Omer, 1620), 3. In early modern England, pseudo-Augustinian texts perpetuate this notion of an interior space of dialogue and meditation. See Julia Staykova, "Pseudo-Augustine and Religious Controversy in Early Modern England," in *Augustine Beyond the Book: Intermediality, Transmediality and Reception,* ed. Karla Pollmann and Meredith J. Gill (Leiden: Brill, 2012), 147–66; also Ian Green, *Print and Protestantism in Early Modern England* (Oxford: Oxford University Press, 2000), esp. 258–59. Rambuss and McKeon explore whether a "closet of the heart" exists solely as a trope or has correlates in real space; see *Closet Devotions,* 120–21, and *Secret History of Domesticity,* 40–43.

51. Patricia Fumerton, *Cultural Aesthetics: Renaissance Literature and the Practice of Social Ornament* (Chicago: University of Chicago Press, 1991), 69.

52. Margaret W. Ferguson also discusses Hamlet's materialization of words in "*Hamlet:* Letters and Spirits," in *Shakespeare and the Question of Theory,* ed. Patricia Parker and Geoffrey Hartman (New York: Methuen, 1985), 292–309. Compare Hamlet's brutal materialism about Polonius's body: "This man shall set me packing" (III.iv.213).

53. Compare Rosencrantz's protest—"there was no such stuff in my thoughts" (II.ii.311)—where "stuff" refers to sexualized women who cause

Hamlet's madness. As Janet Adelman observes in *Suffocating Mothers: Fantasies of Maternal Origin in Shakespeare's Plays, "Hamlet" to "The Tempest"* (New York: Routledge, 1992), "the whore-mother in him betrays him, returning him to his own mixed origin, his contamination by the sexual female within" (30).

54. Just as Alan Stewart contends that secretaries form human equivalents of closets, closets were also secretaries (*OED* definition 2). For "secretari," the earliest known and least assimilated English translation, see *The Imitation of Christ: The First English Translation of the "Imitatio Christi,"* ed. B. J. H. Biggs (Oxford: Oxford University Press, 1997): "So Þou owest to flee into the secretari of Þi herte, bisechinge inwardely the helpe of God" (113; III.43.2). For "secrete place," see Edward Hake's *The Imitation or Following of Christ* (London, 1567): "Even so oughtest thou to flie into the secrete place of thy heart, in calling earnestly vppon Gods helpe" (III.43; 109v). For "closet," see Rogers, *Imitation of Christ,* 208. According to the prefatory "A second Epistle concerning the translation and correction of this Booke," Rogers consulted two Latin sources as well as Hake's 1567 translation, so the choice of *closet* seems to reflect what Rogers believed to be a better rendering of *secretarium* for a 1580 readership.

55. Rambuss, *Closet Devotions,* 122.

56. For more on Augustine's secretarium, see J. E. Merdinger, *Rome and the African Church in the Time of Augustine* (New Haven: Yale University Press, 1997), 69–70, 86. James O'Donnell notes that in 411 C.E., six hundred bishops met in a secretarium adjoining the baths; see *Augustine: A New Biography* (New York: HarperCollins, 2005), 236.

57. Ernest Nash, "Secretarium Senatus," in *In Memoriam Otto J. Brendel: Essays in Archaeology and the Humanities,* ed. Larissa Bonfante and Helga von Heintze (Maintz: Verlag Philipp von Zabern, 1976), 191–204, esp. 192–93. See also *secretarium* entries in Lawrence Richardson Jr., *A New Topographical Dictionary of Ancient Rome* (Baltimore: Johns Hopkins University Press, 1992), 347, 321. For more on court proceedings inside and outside the *velum,* see Saul Lieberman, "Roman Legal Institutions in Early Rabbinics and in the Acta Martyrum," *Jewish Quarterly Review,* n.s., 35, no. 1 (1944): 18–19. For more on the paleo-Christian *secretarium,* see Pierre-Marie Gy, "The Meaning and Function of the Introit," in *Liturgy and the Arts in the Middle Ages: Studies in Honour of C. Clifford Flanigan,* ed. Eva Louise Lillie and Nils Holger Petersen (Copenhagen: Museum Tusculanum Press, 1996), 72–73n1.

58. See Mary Carruthers's work on *secretorium* in *The Book of Memory: A Study of Memory in Medieval Culture,* 2nd ed. (Cambridge: Cambridge University Press, 2008), 46–47. Compare Kate Chedgzoy's analysis of metaphors of memory, including the storehouse and wax tablet (*Women's Writing,* esp. 20–31); also Greenblatt's discussion of memory as a treasure-house and strongbox (*Hamlet in Purgatory,* 215).

59. Francesco Petrarca, *Prose,* ed. G. Martellotti, P. G. Ricci, E. Carrara, and E. Bianchi (Milan: Riccardo Ricciardi, 1955), 26. All Latin transcriptions of *Secretum* come from this source.

60. Francesco Petrarca, *Petrarch's Secret,* trans. William H. Draper (London: Chatto & Windus, 1911), 5. I have chosen an older translation that better retains Petrarch's tropes.

61. Ibid., 5.

62. Victoria Kahn cites memory's relation to reading as a problem raised from *Secretum*'s outset; see "The Figure of the Reader in Petrarch's *Secretum,*" *PMLA* 100, no. 2 (1985): 158–59.

63. Petrarca, *Petrarch's Secret,* 6.

64. Ibid. Petrarch tells his book to be content with staying with him (*mecum mansisse contentus eris*), differentiating it from other books sent into the public realm. Hans Baron argues that Petrarch's gesture toward privacy is not merely rhetorical; see *Petrarch's "Secretum"* (Cambridge, Mass.: Medieval Academy of America, 1985), esp. 185–202.

65. For more on how Augustine uses *secretum,* see David Marsh, *The Quattrocento Dialogue: Classical Tradition and Humanist Innovation* (Cambridge, Mass.: Harvard University Press, 1980), 17; Timothy Kircher claims that Petrarch's *secretum* involves an "inward exchange of ideas"; see *The Poet's Wisdom: The Humanists, the Church, and the Formation of Philosophy in the Early Renaissance* (Leiden: Brill, 2006), 161. For more on Petrarch's literary aims, see Carol Quillen, *Rereading the Renaissance: Petrarch, Augustine, and the Language of Humanism* (Ann Arbor: University of Michigan Press, 1998), esp. 182–216, and Brian Stock, *After Augustine: The Meditative Reader and the Text* (Philadelphia: University of Pennsylvania Press, 2001), 77–78.

66. Compare Julia D. Staykova's linkage of Hamlet's and Augustine's soliloquies as models of early modern interiority; see "The Augustinian Soliloquies of an Early Modern Reader: A Stylistic Relation of Shakespeare's Hamlet?," *Literature and Theology* 23, no. 2 (2009): 121–41.

67. I.xx; Rogers, *Imitation of Christ,* 43. Later in the same section, *cella* is translated as *chamber.*

68. Joseph F. O'Connor, "Architecture," in *Medieval Latin: An Introduction and Bibliographical Guide,* ed. F. A. C. Mantello and A. G. Rigg (Washington, D.C.: Catholic University of America Press, 1996), 438. Dag Norberg traces how *cellarium* became the monastic *cella;* see *Manuel Pratique de Latin Médiéval* (Paris: A. J. Picard, 1968), 55.

69. Carruthers, *Book of Memory,* 41; see Chaucer's Prologue to the Monk's Tale in *The Canterbury Tales.* In *De re aedificatoria,* Alberti calls the study off a husband's bedroom the *libraria cella* (*L'architettura,* ed. Portoghesi, 427; V.17); a *cella obsonaria* is a pantry (425).

70. In contrast, Samuel Weber sees a tension in this scene between "*plot as story* and *plot as stage*"; see *Theatricality as Medium* (New York: Fordham University Press, 2004), 185.

71. Regarding the writing-effect, Daniel Sibony defines it thus: "when the signifier starts to play for itself and its precipitations become dense enough . . . then spoken language is caught by or caught up in writing-effects that slice through it and jam its works" ("Hamlet: A Writing-Effect," 53). Regarding

Ophelia's interiority, compare Juliet Dusinberre's claim that Ophelia is "stifled . . . by the authority of the male world"; see *Shakespeare and the Nature of Women* (London: Macmillan, 1975), 94. In contrast, Elaine Showalter notes how some feminists see Ophelia as "the Story of O—the zero, the empty circle or mystery of feminine difference"; see "Representing Ophelia: Women, Madness, and the Responsibilities of Feminist Criticism," in *Shakespeare and the Question of Theory,* ed. Patricia Parker and Geoffrey Hartman (New York: Methuen, 1985), 78–79.

72. Q2 has "closet" here, but the Folio has "chamber."

73. Compare John Kerrigan's claim that remembrance constitutes the secret heart of Hamlet's mystery; see "Hieronimo, Hamlet and Remembrance," *Essays in Criticism* 31, no. 2 (1981): esp. 116.

74. Geraldo U. de Sousa notes that the adverbial "home" means "to the very heart, deeply, intimately, poignantly" and that Gertrude must touch this center; see *At Home in Shakespeare's Tragedies* (Farnham: Ashgate, 2010), 112.

75. See the *OED* entry for *bestow,* esp. definitions 1, 2, 6, and, to a lesser extent, 3.

76. Augustine, *Confessions,* 315.

77. Polonius echoes Rosencrantz by calling the room "[Hamlet's] mother's closet" (III.iii.27).

78. For great halls used as stages, see Richard Southern, *The Staging of Plays Before Shakespeare* (London: Faber and Faber, 1973), 53–55; Glynne Wickham, *Early English Stages 1300 to 1660,* vol. 1, *1300–1576* (London: Routledge and Kegan Paul), 180. By the end of the sixteenth century, great halls yielded this staging function to great chambers; see Mark Girouard, *Life in the English Country House: A Social and Architectural History* (New Haven: Yale University Press, 1978), 88–94. Yet the structure of great halls continued to inform both commercial and domestic spaces of performance; see Andrew Gurr, *The Shakespearean Stage, 1574–1642,* 4th ed. (Cambridge: Cambridge University Press, 2009), esp. 23; also John Orrell, *The Human Stage: English Theatre Design, 1567–1640* (Cambridge: Cambridge University Press, 1988), 41. With sources dating to the twelfth century, *Hamlet*'s architectural and historical milieu remains complex; the players' reception in Act II, for example, recalls a medieval hospitality toward mummers.

79. Scott Huelin, "Reading, Writing, and Memory in *Hamlet,*" *Religion and Literature* 37, no. 1 (2005): 30. Compare the "closet" cited in Stephen Greenblatt, *Will in the World: How Shakespeare Became Shakespeare* (New York: W. W. Norton, 2004), 137. Anna K. Nardo situates Claudius in "his private chapel"; see "Hamlet, 'A Man to Double Business Bound,' " *Shakespeare Quarterly* 34, no. 2 (1983): 181, 198. Compare Edward IV's exit to his closet after repenting his brother's murder in Act II of Shakespeare's *Richard III.*

80. After Polonius's murder, Claudius asks Rosencrantz and Guildenstern to "bring the body/Into the chapel" (IV.i.36–37). This impersonal ("the") chapel suggests a more public space that a recently unmasked murderer would avoid given the option of his own closet.

81. Knowles, " 'Infinite Riches in a Little Room,' " 21.

82. All five men appear in Claudius's closet in III.iii. Polonius and Hamlet then turn up in Gertrude's closet in III.iv, while Claudius, Rosencrantz, and Guildenstern arrive in IV.i after Hamlet's departure. Only Gertrude and the Ghost do not come from Claudius's closet.

83. Orlin, "Gertrude's Closet," 55–56.

84. John Bickersteth and Robert W. Dunning, *Clerks of the Closet in the Royal Household: Five Hundred Years of Service to the Crown* (Stroud: Alan Sutton, 1991), 5–7. For more on how English closets relate to the Italian chapel and *studiolo,* see Orest Ranum, "The Refuges of Intimacy," in *A History of Private Life III: Passions of the Renaissance,* ed. Roger Chartier, trans. Arthur Goldhammer (Cambridge, Mass.: Belknap Press, 1989), 228.

85. *British Architectural Theory, 1540–1750: An Anthology of Texts,* ed. Caroline Van Eck and Christy Anderson (Aldershot: Ashgate, 2003), 2.

86. Peter McCullough, *Sermons at Court: Politics and Religion in Elizabethan and Jacobean Preaching* (Cambridge: Cambridge University Press, 1998), esp. 1–48. Stephen Orgel similarly posits the king's body as the focal point of theater; see *The Illusion of Power: Political Theater in the English Renaissance* (Berkeley: University of California Press, 1975). For more on royal chapels and closets, see Simon Thurley, *Whitehall Palace: An Architectural History of the Royal Apartments, 1240–1698* (New Haven: Yale University Press, 1999), 67–69; also Howard Colvin, ed., *The History of the King's Works* (London: Her Majesty's Stationery Office, 1963–75), 2:887 and 2:1000. Compare Elizabeth's odd use of her chapel closet during her coronation; see Richard C. McCoy, "'Thou Idol Ceremony': Elizabeth I, *The Henriad,* and the Rites of the English Monarchy," in *Urban Life in the Renaissance,* ed. Susan Zimmerman and Ronald F. E. Weissman (Cranbury, N.J.: Associated University Press, 1989), 240–68, esp. 241–43.

87. Paul Hentzner, *Paul Hentzner's Travels in England, During the Reign of Queen Elizabeth* (London, 1797), 56.

88. McCullough, *Sermons at Court,* 20. At Richmond, however, the king's and queen's closets occupied facing sides above the choir.

89. Michael Cameron Andrews, "His Mother's Closet: A Note on *Hamlet,*" *Modern Philology* 80, no. 2 (1982): 165.

90. Simon Thurley, *The Royal Palaces of Tudor England: Architecture and Court Life, 1460–1547* (New Haven: Yale University Press, 1993), 125–27. *Closet, oratory,* and *chapel* overlap in early modern usage. In *Royal Palaces,* Thurley calls the altar room a "closet" and the kneeling space an "oratory." However, in his more recent *Hampton Court: A Social and Architectural History* (New Haven: Yale University Press, 2003), Thurley labels the altar room a "chapel" and the kneeling place a "privy closet." To avoid confusion, I will term the former a "chapel" and the latter an "oratory," since these terms best describe function; together, both rooms comprise the "privy closet."

91. David Starkey places the privy chamber at the border between public and private; see David Starkey, ed., *The English Court from the Wars of the Roses to the Civil War* (London: Longman, 1987), 8.

92. For more on the layout of English versus European royal suites, see Hugh Murray Baillie, "Etiquette and the Planning of the State Apartments in Baroque Palaces," *Archaeologia*, 2nd ser., 101, no. 51 (1967): 169–200.

93. Thurley, *Royal Palaces*, 125.

94. Ibid. Thurley notes that the king would wait in the gallery before grandly entering the presence chamber with attendants; thus, the most privately spiritual and theatrically political moments hinged upon a transitional space.

95. For the closet as an expansion of locked boxes, see Orlin, "Gertrude's Closet," 65; also Ranum, "The Refuges of Intimacy," 225, 228.

96. As Orlin notes, Ralph Treswell's surveys of London show that modest homes also had closets, often within or next to parlors, bedrooms, or dining rooms ("Gertrude's Closet," 60–61).

97. As secondary spaces, closets are often named in relation to a larger space, such as Ham House's "the Closet within the gallerie" and "my Lords Clossett next the new Library," or Gervase Markham's "inward Closset within the parlor for the Mistresses use, for necessaries." For Ham House, see the National Trust's *Ham House* (London: National Trust, 2002), 25, 28. For Markham, see *The English Husbandman* (London, 1613), B1r.

98. As discussed in chapter 2, Mark Jarzombeck calls the internal corridor "a within in the within"; see "Corridor Spaces," *Critical Inquiry* 36, no. 4 (2010): 746.

99. Ramie Targoff, "The Performance of Prayer: Sincerity and Theatricality in Early Modern England," *Representations*, no. 60 (1997): 65. Compare Rambuss's claim that in the secretary's closet, "an interior, private subjectivity begins to be scripted and secured"; see "The Secretary's Study: The Secret Designs of *The Shepheardes Calender*," *ELH* 59, no. 2 (1992): 321.

100. Jonathan Crary, *Techniques of the Observer: On Vision and Modernity in the Nineteenth Century* (Cambridge, Mass.: MIT Press, 1990), 27.

101. John Locke, *An Essay Concerning Humane Understanding* (London, 1690), 72. Compare Crary, *Techniques of the Observer*, 41–42.

102. Chérubin d'Orléans, *La Dioptrique Oculaire* (Paris, 1671), 17: "Et en effet, cette peinture naturelle, y est si parfaitement ordonné, & conduite, que l'oeil n'y trouve rien à desirer."

103. D'Orléans accepts any vertical plane situated at the correct focal length to serve as the screen, though his image presupposes a room whose dimensions to match exactly the needs of his optical device ("Je suppose en cette figure, le mur opposé à cette fenestre de la chambre, estre en distance requise, pour luy servir de plan" [17]).

104. Simon During, *Modern Enchantments: The Cultural Power of Secular Magic* (Cambridge, Mass.: Harvard University Press, 2002), 282.

105. Ibid. See chapter 1 for more on Alberti's refusal to perform demonstrations.

106. Gilles Deleuze, *The Fold: Leibniz and the Baroque*, trans. Tom Conley (Minneapolis: University of Minnesota Press, 1993). For more on how Deleuze's folds extend Leibniz's monadology, see Anthony Vidler, *Warped Space: Art, Architecture, and Anxiety in Modern Culture* (Cambridge, Mass.: MIT Press, 2000), 219–33.

107. Deleuze, *The Fold,* 120, 10.

108. Ibid., 28.

109. George Herbert, "Confession," in *The Temple* (London, 1633), 118–19.

110. *Hamlet,* I.v.170.

111. Jacques Derrida, *Writing and Difference,* trans. Alan Bass (London: Routledge, 1978), 214.

112. "A Note on the 'Mystic Writing-Pad,'" in *The Standard Edition of the Complete Psychological Works of Sigmund Freud,* trans. James Strachey, vol. 19 (London: Hogarth, 1957), 225–32. Freud analogizes the psyche to a child's wax tablet overlaid first with a waxed paper and then with a celluloid sheet. A stylus that inscribes on the celluloid (top layer) transfers dark marks onto the wax tablet (bottom layer). Traces of these marks remain even after lifting the two covering sheets to clear the surface. Barbara Freedman links Freud's mystic writing pad, Elizabethan table-books, and Shakespeare's notion of the mind in *Staging the Gaze: Postmodernism, Psychoanalysis, and Shakespearean Comedy* (Ithaca: Cornell University Press, 1991), esp. 169–70.

113. David Hillman draws on Norbert Elias's notion of *homo clausus* to explain this bodily closure; see *Shakespeare's Entrails: Belief, Skepticism and the Interior of the Body* (Houndmills: Palgrave, 2007), 89.

114. A royal secretary's main duty is to carry the king's signet seal to authorize public and private documents. See J. Otway-Ruthven, "The King's Secretary in the Fifteenth Century," *Transactions of the Royal Historical Society,* 4th ser., 19 (1936): 81–100; also, L. B. Dibben, "Secretaries in the Thirteenth and Fourteenth Centuries," *English Historical Review* 25, no. 99 (1910): 430–44.

115. Nicholas Royle discusses the mole as a Derridean trace and signifier of the human/animal divide in *The Uncanny: An Introduction* (Manchester: Manchester University Press, 2003), esp. 241–55. Margreta de Grazia shows how *Hamlet*'s mole is crucial to the ideas of Hegel, Marx, Freud, Lacan, and Derrida; see "Teleology, Delay, and the 'Old Mole,'" *Shakespeare Quarterly* 50, no. 3 (1999): 251–67. Reading *Hamlet* via Marx's *Eighteenth Brumaire,* Peter Stallybrass claims that the mole represents "the transformation of the principle of legitimacy—the father and King—into the principle of subversion"; see "'Well Grubbed, Old Mole': Marx, *Hamlet,* and the (Un)fixing of Representation," *Cultural Studies* 12, no. 1 (1998): 11.

116. For more on Semper, see chapter 1. For more on linenfold paneling, see Olive Cook, *The House Through Seven Centuries* (Woodstock, N.Y.: Overlook Press, 1968), 59. Linenfold panels often decorate the exterior of medieval and early Tudor chests, the strongboxes analogous to early modern closets. Paul Hentzer recalls finding, next to Windsor Castle's presence chamber, "a small chapel richly hung with tapestry, where the Queen performs her devotions"; see *Paul Hentzner's Travels in England, During the Reign of Queen Elizabeth* (London, 1797), 56.

117. Smith, *Key of Green,* 239.

118. Compare Margaret W. Ferguson's claim that the "curtain" figures the in-between ("*Hamlet:* Letters and Spirits," 297).

119. Compare Patricia Parker's insight that the councillor/counsellor Polonius evokes a secretary who keeps secrets ("counsel") and serves as a go-between; see *Shakespeare from the Margins,* esp. 183, 255.

120. Huelin, "Reading, Writing, and Memory in *Hamlet,*" 36.

121. The right-hand panel frames its sitter with twenty-two books, many identifiable by title; dozens of other volumes appear in the central family portrait and the left-hand panel, which depicts a teenage Clifford's closet. For more on the Great Picture, see Graham Parry, "The Great Picture of Lady Anne Clifford," in *Art and Patronage in the Caroline Courts: Essays in Honour of Sir Oliver Millar,* ed. David Howarth (Cambridge: Cambridge University Press, 1993), 202–19; Heidi Brayman Hackel, *Reading Material in Early Modern England: Print, Gender, Literacy* (Cambridge: Cambridge University Press, 2005), esp. 221–28; Edith Snook, *Women, Reading, and the Cultural Politics of Early Modern England* (Aldershot: Ashgate, 2005), 1–3.

122. *Ben Jonson,* ed. C. H. Herford, Percy Simpson, and Evelyn Simpson, vol. 6 (Oxford: Clarendon Press, 1938), 320. While mocking this pretentious sitting in state, Jonson's comedy raises the serious possibility that closets serve as formal reception spaces congruent with Gertrude's public and political duties, including curbing her treasonous son. Compare Catherine Richardson's claim that Gertrude's closet revolves around her chair (*Shakespeare and Material Culture,* 104–5 and 118–19).

123. For the stage as "extended altar," see Robert E. Wood, "Space and Scrutiny in *Hamlet,*" *South Atlantic Review* 52, no. 1 (1987): 25. For the arras as marking an altar (Latin *ara*), see Elizabeth S. Watson, "Old King, New King, Eclipsed Sons, and Abandoned Altars in *Hamlet,*" *Sixteenth Century Journal* 35, no. 2 (2004): 487–88.

124. Debora Shuger notes that the kings' portraits function as a mirror of conscience for Gertrude. Rather than produce a reflexive self-consciousness, Shuger believes that early modern mirrors embody the medieval notion that "one encounters one's own likeness in the mirror of the other"; see "The 'I' of the Beholder: Renaissance Mirrors and the Reflexive Mind," in *Renaissance Culture and the Everyday,* ed. Patricia Fumerton and Simon Hunt (Philadelphia: University of Pennsylvania Press, 1999), 37. Paul D. Stegner highlights Hamlet's role as a father confessor who opens up Gertrude's interiority; see "'Try What Repentance Can': *Hamlet,* Confession, and the Extraction of Interiority," *Shakespeare Studies* 35 (2007): 119–20.

125. Spivak, "Introduction" to *Of Grammatology,* xiv.

126. Derrida, *Writing and Difference,* 227.

Chapter Four

1. *Timaeus,* trans. Donald J. Zeyl (Indianapolis: Hackett, 2000), 39 (50c). All citations of Plato come from this edition; I have also provided Stephanus section references in parentheses.

2. Jacques Derrida, "How to Avoid Speaking: Denials," trans. Ken Frieden, in *Derrida and Negative Theology,* ed. Harold G. Coward and Toby Foshay (Albany: SUNY Press, 1992), 105. Edward Casey traces the impact of Plato's

chora on philosophies of space in *The Fate of Place: A Philosophical History* (Berkeley: University of California Press, 1997), esp. 32–49. Anthony Vidler surveys poststructuralist approaches to space in "Nothing to Do with Architecture," *Grey Room,* no. 21 (2005): 112–27. Emanuela Bianchi considers feminist critiques of the chora; see "Receptacle/*Chōra:* Figuring the Errant Feminine in Plato's *Timaeus,*" *Hypatia* 21, no. 4 (2006): 124–46. Edward Soja offers broader musings on women and space in *Thirdspace: Journeys to Los Angeles and Other Real-and-Imagined Places* (Cambridge, Mass.: Blackwell, 1996), 107–25.

3. Judith Butler, *Bodies That Matter: On the Discursive Limits of "Sex"* (New York: Routledge, 1993), 38.

4. Richard Helgerson, *Forms of Nationhood: The Elizabethan Writing of England* (Chicago: University of Chicago Press, 1992), 124.

5. J. B. Harley pioneered the study of maps in terms of political discourse; see "Silences and Secrecy: The Hidden Agenda of Cartography in Early Modern Europe," *Imago Mundi* 40 (1988): 57–76, and "Meaning and Ambiguity in Tudor Cartography," in *English Map-Making, 1500–1650,* ed. Sarah Tyacke (London: British Library, 1983), 22–45. Beyond sources cited elsewhere in this chapter, analyses of English maps and politics include Kenneth Robert Olwig, *Landscape, Nature, and the Body Politic: From Britain's Renaissance to America's New World* (Madison: University of Wisconsin Press, 2002); Bernhard Klein, *Maps and the Writing of Space in Early Modern England and Ireland* (Houndmills: Palgrave, 2001), esp. 137–48; *Monarchs, Ministers, and Maps: The Emergence of Cartography as a Tool of Government in Early Modern Europe,* ed. David Buisseret (Chicago: University of Chicago Press, 1992), 26–98.

6. Richard Mohr, *The Platonic Cosmology* (Leiden: Brill, 1985), 94

7. Plato, *Timaeus,* 37 (48e).

8. John Sallis, *Chorology: On Beginning in Plato's "Timaeus"* (Bloomington: Indiana University Press, 1999), 96. By ideals, I mean the first category of eternal, perfect, and unchanging paradigms; by bodies—and I have deliberately chosen a more loaded term—I mean the instantiation of a specific ideal at a given time and place. Bodies are thus sensible, alterable, imperfect, and impermanent. In contrast, recent debates over this passage have focused on whether the receptacle resembles prime matter or a mirrorlike medium; see Zeyl (*Timaeus,* lvi–lxiv) for an overview.

9. Plato, 39 (50c).

10. Ibid., 41 (52b). Compare Luce Irigaray's reading of "the 'go-between path' that links two 'worlds,' two modes, two methods" in Plato's allegory of the cave; see *Speculum of the Other Woman,* trans. Gillian C. Gill (Ithaca: Cornell University Press, 1985), 246.

11. Plato opposes the chora to a void, that is, "intervals or stretches of vacancy where things are not"; see Francis Cornford, *Plato's Cosmology* (London: Routledge and Kegan Paul, 1937), 200. See also Irigaray, cited above."

12. Plato, 42 (52e).

13. Ibid., 37n50; 42 (52d). However, Plato warns against seeing these elements as truly letters, founding principles (*archai*), or even syllables, since all

elements break down into more basic forms. "Only a very unenlightened person," he claims, would make such a comparison (37; 48c).

14. Ibid., 43 (53b).

15. Ibid., 42 (52e).

16. Ibid., 39 (50b), 40 (50e–51b).

17. Ibid., 40 (50d–e); 40 (50e).

18. Alberto Pérez-Gómez asserts that, since Plato errs in physiology, the chora must be conceived as androgynous; see "Chora: The Space of Architectural Representation," in *Chora: Intervals in the Philosophy of Architecture,* vol. 1, ed. Alberto Pérez-Gómez and Stephen Parcell (Montreal: McGill-Queen's University Press, 1994), 8. Yet gender mistakes count in intellectual history.

19. Max Statkiewicz sees the chora as a canvas for the Demiurge, a function linked to philosopher-artists who clear a space to imprint the city; see *Rhapsody of Philosophy: Dialogues with Plato in Contemporary Thought* (University Park: Pennsylvania State University Press, 2009), 141–42.

20. Irigaray, *Speculum,* 240. She also notes the "incestuously paternal" economy of the self-same Father and son (*Speculum,* 344).

21. See Jacques Lacan's essay "The Signification of the Phallus," in *Ecrits: A Selection,* trans. Bruce Fink (New York: W. W. Norton, 2002), 271–80, esp. 279. Basically, women circulate in patriarchal society as visible and acquirable signifiers of masculine power, as objects of desire that enable men to counter a much-feared lack in themselves.

22. Irigaray, *Ethics,* 34. See the introduction for Michel de Certeau's definitions of space (*espace*) and place (*lieu*).

23. Marcus A. Doel, *Poststructuralist Geographies: The Diabolical Art of Spatial Science* (Edinburgh: Edinburgh University Press, 1999), 87.

24. Plato, *Timaeus,* 41 (52b).

25. Ibid., 41–42 (52b).

26. Jonathan Crewe questions Plato similarly in "What Does Matter Want? Irigaray, Plotinus, and the Human Condition," in *Luce Irigaray and Premodern Culture: Thresholds of History,* ed. Theresa Krier and Elizabeth Harvey (New York: Routledge, 2004), 38–52, esp. 40. Crewe's feminist reading of chora draws on Aristotle's notion of prime matter (*hyle*).

27. Kenneth Sayre believes the chora to be a failed experiment "incoherent from start to finish"; see "The Multilayered Incoherence of Timaeus' Receptacle," in *Plato's "Timaeus" as Cultural Icon,* ed. Gretchen J. Reydams-Schils (Notre Dame: University of Notre Dame Press, 2003), 61.

28. Leon Battista Alberti, *On Painting and On Sculpture: The Latin Texts of "De Pictura" and "De Statua,"* ed. Cecil Grayson (London: Phaidon, 1972), 38–39.

29. Lacan, *Ecrits,* esp. 291–92. Following Roman Jakobson, Lacan distinguishes between diachronic metonyms whose meaning depends on the placement of elements and thus emerges retroactively (syntagmatic) and synchronic metaphors that permit a range of signifiers at any given point (paradigmatic). The metaphor's synchronic nature on a sentence level should not be confused with the metaphor's linkage to temporality on a historical level.

30. Martin Kemp, *The Science of Art: Optical Themes in Western Art from Brunelleschi to Seurat* (New Haven: Yale University Press, 1990), 34.

31. Anne Freire Ashbaugh, *Plato's Theory of Explanation: A Study of the Cosmological Account in the* Timaeus (Albany: SUNY Press, 1988), 104–5.

32. Derrida notes how the *mise en abyme* structure of *Timaeus* forms "receptacles of narrative receptacles, or narrative receptacles of receptacles"; see Derrida, "*Khōra,*" trans. Ian McLeod, in *On the Name,* ed. Thomas Dutoit (Stanford: Stanford University Press, 1995), 117. In a similar encasing of one discourse inside another, Plato's words are ventriloquized through Timaeus to form a "double signature"; see Sallis, *Chorology,* 1.

33. Elizabeth Grosz, *Architecture from the Outside, Essays on Virtual and Real Space* (Cambridge, Mass.: MIT Press, 2001), 91.

34. Gilles Deleuze, *The Fold: Leibniz and the Baroque,* trans. Tom Conley (Minneapolis: University of Minnesota Press, 1993), 10. See chapter 3 for more discussion of the *Zweifalt.*

35. For more on chorography versus cartography, see E. V. Walter, *Placeways: A Theory of the Human Environment* (Chapel Hill: University of North Carolina Press, 1988), 115–20; *English County Histories: A Guide,* ed. C. R. J. Currie and C. P. Lewis (Phoenix Mill: Alan Sutton, 1994), esp. M. W. Greenslade's "Introduction: Country History," 9–25; Lucia Nuti, "Mapping Places: Chorography and Vision in the Renaissance," in *Mappings,* ed. Denis Cosgrove (London: Reaktion Press, 1999), 90–108; Edward S. Casey, *Representing Place: Landscape Painting and Maps* (Minneapolis: University of Minnesota Press, 2002), 154–70; Stan Mendyk, "*Speculum Britanniae": Regional Study, Antiquarianism, and Science in Britain to 1700* (Toronto: University of Toronto Press, 1989), esp. 21–24; John M. Adrian, "Itineraries, Perambulations, and Surveys: The Intersections of Chorography and Cartography in the Sixteenth Century," in *Images of Matter: Essays on British Literature of the Middle Ages and Renaissance,* ed. Yvonne Bruce (Cranbury, N.J.: Associated University Presses, 2005), 29–46.

36. Walter, *Placeways,* 120. I agree with J. E. Malpas that correlating *topos* to place and *chora* to space oversimplifies Plato, especially since the concept of place as a specific location begins with Descartes. See *Place and Experience: A Philosophical Topography* (Cambridge: Cambridge University Press, 1999), 23–29. Compare Francis Cornford's distinction between *topos* as "the place where something is" and *chora* as the container, "the room that is filled," or the position/station held by a person (200n2).

37. Malpas, *Place and Experience,* 23. The Latin *spatium,* derived from the Greek *stadion,* measures the distance between objects.

38. In contrast, F. E. Romer claims that classical sources distinguished geography, chorography, and topography only by scale; see *Pomponius Mela's Description of the World* (Ann Arbor: University of Michigan Press, 1998), 4–5. Yet Mela's own *De chorographia,* perhaps the first Roman text on geography, becomes *De cosmographia* when transcribed by others (Romer, *Pomponius Mela's Description of the World,* 5). The first English edition of *De chorographia* identifies Mela as a cosmographer and never mentions

chorography; see *The Worke of Pomponius Mela, the Cosmographer, Concerninge the Situation of the World,* trans. Arthur Golding (London, 1585). This confusion over scope and genre reveals how quantitative differences can never be separated from qualitative differences.

39. As Svetlana Alpers points out, Ptolemy assigns geography—his own project—a superior epistemological power; see *The Art of Describing: Dutch Art in the Seventeenth Century* (Chicago: University of Chicago Press, 1983), 133–36. Indeed, Girolamo Ruscelli, a sixteenth-century translator of *Timaeus* and commentator on Ptolemy, criticizes *Geographia* for its deficiencies in chorographic description; see Denis Cosgrove, *Apollo's Eye: A Cartographic Genealogy of the Earth in the Western Imagination* (Baltimore: Johns Hopkins Press, 2001), 147–48.

40. A unit of distance consisting of five Roman feet, a *passus* suggests a more extended step.

41. *The Geography of Claudius Ptolemy,* trans. and ed. Edward Luther Stevenson (New York: New York Public Library, 1932), 26.

42. William Cuningham, *The Cosmographical Glasse* (London, 1559), 7.

43. For Jakobson, *metonymy* describes a relation where two spaces happen to be adjacent, while *metaphor* is linked to causal relationships, temporality, and similarity; see Roman Jakobson and Morris Halle, *Fundamentals of Language* ('S-Gravenhage: Mouton, 1956). Although Helgerson treats chorography and chronicle as opposite genres, he notes that early modern writers failed to distinguish *survey, description,* and *chorography* (*Forms of Nationhood,* 131–32). John Adrian adds *itinerary, view, perambulation, breviary,* and *account* to this list ("Itineraries, Perambulations, and Surveys," 30). Stan Mendyk defines chorography as "topographical-historical" in "Early British Chorography," *Sixteenth Century Journal* 17, no. 4 (1986): 459; his book, however, stresses the aspects of local history or antiquarianism ("*Speculum Britanniae,*" x and passim). Lesley Cormack also defines chorography as local history, but includes many examples that transcend these parameters; see *Charting an Empire: Geography at the English Universities, 1580–1620* (Chicago: University of Chicago Press, 1997), 165. Howard Marchitello claims that chorography is "typically narrative and only occasionally graphic"; see *Narrative and Meaning in Early Modern England: Browne's Skull and Histories* (Cambridge: Cambridge University Press, 1997), 78.

44. Cuningham, *Cosmographical Glasse,* 7.

45. Apian, *Cosmographia,* 2r.

46. Cuningham, *Cosmographical Glasse,* 6.

47. Ibid., "Praeface."

48. Holinshed, *Chronicles* (London, 1577), 36r.

49. John Leland, *The Laboryouse Iourney [and] Serche of Iohan Leylande, for Englandes Antiquitees,* ed. John Bale (1549), B3v. Leland lapsed into madness shortly after presenting an early version of his project to Henry VIII in 1546. John Bale published Leland's notes as *The Laboryouse Iourney* (1549), adding commentary, two prefaces, and (probably) a conclusion.

50. Ibid., B8v. These are Bale's words.

51. From a letter to Thomas Cromwell, now lost, dated July 16, 1536. See Anthony à Wood, *Athenae Oxonienses,* vol. 1 (London, 1691), 68.

52. Leland, *Laboryouse Iourney,* A2v (Bale's words). While Leland slips between *English* and *British,* I will reserve *Britain* for the England and Wales that Leland considers yoked into a royal "realm." The 1536 Act of Union made Wales subject to English policies such as the Suppression of Monasteries. Compare Bale's reference to "thys oure Englyshe or Bryttyshe nacyon" in his Preface (ibid., B3v). For more on Leland's usage of *Britain,* see Cathy Shrank, *Writing the Nation in Reformation England, 1530–1580* (Oxford: Oxford University Press, 2004), 71.

53. Leland often uses the term *monuments* to describe texts as well. Shrank discusses the "depopulation of the libraries" (*bibliothecae depopulatoribus*), which Leland diplomatically attributes to marauding outsiders rather than Henry's actions (*Writing the Nation,* 100). See also James P. Carley and Pierre Petitmengin, "Pre-Conquest Manuscripts from Malmesbury Abbey and John Leland's Letter to Beatus Rhenanus Concerning a Lost Copy of Tertullian's Works," *Anglo-Saxon England* 33 (2004): 195–223.

54. Leland, *Laboryouse Iourney,* C2r.

55. Ibid., C6v. Leland's notes toward this unfinished project were published as *Commentarii de Scriptoribus Britannicis,* ed. Anthony Hall (Oxford, 1709).

56. Ibid., D4r.

57. Ibid. Bale compares Leland to "Strabo, Pliny, Ptholome [Ptolemy], and other Geographers" (D5r).

58. Ibid., D5r (Bale's words); D5v. Leland compares this "quadrate table" to Charlemagne's silver tables depicting Constantinople, Rome, and the world; Leland uses the terms *site, figure,* and *description*—respectively—to characterize these earlier treasures. If Charlemagne's tables follow the Ptolemaic distinction between chorographic view and geographical map, then Leland's table likely falls into the former category as a limited "pycturinge out of the vniuersall worlde." For more on this table, see Philip Schwyzer, "John Leland and His Heirs: The Topography of England," in *The Oxford Handbook of Tudor Literature, 1485–1603,* ed. Mike Pincombe and Cathy Shrank (Oxford: Oxford University Press, 2009), 244n5.

59. Jennifer Summit, "Leland's *Itinerary* and the Remains of the Medieval Past," in *Reading the Medieval in Early Modern England,* ed. Gordon McMullan and David Matthews (Cambridge: Cambridge University Press, 2007), 162 and passim. For more on English reactions to monastic ruins, see Margaret Aston, "English Ruins and English History: The Dissolution and the Sense of the Past," *Journal of the Warburg and Courtauld Institutes* 36 (1973): 231–55.

60. Summit, "Leland's *Itinerary,*" 166. For more on Leland's architectural observations and reused materials, see Maurice Howard, *The Early Tudor Country House: Architecture and Politics, 1490–1550* (London: George Philip, 1987), 21–23.

61. Walter Benjamin, *The Origin of German Tragic Drama,* trans. John Osborne (London: Verso, 1998), 177–78.

62. Leland, *Laboryouse Iourney,* D5r. Bale describes the author as a "second father" to the original event ("Conclusyon," A8v).

63. Jacques Derrida, *Memoirs of the Blind: The Self-Portrait and Other Ruins,* trans. Pascale-Anne Brault and Michael Naas (Chicago: University of Chicago Press, 1993), 68.

64. Leland, *Laboryouse Iourney,* D5v (Bale's words).

65. For more on Lambarde's position in chorographical history, see R. C. Richardson, "Introduction: The Changing Face of English Local History," in *The Changing Face of English Local History,* ed. R. C. Richardson (Aldershot: Ashgate, 2000), 1. See also Richard Church's introduction to Lambarde's *Perambulation of Kent* (Bath: Adams and Dart, 1970).

66. William Lambarde, *Perambulations of Kent* (London, 1596), A2v, A2r. From an Epistle to Thomas Wotton found in the second edition but absent from the 1576 text.

67. Ibid., A2r.

68. Ibid., 8.

69. Ibid., 23.

70. Ibid., 24–25.

71. Henry Wotton, *The Elements of Architecture* (London, 1624), 4. The early modern term *perambulation* itself denotes a walk around the perimeter of a property.

72. Lambarde, *Perambulation,* A3v. See also Church's introduction to *Perambulation,* viii–ix. Lambarde includes himself in a list of Kentish gentry near the beginning of *Perambulation,* though he does not dwell on a reference to Westcombe, the site of his inherited estate (388).

73. John M. Adrian argues that the text promotes a gentry order while making Lambarde, a draper's son, a gentleman; see "Tudor Centralization and Gentry Visions of Local Order in Lambarde's *Perambulation of Kent,*" *English Literary Renaissance* 36, no. 3 (2006): 307–34.

74. Lambarde, *Perambulation,* 172. This section on St. Nicholas's Chapel first appears in 1596; while Lambarde claims to criticize past Catholic practices only if the opportunity arose, the second edition shows a willingness to choose locations solely to launch religious invective.

75. Ibid., 173, 172. See also Adrian, "Itineraries, Perambulations, and Surveys," 320–21.

76. Ibid., 526. The second quote also appears in the 1576 edition (387).

77. William Camden, *Britannia* (London, 1586), A4v.

78. Camden, *Britannia* (London, 1610), "To the Reader." This is the first English edition.

79. Ibid. The 1600 edition seems to be the first with a map on the frontispiece; later editions feature a similar engraving by William Hole. Helgerson also notes a schism between the map and personification of Britannia; see *Forms of Nationhood,* 120. Stuart Piggot notes that Camden's father, known as a *pictor,* may have influenced his son's "markedly visual approach to antiquities"; see "William Camden and the Britannia," in *The Changing Face of English Local History,* ed. R. C. Richardson (Aldershot: Ashgate, 2002), 13.

80. For more on sieve portraits and chastity, see Roy Strong's *Gloriana: The Portraits of Queen Elizabeth I* (London: Thames and Hudson, 1987), 94–107. Frances Yates links the queen to Vestal Virgins in tilt imagery and sieve portraits; see *Astraea: The Imperial Theme in the Sixteenth Century* (London: Routledge and Kegan Paul, 1975), esp. 102–3, 113–18.

81. For more on Elizabeth's imagery and Tuccia, see chapter 11 in Marina Warner's *Monuments and Maidens: The Allegory of the Female Form* (New York: Atheneum, 1985), esp. 373.

82. William Camden, *Remaines of a Greater Worke, Concerning Britaine* (London, 1605), 164.

83. Derrida, "*Khōra,*" 94. Carla Freccero's *Queer/Early/Modern* (Durham: Duke University Press, 2006) pioneered the study of queer temporality in early modern culture.

84. Yates notes how Elizabeth's sieve portraits also situate her as the Imperial Virgin, or "the Virgin of expanded empire" (*Astraea,* 117). Andrew and Catherine Belsey discuss Elizabeth's martial, sieve-like chastity in "Icons of Divinity: Portraits of Elizabeth I," in *Renaissance Bodies: The Human Body in English Culture, 1540–1660,* ed. Lucy Gent and Nigel Llewellyn (London: Reaktion Books, 1990), 15–16. For Gail Kern Paster, Elizabeth's continence implies leakiness as the "normal punitive condition for women"; see *The Body Embarrassed: Drama and the Disciplines of Shame in Early Modern England* (Ithaca: Cornell University Press, 1993), 50.

85. Though variously attributed, this portrait bears the notation "1583. Q. Massys | Ant." on the globe's base; see *Dynasties: Painting in Tudor and Jacobean England, 1530–1630,* ed. Karen Hearn (New York: Rizzoli, 1995), 85. The artist's name can be spelled "Metsys" or "Massys."

86. Lowell Gallagher, *Medusa's Gaze: Casuistry and Conscience in the Renaissance* (Stanford: Stanford University Press, 1991), 132. Compare Donald Stump's counterintuitive claim that Elizabeth "seems to have little regard for the sieve"; see "Marlowe's Travesty of Virgil: Dido and Elizabethan Dreams of Empire," *Comparative Drama* 34, no. 1 (2000): 83. Karen Green even rejects identifying the sieve with chastity; see "Phronesis Feminised: Prudence from Christine de Pizan to Elizabeth I," in *Virtue, Liberty, and Toleration: Political Ideas of European Women, 1400–1800,* ed. Jacqueline Broad and Karen Green (Dordrecht: Springer, 2007), 32–34.

87. As Strong notes in *Gloriana,* three versions of this 1579 painting existed; the Folger Library owns the so-called Plimpton Sieve Portrait discussed here.

88. Deanne Williams, "Dido, Queen of England," *ELH* 73, no. 1 (2006): 39. Louis Montrose similarly compares the pearl that hangs below Elizabeth's bodice in the Armada portrait to Henry VIII's codpiece; see "The Elizabethan Subject and the Spenserian Text," in *Literary Theory/Renaissance Texts,* ed. Patricia Parker and David Quint (Baltimore: Johns Hopkins University Press, 1966), 312–15.

89. Like Strong, Doris Adler situates the Siena Portrait in Elizabeth's failed marriage negotiations with the Duke of Anjou; see "The Riddle of the Sieve: The Siena Sieve Portrait of Queen Elizabeth," *Renaissance Papers* (1978):

1–10. Walter Oakeshott and [Constance] Anson Jordan link the painting to various marriage suits, noting that an inscription on the sieve—"A terra il ben mal dimora insella" (literally "to earth the good, bad remains in the saddle")—may refer to Robert Dudley, who was master of the horse. See "The Siena Portrait of Queen Elizabeth I," *Apollo* 124 (October 1986): 306–9. Jordan further notes that this inscription subverts virginity not only with the sexual connotations of a saddle, but also by letting the good fall through the holes; see "Representing Political Androgyny," in *The Renaissance Englishwoman in Print: Counterbalancing the Canon,* ed. Anne M. Haselkorn and Betty S. Travitsky (Amherst: University of Massachusetts Press, 1990), 166–68.

90. For more on Hatton's links to John Dee and empire, see Strong's *Gloriana,* 101–3; Susan Doran "Virginity, Divinity and Power: The Portraits of Elizabeth I," in *The Myth of Elizabeth,* ed. Susan Doran and Thomas S. Freeman (Houndmills: Palgrave Macmillan, 2003), 187.

91. For more on the elderly woman's role as duenna, see Jordan, "Representing Political Androgyny," 171. For more on this group's sexual roles, see Jonathan Goldberg, *Sodometries: Renaissance Texts, Modern Sexualities* (Stanford: Stanford University Press, 1992), 43–47.

92. Elizabeth wears a similar necklace in the Darnley portrait (c. 1575). This double loop, while lacking an overt iconographic meaning, nevertheless contributes to the portrait's formal logic.

93. Deanne Williams's "Dido, Queen of England" extends the work of Stephen Orgel, who raises the tangled history of Dido/Elissa in relation to the Siena Portrait in "Shakespeare and the Cannibals," in *Cannibals, Witches, and Divorce: Estranging the Renaissance,* ed. Marjorie Garber (Baltimore: Johns Hopkins University Press, 1987), 58–62.

94. Typically, viewers first identify the roundel with Dido burning at stake, located in the middle of the highest row, then work backward and forward from this climax to map vignettes onto memories of the *Aeneid.* Strong identifies the entire sequence of images, based on engravings by Marcantonio Raimondi, in *Gloriana,* 107.

95. Williams, "Dido, Queen of England," 42.

96. Derrida, "*Khōra,*" 91.

97. Gilles Deleuze, *The Fold: Leibniz and the Baroque,* trans. Tom Conley (Minneapolis: University of Minnesota Press, 1993), 10. See chapter 3 for more on the *Zweifalt.*

98. Case insists on women's natural virtue, concluding "faeminarum imperio ergo subscribas" (thus you should subscribe to the authority of women). See *Sphaera Civitatis* (Oxford, 1588), 34. Case tackles the broader question of female sovereignty in Book I, Chapter III, Question 4. For more on Case's relation to Aristotle, see Charles Schmitt's *John Case and Aristotelianism in Renaissance England* (Montreal: McGill-Queen's University Press, 1983).

99. For critique of pseudo-Albertus Magnus's *De faeminarum secretis,* also known as *De secretis mulieribus,* see Case, *Sphaera Civitatis,* 4. Case repeatedly observes that women are "libera" by nature (e.g., 18, 33), disputing that women should be treated as chattels or slaves (18–19).

100. From Kaara L. Peterson's unpublished paper, "Ministering to Herself: Elizabeth I, *All's Well That Ends Well,* and the Dialectics of Virginity," delivered at the Midwest Modern Languages Association Conference, 2003.

101. For Goldberg, this image is "at once, phallic and virginal, as endlessly prevaricating the relationship between inside and outside"; see *Sodometries,* 40. Rhonda Lemke Sanford notes that the rings "make invasion a matter of degrees"; see *Maps and Memory in Early Modern England: A Sense of Place* (New York: Palgrave, 2002), 57.

102. Tom Conley, *The Self-Made Map: Cartographic Writing in Early Modern France* (Minneapolis: University of Minnesota Press, 1996), 9.

103. For Strong, the queen "seems to embrace" the world before her; see *Gloriana,* 133.

104. Gilles Deleuze, *The Logic of Sense,* trans. Mark Lester with Charles Stivale, ed. Constantin V. Boundas (New York: Columbia University Press, 1990), 87.

105. Strong identifies the print as depicting Elizabeth (*Portraits,* 114), despite the sixteenth-century tradition of Europa-Virgo maps that allegorize the Spanish Hapsburg Empire. Indeed, given the mocking title "Het Spaens Europa" ("The Spanish Europa"), the figure could show a *Spanish* Europa whose recent military defeats are marked on the map. The best source on Europa-Virgo maps is H. A. M. van der Heijden, *De Oudste Gedrukte Kaarten van Europa* (Alphen aan den Rijn: Canaletto, 1992), 118–35; in English, see Bernhard Klein, *Maps and the Writing of Space,* 36–39, 193n36, and Michael Wintle, *The Image of Europe: Visualizing Europe in Cartography and Iconography Throughout the Ages* (Cambridge: Cambridge University Press, 2009), 247–52.

106. Compare Michael Camille's discussion of the schizo-body in relation to the anthropomorphic maps of Opicinus de Canistris, a fourteenth-century cleric who may have suffered psychotic delusions; see "The Image and the Self: Unwriting Late Medieval Bodies," in *Framing Medieval Bodies,* ed. Sarah Kay and Miri Rubin (Manchester: Manchester University Press, 1994), 62–99, esp. 87–95.

107. Jodi Mikalachki, *The Legacy of Boadicea: Gender and Nation in Early Modern England* (London: Routledge, 1998), 18–67.

Chapter Five

An earlier version of this chapter, along with sections now in chapter 4, appeared in *PMLA* 122, no. 1 (2007): 72–88.

1. Ben Jonson, *The Workes of Ben Jonson,* vol. 2 (London, 1641), 57. Also discussed in Richard Barbour, "'When I Acted Young Antinous': Boy Actors and the Erotics of Jonsonian Theater," *PMLA* 110, no. 5 (1995): 1006–22. To illustrate this inability to "make the difference," Jonson cites the example of male and female animals mixed in a group, or a species of animal construed as one gender no matter what the biological sex; thus, all doves are seen as feminine.

2. See the *OED* entry for *epicene,* esp. definitions A2 and B. As Barbara Millard notes, the early modern term *androgynous* often connoted

hermaphroditism, thus forming a synonym to *epicoene* in referring to deviant sexuality. See "'An Acceptable Violence': Sexual Contest in Jonson's *Epicoene*," *Medieval and Renaissance Drama in England* 1 (1984): 143, 157–58n5.

3. Yet few critics analyze the play using queer theory. A notable exception is Mario di Gangi's "Asses and Wits: The Homoerotics of Mastery in Satiric Comedy," *English Literary Renaissance* 25, no. 2 (1995): 179–208.

4. All *Epicoene* citations come from *Ben Jonson: Works*, ed. C. H. Herford and Percy Simpson, vol. 5 (Oxford: Clarendon Press, 1937).

5. As Barbara J. Baines and Mary C. Williams note, Jonson reverses the New Comedy plotline by staging a wedding mid-play, then ending with the bond's dissolution; see "The Contemporary and Classical Antifeminist Tradition in Jonson's *Epicoene*," *Renaissance Papers* (1977): 49. Since Dauphine has no plans to wed, the marital institution cannot be redeemed through another lineage. See Marjorie Swann, "Refashioning Society in Ben Jonson's *Epicoene*," *Studies in the English Language* 38 (1998): 300; also Mary Beth Rose, *The Expense of Spirit: Love and Sexuality in English Renaissance Drama* (Ithaca: Cornell University Press, 1988), 63.

6. Edward Partridge, *The Broken Compass: A Study of the Major Comedies of Ben Jonson* (New York: Columbia University Press, 1958), 162. Partridge reads *epicene* as a binary inversion that governs Jonson's comedies (63–69). Compare Philip Mirabelli's remarks on "Jonson's semantically innovative use" of *epicoene* in "Silence, Wit, and Wisdom in *The Silent Woman*," *SEL* 29 (1989): 312. Sandra Clark argues that the play does not concern literal epicenity, which she links to masculine women; see "'Hic Mulier,' 'Haec Vir,' and the Controversy over Masculine Women," *Studies in Philology* 82, no. 2 (1985): esp. 162.

7. Partridge, *Broken Compass*, 162.

8. As W. David Kay points out, Jonson's first attempt to satirize London society comes in *Everyman Out of His Humour* (1st quarto, 1600), which moves from country to city; see "*Epicoene*, Lady Compton, and the Gendering of Jonsonian Satire on Extravagance," *Ben Jonson Journal* 6 (1999): 4. Jonson finally accepts London as his latent urban template when he transplants *Every Man in His Humour* from Italy (1601 quarto) to London (1616 folio).

9. Between 1500 and 1700, London swelled from an estimated forty thousand to three hundred thousand people; see Peter Clark and Paul Slack, *English Towns in Transition, 1500–1700* (London: Oxford University Press, 1976), esp. 63–64. Compare Peter Borsay, *The English Urban Renaissance: Culture and Society on the Provincial Town* (Oxford: Clarendon Press, 1989), 10, 22.

10. P. K. Ayers contrasts the "town" setting of polite society to the business "city"; see "Dreams of the City: The Urban and the Urbane in Jonson's *Epicoene*," *Philological Quarterly* 66, no. 1 (1987): 74. Yet Janette Dillon rightly observes that Morose "cannot banish [the city] from his mindset, and it continues to shape his thinking inexorably"; see *Theatre, Court and City, 1595–1610: Drama and Social Space in London* (Cambridge: Cambridge University Press, 2000), 125.

11. As L. G. Salingar notes, Clerimont, Daw and Mrs. Otter all live near Amorous La-Foole, who in turn resides on the aristocratic Strand; since Morose's house is "but ouer the way, hard by" Mrs. Otter's house (III.iii.69–70), the wedding revelers can carry their feast from her house to his. See "Farce and Fashion in *The Silent Woman*," *Essays and Studies* 20 (1967): 44.

12. Frances Teague, "Ben Jonson's Stagecraft in *Epicoene*," *Renaissance Drama* 9 (1978): 175–92.

13. For more on the Whitefriars theater, see Glynne Wickham, Herbert Berry, and William Ingram's *English Professional Theatre, 1530–1660* (Cambridge: Cambridge University Press, 2000), 547–64; Jean MacIntyre, "Production Resources at the Whitefriars Playhouse, 1609–1612," *Early Modern Literary Studies* 2, no. 3 (1996): 2.1–35, http://purl.oclc.org/emls/02–3/maciwhit.html; Glynne Wickham, *Early English Stages, 1300–1660*, vol. 2, pt. 2 (London: Routledge & Kegan Paul, 1972), 122–23. For more on *Epicoene*'s staging at Whitefriars, see Richard Dutton's introduction to *Epicene, or The Silent Woman* (Manchester: Manchester University Press, 2003), 52–58; Tim Fitzpatrick, *Playwright, Space and Place in Early Modern Performance: Shakespeare and Company* (Farnham: Ashgate, 2011), 44–53.

14. Teague, "Ben Jonson's Stagecraft," 176. Teague estimates that auditors would sit within twenty-one yards of the stage. Karen Newman similarly notes that early modern audiences would both laugh at and empathize with Morose's reaction to these urban noises; see *Cultural Capitals: Early Modern London and Paris* (Princeton: Princeton University Press, 2007), 89. Dutton claims the opposite effect: "The theatre itself, at its quietest, becomes the equivalent of the double- and triple-insulated room he [Morose] has created" (Jonson, *Epicene*, 53). But does an early modern theater ever reach such levels of silence?

15. For more on Whitefriars as a touristic district of vice, see Mary Bly, "Playing the Tourist in Early Modern London: Selling the Liberties Onstage," *PMLA* 122, no. 1 (2007): 61–71. Compare Bly's *Queer Virgins and Virgin Queans on the Early Modern Stage* (Oxford: Oxford University Press, 2000), esp. 139–42. In contrast, John Stow describes Whitefriars as gentrified: "In place of this Fryars church bee now many fayre houses builded, lodginges for noble men and others." See Stowe's *A Suruay of London* (London, 1598), 324. Bly notes the social divisions among those invited to Jonson's feast, while Alison Findlay sees Jonson as catering to female spectators with urban tastes; see *A Feminist Perspective on Renaissance Drama* (Oxford: Blackwell, 1999), 109.

16. Bly notes that the reference to prostitutes is "double gendered," encompassing both "men *and* daughters of Whitefriars" (*Queer Virgins*, 141).

17. For more on this boys' company, see Lucy Munro's *Children of the Queen's Revels: A Jacobean Theatre Repertory* (Cambridge: Cambridge University Press, 2005). Munro notes the troupe's penchant for plays that feature a cross-dressed young man (50).

18. Dillon, *Theatre, Court and City*, 126. Compare Steven Mullaney's study of London theater and the margins, *The Place of the Stage: License, Play, and Power in Renaissance England* (Chicago: University of Chicago Press, 1988).

Some confusion exists over whether the liberty of Whitefriars stood within city walls in this period, as Bly believes (*Queer Virgins*, 139). If Whitefriars was located just west of city walls, there may still be a monastic perimeter wall.

19. Ian Donaldson's *Jonson's Magic Houses: Essays in Interpretation* (Oxford: Clarendon Press, 1997), notably chapter 5, explores building analogies in Jonson's canon. In *Ben Jonson: Poetry and Architecture* (Oxford: Clarendon Press, 1994), A. W. Johnson makes a formalist comparison between Vitruvian principles and the structure of Jonson's poetry and masques. Similarly, Elizabeth T. Jordan traces the philosophical tradition shared by architecture and writing; see "Inigo Jones and the Architecture of Poetry," *Renaissance Quarterly* 44, no. 2 (1991): 280–319.

20. Jonson, *Ben Jonson: Works*, ed. C. H. Herford, Percy Simpson, and Evelyn Simpson, vol. 8 (Oxford: Clarendon Press, 1970), 623.

21. Thomas Rymer, *A Short View of Tragedy* (London, 1693), 161.

22. The notion of Morose's disability was first suggested to me by Lindsey Row-Heyveld.

23. *Windore* or *wind-door* may simply be another term for *window;* Richard Dutton notes that Jonson consistently uses *windore* across his plays (*Epicene*, 128n174). Yet the fact that Morose lives by candlelight after closing and caulking his *windores* suggests a specific reference to shuttered windows, glazed or not. Rayna Kalas traces a shift from lattice, horn, oiled-cloth, and leaded windows to those of plate glass in *Frame, Glass, Verse: The Technology of Poetic Invention in the English Renaissance* (Ithaca: Cornell University Press, 2007), 189–90.

24. Clerimont uses *wind-fucker,* which means "kestrel," to insult Amorous La-Foole, whose empty speech is mere noise. Jonson's term nods to both the Amorous and La-Foole aspects of the name.

25. Lorna Hutson, "Civility and Virility in Ben Jonson," *Representations*, no. 78 (2002): 3. Hutson also notes how Jonson attends to architectural details like *windores.*

26. Laura Levine, *Men in Women's Clothing: Anti-Theatricality and Effeminization, 1579–1642* (Cambridge: Cambridge University Press, 1994), 80. Similarly, William Slights links Morose's spatial enclosure to a female rape, noting that most of the action "is laid out on the model of the closed and hence, in this play, feminized space"; see *Ben Jonson and the Art of Secrecy* (Toronto: University of Toronto Press, 1994), 99.

27. James Mardock claims that Morose enacts a "complete domestic prophylaxis" in *Our Scene Is London: Ben Jonson's City and the Space of the Author* (New York: Routledge, 2008), 73.

28. William Lithgow, *The Totall Discourse* (London, 1632), frontispiece. For more on Lithgow's turban, see Clifford Edmund Bosworth, *An Intrepid Scot: William Lithgow of Lanark's Travels in the Ottoman Lands, North Africa, and Central Europe, 1609–21* (Aldershot: Ashgate, 2006), 49–50. On a Shrove Sunday in 1510, Henry VIII "with the earle of Essex, came in apparelled after the Turkie fashion, in long robes of baudekin, powdered with gold,

hats on their heds of crimsin veluet, with great rolles of gold, girded with two swords called cimiteries, hanging by great bauderiks of gold"; see Holinshed's *Chronicles,* vol. 3 (London, 1587), 805.

29. Thomas M. Greene, "Ben Jonson and the Centered Self," *SEL* 10 (1970): 335. For a differing view, see Ann C. Christensen's "Reconsidering Ben Jonson and the 'Centered Self,'" *South Central Review* 13, no. 1 (1996): 1–16; Christensen notes the "enigmatic vulnerability of Jonson's houses" (6).

30. Dauphine uses the phrase "waking dreames" to describe Truewit's plots (IV.vii.42).

31. See Barbara Sebek, "Morose's Turban," *Shakespeare Studies* 35 (2007): 32–38. While Sebek opposes Morose's "turbanization" to his urbanization and emasculation, I argue the opposite.

32. Douglas Lanier sees Morose's extremes of silence/speech as reflecting upon Jonson's own master *logos* as a manly poet, a *logos* that turns out to be *epicoene;* see "Masculine Silence: *Epicoene* and Jonsonian Stylistics," *College Literature* 21, no. 2 (1994): 1–18.

33. For more on the play's links to dumb-show, see Adrian Curtin, "Dumb Reading: The Noise of the Mute in Jonson's *Epicene,*" *Comparative Drama* 43, no. 1 (2009): 45–62.

34. For more on how early modern Turks are depicted, see Barbara Fuchs, *Mimesis and Empire: The New World, Islam, and European Identities* (Cambridge: Cambridge University Press, 2001); Nabil Matar, *Islam in Britain, 1558–1685* (Cambridge: Cambridge University Press, 1998), esp. chapter 2; and Daniel Vitkus, *Turning Turk: English Theater and the Multicultural Mediterranean, 1570–1630* (New York: Palgrave Macmillan, 2003), esp. chapters 3 and 5.

35. Gail Kern Paster, *The Idea of the City in the Age of Shakespeare* (Athens: University of Georgia Press, 1985), 162–63. Karen Newman characterizes Morose's various treaties as an act of "urban zoning" (*Cultural Capitals,* 86).

36. George Puttenham, *The Arte of English Poesie* (London, 1589), 4. In this origin myth centered on "two Poets of the first ages," Puttenham describes how Amphion's brother Orpheus tames herds of beasts and civilizes "the rude and savage people" through his own music. Curiously, Alberti describes stones in musical terms as well, advising that "some are living, juicy, and strong . . . which by Nature are heavy and sonorous; others are exhausted, light, and dead sounding" (45 in Leoni edition; III.iv). In choosing stones for construction, the builder thus assembles a harmonious and strong set of blocks that will rise a long way without mortar.

37. Compare Cicero's question whether "mankind, dispersed originally in mountains and woods, inclosed themselves in towns and walls, not so much from being convinced by the counsels of the wise, as from being charmed by the speeches of the eloquent?" See *Cicero on Oratory and Orators,* trans. and ed. J. S. Watson (Carbondale: Southern Illinois University Press, 1970), 14–15.

38. Like Morose's Turkish model of authority, the sovereign on Hobbes's title page may be inspired by Jean-François Niceron's anamorphic illusion of Ottoman sultans. When seen through a special tube, these sultans comprise a

portrait of Louis XIII; see Noel Malcolm, *Aspects of Hobbes* (Oxford: Clarendon Press, 2002), 200–233, esp. 213.

39. British Library, Shelfmark G11548.

40. The reference to John Foxe's *Actes and Monuments* (London, 1563), which details Queen Mary's brutality toward Protestants, recalls Morose's heretical lifestyle. Morose's censure of these "ridiculous" acts and monuments thus aligns him with a bloody Catholic tyrant. Yet since Foxe's martyrs have become exemplars of faith in Jacobean times, might a similar regime change legitimate Morose's Turkish ways in the future?

41. James Mardock, "Hermaphroditical Authority in Jonson's City Comedies," *Ben Jonson Journal* 9 (2002): 71. As Clerimont's page shows in the first scene, the play does not confine cross-dressing to a theatrical domain.

42. Adam Zucker, "The Social Logic of Ben Jonson's *Epicoene*," *Renaissance Drama*, n.s., 33 (2004): 56.

43. Robert N. Watson also notes that Jonson "refunctions" male cross-dressing to undercut theater and "unsettle the inert literary heritage of his audience"; see *Ben Jonson's Parodic Strategy: Literary Imperialism in the Comedies* (Cambridge, Mass.: Harvard University Press, 1987), 100.

44. This noisy invasion evokes a charivari in which neighbors punish socially unpalatable acts. See Ian Donaldson, *The World Upside-Down: Comedy from Jonson to Fielding* (Oxford: Oxford University Press, 1970), 39–40; Bruce Boehrer, "*Epicoene*, Charivari, Skimmington," *English Studies* 75, no. 1 (1994): 17–33.

45. See Mardock, *Our Scene Is London*, 77.

46. David Henry Hwang, *M. Butterfly* (New York: Penguin Books, 1986), 63. As in *Epicoene*, tragedy arises in *M. Butterfly* because the cross-dressed Chinese man's voice is misinterpreted as the voice of a feminized Orient, the voice of a place, or rather, the idea of a place. When Song ultimately disrobes to reveal a male body, his Western husband realizes his own subject position as feminine and thus commits suicide. Likewise, Jonson's exposure of Epicoene makes Morose see his orientalist fantasy as self-castrating: it is Morose who finally assumes the role of a silent woman, walking off the stage humiliated and ceding all voice to his nephew.

47. Michel Foucault, *The Order of Things: An Archaeology of the Human Sciences* (New York: Random House, 1970), 51.

48. Hiromi Fuji, "Dispersed, Multi-Layered Space," trans. Hiroshi Watanabe, *Deconstruction II*, ed. Andrea Papadakis (New York: St Martin's Press, 1989), 68.

49. Rudolf Wittkower, *Architectural Principles in the Age of Humanism* (New York: Random House, 1962), 101–54. See also chapter 2, esp. note 102.

50. Luce Irigaray, *This Sex Which Is Not One*, trans. Catherine Porter and Carolyn Burke (Ithaca: Cornell University Press, 1985), 120.

51. Besides essays mentioned elsewhere, see Susan Wells, "Jacobean City Comedy and the Ideology of the City," *ELH* 48, no. 1 (1981): 37–60; Alison Findlay, *A Feminist Perspective on Renaissance Drama* (Oxford: Blackwell, 1999), 109–16; Rebecca Merrens, "'Ignoring the Men': Female Speech and

Male Anxiety in Cavendish's *The Female Academy* and Jonson's *Epicoene,*" *In-Between: Essays and Studies in Literary Criticism* 9 (2000): 243–60.

52. Karen Newman, "City Talk: Women and Commodification in Jonson's *Epicoene,*" *ELH* 56, no. 3 (1989): 509. Compare Heather C. Easterling's chapter on "*Epicoene,* Women, and the Language of the City," in *Parsing the City: Jonson, Middleton, Dekker, and City Comedy's London as Language* (New York: Routledge, 2007), 47–80.

53. Salingar, "Farce and Fashion," 35.

54. For more on proleptic dreams, see Carole Levin, *Dreaming the English Renaissance: Politics and Desire in Court and Culture* (New York: Palgrave Macmillan, 2008), esp. chapter 2.

55. William Austin, *Haec Homo* (London, 1637), 5–6.

56. Ibid., 81.

57. Ibid., 93.

58. See the *OED* definition 2 and 2a for *him.*

59. For Mathew Martin, the "collegiates' time of consumption negates the reproductive time of patriarchy"; see "Wasting Time in Ben Jonson's *Epicoene,*" *Studies in Philology* 105, no. 1 (2008): 91.

60. Voices rule Morose's divorce "hearing"; see Keith M. Botelho, *Renaissance Earwitnesses: Rumor and Early Modern Masculinity* (New York: Palgrave Macmillan, 2009), 103–4.

61. Judith Butler, *Bodies That Matter: On the Discursive Limits of "Sex"* (New York: Routledge, 1993), 50.

62. I draw on Derrida's notion of a dialogic text that solicits countersignatures from readers. John Brannigan defines the countersignature as "the application of one's self to the other, not as a projection of one's self onto the other, but as a way of exposing the self to the arrival of the other"; see "'We Have Nothing to Do with Literature': Derrida and Surrealist Writing," in *The French Connections of Jacques Derrida,* ed. Julian Wolfreys, John Brannigan, and Ruth Robbins (Albany: SUNY Press, 1999), 68. Derrida also posits the countersignature as a response to the text of an other (66–67), and as a filial relation (315–16); see *Acts of Literature,* ed. Derek Attridge (New York: Routledge, 1992).

63. Andrew Gurr notes the intense noise produced by early modern audiences wishing to interact with performers; see *Playgoing in Shakespeare's London,* 3rd ed. (Cambridge: Cambridge University Press, 2004), 51–57.

64. See Jonson's dedication to Francis Stuart (*Ben Jonson,* 161).

65. Gurr believes that hall playhouses were generally quieter than amphitheaters (*Playgoing,* 54). However, Whitefriars was much smaller than indoor theaters like Blackfriars.

Chapter Six

1. Klakse Muizelaar and Derek Phillips provide an overview of Dutch seventeenth-century room types in *Picturing Men and Women in the Dutch Golden Age: Paintings and People in Historical Perspective* (New Haven: Yale University Press, 2003), 25–42. See also Mariet Westermann, "'Costly and Curious, Full Off Pleasure and Home Contentment': Making Home in the

Dutch Republic," in *Art and Home: Dutch Interiors in the Age of Rembrandt,* ed. Mariet Westermann (Zwolle: Denver Art Museum, Newark Museum, and Waanders Publishers, 2001), 15–82. Like the English great hall, the *voorhuis* gradually shrank from being the main gathering place to an entrance hallway. Hoogstraten's *voorhuis* has already reduced to about half the house's width.

2. The box measures 58 × 88 × 63.5 cm. See Neil MacLaren and Christopher Brown's *The Dutch School: 1600–1900,* vol. 1 (London: National Gallery Publications, 1991), 205.

3. Following other critics, I designate the open side as the front (other panels are thus the left, back, right, bottom, and top). However, the front of Hoogstraten's box is not the same as the front of Hoogstraten's house; this latter role falls to the right panel, which shows the inside of a street facade. The box's intended orientation remains unclear: for example, viewers who approach from the "back" would not see the open side, thus keeping the inside a greater surprise.

4. Compare Susan Koslow, "De wonderlijke Perspectyfkas: An Aspect of Seventeenth Century Dutch Painting," *Oud Holland* 82 (1967): 36. Unlike a feminine dollhouse, the perspective box requires a masculine, mathematical precision (Westermann, "Costly and Curious," 45). Thus, perspective boxes were an "experimental demonstration"; see Celeste Brusati, *Artifice and Illusion: The Art and Writing of Samuel van Hoogstraten* (Chicago: University of Chicago Press, 1995), 172.

5. David Bomford, "Perspective and Peepshow Construction," *National Gallery Technical Bulletin* 11 (1987): 68. Bomford is defining perspective boxes in general.

6. Hoogstraten's art treatise, *Inleyding tot de Hooge Schoole der Schilderkonst* (Rotterdam, 1678), explains how perspective boxes make "a finger-length figure appear to be life-sized" (Brusati, *Artifice and Illusion,* 169).

7. Bomford, "Perspective and Peepshow Construction," 76.

8. Koslow's "De wonderlijke Perspectyfkas" surveys the extant perspective boxes in Denmark, the Netherlands, and England. Wolfgang Born compares theatrical models to peepboxes in "Early Peep-Shows and the Renaissance Stage," *Connoisseur* 107 (1941): 67–71, 161–64, 180.

9. Jacques Lacan, *The Ethics of Psychoanalysis,* trans. Dennis Porter (New York: W. W. Norton, 1992), 136. See also 140–41.

10. Tied to Žižek's notion of the blot, discussed in chapter 1, Lacan's *objet petit a* sustains the subject by forming an unattainable object of desire. As a remainder of the Real that cannot be sutured into the Symbolic, the *objet petit a* thus appears as a hole or stain in the visual field.

11. Margreta de Grazia notes an epistemic shift in the late seventeenth century when the proscenium arch starts framing the *scene* into the *seen;* see "World Pictures, Modern Periods, and the Early Stage," in *A New History of Early English Drama,* ed. John D. Cox and David Scott Kastan (New York: Columbia University Press, 1997), 19–20.

12. Hoogstraten likely knew Alberti's *De pictura* from a 1649 Amsterdam edition, which also contained an annotated Vitruvius's *De architectura.* See

Arthur K. Wheelock Jr., *Perspective, Optics and Delft Artists Around 1650* (London: Garland Press, 1977), 25, 54n5.

13. *The Diary of Samuel Pepys,* ed. Robert Latham and William Mathews, vol. 4 (Berkeley: University of California Press, 1995), 26. In a July 1, 1663, entry about Povey's house, John Evelyn admires a "perspective in his court, painted by Streater" and "the inlaying of his closet."

14. Brusati, *Artifice and Illusion,* 201.

15. See Evelyn's entry of February 29, 1676, and Pepys's entry of January 19, 1663. Pepys apparently saw the painting twice in a month.

16. See Evelyn's diary entry of February 29, 1676. Povey often appears in both Evelyn's and Pepys's diaries as a host. In the January 19, 1663, entry mentioned above, Pepys describes how Povey shows various "delicate pictures" to his visitors after a dinner of prawns, swan, and venison: culinary delicacies to match his artistic ones.

17. See the *Leonis Baptistae de Albertis Vita,* in *Opere Volgari di Leon Battista Alberti,* vol. 1, ed. Anicio Bonucci (Florence: Tipographia Galileiana, 1843), 102–4.

18. See Alberti, *Opere Volgari,* cii–iv: "Videsses illic montes maximos, vastasque provincias, sinum immanem maris ambientis, tum e conspectu longe sepositas regiones usque adeo remotissimas, ut visenti acies deficeret." These sights may belong to one or several pictures.

19. Roger Hinks, "Peepshow and Roving Eye," *Architectural Review* 118, no. 705 (September 1955): 163. Lisa Jardine calls Hoogstraten's box an "inside-out *camera obscura*"; see *Ingenious Pursuits: Building the Scientific Revolution* (New York: Anchor Books, 2000), 107.

20. Brusati, *Artifice and Illusion,* 177.

21. For more on these scenes, see Joanne Woodall, "Love Is in the Air—*Amor* as Motivation and Message in Seventeenth-Century Netherlandish Painting," *Art History* 19 (1996): 208–46.

22. Compare Richard Helgerson's claim that genre painters "simply understood that well-to-do male householders did not belong in such scenes," though these men were presumed spectators. See "Soldiers and Enigmatic Girls: The Politics of Dutch Domestic Realism, 1650–1672," *Representations,* no. 58 (1997): 55.

23. Brusati, *Artifice and Illusion,* 177.

24. Hoogstraten himself employs the letter-signature trick in several paintings, including *Perspective from a Threshold.* See Clotilde Misme, "Deux 'Boîtes-à-Perspective' Hollandaises du XVIIe Siècle," *Gazette des Beaux-Arts* 11 (1925): 159; Brusati, *Artifice and Illusion,* 69, 364.

25. Bomford, "Perspective and Peepshow Construction," 74–75.

26. See Danielle Lokin's "Life and Work in Seventeenth-Century Delft," in *The Public and the Private in the Age of Vermeer,* ed. Arthur Wheelock Jr. (London: Philip Wilson, 2000), esp. 38–41. Also C. Willemijn Fock's "The Décor of Domestic Entertaining at the Time of the Dutch Republic," *Netherlands Yearbook for History of Art* 51 (2001): 103–35.

27. Woodall praises how "the Dutch interior of the perspective box can be seen as a marvellous, mirror-like illusion of 'reality'" ("Love Is in the Air," 237). John Loughman and John Michael Montias look to the perspective box for evidence of how actual Dutch interiors were organized; see *Public and Private Spaces: Works of Art in Seventeenth-Century Dutch Houses* (Zwolle: Waanders Publishers, 2000), 9–12.

28. Brusati, *Artifice and Illusion,* 175, 190. See esp. her fig. 123.

29. Svetlana Alpers, *The Art of Describing* (Chicago: University of Chicago Press, 1983), 163. See also her analysis of Hoogstraten (61–62).

30. Compare Bomford, "Perspective and Peepshow Construction," 74.

31. The two peepholes are roughly the same height and distance from the front edge, but the right peephole has beveling that directs the gaze more sharply toward the opposite rear corner.

32. For more on the box's original appearance, see Bomford, "Perspective and Peepshow Construction," 70, 75. Traces of paper have been found around the front edges, and a secondary frame may have slotted into the opening.

33. Gilles Deleuze and Félix Guattari, *A Thousand Plateaus: Capitalism and Schizophrenia,* trans. Brian Massumi (Minneapolis: University of Minnesota Press, 1987), 287.

34. Ibid.

35. Compare Brusati's notion that the perspective box aims for an "aesthetic conquest" intended to delineate "the artifice of vision itself" (*Artifice and Illusion,* 181).

36. Kaja Silverman offers an account of cinematic suture in chapter 5 of *The Subject of Semiotics* (New York: Oxford University Press, 1983). For Daniel Dayan, a viewer's awareness of the frame "radically transforms his mode of participation—the unreal space between characters and/or objects is no longer perceived as pleasurable. . . . He discovers that he is only authorized to see what happens to be in the axis of the gaze of another spectator, who is ghostly or absent"; see "The Tutor-Code of Classical Cinema," in *Film Theory and Criticism,* 4th ed., ed. Gerald Mast, Marshall Cohen, and Leo Braudy (New York: Oxford University Press, 1992), 179–91.

37. Misme, "Deux 'Boîtes-à-Perspective,'" 165: "Elle rayonne . . . de simplicité digne, d'ordre et de propreté" (It radiates a dignified simplicity, order, and propriety).

38. Fred Leeman, *Hidden Images,* trans. Joost Elfers and Margaret L. Kaplan (New York: Harry Abrams, 1976), 9.

39. Deleuze and Guattari, *A Thousand Plateaus,* 168.

40. Richard Helgerson, "Soldiers and Enigmatic Girls: The Politics of Dutch Domestic Realism, 1650–1672," *Representations* 58 (1997): 80.

41. Bomford, "Perspective and Peepshow Construction," 75.

42. In this regard, the letter resembles the sharply raked image of Venus and Cupid on top of the box, an anamorphic experiment generally considered a failure.

43. Deleuze and Guattari, *A Thousand Plateaus,* 287.

SELECTED BIBLIOGRAPHY

Adelman, Janet. *Suffocating Mothers: Fantasies of Maternal Origin in Shakespeare's Plays, "Hamlet" to "The Tempest."* New York: Routledge, 1992.

Adler, Doris. "The Riddle of the Sieve." *Renaissance Papers* (1978): 1–10.

Adrian, John M. "Itineraries, Perambulations, and Surveys: The Intersections of Chorography and Cartography in the Sixteenth Century." In *Images of Matter: Essays on British Literature of the Middle Ages and Renaissance,* edited by Yvonne Bruce, 29–46. Cranbury, N.J.: Associated University Presses, 2005.

———. "Tudor Centralization and Gentry Visions of Local Order in Lambarde's *Perambulation of Kent.*" *English Literary Renaissance* 36, no. 3 (2006): 307–34.

Agamben, Giorgio. *Homo Sacer: Sovereign Power and Bare Life.* Translated by Daniel Heller-Roazen. Stanford: Stanford University Press, 1998.

Airs, Malcolm. *The Making of the English Country House, 1500–1640.* London: Architectural Press, 1975.

Albano, Caterina. "Visible Bodies: Cartography and Anatomy." In *Literature, Mapping, and the Politics of Space in Early Modern Britain,* edited by Andrew Gordon and Bernhard Klein, 89–106. Cambridge: Cambridge University Press, 2001.

Alberti, Leon Battista. *L'Architettura.* Translated by Paolo Portoghesi. Milan: Edizioni Il Polifilo, 1966.

———. *On Painting and On Sculpture: The Latin Texts of "De Pictura" and "De Statua."* Edited by Cecil Grayson. London: Phaidon, 1972.

———. *On the Art of Building in Ten Books.* Translated by Joseph Rykwert, Neil Leach, and Robert Tavernor. Cambridge, Mass.: MIT Press, 1988.

———. *Opere Volgari di Leon Battista Alberti.* Vol. 1. Edited by Anicio Bonucci. Florence: Tipographia Galileiana, 1843.

———. *The Ten Books of Architecture.* 1755. Translated by Cosimo Bartoli and James Leoni. New York: Dover, 1986.

Alpers, Svetlana. *The Art of Describing: Dutch Art in the Seventeenth Century.* Chicago: University of Chicago Press, 1983.

Anderson, Christy. *Inigo Jones and the Classical Tradition.* Cambridge: Cambridge University Press, 2007.

———. "Learning to Read Architecture in the English Renaissance." In *Albion's Classicism: Britain and the Visual Arts, 1550–1650,* edited by Lucy Gent, 239–86. New Haven: Yale University Press, 1995.

———. "Monstrous Babels: Language and Architectural Style in the English Renaissance." In *Architecture and Language: Constructing Identity in*

European Architecture c. 1000–c. 1650, edited by Georgia Clarke and Paul Crossley, 148–61. Cambridge: Cambridge University Press, 2000.

———. "Palladio in England: The Dominance of the Classical in a Foreign Land." In *Palladio and Northern Europe: Books, Travellers, Architects,* 122–29. Milan: Skira, 1999.

Andrewes, Lancelot. *XCVI Sermons.* London, 1629.

Andrews, Michael Cameron. "His Mother's Closet: A Note on *Hamlet.*" *Modern Philology* 80, no. 2 (1982): 164–66.

Anstey, T. A. "Fictive Harmonies: Music and the Tempio Malatestiano." *RES: Anthropology and Aesthetics,* no. 36 (1999): 187–204.

Apian, Peter. *Cosmographia, Sive Descriptio Vniversi Orbis.* Antwerp, 1553.

Arendt, Hannah. *The Human Condition.* Chicago: University of Chicago Press, 1958.

Armstrong, Philip. *Shakespeare in Psychoanalysis.* New York: Routledge, 2001.

Ashbaugh, Anne Freire. *Plato's Theory of Explanation: A Study of the Cosmological Account in the "Timaeus."* Albany: SUNY Press, 1988.

Aston, Margaret. "English Ruins and English History: The Dissolution and the Sense of the Past." *Journal of the Warburg and Courtauld Institutes* 36 (1973): 231–55.

Augustine. *The Confessions of the Incomparable Doctour S. Augustine.* Translated by Tobie Matthew. St. Omer, 1620.

Austin, William. *Haec Homo, Wherein the Excellency of the Creation of Woman is Described, by Way of an Essay.* London, 1637.

Ayers, P. K. "Dreams of the City: The Urban and the Urbane in Jonson's *Epicoene.*" *Philological Quarterly* 66, no. 1 (1987): 73–86.

———. "Reading, Writing, and *Hamlet.*" *Shakespeare Quarterly* 44, no. 4 (1993): 423–39.

Bacon, Francis. *The Essayes or Counsels, Ciuill and Morall, of Francis Lo. Verulam, Viscount St. Alban.* London, 1625.

———. *Sylua Syluarum.* London, 1627.

Baillie, Hugh Murray. "Etiquette and the Planning of the State Apartments in Baroque Palaces." *Archaeologia,* 2nd ser., 101, no. 51 (1967): 169–200.

Baines, Barbara J., and Mary C. Williams. "The Contemporary and Classical Antifeminist Tradition in Jonson's *Epicoene.*" *Renaissance Papers* (1977): 43–58.

Barasch, Moshe. *The Language of Art: Studies in Interpretation.* New York: NYU Press, 1997.

Barbon, Nicholas. *An Apology for the Builder, or, A Discourse Shewing the Cause and Effects of the Increase of Building.* London, 1685.

Barbour, Richard. "'When I Acted Young Antinous': Boy Actors and the Erotics of Jonsonian Theater." *PMLA* 110, no. 5 (1995): 1006–22.

Barkan, Leonard. *Nature's Work of Art: The Human Body as Image of the World.* New Haven: Yale University Press, 1975.

Barker, Francis. *The Tremulous Private Body: Essays on Subjection.* Ann Arbor: University of Michigan Press, 1995.

Barley, Maurice. *Houses and History.* London: Faber and Faber, 1986.

Baron, Hans. *Petrarch's "Secretum."* Cambridge, Mass.: Medieval Academy of America, 1985.

Barthes, Roland. *Camera Lucida: Reflections on Photography.* Translated by Richard Howard. New York: Hill and Wang, 1981.

Batho, Gordon. "The Library of the 'Wizard Earl': Henry Percy Ninth Earl of Northumberland (1564–1632)." *The Library,* 5th ser., 15 (1960): 246–61.

Belsey, Andrew, and Catherine Belsey. "Icons of Divinity: Portraits of Elizabeth I." In *Renaissance Bodies: The Human Body in English Culture, 1540–1660,* edited by Lucy Gent and Nigel Llewellyn, 11–35. London: Reaktion Books, 1990.

Belsey, Catherine. "Making Space: Perspective Vision and the Lacanian Real." *Textual Practice* 16, no. 1 (2002): 31–55.

———. *The Subject of Tragedy: Identity and Difference in Renaissance Drama.* London: Methuen, 1985.

Bennett, J. A. "Architecture and Mathematical Practice in England, 1550–1650." In *English Architecture Public and Private,* edited by John Bold and Edward Chaney, 22–30. London: Hambledon, 1993.

Bianchi, Emanuela. "Receptacle/*Chōra:* Figuring the Errant Feminine in Plato's *Timaeus.*" *Hypatia* 21, no. 4 (2006): 124–46.

Bickersteth, John, and Robert W. Dunning. *Clerks of the Closet in the Royal Household: Five Hundred Years of Service to the Crown.* Stroud: Alan Sutton, 1991.

Bickham, George. *The British Monarchy: Or a New Chorographical Description of All the Dominions Subject to the King of Great Britain.* London, 1743.

Biddle, Martin. "The Gardens of Nonsuch: Sources and Dating." *Garden History* 27, no. 1 (1999): 145–83.

———. "Nicholas Bellin of Modena." *Journal of the British Archaeological Association,* 3rd ser., 29 (1966): 106–21.

———. *Nonsuch: The Material Culture of a Noble Restoration Household.* Oxford: Oxbow, 2005.

———. "The Stuccoes of Nonsuch." *Burlington Magazine* 126, no. 976 (1984): 411–17.

Blount, Thomas. *Glossographia.* London, 1656.

Bly, Mary. "Playing the Tourist in Early Modern London: Selling the Liberties Onstage." *PMLA* 122, no. 1 (2007): 61–71.

———. *Queer Virgins and Virgin Queans on the Early Modern Stage.* Oxford: Oxford University Press, 2000.

Bodin, Jean. *The Six Bookes of a Commonweale.* Translated by Richard Knolles. London, 1606.

Boehrer, Bruce. "*Epicoene,* Charivari, Skimmington." *English Studies* 75, no. 1 (1994): 17–33.

Bold, John. "Privacy and the Plan." In *English Architecture Public and Private,* edited by John Bold and Edward Chaney, 107–19. London: Hambledon, 1993.

Bomford, David. "Perspective and Peepshow Construction." *National Gallery Technical Bulletin* 11 (1987): 65–77.

Boorde, Andrew. *The Boke for to Lerne a Man to be Wyse in Buyldyng of His Howse for the Helth of Body and to Holde Quyetnes for the Helth of his Soule, and Body*. London, 1540[?].

Born, Wolfgang. "Early Peep-Shows and the Renaissance Stage." *Connoisseur* 107 (1941): 67–71, 161–64, 180.

Borsay, Peter. *The English Urban Renaissance: Culture and Society on the Provincial Town*. Oxford: Clarendon Press, 1989.

Borsi, Franco. *Leon Battista Alberti: The Complete Works*. Translated by Rudolf G. Carpanini. London: Faber and Faber, 1989.

Bosse, Abraham. *Traité des manières de dessiner les ordres de l'architecture antique*. Paris, 1664.

Bosworth, Clifford Edmund. *An Intrepid Scot: William Lithgow of Lanark's Travels in the Ottoman Lands, North Africa, and Central Europe, 1609–21*. Aldershot: Ashgate, 2006.

Botelho, Keith M. *Renaissance Earwitnesses: Rumor and Early Modern Masculinity*. New York: Palgrave Macmillan, 2009.

Brannigan, John. "'We Have Nothing to Do with Literature': Derrida and Surrealist Writing." In *The French Connections of Jacques Derrida*, edited by Julian Wolfreys, John Brannigan, and Ruth Robbins, 53–70. Albany: SUNY Press, 1999.

Broadbent, Geoffrey. "A Plain Man's Guide to the Theory of Signs." In *Theorizing a New Agenda for Architecture: An Anthology of Architectural Theory, 1965–95*, edited by Kate Nesbitt, 124–41. New York: Princeton Architectural Press, 1996.

Brotton, Jerry. "Ways of Seeing *Hamlet*." In *Hamlet: New Critical Essays*, edited by Arthur F. Kinney, 161–76. New York: Routledge, 2002.

Brown, Keith. "'Form and Cause Conjoin'd': *Hamlet* and Shakespeare's Workshop." *Shakespeare Survey* 26 (1973): 11–20.

Brusati, Celeste. *Artifice and Illusion: The Art and Writing of Samuel van Hoogstraten*. Chicago: University of Chicago Press, 1995.

Bryan, Jennifer. *Looking Inward: Devotional Reading and the Private Self in Late Medieval England*. Philadelphia: University of Pennsylvania Press, 2007.

Bryson, Norman. "The Gaze in the Expanded Field." In *Vision and Visuality*, edited by Hal Foster, 87–114. Seattle: Bay Press, 1988.

———. *Vision and Painting: The Logic of the Gaze*. New Haven: Yale University Press, 1983.

Buisseret, David, ed. *Monarchs, Ministers, and Maps: The Emergence of Cartography as a Tool of Government in Early Modern Europe*. Chicago: University of Chicago Press, 1992.

Bulgarelli, Massimo. "L'architettura." In *Il Tempio Malatestiano a Rimini*, vol. 1, edited by Antonio Paolucci, 49–121. Modena: Franco Cosimo Panini, 2010.

Burnett, David. *Longleat: The Story of an English Country House*. London: Collins, 1978.

Burroughs, Charles. "The Building's Face and the Herculean Paradigm: Agendas and Agency in Roman Renaissance Architecture." *RES: Anthropology and Aesthetics* 23 (1993): 7–30.

———. *From Signs to Design: Environmental Process and Reform in Early Renaissance Rome*. Cambridge, Mass.: MIT, 1990.

———. *The Italian Renaissance Palace Façade: Structures of Authority, Surfaces of Sense*. Cambridge: Cambridge University Press, 2002.

Butler, Judith. *Bodies That Matter: On the Discursive Limits of "Sex."* New York: Routledge, 1993.

———. *Gender Trouble: Feminism and the Subversion of Identity*. New York: Routledge, 1990.

Callebat, L., and P. Bouet, Ph. Fleury, M. Zuinghedau, eds. *Vitruve "De architectura" Concordance*. Part 1. Hildesheim-Zurich-New York: Olms-Weidmann, 1984.

Camden, William. *Britain, or A Chorographicall Description of the Most Flourishing Kingdomes, England, Scotland, and Ireland, and the Ilands Adjoyning*. Translated by Philemon Holland. London, 1610.

———. *Britannia Siue Florentissimorum Regnorum, Angliae, Scotiae, Hiberniae, et Insularum Adiacentium Ex Intima Antiquitate Chorographica Descriptio*. London, 1586.

———. *Remaines of a Greater Worke, Concerning Britaine, the Inhabitants Thereof, Their Languages, Names, Surnames, Empreses, Wise Speeches, Poësies, and Epitaphes*. London, 1605.

Camille, Michael. "The Image and the Self: Unwriting Late Medieval Bodies." In *Framing Medieval Bodies*, edited by Sarah Kay and Miri Rubin, 62–99. Manchester: Manchester University Press, 1994.

Carley, James P., and Pierre Petitmengin. "Pre-Conquest Manuscripts from Malmesbury Abbey and John Leland's Letter to Beatus Rhenanus Concerning a Lost Copy of Tertullian's Works." *Anglo-Saxon England* 33 (2004): 195–223.

Carpo, Mario. *Architecture in the Age of Printing: Orality, Writing, Typography, and Printed Images in the History of Architectural Theory*. Translated by Sarah Benson. Cambridge, Mass.: MIT Press, 2001.

Carruthers, Mary. *The Book of Memory: A Study of Memory in Medieval Culture*. 2nd ed. Cambridge: Cambridge University Press, 2008.

Casey, Edward S. *The Fate of Place: A Philosophical History*. Berkeley: University of California Press, 1997.

———. *Representing Place: Landscape Painting and Maps*. Minneapolis: University of Minnesota Press, 2002.

———. *The World at a Glance*. Bloomington: Indiana University Press, 2007.

Cassani, Alberto G. "Per foramina obductae personae: Una fonte inedita per la facciata del tempio Malatestiano." *Albertiana* 5 (2002): 61–76.

Certeau, Michel de. *The Practice of Everyday Life*. Translated by Steven Rendall. Berkeley: University of California Press, 1984.

Chaney, Edward, ed. *Inigo Jones's "Roman Sketchbook."* 2 vols. London: Roxburghe Club, 2006.

Charney, Maurice. "The Closet-Scene Access." In *Approaches to Teaching Shakespeare's Hamlet,* edited by Bernice W. Kliman, 180–83. New York: MLA, 2002.

Chedgzoy, Kate. *Women's Writing in the British Atlantic World: Memory, Place, and History, 1550–1700.* Cambridge: Cambridge University Press, 2007.

Choay, Françoise. *The Rule and the Model: On the Theory of Architecture and Urbanism.* Edited by Denise Bratton. Cambridge, Mass.: MIT Press, 1997.

Christensen, Ann C. "Reconsidering Ben Jonson and the 'Centered Self.'" *South Central Review* 13, no. 1 (1996): 1–16.

Cicero, Marcus Tullius. *Cicero on Oratory and Orators* [*De Oratore*]. Translated and edited by J. S. Watson. Carbondale: Southern Illinois University Press, 1970.

Clark, Peter, and Paul Slack. *English Towns in Transition, 1500–1700.* London: Oxford University Press, 1976.

Clark, Sandra. "'Hic Mulier,' 'Haec Vir,' and the Controversy over Masculine Women." *Studies in Philology* 82, no. 2 (1985): 157–83.

Clarke, Elizabeth, and Erica Longfellow. "'[E]xamine My Life': Writing the Self in the Early Seventeenth Century." *Constructing Elizabeth Isham, 1609–1654.* Last modified June 11, 2012. http://www2.warwick.ac.uk/fac/arts/ren/projects/isham/texts.

Cliffe, J. T. *The World of the Country House in Seventeenth-Century England.* New Haven: Yale University Press, 1999.

Colie, Rosalie. *"My Ecchoing Song": Andrew Marvell's Poetry of Criticism.* Princeton: Princeton University Press, 1970.

Colvin, Howard, ed. *The History of the King's Works.* 6 vols. London: H. M. Stationery Office, 1963–82.

———. "Recycling the Monasteries: Demolition and Reuse by the Tudor Government, 1536–47." In *Essays in English Architectural History,* 52–66. New Haven: Yale University Press, 1999.

Conley, Tom. *The Self-Made Map: Cartographic Writing in Early Modern France.* Minneapolis: University of Minnesota Press, 1996.

Cook, Olive. *The English House Through Seven Centuries.* Woodstock, N.Y.: Overlook Press, 1968.

Cooper, Nicholas. *Houses of the Gentry, 1480–1680.* New Haven: Yale University Press, 1999.

Cormack, Lesley. *Charting an Empire: Geography at the English Universities, 1580–1620.* Chicago: University of Chicago Press, 1997.

Cornford, Francis. *Plato's Cosmology.* London: Routledge and Kegan Paul, 1937.

Cosgrove, Denis. *Apollo's Eye: A Cartographic Genealogy of the Earth in the Western Imagination.* Baltimore: Johns Hopkins Press, 2001.

Cotgrave, Randle. *A Dictionarie of the French and English Tongues.* London, 1611.

Crary, Jonathan. *Techniques of the Observer: On Vision and Modernity in the Nineteenth Century.* Cambridge, Mass.: MIT Press, 1990.

Crawford, Julie. "Women's Secretaries." In *Queer Renaissance Historiography: Backward Gaze,* edited by Stephen Guy-Bray, Vin Nardizzi, and Will Stockton, 111–34. Aldershot: Ashgate, 2009.

Crewe, Jonathan. "What Does Matter Want? Irigaray, Plotinus, and the Human Condition." In *Luce Irigaray and Premodern Culture: Thresholds of History,* edited by Theresa Krier and Elizabeth Harvey, 38–52. New York: Routledge, 2004.

Cuningham, William. *The Cosmographical Glasse Conteinyng the Pleasant Principles of Cosmographie, Geographie, Hydrographie, or Nauigation.* London, 1559.

Currie, C. R. J., and C. P. Lewis, eds. *English County Histories: A Guide.* Phoenix Mill: Alan Sutton, 1994.

Curtin, Adrian. "Dumb Reading: The Noise of the Mute in Jonson's *Epicene.*" *Comparative Drama* 43, no. 1 (2009): 45–62.

Damisch, Hubert. *The Origin of Perspective.* Translated by John Goodman. Cambridge, Mass.: MIT Press, 1994.

Day, Angel. *The English Secretary.* 2nd ed. London, 1599.

Dayan, Daniel. "The Tutor-Code of Classical Cinema." In *Film Theory and Criticism,* 4th ed., edited by Gerald Mast, Marshall Cohen, and Leo Braudy, 179–91. New York: Oxford University Press, 1992.

Dee, John. Preface to *The Elements of Geometrie of the Most Auncient Philosopher Euclide of Megara.* Translated by H. Billingsley. London, 1570.

De Grazia, Margreta. *"Hamlet" Without Hamlet.* Cambridge: Cambridge University Press, 2007.

———. "Teleology, Delay, and the 'Old Mole.'" *Shakespeare Quarterly* 50, no. 3 (1999): 251–67.

———. "World Pictures, Modern Periods, and the Early Stage." In *A New History of Early English Drama,* edited by John D. Cox and David Scott Kastan, 7–21. New York: Columbia University Press, 1997.

Deleuze, Gilles. *The Fold: Leibniz and the Baroque.* Translated by Tom Conley. Minneapolis: University of Minnesota Press, 1993.

———. *The Logic of Sense.* Translated by Mark Lester with Charles Stivale. Edited by Constantin V. Boundas. New York: Columbia University Press, 1990.

Deleuze, Gilles, and Félix Guattari. *Kafka: Toward a Minor Literature.* Translated by Dana Polan. Minneapolis: University of Minnesota Press, 1986.

———. *A Thousand Plateaus: Capitalism and Schizophrenia.* Translated by Brian Massumi. Minneapolis: University of Minnesota Press, 1987.

———. *What Is Philosophy?* Translated by Graham Burchell III. New York: Columbia University Press, 1994.

Dent, John. *The Quest for Nonsuch.* London: Hutcheson & Co., 1962.

Derrida, Jacques. *Acts of Literature.* Edited by Derek Attridge. New York: Routledge, 1992.

———. *Chora L Work*. Translated by Ian McCloud. New York: Monacelli Press, 1997.

———. *Memoirs of the Blind: The Self-Portrait and Other Ruins*. Translated by Pascale-Anne Brault and Michael Naas. Chicago: University of Chicago Press, 1993.

———. *Of Grammatology*. Translated by Gayatri Chakravorty Spivak. Baltimore: Johns Hopkins Press, 1974.

———. *On the Name*. Edited by Thomas Dutoit. Translated by David Wood, John P. Leavey Jr., and Ian McLeod. Stanford: Stanford University Press, 1995.

———. *The Truth in Painting*. Translated by Geoff Bennington and Ian McLeod. Chicago: University of Chicago Press, 1987.

Di Gangi, Mario. "Asses and Wits: The Homoerotics of Mastery in Satiric Comedy." *English Literary Renaissance* 25, no. 2 (1995): 179–208.

Dibben, L. B. "Secretaries in the Thirteenth and Fourteenth Centuries." *English Historical Review* 25, no. 99 (1910): 430–44.

Dillon, Janette. *Theatre, Court and City, 1595–1610: Drama and Social Space in London*. Cambridge: Cambridge University Press, 2000.

Doel, Marcus A. *Poststructuralist Geographies: The Diabolical Art of Spatial Science*. Edinburgh: Edinburgh University Press, 1999.

Dollimore, Jonathan. *Radical Tragedy: Religion, Ideology, and Power in the Drama of Shakespeare and His Contemporaries*. Chicago: Chicago University Press, 1984.

Donaldson, Ian. *Jonson's Magic Houses: Essays in Interpretation*. Oxford: Clarendon Press, 1997.

———. *The World Upside-Down: Comedy from Jonson to Fielding*. Oxford: Oxford University Press, 1970.

Doran, Susan. "Virginity, Divinity and Power: The Portraits of Elizabeth I." In *The Myth of Elizabeth*, edited by Susan Doran and Thomas S. Freeman, 171–99. Houndmills: Palgrave Macmillan, 2003.

D'Orléans, Chérubin. *La Dioptrique Oculaire*. Paris, 1671.

Drayton, Michael. *The Poly-Olbion: A Chorographicall Description of Great Britain*. London, 1622.

Dunlop, Ian. "Nonsuch Palace." *Connoisseur* 128 (1951): 113–15, 127.

During, Simon. *Modern Enchantments: The Cultural Power of Secular Magic*. Cambridge, Mass.: Harvard University Press, 2002.

Dusinberre, Juliet. *Shakespeare and the Nature of Women*. London: Macmillan, 1975.

Eagleton, Terry. *William Shakespeare*. Oxford: Blackwell, 1986.

Eamon, William. *Science and the Secrets of Nature: Books of Secrets in Medieval and Early Modern Culture*. Princeton: Princeton University Press, 1994.

Easterling, Heather C. *Parsing the City: Jonson, Middleton, Dekker, and City Comedy's London as Language*. New York: Routledge, 2007.

Eco, Umberto. *The Open Work*. Translated by Anna Cancogni. Cambridge, Mass.: Harvard University Press, 1989.

Edgerton, Samuel Y., Jr. *The Renaissance Rediscovery of Linear Perspective.* New York: Basic Books, 1975.

Elet, Yvonne. "Seats of Power: The Outdoor Benches of Early Modern Florence." *Journal of the Society of Architectural Historians* 61, no. 4 (2002): 444–69.

Elkins, James. "Piero della Francesca and the Renaissance Proof of Linear Perspective." *Art Bulletin* 69, no. 2 (1987): 220–30.

———. *The Poetics of Perspective.* Ithaca: Cornell University Press, 1994.

———. "Renaissance Perspectives." *Journal of the History of Ideas* 53, no. 2 (1992): 209–30.

Elyot, Thomas. *Bibliotheca Eliotae.* London, 1542.

———. *The Boke Named the Gouernour.* London, 1537.

Eriksen, Roy. *The Building in the Text: Alberti to Shakespeare and Milton.* University Park: Pennsylvania State University Press, 2001.

Ettlinger, Helen S. "The Sepulchre on the Facade: A Re-Evaluation of Sigismondo Malatesta's Rebuilding of San Francesco in Rimini." *Journal of the Warburg and Courtauld Institutes* 53 (1990): 133–43.

Evelyn, John. *The Diary of John Evelyn.* Edited by E. S. de Beer. Oxford: Clarendon Press, 1955.

Farmer, Norman K., Jr. *Poets and the Visual Arts in Renaissance England.* Austin: University of Texas Press, 1984.

Ferguson, Margaret W. "*Hamlet:* Letters and Spirits." In *Shakespeare and the Question of Theory,* edited by Patricia Parker and Geoffrey Hartman, 292–309. New York: Methuen, 1985.

Ferrarius, Johannes. *A Woorke of Ioannes Ferrarius Montanus, Touchynge the Good Orderynge of a Common Weale.* Translated by William Bauande [Bavande]. London, 1559.

Ficino, Marsilio. *The Platonic Theology.* Vol. 1. Translated by Michael J. B. Allen. Edited by James Hankins. Cambridge, Mass.: Harvard University Press, 2001.

Field, J. V. *The Invention of Infinity: Mathematics and Art in the Renaissance.* Oxford: Oxford University Press, 1997.

Findlay, Alison. *A Feminist Perspective on Renaissance Drama.* Oxford: Blackwell, 1999.

———. *Playing Spaces in Early Modern Women's Drama.* Cambridge: Cambridge University Press, 2006.

Fitzpatrick, Tim. *Playwright, Space and Place in Early Modern Performance: Shakespeare and Company.* Farnham: Ashgate, 2011.

Fock, C. Willemijn. "The Décor of Domestic Entertaining at the Time of the Dutch Republic." *Netherlands Yearbook for History of Art* 51 (2001): 103–35.

Forster, Kurt W. "The Palazzo Rucellai and Questions of Typology in the Development of Renaissance Buildings." *Art Bulletin* 58, no. 1 (1976): 109–13.

Fossati, Carlo Giuseppe. *Le Temple de Malateste de Rimini: Architecture de Leon Baptiste Alberti de Florence.* Fuligno, 1794.

Foucault, Michel. *The History of Sexuality.* Vol. 1, *An Introduction.* New York: Vintage, 1990.

———. *The Order of Things: An Archaeology of the Human Sciences.* New York: Random House, 1970.

———. "Space, Knowledge, Power." Translated by Christian Hubert. In *Architecture Theory Since 1968,* edited by Michael Hays, 428–39. Cambridge, Mass.: MIT Press, 2000.

Fowler, Alastair. *The Country House Poem: A Cabinet of Seventeenth-Century Estate Poems and Related Items.* Edinburgh: Edinburgh University Press, 1994.

Frangenberg, Thomas. *Der Betrachter, Studien zur florentinischen Kunstliteratur des 16. Jahrunderts.* Berlin: Gebr. Mann, 1990.

———. "The Image and the Moving Eye: Jean Pélerin (Viator) to Guidobaldo del Monte." *Journal of the Warburg and Courtauld Institutes* 49 (1986): 150–71.

Freccero, Carla. *Queer/Early/Modern.* Durham: Duke University Press, 2006.

Freedman, Barbara. *Staging the Gaze: Postmodernism, Psychoanalysis, and Shakespearean Comedy.* Ithaca: Cornell University Press, 1991.

Freud, Sigmund. *The Standard Edition of the Complete Psychological Works of Sigmund Freud.* Translated by James Strachey. London: Hogarth, 1957.

Friedberg, Anne. *The Virtual Window: From Alberti to Microsoft.* Cambridge, Mass.: MIT Press, 2006.

Friedman, Alice T. "Architecture, Authority, and the Female Gaze: Planning and Representation in the Early Modern Country House." *Assemblage,* no. 18 (1992): 40–61.

———. *House and Household in Elizabethan England: Wollaton Hall and the Willoughby Family.* Chicago: University of Chicago Press, 1989.

Friedman, David. "Palaces and the Street in Late-Medieval and Renaissance Italy." In *Urban Landscapes: International Perspectives,* edited by J. W. R. Whitehand and P. J. Larkham, 69–113. London: Routledge, 1992.

Fuchs, Barbara. *Mimesis and Empire: The New World, Islam, and European Identities.* Cambridge: Cambridge University Press, 2001.

Fuji, Hiromi. "Dispersed, Multi-Layered Space." Translated by Hiroshi Watanabe. In *Deconstruction II,* edited by Andrea Papadakis, 67–75. New York: St. Martin's Press, 1989.

Fumerton, Patricia. *Cultural Aesthetics: Renaissance Literature and the Practice of Social Ornament.* Chicago: University of Chicago Press, 1991.

Gallagher, Lowell. *Medusa's Gaze: Casuistry and Conscience in the Renaissance.* Stanford: Stanford University Press, 1991.

Gapper, Claire. "What Is 'Stucco'? English Interpretations of an Italian Term." *Architectural History* 42 (1999): 333–43.

Gent, Lucy. *Picture and Poetry, 1560–1620.* Leamington Spa: James Hall, 1981.

———. "'The Rash Gazer': Economies of Vision in Britain, 1550–1660." In *Albion's Classicism: The Visual Arts in Britain, 1550–1660,* edited by Lucy Gent, 377–93. New Haven: Yale University Press, 1995.

Girouard, Mark. *Elizabethan Architecture: Its Rise and Fall, 1540–1640.* New Haven: Yale University Press, 2009.
———. *Life in the English Country House: A Social and Architectural History.* New Haven: Yale University Press, 1978.
———. *Robert Smythson and the Elizabethan Country House.* New Haven: Yale University Press, 1983.
———, ed. *The Smythson Collection of the Royal Institute of British Architects.* Special issue, *Architectural History* 5 (1962): 23–184.
Godfrey, Eleanor. *The History of English Glassmaking, 1560–1640.* Oxford: Clarendon Press, 1975.
Godwin, Joscelyn. *The Pagan Dream of the Renaissance.* Grand Rapids: Phanes, 2002.
Goldberg, Jonathan. "Hamlet's Hand." *Shakespeare Quarterly* 39, no. 3 (1988): 307–27.
———. *Sodometries: Renaissance Texts, Modern Sexualities.* Stanford: Stanford University Press, 1992.
———. *Voice Terminal Echo: Postmodernism and English Renaissance Texts.* New York: Methuen, 1986.
———. *Writing Matter: From the Hands of the English Renaissance.* Stanford: Stanford University Press, 1990.
Goldthwaite, Richard. "The Florentine Palace as Domestic Architecture." *American Historical Review* 77, no. 4 (1972): 977–1012.
Gomme, Andor. "Halls into Vestibules." In *The Renaissance Villa in Britain, 1500–1700,* edited by Malcolm Airs and Geoffrey Tyack, 38–63. Reading: Spire, 2007.
Gomme, Andor, and Alison Maguire. *Design and Plan in the Country House: From Castle Donjons to Palladian Boxes.* New Haven: Yale University Press, 2008.
Gotch, J. Alfred. "The Development of House Design in the Reigns of Elizabeth and James, as Illustrated by Contemporary Architectural Drawings." *Journal of the Royal Institute of British Architects,* 3rd ser., 16, no. 2 (1908): 41–66.
———. *Early Renaissance Architecture in England: A Historical and Descriptive Account of the Tudor, Elizabethan, and Jacobean Periods, 1500–1625.* London: B. T. Batsford, 1901.
Goyet, Francis. "Hamlet, étudiant du XVIe siècle." *Poétique,* no. 113 (1998): 3–15.
Grafton, Anthony. *Leon Battista Alberti: Master Builder of the Italian Renaissance.* New York: Hill and Wang, 2000.
Grayson, Cecil. *An Autograph Letter from Leon Battista Alberti to Matteo de' Pasti: November 18, 1454.* New York: Pierpont Morgan Library, 1957.
———. *Studi su Leon Battista Alberti.* Edited by Paola Claut. Mantua: Leo S. Olschki, 1998.
Green, Ian. *Print and Protestantism in Early Modern England.* Oxford: Oxford University Press, 2000.
Green, Karen. "Phronesis Feminised: Prudence from Christine de Pizan to Elizabeth I." In *Virtue, Liberty, and Toleration: Political Ideas of European*

Women, 1400–1800, edited by Jacqueline Broad and Karen Green, 23–38. Dordrecht: Springer, 2007.

Greenblatt, Stephen. *Hamlet in Purgatory.* Princeton: Princeton University Press, 2002.

———. *Will in the World: How Shakespeare Became Shakespeare.* New York: W. W. Norton, 2004.

Greene, Thomas M. "Ben Jonson and the Centered Self." *SEL* 10, no. 2 (1970): 325–48.

Greenstein, Jack M. "On Alberti's 'Sign': Vision and Composition in Quattrocento Painting." *Art Bulletin* 79, no. 4 (1997): 669–98.

Grosz, Elizabeth. *Architecture from the Outside, Essays on Virtual and Real Space.* Cambridge, Mass.: MIT Press, 2001.

Guillen, Claudio. "On the Concept and Metaphor of Perspective." In *Comparatists at Work: Studies in Comparative Literature,* edited by Stephen G. Nichols Jr. and Richard B. Vowles, 28–90. Waltham, Mass.: Blaisdell Publishing, 1968.

Gurr, Andrew. *Playgoing in Shakespeare's London.* 3rd ed. Cambridge: Cambridge University Press, 2004.

———. *The Shakespearean Stage, 1574–1642.* 4th ed. Cambridge: Cambridge University Press, 2009.

Gy, Pierre-Marie. "The Meaning and Function of the Introit." In *Liturgy and the Arts in the Middle Ages: Studies in Honour of C. Clifford Flanigan,* edited by Eva Louise Lillie and Nils Holger Petersen, 64–74. Copenhagen: Museum Tusculanum Press, 1996.

Habermas, Jürgen. *The Structural Transformation of the Public Sphere: An Inquiry into a Category of Bourgeois Society.* Translated by Thomas Burger and Frederic Lawrence. Cambridge, Mass.: MIT Press, 1989.

Hackel, Heidi Brayman. *Reading Material in Early Modern England: Print, Gender, Literacy.* Cambridge: Cambridge University Press, 2005.

Hake, Edward. *The Imitation or Following of Christ.* London, 1567.

Hakewill, George. *An Apologie or Declaration of the Power and Providence of God in the Government of the World.* Oxford, 1627.

Hale, John. *The Civilization of Europe in the Renaissance.* New York: Touchstone, 1993.

Halpern, Richard. *Shakespeare Among the Moderns.* Ithaca: Cornell University Press, 1997.

Hanson, Elizabeth. *Discovering the Subject in Renaissance England.* Cambridge: Cambridge University Press, 1998.

Harley, J. B. "Meaning and Ambiguity in Tudor Cartography." In *English Map-Making, 1500–1650,* edited by Sarah Tyacke, 22–45. London: British Library, 1983.

———. "Silences and Secrecy: The Hidden Agenda of Cartography in Early Modern Europe." *Imago Mundi* 40 (1988): 57–76.

Harris, Eileen, with Nicholas Savage. *British Architectural Books and Writers, 1556–1785.* Cambridge: Cambridge University Press, 1990.

Hart, Vaughan. *Art and Magic in the Court of the Stuarts*. London: Routledge, 1994.

———. "From Virgin to Courtesan in Early English Vitruvian Books." In *Paper Palaces: The Rise of the Renaissance Architectural Treatise,* edited by Vaughan Hart and Peter Hicks, 297–318. New Haven: Yale University Press, 1998.

Harvey, Elizabeth D., and Theresa Krier, eds. *Luce Irigaray and Premodern Culture: Thresholds of History*. New York: Routledge, 2004.

Hawkins, Henry. *Partheneia Sacra*. Rouen, 1633.

Hearn, Karen, ed. *Dynasties: Painting in Tudor and Jacobean England, 1530–1630*. New York: Rizzoli, 1995.

Heath, Stephen. "Joan Riviere and the Masquerade." In *Formations of Fantasy,* edited by Victor Burgin, James Donald, and Cora Kaplan, 45–61. London: Methuen, 1986.

Heidegger, Martin. "Building, Dwelling, Thinking." In *Poetry, Language, Thought,* translated by A. Hofstadter, 143–61. New York: Harper and Row, 1971.

Heijden, H. A. M. van der. *De Oudste Gedrukte Kaarten van Europa*. Alphen aan den Rijn: Canaletto, 1992.

Helgerson, Richard. *Forms of Nationhood: The Elizabethan Writing of England*. Chicago: University of Chicago Press, 1992.

———. "Soldiers and Enigmatic Girls: The Politics of Dutch Domestic Realism, 1650–1672." *Representations,* no. 58 (Spring 1997): 49–87.

Henderson, Paula. *The Tudor House and Garden: Architecture and Landscape in the Sixteenth and Early Seventeenth Centuries*. New Haven: Yale University Press, 2005.

Hentzner, Paul. *Paul Hentzner's Travels in England, During the Reign of Queen Elizabeth*. London, 1797.

Herrtage, Sidney J., ed. *England in the Reign of King Henry the Eighth*. Part 1, *Starkey's Life and Letters*. Early English Text Society, Extra Series 32. London: N. Trübner, 1878.

Hibbard, G. R. "The Country House Poem of the Seventeenth Century." *Journal of the Warburg and Courtauld Institutes* 19 (1956): 159–74.

Higgott, Gordon. "'Varying with Reason': Inigo Jones's Theory of Design." *Architectural History* 35 (1992): 51–77.

Hill, Gillian. *Cartographical Curiosities*. London: British Library, 1978.

Hillman, David. *Shakespeare's Entrails: Belief, Skepticism and the Interior of the Body*. Houndmills: Palgrave, 2007.

Hinks, Roger. "Peepshow and Roving Eye." *Architectural Review* 118, no. 705 (September 1955): 161–64.

Historical Manuscripts Commission. *The Manuscripts of His Grace, the Duke of Rutland, K. G., Preserved at Belvoir Castle*. Vol. 4. London: H. M. Stationery Office, 1905.

Holinshed, Raphael. *Chronicles*. London, 1577 (2 vols., 1st ed.) and 1587 (3 vols., 2nd ed.).

Hollingsworth, Mary. "Art Patronage in Renaissance Urbino, Pesaro, and Rimini." In *The Court Cities of Northern Italy: Milan, Parma, Piacenza, Mantua, Ferrara, Bologna, Urbino, Pesaro, and Rimini,* edited by Charles M. Rosenberg, 325–68. Cambridge: Cambridge University Press, 2010.

Hope, Charles. "The Early History of the Tempio Malatestiano." *Journal of the Warburg and Courtauld Institutes* 55 (1992): 51–154.

Hoskins, W. G. "The Rebuilding of Rural England, 1570–1640." *Past and Present,* no. 4 (1953): 44–59.

Howard, Maurice. *The Early Tudor Country House: Architecture and Politics, 1490–1550.* London: George Philip, 1987.

———. "The Ideal House and Healthy Life: The Origins of Architectural Theory in England." In *Les traités d'architecture de la Renaissance,* edited by Jean Guillaume, 425–35. Paris: Picard, 1988.

Howarth, David. *Images of Rule: Art and Politics in the English Renaissance, 1485–1649.* Berkeley: University of California Press, 1997.

Huebert, Ronald. "The Gendering of Privacy." *Seventeenth Century* 16, no. 1 (2001): 37–67.

Huelin, Scott. "Reading, Writing, and Memory in *Hamlet*." *Religion and Literature* 37, no. 1 (2005): 25–44.

Huloet, Richard, and John Higgins. *Huloets Dictionarie Newelye Corrected.* London, 1572.

Hulse, Clark. *The Rule of Art: Literature and Painting in the Renaissance.* Chicago: University of Chicago Press, 1990.

Hutson, Lorna. "Civility and Virility in Ben Jonson." *Representations,* no. 78 (2002): 1–27.

Hwang, David Henry. *M. Butterfly.* New York: Penguin Books, 1986.

Ingraham, Catherine. *Architecture, Animal, Human: The Asymmetric Condition.* New York: Routledge, 2006.

———. *Architecture and the Burdens of Linearity.* New Haven: Yale University Press, 1998.

Irigaray, Luce. *An Ethics of Sexual Difference.* Translated by Carolyn Burke and Gillian C. Gill. Ithaca: Cornell University Press, 1984.

———. *Speculum of the Other Woman.* Translated by Gillian C. Gill. Ithaca: Cornell University Press, 1985.

———. *This Sex Which Is Not One.* Translated by Catherine Porter and Carolyn Burke. Ithaca: Cornell University Press, 1985.

Ivins, William M., Jr. *Art and Geometry: A Study in Space Intuitions.* Cambridge, Mass.: Harvard University Press, 1946.

Jagodzinski, Cecile M. *Privacy and Print: Reading and Writing in Seventeenth-Century England.* Charlottesville: University of Virginia Press, 1999.

Jakobson, Roman, and Morris Halle. *Fundamentals of Language.* 'S-Gravenhage: Mouton, 1956.

Jardine, Lisa. *Ingenious Pursuits: Building the Scientific Revolution.* New York: Anchor Books, 2000.

———. *Reading Shakespeare Historically.* London: Routledge, 1996.

Jardine, Lisa, and William Sherman. "Pragmatic Readers: Knowledge Transactions and Scholarly Services in Late Elizabethan England." In *Religion, Culture, and Society in Early Modern Britain: Essays in Honour of Patrick Collinson,* edited by Anthony Fletcher and Peter Roberts, 102–24. Cambridge: Cambridge University Press, 1994.

Jarzombek, Mark. "Corridor Spaces." *Critical Inquiry* 36, no. 4 (2010): 728–70.

———. *On Leon Baptista Alberti: His Literary and Aesthetic Theories.* Cambridge, Mass.: MIT Press, 1989.

Jay, Martin. "Scopic Regimes of Modernity." In *Vision and Visuality,* edited by Hal Foster, 3–23. Seattle: Bay Press, 1988.

Jed, Stephanie. *Chaste Thinking: The Rape of Lucretia and the Birth of Humanism.* Bloomington: Indiana University Press, 1989.

Jenks, Chris. "The Centrality of the Eye in Western Culture: An Introduction." In *Visual Culture,* edited by Chris Jenks, 1–25. New York: Routledge, 1995.

Johnson, A. W. *Ben Jonson: Poetry and Architecture.* Oxford: Clarendon Press, 1994.

Johnston, Mark Albert. "Prosthetic Absence in Ben Jonson's *Epicoene, The Alchemist,* and *Bartholomew Fair.*" *English Literary Renaissance* 37, no. 3 (2007): 401–28.

Jonson, Ben. *Ben Jonson: Works.* 11 vols. Edited by C. H. Herford, Percy Simpson, and Evelyn Simpson. Oxford: Clarendon Press, 1925–52.

———. *Epicene, or The Silent Woman.* Edited by Richard Dutton. Manchester: Manchester University Press, 2003.

———. *The Workes of Ben Jonson.* 2 vols. London, 1640–41.

Jordan, Constance. "Representing Political Androgyny." In *The Renaissance Englishwoman in Print: Counterbalancing the Canon,* edited by Anne M. Haselkorn and Betty S. Travitsky, 157–76. Amherst: University of Massachusetts Press, 1990.

Jordan, Elizabeth T. "Inigo Jones and the Architecture of Poetry." *Renaissance Quarterly* 44, no. 2 (1991): 280–319.

Kahn, Victoria. "The Figure of the Reader in Petrarch's *Secretum.*" *PMLA* 100, no. 2 (1985): 154–66.

Kalas, Rayna. *Frame, Glass, Verse: The Technology of Poetic Invention in the English Renaissance.* Ithaca: Cornell University Press, 2007.

Kay, W. David. "*Epicoene,* Lady Compton, and the Gendering of Jonsonian Satire on Extravagance." *Ben Jonson Journal* 6 (1999): 1–33.

Kemp, Martin. *The Science of Art: Optical Themes in Western Art from Brunelleschi to Seurat.* New Haven: Yale University Press, 1990.

Kempis, Thomas à. *The Imitation of Christ: The First English Translation of the "Imitatio Christi."* Edited by B. J. H. Biggs. Oxford: Oxford University Press, 1997.

Kent, Dale. *Cosimo de' Medici and the Florentine Renaissance: The Patron's Oeuvre.* New Haven: Yale University Press, 2000.

Kent, F. W. "Palaces, Politics and Society in Fifteenth-Century Florence." *I Tatti Studies: Essays in the Renaissance* 2 (1987): 41–70.

Kerrigan, John. "Hieronimo, Hamlet and Remembrance." *Essays in Criticism* 31, no. 2 (1981): 105–26.

Kircher, Timothy. *Poet's Wisdom: The Humanists, the Church, and the Formation of Philosophy in the Early Renaissance.* Leiden: Brill, 2006.

Kitson, Anthony [?]. *The Secrete of Secretes.* London, 1572.

Klein, Bernhard. *Maps and the Writing of Space in Early Modern England and Ireland.* Houndmills: Palgrave, 2001.

Klein, Robert. "Studies on Perspective in the Renaissance." In *Form and Meaning: Essays on the Renaissance and Modern Art,* translated by Madeline Jay and Leon Wieseltier, 129–40. Princeton: Princeton University Press, 1970.

Kliman, Bernice. "The Bed in *Hamlet*'s Closet Scene: Rowe 1709 and 1714." *Shakespeare Newsletter* 43, no. 1 (1993): 8–9.

Knoppers, Laura Lunger. "Opening the Queen's Closet: Henrietta Maria, Elizabeth Cromwell, and the Politics of Cookery." *Renaissance Quarterly* 60, no. 2 (2007): 464–99.

Knowles, James. "'Infinite Riches in a Little Room:' Marlowe and the Aesthetics of the Closet." In *Renaissance Configurations: Voices/Bodies/Spaces, 1580–1690,* edited by Gordon McMullan, 3–29. Houndmills: MacMillan, 1998.

Knowles, Ric. Review of *Author's Pen and Actor's Voice: Playing and Writing in Shakespeare's Theatre,* by Robert Weimann, edited by Helen Higbee and William West. *Early Theatre* 8, no. 1 (2005): 145–48.

Koslow, Susan. "De wonderlijke Perspectyfkas: An Aspect of Seventeenth Century Dutch Painting." *Oud Holland* 82 (1967): 35–56.

Krautheimer, Richard. "Alberti and Vitruvius." In *Studies in Early Christian, Medieval, and Renaissance Art,* 323–30. New York: NYU Press, 1969.

Krinsky, Carol Herselle. "Seventy-Eight Vitruvius Manuscripts." *Journal of the Warburg and Courtauld Institutes* 30 (1967): 36–70.

Kristeva, Julia. *Revolution in Poetic Language.* Translated by Margaret Waller. New York: Columbia University Press, 1984.

Kruft, Hanno-Walter. *A History of Architectural Theory from Vitruvius to the Present.* Translated by Ronald Taylor, Elsie Callander, and Anthony Wood. New York: Princeton Architectural Press, 1994.

Kunin, Aaron. "From the Desk of Anne Clifford." *ELH* 71, no. 3 (2004): 587–608.

Lacan, Jacques. *The Ethics of Psychoanalysis.* Translated by Dennis Porter. New York: W. W. Norton, 1992.

———. "The Instance of the Letter in the Unconscious, or Reason Since Freud." In *Ecrits: A Selection,* translated by Bruce Fink, 138–68. New York: W. W. Norton, 2002.

———. *The Seminar of Jacques Lacan, Book IX: The Four Fundamental Concepts of Psychoanalysis.* Edited by Jacques-Alain Miller. Translated by Alan Sheridan. New York: W. W. Norton, 1981.

Lambarde, William. *A Perambulation of Kent.* 2nd ed. London, 1596.

———. *A Perambulation of Kent.* Introduction by Richard Church. Bath: Adams and Dart, 1970.

Leeman, Fred. *Hidden Images.* Translated by Joost Elfers and Margaret L. Kaplan. New York: Harry Abrams, 1976.

Lefebvre, Henri. *The Production of Space.* Translated by Donald Nicholson-Smith. Oxford: Basil Blackwell, 1991.

Lehmann, Phyllis Williams. "Alberti and Antiquity: Additional Observations." *Art Bulletin* 70, no. 3 (1988): 388–400.

Leland, John. *Commentarii de Scriptoribus Britannicis.* Edited by Anthony Hall. Oxford, 1709.

———. *The Laboryouse Iourney [and] Serche of Iohan Leylande, for Englandes Antiquitees.* Edited by John Bale. London, 1549.

Levin, Carole. *Dreaming the English Renaissance: Politics and Desire in Court and Culture.* New York: Palgrave Macmillan, 2008.

Levine, Laura. *Men in Women's Clothing: Anti-Theatricality and Effeminization, 1579–1642.* Cambridge: Cambridge University Press, 1994.

Lieberman, Saul. "Roman Legal Institutions in Early Rabbinics and in the Acta Martyrum." *Jewish Quarterly Review,* n.s., 35, no. 1 (1944): 1–57.

Lin, Erika. "Performance Practice and Theatrical Privilege: Rethinking Weimann's Concepts of *Locus* and *Platea.*" *New Theatre Quarterly* 22, no. 3 (2006): 283–98.

Lindberg, David C. *Theories of Vision from Al-Kindi to Kepler.* Chicago: University of Chicago Press, 1981.

Lithgow, William. *The Totall Discourse, of the Rare Aduentures, and Painefull Peregrinations of Long Nineteene Yeares Trauayles, from Scotland, to the Most Famous Kingdomes in Europe, Asia, and Affrica.* London, 1632.

Lochrie, Karma. *Covert Operations: The Medieval Uses of Secrecy.* Philadelphia: University of Pennsylvania Press, 1999.

Lokin, Danielle. "Life and Work in Seventeenth-Century Delft." In *The Public and the Private in the Age of Vermeer,* edited by Arthur Wheelock Jr., 33–43. London: Philip Wilson, 2000.

Longfellow, Erica. "Public, Private, and the Household in Early Seventeenth-Century England." *Journal of British Studies* 45, no. 2 (2006): 313–34.

Loughman, John, and John Michael Montias. *Public and Private Spaces: Works of Art in Seventeenth-Century Dutch Houses.* Zwolle: Waanders Publishers, 2000.

Lücke, Hans-Karl. *Alberti Index: Leon Battista Alberti, "De re aedificatoria," Florenz 1485; Index verborum.* Munich: Prestel, 1975.

Lupton, Julia Reinhard. "Hamlet, Prince: Tragedy, Citizenship, Political Theology." In *Alternative Shakespeares 3,* edited by Diana Henderson, 181–203. New York: Routledge, 2007.

MacIntyre, Jean. "Production Resources at the Whitefriars Playhouse, 1609–1612." *Early Modern Literary Studies* 2, no. 3 (1996): 2.1–35. http://purl.oclc.org/emls/02–3/maciwhit.html. Accessed August 23, 2010.

Mack, Charles Randall. "The Rucellai Palace: Some New Proposals." *Art Bulletin* 56, no. 4 (1974): 517–29.
MacLaren, Neil, and Christopher Brown. *The Dutch School: 1600–1900*. Vol. 1. London: National Gallery Publications, 1991.
Malcolm, Noel. *Aspects of Hobbes*. Oxford: Clarendon Press, 2002.
Malpas, J. E. *Place and Experience: A Philosophical Topography*. Cambridge: Cambridge University Press, 1999.
Mancini, Girolamo. *Vita di Leon Battista Alberti*. 2nd ed. Florence: G. Carnesecchi, 1911.
Manetti, Antonio di Tuccio. *The Life of Brunelleschi*. Edited by Howard Saalman. Translated by Catherine Enggass. University Park: Pennsylvania State University Press, 1970.
Manzalaoui, M. A. *"Secretum Secretorum": Nine English Versions*. Early English Text Society No. 276. Oxford: Oxford University Press, 1977.
Marchitello, Howard. *Narrative and Meaning in Early Modern England: Browne's Skull and Histories*. Cambridge: Cambridge University Press, 1997.
Mardock, James. "Hermaphroditical Authority in Jonson's City Comedies." *Ben Jonson Journal* 9 (2002): 69–85.
———. *Our Scene Is London: Ben Jonson's City and the Space of the Author*. New York: Routledge, 2008.
Marin, Louis. "Classical, Baroque: Versailles, or The Architecture of the Prince." *Yale French Studies*, no. 80 (1991): 167–82.
Markham, Gervase. *The English Husbandman*. London, 1635.
Marotti, Arthur. *Manuscript, Print, and the English Renaissance Lyric*. Ithaca: Cornell University Press, 1995.
Marsh, David. *The Quattrocento Dialogue: Classical Tradition and Humanist Innovation*. Cambridge: Harvard University Press, 1980.
Martin, Mathew. "Wasting Time in Ben Jonson's *Epicoene*." *Studies in Philology* 105, no. 1 (2008): 83–102.
Marvell, Andrew. *Miscellaneous Poems*. London, 1681.
Masheck, Joseph. "Alberti's 'Window': Art-Historiographic Notes on an Antimodernist Misprision." *Art Journal* 50, no. 1 (1991): 35–41.
Matar, Nabil. *Islam in Britain, 1558–1685*. Cambridge: Cambridge University Press, 1998.
Maus, Katharine Eisaman. *Inwardness and Theater in the English Renaissance*. Chicago: University of Chicago Press, 1995.
Mayer, Thomas F. *Thomas Starkey and the Commonweal: Humanist Politics and Religion in the Reign of Henry VIII*. Cambridge: Cambridge University Press, 1989.
McBride, Kari Boyd. *Country House Discourse in Early Modern England: A Cultural Study of Landscape and Legitimacy*. Aldershot: Ashgate, 2001.
McClung, William A. *The Architecture of Paradise: Survivals of Eden and Jerusalem*. Berkeley: University of California Press, 1983.
McCoy, Richard C. "'Thou Idol Ceremony': Elizabeth I, *The Henriad*, and the Rites of the English Monarchy." In *Urban Life in the Renaissance*, edited

by Susan Zimmerman and Ronald F. E. Weissman, 240–68. Cranbury, N.J.: Associated University Press, 1989.

McCullough, Peter. *Sermons at Court: Politics and Religion in Elizabethan and Jacobean Preaching.* Cambridge: Cambridge University Press, 1998.

McEwen, Indra Kagis. *Vitruvius: Writing the Body of Architecture.* Cambridge, Mass.: MIT Press, 2003.

McKeon, Michael. *The Secret History of Domesticity: Public, Private, and the Division of Knowledge.* Baltimore: Johns Hopkins University Press, 2005.

McLeod, Mary. "'Other' Spaces and 'Others.'" In *The Sex of Architecture,* edited by Diana Agrest, Patricia Conway, and Leslie Kanes Weisman, 15–28. New York: Harry N. Abrams, 1996.

Mendyk, Stan. "Early British Chorography." *Sixteenth Century Journal* 17, no. 4 (1986): 459–81.

———. *"Speculum Britanniae": Regional Study, Antiquarianism, and Science in Britain to 1700.* Toronto: University of Toronto Press, 1989.

Merrens, Rebecca. "'Ignoring the Men': Female Speech and Male Anxiety in Cavendish's *The Female Academy* and Jonson's *Epicoene.*" *In-Between: Essays and Studies in Literary Criticism* 9 (2000): 243–60.

Mikalachki, Jodi. *The Legacy of Boadicea: Gender and Nation in Early Modern England.* London: Routledge, 1998.

Millard, Barbara. "'An Acceptable Violence': Sexual Contest in Jonson's *Epicoene.*" *Medieval and Renaissance Drama in England* 1 (1984): 143–58.

Mirabelli, Philip. "Silence, Wit, and Wisdom in *The Silent Woman.*" *SEL* 29, no. 2 (1989): 309–36.

Misme, Clotilde. "Deux 'Boîtes-à-Perspective' Hollandaises du XVIIe Siècle." *Gazette des Beaux-Arts* 11 (1925): 156–66.

Mohr, Richard. *The Platonic Cosmology.* Leiden: Brill, 1985.

Montrose, Louis. "The Elizabethan Subject and the Spenserian Text." In *Literary Theory/Renaissance Texts,* edited by Patricia Parker and David Quint, 303–40. Baltimore: Johns Hopkins Press, 1966.

Mowl, Timothy, and Brian Earnshaw. *Architecture Without Kings: The Rise of Puritan Classicism Under Cromwell.* Manchester: Manchester University Press, 1995.

Muizelaar, Klakse, and Derek Phillips. *Picturing Men and Women in the Dutch Golden Age: Paintings and People in Historical Perspective.* New Haven: Yale University Press, 2003.

Munro, Lucy. *Children of the Queen's Revels: A Jacobean Theatre Repertory.* Cambridge: Cambridge University Press, 2005.

Murray, Timothy, ed. *Mimesis, Masochism, and Mime: The Politics of Theatricality in Contemporary French Thought.* Ann Arbor: University of Michigan Press, 1997.

Nardo, Anna K. "Hamlet, 'A Man to Double Business Bound.'" *Shakespeare Quarterly* 34, no. 2 (1983): 181–99.

Nash, Ernest. "Secretarium Senatus." In *In Memoriam Otto J. Brendel: Essays in Archaeology and the Humanities,* edited by Larissa Bonfante and Helga von Heintze, 191–204. Maintz: Verlag Philipp von Zabern, 1976.

National Trust. *Ham House*. London: National Trust, 2002.

Newman, John. "Inigo Jones's Architectural Education Before 1614." *Architectural History* 35 (1992): 18–50.

Newman, Karen. "City Talk: Women and Commodification in Jonson's *Epicoene*." *ELH* 56, no. 3 (1989): 503–18.

———. *Cultural Capitals: Early Modern London and Paris*. Princeton: Princeton University Press, 2007.

Norberg, Dag. *Manuel Pratique de Latin Médiéval*. Paris: A. J. Picard, 1968.

North, Roger. *Of Building: Roger North's Writings on Architecture*. Edited by Howard Colvin and John Newman. Oxford: Clarendon Press, 1981.

Nuñez, Javier Fresnillo. *Leon Battista Alberti "De re aedificatoria": A Lemmatized Concordance*. Part 1. Hildesheim-Zurich-New York: Olms-Weidmann, 1996.

Nuti, Lucia. "Mapping Places: Chorography and Vision in the Renaissance." In *Mappings*, edited by Denis Cosgrove, 90–108. London: Reaktion Press, 1999.

Oakeshott, Walter, and [Constance] Anson Jordan. "The Siena Portrait of Queen Elizabeth I." *Apollo* 124 (Oct. 1986): 306–9.

O'Connor, Joseph F. "Architecture." In *Medieval Latin: An Introduction and Bibliographical Guide*, edited by F. A. C. Mantello and A. G. Rigg, 436–42. Washington, D.C.: Catholic University of America Press, 1996.

OED Online. Last updated March 2013. Oxford University Press. http://www.oed.com.

Olwig, Kenneth Robert. *Landscape, Nature, and the Body Politic: From Britain's Renaissance to America's New World*. Madison: University of Wisconsin Press, 2002.

Orgel, Stephen. *The Illusion of Power: Political Theater in the English Renaissance*. Berkeley: University of California Press, 1975.

———. "Shakespeare and the Cannibals." In *Cannibals, Witches, and Divorce: Estranging the Renaissance*, edited by Marjorie Garber, 40–66. Baltimore: Johns Hopkins Press, 1987.

Orlin, Lena Cowen. "Gertrude's Closet." *Shakespeare Jahrbuch* 134 (1998): 44–67.

———. *Locating Privacy in Tudor London*. Oxford: Oxford University Press, 2007.

———. *Private Matters and Public Culture in Post-Reformation England*. Ithaca: Cornell University Press, 1994.

Orrell, John. *The Human Stage: English Theatre Design, 1567–1640*. Cambridge: Cambridge University Press, 1988.

Otway-Ruthven, J. "The King's Secretary in the Fifteenth Century." *Transactions of the Royal Historical Society*, 4th ser., 19 (1936): 81–100.

Panofsky, Erwin. *Perspective as Symbolic Form*. Edited by Christopher S. Wood. New York: Zone Books, 1991.

Parker, Patricia. *Shakespeare from the Margins: Language, Culture, Context*. Chicago: University of Chicago Press, 1996.

Parry, Graham. "The Great Picture of Lady Anne Clifford." In *Art and Patronage in the Caroline Courts: Essays in Honour of Sir Oliver Millar,* edited by David Howarth, 202–19. Cambridge: Cambridge University Press, 1993.

Partridge, Edward. *The Broken Compass: A Study of the Major Comedies of Ben Jonson.* New York: Columbia University Press, 1958.

Pasini, Pier Giorgio. "La facciata 'prospettica' dell Tempio Malatestiano." *Romagna: Arte e Storia* 1, no. 2 (1981): 21–34.

Paster, Gail Kern. *The Body Embarrassed: Drama and the Disciplines of Shame in Early Modern England.* Ithaca: Cornell University Press, 1993.

———. *The Idea of the City in the Age of Shakespeare.* Athens: University of Georgia Press, 1985.

Payne, Alina A. *The Architectural Treatise in the Italian Renaissance: Architectural Invention, Ornament, and Literary Culture.* Cambridge: Cambridge University Press, 1999.

Peacock, John. *The Stage Designs of Inigo Jones: The European Context.* Cambridge: Cambridge University Press, 1995.

Pepys, Samuel. *The Diary of Samuel Pepys.* Edited by Robert Latham and William Mathews. Berkeley: University of California Press, 1995.

Pérez-Gómez, Alberto. "Chora: The Space of Architectural Representation." In *Chora: Intervals in the Philosophy of Architecture,* vol. 1., edited by Alberto Pérez-Gómez and Stephen Parcell, 1–34. Montreal and Kingston: McGill-Queen's University Press, 1994.

Pérez-Gómez, Alberto, and Louise Pelletier. *Architectural Representation and the Perspective Hinge.* Cambridge, Mass.: MIT Press, 1997.

Petrarca, Francesco. *Petrarch's Secret.* Translated by William H. Draper. London: Chatto & Windus, 1911.

———. *Prose.* Edited by G. Martellotti, P. G. Ricci, E. Carrara, and E. Bianchi. Milan: Riccardo Ricciardi, 1955.

Piggott, Stuart. "William Camden and the Britannia." In *The Changing Face of English Local History,* edited by R. C. Richardson, 12–29. Aldershot: Ashgate, 2002.

Pius II. *Commentaries.* Vol. 1. Edited by Margaret Meserve and Marcello Simonetta. Cambridge, Mass.: Harvard University Press, 2003.

Plato. *Timaeus.* Translated by Donald J. Zeyl. Indianapolis: Hackett, 2000.

———. *The Timaeus of Plato.* Edited by R. D. Archer-Hind. New York: Arno Press, 1973.

Platt, Colin. *The Great Rebuildings of Tudor and Stuart England: Revolutions in Architectural Taste.* London: UCL Press, 1994.

Poole, Kristen. "'The Fittest Closet for All Goodness': Authorial Strategies of Jacobean Mothers' Manuals." *SEL* 35, no. 1 (1995): 69–88.

Pratt, Roger. *The Architecture of Sir Roger Pratt, Charles II's Commissioner for the Rebuilding of London After the Great Fire.* Edited by R. T. Gunther. Oxford: R. T. Gunther, 1928.

Preyer, Brenda. "L'architettura del Palazzo Mediceo." In *Il Palazzo Medici Riccardi di Firenze,* edited by Giovanni Cherubini and Giovanni Fanelli, 58–73. Florence: Giunti, 1990.

———. "The Rucellai Palace." In *Giovanni Rucellai ed il suo zibaldone, II: A Florentine Patrician and His Palace,* edited by F. W. Kent et al., 155–228. London: Warburg Institute, 1981.

Ptolemy. *The Geography of Claudius Ptolemy.* Translated and edited by Edward Luther Stevenson. New York: New York Public Library, 1932.

Puttenham, George. *The Arte of English Poesie.* London, 1589.

Puttfarken, Thomas. *The Discovery of Pictorial Composition: Theories of Visual Order in Painting, 1400–1800.* New Haven: Yale University Press, 2000.

Quillen, Carol E. *Rereading the Renaissance: Petrarch, Augustine, and the Language of Humanism.* Ann Arbor: University of Michigan Press, 1998.

Rajchman, John. *Constructions.* Cambridge, Mass.: MIT Press, 1998.

Rambuss, Richard. *Closet Devotions.* Durham: Duke University Press, 1998.

———. "The Secretary's Study: The Secret Designs of *The Shepheardes Calender.*" *ELH* 59, no. 2 (1992): 313–35.

Ranum, Orest. "The Refuges of Intimacy." In *A History of Private Life III: Passions of the Renaissance,* edited by Roger Chartier, translated by Arthur Goldhammer, 207–63. Cambridge, Mass.: Belknap Press of Harvard University Press, 1989.

Richardson, Catherine. *Shakespeare and Material Culture.* Oxford: Oxford University Press, 2011.

Richardson, Lawrence, Jr. *A New Topographical Dictionary of Ancient Rome.* Baltimore: Johns Hopkins University Press, 1992.

Richardson, R. C. "Introduction: The Changing Face of English Local History." In *The Changing Face of English Local History,* edited by R. C. Richardson, 1–11. Aldershot: Ashgate, 2000.

Riviere, Joan. "Womanliness as a Masquerade." *International Journal of Psycho-Analysis* 10 (1929): 303–13.

Roberts, Sasha. "Shakespeare 'Creepes into the Womens Closets About Bedtime': Women Reading in a Room of Their Own." In *Renaissance Configurations: Voices/Bodies/Spaces, 1580–1690,* edited by Gordon McMullan, 30–63. Houndmills: MacMillan, 1998.

Robinson, Hilary. *Reading Art, Reading Irigaray: The Politics of Art by Women.* London: I. B. Taurus, 2006.

Rogers, Thomas. *Of the Imitation of Christ.* London, 1580.

Romer, F. E. *Pomponius Mela's Description of the World.* Ann Arbor: University of Michigan Press, 1998.

Rose, Mary Beth. *The Expense of Spirit: Love and Sexuality in English Renaissance Drama.* Ithaca: Cornell University Press, 1988.

Royle, Nicholas. *The Uncanny: An Introduction.* Manchester: Manchester University Press, 2003.

Rubin, Patricia Lee. *Images and Identity in Fifteenth-Century Florence.* New Haven: Yale University Press, 2007.

Rykwert, Joseph. *The Dancing Column: On Order in Architecture*. Cambridge, Mass.: MIT Press, 1996.

———. "Theory as Rhetoric: Leon Battista Alberti in Theory and in Practice." In *Paper Palaces: The Rise of the Renaissance Architectural Treatise*, edited by Vaughan Hart and Peter Hicks, 33–50. New Haven: Yale University Press, 1998.

Rymer, Thomas. *A Short View of Tragedy*. London, 1693.

Saalman, Howard. Review of *Giovanni Rucellai ed il suo zibaldone, II: A Florentine Patrician and His Palace*, edited by F. W. Kent et al. *Journal of the Society of Architectural Historians* 47, no. 1 (1988): 82–90.

———. "Tommaso Spinelli, Michelozzo, Manetti, and Rossellino." *Journal of the Society of Architectural Historians* 25, no. 3 (1966): 151–64.

Salingar, L. G. "Farce and Fashion in *The Silent Woman*." *Essays and Studies* 20 (1967): 29–46.

Sallis, John. *Chorology: On Beginning in Plato's "Timaeus."* Bloomington: Indiana University Press, 1999.

Sayre, Kenneth. "The Multilayered Incoherence of Timaeus' Receptacle." In *Plato's "Timaeus" as Cultural Icon*, edited by Gretchen J. Reydams-Schils, 60–79. Notre Dame: University of Notre Dame Press, 2003.

Schmitt, Carl. *The* Nomos *of the Earth: In the International Law of Jus Publicum Europaeum*. Translated by G. L. Ulmen. New York: Telos Press, 2006.

Schmitt, Charles. *John Case and Aristotelianism in Renaissance England*. Montreal: McGill-Queen's University Press, 1983.

Schwyzer, Philip. "John Leland and His Heirs: The Topography of England." In *The Oxford Handbook of Tudor Literature, 1485–1603*, edited by Mike Pincombe and Cathy Shrank, 238–53. Oxford: Oxford University Press, 2009.

Scott, Charlotte. *Shakespeare and the Idea of the Book*. Oxford: Oxford University Press, 2007.

Sebek, Barbara. "Morose's Turban." *Shakespeare Studies* 35 (2007): 32–38.

Sedgwick, Eve Kosofsky. *Epistemology of the Closet*. Berkeley: University of California Press, 1990.

Semper, Gottfried. *The Four Elements of Architecture and Other Writings*. Translated by Harry Francis Mallgrave and Wolfgang Herrmann. Cambridge: Cambridge University Press, 1989.

Serlio, Sebastiano. *The Five Books of Architecture*. Translated by Robert Peake [?]. London, 1611.

———. *Sebastiano Serlio on Architecture*. 2 vols. Translated and edited by Vaughan Hart and Peter Hicks. New Haven: Yale University Press, 1996.

Shakespeare, William. *Hamlet*. Edited by Harold Jenkins. London: Routledge, 1982.

Showalter, Elaine. "Representing Ophelia: Women, Madness, and the Responsibilities of Feminist Criticism." In *Shakespeare and the Question of Theory*, edited by Patricia Parker and Geoffrey Hartman, 77–94. New York: Methuen, 1985.

Shrank, Cathy. *Writing the Nation in Reformation England, 1530–1580.* Oxford: Oxford University Press, 2004.

Shuger, Debora. "The 'I' of the Beholder: Renaissance Mirrors and the Reflexive Mind." In *Renaissance Culture and the Everyday,* edited by Patricia Fumerton and Simon Hunt, 21–41. Philadelphia: University of Pennsylvania Press, 1999.

Shute, John. *The First and Chief Groundes of Architecture.* London, 1563.

———. *The First and Chief Groundes of Architecture.* Edited by Lawrence Weaver. London: Country Life, 1912.

Sibony, Daniel. "Hamlet: A Writing-Effect." *Yale French Studies,* nos. 55–56 (1977): 53–93.

Sidney, Philip. *An Apologie for Poetry.* London, 1595.

Silverman, Kaja. *Male Subjectivity at the Margins.* New York: Routledge, 1992.

———. *The Subject of Semiotics.* New York: Oxford University Press, 1983.

Simpson, W. Douglas. "Dudley Castle, the Renaissance Buildings." *Archaeological Journal* 101 (1944): 119–25.

Slights, William W. E. *Ben Jonson and the Art of Secrecy.* Toronto: University of Toronto Press, 1994.

Smith, Bruce R. *The Key of Green: Passion and Perception in Renaissance Culture.* Chicago: University of Chicago Press, 2009.

Smith, Christine. *Architecture in the Culture of Early Humanism: Ethics, Aesthetics, and Eloquence, 1400–1470.* Oxford: Oxford University Press, 1992.

Snook, Edith. *Women, Reading, and the Cultural Politics of Early Modern England.* Aldershot: Ashgate, 2005.

Soja, Edward. *Thirdspace: Journeys to Los Angeles and Other Real-and-Imagined Places.* Cambridge, Mass.: Blackwell, 1996.

Sousa, Geraldo U. *At Home in Shakespeare's Tragedies.* Farnham: Ashgate, 2010.

Southern, Richard. *The Staging of Plays Before Shakespeare.* London: Faber and Faber, 1973.

Speed, John. *The Theatre of Great Britaine.* London: 1611.

Stallybrass, Peter. "Patriarchal Territories: The Body Enclosed." In *Rewriting the Renaissance: The Discourse of Sexual Difference in Early Modern Europe,* edited by Margaret W. Ferguson, Maureen Quilligan, and Nancy J. Vickers, 123–42. Chicago: University Chicago Press, 1986.

———. "'Well Grubbed, Old Mole': Marx, *Hamlet,* and the (Un)fixing of Representation." *Cultural Studies* 12, no. 1 (1998): 3–14.

Stallybrass, Peter, Roger Chartier, J. Franklin Mowery, and Heather Wolfe. "Hamlet's Tables and the Technologies of Writing in Renaissance England." *Shakespeare Quarterly* 55, no. 4 (2004): 379–419.

Starkey, David, ed. *The English Court: From the Wars of the Roses to the Civil War.* London: Longman, 1987.

Staykova, Julia D. "The Augustinian Soliloquies of an Early Modern Reader: A Stylistic Relation of Shakespeare's Hamlet?" *Literature and Theology* 23, no. 2 (2009): 121–41.

———. "Pseudo-Augustine and Religious Controversy in Early Modern England." In *Augustine Beyond the Book: Intermediality, Transmediality and Reception*, edited by Karla Pollmann and Meredith J. Gill, 147–66. Leiden: Brill, 2012.

Steadman, Philip. *The Evolution of Designs: Biological Analogy in Architecture and the Applied Arts*. Rev. ed. New York: Routledge, 2008.

Stegner, Paul D. "'Try What Repentance Can': *Hamlet*, Confession, and the Extraction of Interiority." *Shakespeare Studies* 35 (2007): 105–29.

Stewart, Alan. *Close Readers: Humanism and Sodomy in Early Modern England*. Princeton: Princeton University Press, 1997.

———. "The Early Modern Closet Discovered." *Representations*, no. 50 (1995): 76–100.

———. *Shakespeare's Letters*. Oxford: Oxford University Press, 2008.

Stock, Brian. *After Augustine: The Meditative Reader and the Text*. Philadelphia: University of Pennsylvania Press, 2001.

Stone, Lawrence. *The Family, Sex and Marriage in England, 1500–1800*. New York: Harper & Row, 1977.

Straznicky, Marta. *Privacy, Playreading, and Women's Closet Drama, 1550–1700*. Cambridge: Cambridge University Press, 2004.

Strong, Roy. *Gloriana: The Portraits of Queen Elizabeth I*. London: Thames and Hudson, 1987.

Stump, Donald. "Marlowe's Travesty of Virgil: Dido and Elizabethan Dreams of Empire." *Comparative Drama* 34, no. 1 (2000): 79–107.

Summers, David. *Vision, Reflection, and Desire in Western Painting*. Chapel Hill: University of North Carolina Press, 2007.

Summerson, John. *Architecture in Britain, 1530–1830*. 9th ed. New Haven: Yale University Press, 1993.

———. "John Thorpe and the Thorpes of Kingscliffe." In *The Unromantic Castle and Other Essays*, 17–40. London: Thames and Hudson, 1990.

———. "Three Elizabethan Architects." *Bulletin of the John Rylands Library* 40, no. 1 (1957): 202–28.

Summit, Jennifer. "Leland's *Itinerary* and the Remains of the Medieval Past." In *Reading the Medieval in Early Modern England*, edited by Gordon McMullan and David Matthews, 159–78. Cambridge: Cambridge University Press, 2007.

Swann, Marjorie. "Refashioning Society in Ben Jonson's *Epicoene*." *SEL* 38, no. 2 (1998): 297–315.

Tafuri, Manfredo. "Discordant Harmony from Alberti to Zuccari." *Architectural Design* 49, nos. 5–6 (1979): 36–44.

Targoff, Ramie. "The Performance of Prayer: Sincerity and Theatricality in Early Modern England." *Representations*, no. 60 (1997): 49–69.

Tavernor, Robert. *On Alberti and the Art of Building*. New Haven: Yale University Press, 1998.

———. *Palladio and Palladianism*. London: Thames and Hudson, 1991.

Teague, Frances. "Ben Jonson's Stagecraft in *Epicoene*." *Renaissance Drama*, n.s., 9 (1978): 175–92.

Thorpe, John. *The Book of Architecture of John Thorpe in Sir John Soane's Museum.* Edited by John Summerson. Glasgow: Walpole Society, 1966.

Thurley, Simon. *The Royal Palaces of Tudor England: Architecture and Court Life, 1460–1547.* New Haven: Yale University Press, 1993.

———. *Whitehall Palace: An Architectural History of the Royal Apartments, 1240–1698.* New Haven: Yale University Press, 1999.

Turner, Henry. *The English Renaissance Stage: Geometry, Poetics, and the Practical Spatial Arts, 1580–1630.* Oxford: Oxford University Press, 2006.

Van Eck, Caroline, with Christy Anderson, eds. *British Architectural Theory, 1540–1750: An Anthology of Texts.* Aldershot: Ashgate, 2003.

Vasari, Giorgio. *The Lives of the Artists.* Translated by Julia Conaway Bondanella and Peter Bondanella. Oxford: Oxford University Press, 1991.

Vidler, Anthony. "Nothing to Do with Architecture." *Grey Room,* no. 21 (2005): 112–27.

———. *Warped Space: Art, Architecture, and Anxiety in Modern Culture.* Cambridge, Mass.: MIT Press, 2000.

Vitkus, Daniel. *Turning Turk: English Theater and the Multicultural Mediterranean, 1570–1630.* New York: Palgrave Macmillan, 2003.

Vitruvius. *An Abridgment of the Architecture of Vitruvius.* Translated and edited by Abel Boyer [?]. London, 1692.

———. *The Architecture of M. Vitruvius Pollio.* Translated and edited by William Newton. Vol. 1. London, 1771.

———. *De l'architecture.* Translated by Philippe Fleury. Paris: Les Belles Lettres, 1990.

———. *On Architecture.* Translated by Frank Granger. 2 vols. London: William Heinemann, 1931.

———. *Ten Books on Architecture.* Translated by Ingrid D. Rowland, with commentary by Thomas Noble Howe, Ingrid D. Rowland, and Michael J. Dewar. Cambridge: Cambridge University Press, 1999.

Wall, Wendy. *Staging Domesticity: Household Work and English Identity in Early Modern Drama.* Cambridge: Cambridge University Press, 2002.

Walter, E. V. *Placeways: A Theory of the Human Environment.* Chapel Hill: University of North Carolina Press, 1988.

Walton, Izaak. "The Life of Sir Henry Wotton." In *Reliquiae Wottonianae,* b1r–c12v. London, 1651.

Warner, Marina. *Monuments and Maidens: The Allegory of the Female Form.* New York: Atheneum, 1985.

Watson, Elizabeth S. "Old King, New King, Eclipsed Sons, and Abandoned Altars in *Hamlet.*" *Sixteenth Century Journal* 35, no. 2 (2004): 475–91.

Watson, Robert N. *Ben Jonson's Parodic Strategy: Literary Imperialism in the Comedies.* Cambridge, Mass.: Harvard University Press, 1987.

Wayne, Don. *Penshurst: The Semiotics of Place and the Poetics of History.* Madison: University of Wisconsin Press, 1984.

Weber, Samuel. *Theatricality as Medium.* New York: Fordham University Press, 2004.

Weimann, Robert. *Shakespeare and the Popular Tradition in the Theatre: Studies in the Social Dimension of Dramatic Form and Function.* Edited by Robert Schwartz. Baltimore: Johns Hopkins University Press, 1978.

Wells, Susan. "Jacobean City Comedy and the Ideology of the City." *ELH* 48, no. 1 (1981): 37–60.

Westermann, Mariet. "'Costly and Curious, Full of Pleasure and Home Contentment': Making Home in the Dutch Republic." In *Art and Home: Dutch Interiors in the Age of Rembrandt,* edited by Mariet Westermann, 15–82. Zwolle: Denver Art Museum, Newark Museum, and Waanders Publishers, 2001.

Wheelock, Arthur K., Jr. *Perspective, Optics and Delft Artists Around 1650.* London: Garland Press, 1977.

White, John. *Birth and Rebirth of Pictorial Space.* London: Faber and Faber, 1957.

Wickham, Glynne. *Early English Stages 1300 to 1600.* Vol. 1, *1300–1576.* London: Routledge and Kegan Paul.

Wickham, Glynne, Herbert Berry, and William Ingram. *English Professional Theatre, 1530–1660.* Cambridge: Cambridge University Press, 2000.

Wigley, Mark. *The Architecture of Deconstruction: Derrida's Haunt.* Cambridge, Mass.: MIT Press, 1993.

———. "Untitled: The Housing of Gender." In *Sexuality and Space,* edited by Beatriz Colomina, 326–89. New York: Princeton Architectural Press, 1992.

Williams, Deanne. "Dido, Queen of England." *ELH* 73, no. 1 (2006): 31–59.

Williams, Steven J. *The Secret of Secrets: The Scholarly Career of a Pseudo-Aristotelian Text in the Latin Middle Ages.* Ann Arbor: University of Michigan Press, 2003.

Willis, Cloudesley S. *A Short History of Ewell and Nonsuch.* Epsom: Pullinger, 1932.

Wilton-Ely, John. "The Rise of the Professional Architect in England." In *The Architect: Chapters in the History of the Profession,* edited by Spiro Kostof, 180–208. Berkeley: University of California Press, 2000.

Wintle, Michael. *The Image of Europe: Visualizing Europe in Cartography and Iconography Throughout the Ages.* Cambridge: Cambridge University Press, 2009.

Wittkower, Rudolf. *Architectural Principles in the Age of Humanism.* New York: Random House, 1962.

———. *Palladio and Palladianism.* New York: G. Braziller, 1974.

Wood, Anthony à. *Athenae Oxonienses.* Vol. 1. London, 1691.

Wood, Margaret. *The English Mediaeval House.* London: Studio Editions, 1965.

Wood, Robert E. "Space and Scrutiny in *Hamlet.*" *South Atlantic Review* 52, no. 1 (1987): 25–42.

Woodall, Joanne. "Love Is in the Air—*Amor* as Motivation and Message in Seventeenth-Century Netherlandish Painting." *Art History* 19, no. 2 (1996): 208–46.

Wotton, Henry. *The Elements of Architecture.* London, 1624.
Yates, Frances. *Astraea: The Imperial Theme in the Sixteenth Century.* London: Routledge and Kegan Paul, 1975.
———. *Theatre of the World.* Chicago: University of Chicago Press, 1969.
Yeo, Richard. "Notebooks as Memory Aids: Precepts and Practices in Early Modern England," *Memory Studies* 1, no. 1 (2008): 115–36.
Young, Alan. *Hamlet and the Visual Arts, 1709–1900.* Newark: University of Delaware Press, 2002.
Ziegler, Georgianna. "My Lady's Chamber: Female Space, Female Chastity in Shakespeare." *Textual Practice* 4, no. 1 (1990): 73–90.
Žižek, Slavoj. *Looking Awry: An Introduction to Jacques Lacan Through Popular Culture.* Cambridge, Mass.: MIT Press, 1991.
Zucker, Adam. "The Social Logic of Ben Jonson's *Epicoene.*" *Renaissance Drama,* n.s., 33 (2004): 37–62.

INDEX

Page numbers in italics refer to illustrations.